ADVANCED POWERBUILDER 5.0

ADVANCED POWERBUILDER 5.0

Derek C.R. Ball

INTERNATIONAL THOMSON COMPUTER PRESS
I(T)P™ An International Thomson Publishing Company

London • Bonn • Boston • Johannesburg • Madrid • Melbourne • Mexico City • New York • Paris
Singapore • Tokyo • Toronto • Albany, NY • Belmont, CA • Cincinnati, OH • Detroit, MI

Copyright ©1996 International Thomson Computer Press

I(T)P™ A division of International Thomson Publishing Inc.
The ITP Logo is a trademark under license.

Printed in the United States of America.

For more information, contact:

International Thomson Computer Press
20 Park Plaza, 13th Floor
Boston, MA 02116
USA

International Thomson Publishing GmbH
Königswinterer Strasse 418
53227 Bonn
Germany

International Thomson Publishing Europe
Berkshire House 168-173
High Holborn
London WCIV 7AA
England

International Thomson Publishing Asia
221 Henderson Road #05-10
Henderson Building
Singapore 0315

Thomas Nelson Australia
102 Dodds Street
South Melbourne, 3205
Victoria, Australia

International Thomson Publishing Japan
Hirakawacho Kyowa Building, 3F
2-2-1 Hirakawacho
Chiyoda-ku, 102 Tokyo
Japan

Nelson Canada
1120 Birchmount Road
Scarborough, Ontario
Canada M1K 5G4

International Thomson Editores
Campos Eliseos 385, Piso 7
Col. Polanco
11560 Mexico D.F. Mexico

International Thomson Publishing Southern Africa
Bldg. 19, Constantia Park
239 Old Pretoria Road, P.O. Box 2459
Halfway House, 1685 South Africa

International Thomson Publishing France
1, rue st. Georges
75 009 Paris France

All rights reserved. No part of this work covered by the copyright hereon may be reproduced or used in any form or by any means—graphic, electronic, or mechanical, including photocopying, recording, taping, or information storage and retrieval systems—without the written permission of the Publisher.

Products and services that are referred to in this book may be either trademarks and/or registered trademarks of their respective owners. The Publisher(s) and Author(s) make no claim to these trademarks.

While every precaution has been taken in the preparation of this book, the Publisher and the Author assume no responsibility for errors or omissions, or for damages resulting from the use of information contained herein. In no event shall the Publisher and the Author be liable for any loss of profit or any other commercial damage, including but not limited to special, incidental, consequential, or other damages.

2 3 4 5 6 7 8 9 10 01 00 99 98 97 96

Library of Congress Cataloging-in-Publication Data
Ball, Derek C.R., 1970
    Advanced PowerBuilder 5.0 : tools for the enterprise / Derek C.R. Ball
       p.   cm.
    Includes index.
    ISBN: 1-85032-855-2 (alk. paper)
    1. Application software--Development. 2. PowerBuilder.
I. Title.
QA76.76.A65B35   1996
005.2--dc20
                             96-2909
                                CIP

Publisher/Vice President: Jim DeWolf, ITCP/Boston
Project Director: Chris Grisonich, ITCP/Boston
Marketing Manager: Kathleen Raftery, ITCP/Boston
Production: Jo-Ann Campbell • mle design • 562 Milford Point Rd. • Milford, CT 06460
Index: Lori Lathrop • Lathrop Media Services • 303-567-4447 ex. 28

DEDICATION

To my wonderful wife, Lesley, without whose patience and understanding this book would never have been completed.

And to my parents, Bert and Fay, for always encouraging me to chase my dreams.

TABLE OF CONTENTS

	PREFACE	**XV**
CHAPTER 1	**INTRODUCTION**	**1**

1.1 PowerBuilder in the Enterprise — 1
1.2 How This Book is Organized — 2
1.3 Who Should Read This Book — 3
1.4 What is on the Companion CD — 4
  1.4.1 How to Install the Sample Files — 4
  1.4.2 Setting Up the Sample Files — 4
  1.4.3 Setting Up the Distributed PowerBuilder Example — 5
  1.4.4 Setting Up the OLE Automation Example — 6
1.5 What's Next — 6

CHAPTER 2	**THE DEVELOPMENT METHODOLOGY FOR ENTERPRISE POWERBUILDER**	**9**

2.1 The Evolution of Client/Server Development
  Methodologies — 9

viii   *Table of Contents*

2.2 THE WATERFALL RUNS DRY   11
2.3 THE SPIRAL METHODOLOGY   13
2.4 THE ITERATIVE METHODOLOGY   15
2.5 THE FLATTENED SPIRAL METHODOLOGY   17
   2.5.1 The First Iteration   19
   2.5.2 The Second Iteration   24
   2.5.3 The Third (and Final) Iteration   29
   2.5.4 Implementation   34
2.6 WHERE TO GO FROM HERE   36

CHAPTER 3   ARCHITECTURES FOR DEVELOPMENT   37

3.1 TWO-TIERED ARCHITECTURES   38
3.2 THREE-TIERED ARCHITECTURES   40
3.3 N-TIERED ARCHITECTURES   42
3.4 SERVICE-BASED ARCHITECTURES   42
3.5 SELECTING THE RIGHT ARCHITECTURE   44

CHAPTER 4   DESIGNING A POWERBUILDER APPLICATION   45

4.1 THE DATA MODEL   45
4.2 THE USER INTERFACE   46
   4.2.1 User Centric Design   46
   4.2.2 The Overall Design   47
   4.2.3 User Analysis Matrix   48
   4.2.4 MDI or SDI?   50
   4.2.5 Choosing the Correct Window Type   54
   4.2.6 Providing Feedback to the User   60
4.3 PROCESS OBJECTS   62
   4.3.1 Application Security   62
   4.3.2 Other Process Objects   63
4.4 ONLINE HELP   64
4.5 SUMMARY   64

CHAPTER 5   OBJECT-ORIENTED POWERBUILDER   65

5.1 WHAT DOES USING OO MEAN?   66
5.2 WHY USE OO WITH POWERBUILDER?   67
5.3 OBJECTS   68

Table of Contents ix

5.4 PROPERTIES	69
5.5 METHODS	70
5.6 CLASSES	71
5.7 INSTANCE	74
5.8 CONTROLS	75
5.9 INHERITANCE	75
5.10 ENCAPSULATION	77
5.11 POLYMORPHISM	81
5.12 SUMMARY	83

CHAPTER 6   CLASS LIBRARIES AND FRAMEWORKS   85

6.1 A SINGLE LIBRARY SHOULD SUPPORT ALL YOUR ENTERPRISE APPLICATIONS	86
6.2 THE BUILD VERSUS BUY DILEMMA	88
6.3 BUILDING YOUR OWN	88
6.4 PURCHASING THIRD PARTY	89
6.5 WHAT KINDS OF OBJECTS SHOULD A LIBRARY HAVE?	91
6.5.1 Visual Objects	91
6.5.2 Business Objects	92
6.5.3 Service/Non-Visual Objects	93
6.6 CONCLUSION	93

CHAPTER 7   WHAT'S NEW IN POWERBUILDER 5.0   95

7.1 NATIVE COMPILED CODE	95
7.2 DISTRIBUTED POWERBUILDER	99
7.2.1 Distributed PowerBuilder Concept	99
7.2.2 New Objects for Distributed Computing	102
7.2.3 Other Issues	109
7.2.4 Distributed Example	109
7.3 INBOUND OLE AUTOMATION	120
7.4 POWERBUILDER FOUNDATION CLASS LIBRARY	123
7.4.1 The PFC Libraries	124
7.4.2 The Extension Layer Libraries	125
7.5 DATAWINDOW ENHANCEMENTS	125
7.5.1 Two New DataWindow Object Presentation Styles	126
7.5.2 Changes to the DataWindow Painter	144
7.5.3 DataWindow Control Scripting Changes	159

x *Table of Contents*

7.5.4 Performance Enhancements	163
7.6 POWERSCRIPT PAINTER	165
7.7 POWERSCRIPT CODE ENHANCEMENTS	171
7.7.1 Keywords	171
7.7.2 Variable Declaration	173
7.7.3 Read Only Function Arguments	173
7.7.4 GetParent Function	174
7.7.5 Registry Functions	174
7.8 WINDOW PAINTER	178
7.8.1 New Toolbars and Icons	178
7.8.2 Property Sheets	179
7.8.3 New Controls	180
7.9 MENU PAINTER ENHANCEMENTS	189
7.9.1 Drop Down Toolbar	190
7.9.2 Creating Multiple Docking Toolbars	192
7.10 APPLICATION PAINTER	192
7.11 TABLE PAINTER	193
7.12 PIPELINE PAINTER	194
7.13 DEBUGGER	194
7.14 OBJECT BROWSER	196
7.15 OBJECT-ORIENTED ENHANCEMENTS	198
7.15.1 Function Overloading	198
7.15.2 Event Parameters and Function Posting	198
7.16 DATABASE ENHANCEMENTS	200
7.16.1 Native Enhancements	201
7.16.2 ODBC Enhancements	201
7.17 INTERNATIONALIZATION	202
7.18 COMPONENT LIBRARY	202
7.19 SUMMARY	203

CHAPTER 8 ADVANCED DEVELOPMENT CONCEPTS 205

8.1 SETTING UP OBJECT EVENTS	205
8.1.1 Predefined System Events	206
8.1.2 Undefined System Events	210
8.1.3 Custom Events	213
8.1.4 User Defined Events	215
8.2 FUNCTIONING WITH FUNCTIONS	216
8.2.1 PowerScript Functions	217

Table of Contents **xi**

8.2.2 User Defined Functions	218
8.2.3 External Functions	226
8.3 CALLING EVENTS AND FUNCTIONS FROM SCRIPTS	234
8.3.1 Triggering an Event	236
8.3.2 Posting an Event	237
8.3.3 Posting Functions	237
8.3.4 Triggering Functions	238
8.4 IMPLEMENTING DRAG AND DROP	238
8.4.1 What Is Drag and Drop?	239
8.4.2 How Should Drag and Drop Be Used?	239
8.4.3 How Does Drag and Drop Work?	243
8.4.4 The Drag and Drop Events	243
8.4.5 Drag Properties	245
8.4.6 Drag Mode	245
8.4.7 Setting the Drag Icon	249
8.4.8 Looking at the Code—w_drag_drop	249
8.5 SUMMARY	253

CHAPTER 9 DATAWINDOW COMPONENTS 255

9.1 BUFFERS	255
9.1.1 Primary	256
9.1.2 Filter	256
9.1.3 Delete	257
9.1.4 Original	257
9.2 MANIPULATING DATA STORED IN BUFFERS	257
9.2.1 Copying Data	257
9.3 UPDATING DATAWINDOWS	261
9.3.1 Advanced Updating	261
9.3.2 Status Flags	271
9.4 INTRODUCING DATASTORES	279
9.5 SUMMARY	281

CHAPTER 10 ADVANCED DATAWINDOW TECHNIQUES 283

10.1 DROP DOWN DATAWINDOWS	283
10.1.1 Drop Down DataWindow Example	284
10.2 CHILD DATAWINDOWS	291
10.2.1 Using the GetChild() Function	291

xii   *Table of Contents*

10.3 SLIDING COLUMNS	299
10.4 EDIT STYLES AND DISPLAY FORMATS	302
10.4.1 Display Formats	302
10.4.2 Edit Styles	310
10.5 CREATING DATAWINDOWS DYNAMICALLY	327
10.5.1 Building the Data Object Syntax	327
10.5.2 Rolling It All Together	329
10.5.3 Creating the Object	330
10.5.4 Using a .PBL For Runtime Ad-Hoc Query Storage	331
10.6 MODIFYING DATAWINDOWS DYNAMICALLY	331
10.6.1 Describe	332
10.6.2 Modify	333
10.7 DEALING WITH LARGE RESULT SETS	336
10.7.1 Retrieve As Needed	337
10.7.2 Limiting the User's Query	339
10.7.3 Perform a Count(*) Calculation	339
10.7.4 The RetrieveRow Event	340
10.7.5 Storing Data to Disk	341
10.7.6 Provide a Cancel Retrieval Option	341
10.8 SHARING RESULT SETS	342
10.9 USING BITMAPS	346
10.9.1 Display As Picture	346
10.9.2 Pictures in Computed Fields	347
10.10 USING THE SQLPREVIEW EVENT	348
10.11 SUMMARY	352

CHAPTER 11   ADVANCED REPORTING   353

11.1 NESTED REPORTS	353
11.1.1 Creating a Nested Report	355
11.1.2 Using the Report Objects Properties Page	364
11.1.3 Referencing a Nested Report In Your Script	375
11.2 COMPOSITE REPORTS	376
11.2.1 Creating a Composite DataWindow	376
11.2.2 Properties for Composite Reports	384
11.3 GRAPHS	386
11.3.1 How Do I Add a Graph to My Application	387
11.3.2 Components of PowerBuilder Graphs	387

Table of Contents **xiii**

11.3.3 2 Dimensions or 3?	389
11.3.4 Graph Properties	390
11.3.5 Types of Graphs	410
11.3.6 Building a Graph Presentation Style DataWindow	419
11.3.7 Using Overlays	423
11.3.8 Runtime Graph Manipulation with PowerScript Functions	425
11.3.9 Creating a Drill Down Graph with PowerScript	426
11.4 CROSSTABS	430
11.4.1 Creating a Crosstab	431
11.4.2 Dynamic vs. Static Crosstabs	442
11.5 SUMMARY	445

CHAPTER 12   USER OBJECTS **447**

12.1 VISUAL USER OBJECTS	447
12.1.1 Visual: Standard	448
12.1.2 Visual: Custom	452
12.1.3 Visual: External	456
12.1.4 Visual: VBX	457
12.2 CLASS (NON-VISUAL) USER OBJECTS	458
12.2.1 Class: Standard	458
12.2.2 Class: Custom	461
12.3 CREATING USER OBJECTS	464
12.3.1 Instantiating a Visual User Object	464
12.3.2 Instantiating a Non-Visual User Object	466
12.4 SUMMARY	472

INDEX **473**

Preface

This book is intended to present a concise reference for PowerBuilder developers who have either taken the Introduction or FastTrack to PowerBuilder course, worked with PowerBuilder on at least one project, and are ready to try and advance their skills to the next level. You may have achieved this level of experience through self education from other books or computer based training modules. Either way, you have the basics down pat and need to progress to the next stage.

This book is not intended to be the definitive bible for the PowerBuilder master. Many of the topics discussed here the PowerBuilder master should already be familiar with. Instead, we focus on taking the intermediate level PowerBuilder developer into the realm of the advanced developer.

Much of the new material in PowerBuilder 5.0 is presented in a very dense format in Chapter 7, although just discussing the transition from PowerBuilder 4.0 to PowerBuilder 5.0 would represent enough material for a book all on its own.

The walk throughs of specific techniques are intended to allow you to either follow along with the process mentally, if you are that familiar with PowerBuilder, or to actually follow along and build the walk through as you proceed through it.

xvi   *Preface*

ACKNOWLEDGMENTS

The fact that you are holding this book in your hands right now is the result of an intense team effort to get it there. There are many people who I need to thank for making this book a reality. Thanks to Dave Cinderella for keeping me in line technically and helping me bring the manuscript to completion with his knowledge of distributed PowerBuilder and OLE Automation.

Thanks to Kouros Gorgani and Oscar Ramirez who provided the technical review of the material.

Thanks to Sandy Emerson of Sybase Press for helping to iron out any wrinkles and for her support. From International Thomson, thanks to Rebecca Springer and Jim Dewolf for making the publication process seem easy. And to Carol Mclendan and the folks at Waterside Productions for getting me hooked up with the right people.

Finally, I need to extend the biggest thanks of all to my wife Lesley, who has put up with my late nights and huge mess I made while writing this book. Your unending support and understanding made this all possible.

To everyone else that I haven't mentioned, thank you all. I have appreciated all the help and advice. In the event you find any technical inaccuracies in this book, those errors are mine and mine alone.

ABOUT THE AUTHOR

Derek Ball is the Director of Technology for Visionary Solutions, an advanced technology consulting firm in the pacific northwest. Derek is a much sought after speaker, mentor and instructor in the arena of client/server technology and application development. His favorite tool in this field is PowerBuilder from Powersoft. Derek has been working with PowerBuilder for many years and has spent the last three years as an advanced Certified PowerBuilder Instructor teaching hundreds of people how to use PowerBuilder in all the corners of the globe from Istanbul to San Francisco.

Derek has worked with many Fortune 500 firms, helping to mentor and train their personnel in the correct techniques to be successful with client/server technology and PowerBuilder. Derek believes that learning to use PowerBuilder correctly goes beyond just how to program and write code. A successful development team has to understand the correct development methodology and architecture that will suit their environment and system requirements.

You may be familiar with some of Derek's earlier works. He has co-authored two best selling books on PowerBuilder 3.0 and 4.0 and is a member of the editorial board of the *PowerBuilder Developers Journal*. He is a frequent contributor to the PBDJ and also has a regular column entitled "Into the Looking Glass" in the *PowerBuilder Advisor*. He also writes for a number of other publications including *Computing Canada*, *Visionary Times*, *Technology in Government* and *Powerline*.

When not traveling the globe mentoring and training, Derek lives in Calgary, Canada with his wife Lesley.

CHAPTER 1

Introduction

*I*nformation technology is an exciting place to work these days. Many organizations are realizing that technology holds the key to their long term success and ultimately their viability as an organization. This drive to utilize technology as a tool to achieve competitive and strategic advantage has fueled a massive industry revolving around information technology solutions. The current rush of activity is centered around client/server architectures and graphical user interfaces.

Over the past ten years, client/server architectures have made the transition from 'rare' and 'unusual' to 'fundamental' and 'mainstream.' The bulk of new systems being developed in business today are being rolled out in a client/server environment.

1.1 POWERBUILDER IN THE ENTERPRISE

Over the last five years, PowerBuilder has swept the industry, becoming the most widely used application development tool for enterprise client/server applications. Windows developers quickly adopted PowerBuilder and praised it for the improved productivity and ease of development that it provided.

2 *Advanced PowerBuilder 5.0*

Many non-windows programmers discovered that PowerBuilder demystified the graphical user interface (GUI) and PC based Windows development. A new generation of client/server GUI application developers was rising like a phoenix from the ashes of our character based legacy systems.

1.2 HOW THIS BOOK IS ORGANIZED

The sections of this book are laid out to help you become a better and more skilled PowerBuilder developer. It assumes that you know the basics of developing with PowerBuilder, at least to the level of having completed and understood all the materials from the Getting Started tutorial and hopefully an Introduction to PowerBuilder course.

We begin by discussing some of the critical and much neglected areas of enterprise PowerBuilder projects; methodologies and architectures. People tend to jump into enterprise PowerBuilder projects like they were building a system to keep track of their stamp collection at home. Much more care and deliberation needs to be applied when the project is a mission critical system upon which your organization is betting its future!

Next we examine other pre development considerations that need to be worked through in the enterprise environment; how to design your application, take advantage of object orientation and what kind of a class library should you use? These are critical components that need to be addressed before you begin the build cycle of your enterprise application.

Then in Chapter 7, we examine all the great new features that PowerBuilder 5.0 brings us and we apply them to practical situations. If you are an experienced PowerBuilder 4.0 developer and want to jump right in to 5.0, this is a good place to start. You can see all the new objects and techniques put to use in the sample application that comes on the companion CD.

Chapters 8 through 11 address advanced development concepts. These are concepts that go beyond the basic tutorials and Introduction to PowerBuilder courses (now called FastTrack to PowerBuilder). We teach you the techniques of the pros and show you how to use them in the enterprise environment.

In Chapter 12 we round out your knowledge by examining the different types of user objects and how they should be integrated into your application. You will review a number of examples of non-visual objects.

If you are relatively new to enterprise projects with PowerBuilder, you will probably get the most benefit from this book by reading the chapters in order. If you are already a fairly experienced enterprise developer, you can easily jump from section to section and reference the information that you currently require! Make use of the index because I have tried to avoid any duplication of information. For example, using Rich Text DataWindows is an Advanced Reporting topic and you might expect to find it in Chapter 11, but it is discussed in depth in Chapter 7 because it is a new feature of PowerBuilder 5.0.

This book is focused on specific techniques instead of examining a single application that you build on as you go through the book. Each of the chapters here are discrete and stand alone. Often you will learn about more than one technique allowing you to select the one that is appropriate for your situation.

1.3 WHO SHOULD READ THIS BOOK

This book is intended to provide a valuable resource to PowerBuilder developers who have a need to develop applications in the enterprise environment. It is *not* a beginners book and will not teach you how to paint the different controls into the window painter. We will be focusing instead upon the techniques necessary to proceed from being an intermediate developer to an advanced one. This includes advanced techniques and knowledge which is incremental to the knowledge that we expect you already have. I would expect intermediate and experienced PowerBuilder developers would benefit most from this book.

This book will help to round out your PowerBuilder knowledge by providing you with methodologies and architectures that work for enterprise development projects. We will look at design issues for enterprise applications and discuss the concepts that will help you to make your applications more object oriented.

We will also go into substantial depth on the new PowerBuilder 5.0 features and how to use them. This chapter alone should make this book worthwhile for all existing PowerBuilder 4.0 developers.

The advanced techniques that follow will include details of how to develop the best DataWindows around, taking advantage of nested reports, drop down DataWindows, child DataWindows, sliding columns and many other advanced features.

You will learn how to construct and use non-visual business and service objects, integrate OLE 2.0 .OCX controls and much more.

1.4 WHAT IS ON THE COMPANION CD

The companion CD contains sample files that are referenced throughout the book. There are examples of all the new PowerBuilder 5.0 features such as distributed objects, native compiled code, single level function overloading, direct DataWindow manipulation and more! A compiled version of the sample application is included as well as all the source code. The sample application uses the PowerBuilder sample database in SQLAnywhere, so you must have SQLAnywhere installed on your system (the database file is included on the CD in case you didn't install the sample database when you installed PowerBuilder).

The examples on the companion CD, like the chapters themselves, are discrete examples of specific techniques. To keep the examples as straightforward and easy to understand the code that has been used will not follow pure object-oriented and proper coding techniques.

1.4.1 HOW TO INSTALL THE SAMPLE FILES

To install the sample files, run the SETUP.EXE program from the CD drive. This will create a directory called TFTE in your root directory. Within TFTE it will create three subdirectories:

- C:\TFTE\SAMPLES—contains all the source and compiled sample application objects. The database, if selected, is also installed here.

- C:\TFTE\DISTRIB—contains all the source and compiled files for the distributed PowerBuilder examples.

- C:\TFTE\OLEAUTO—contains all the source and compiled files for the OLE Automation example.

1.4.2 SETTING UP THE SAMPLE FILES

To set up the sample files, simple open PowerBuilder 5.0 and open the application object in the TOOLS.PBL library. Be sure to make your current database connection to the PowerBuilder Demo Database. You can install this database from the CD if you don't have it installed.

From here you can run or compile the application as you choose.

1.4.3 SETTING UP THE DISTRIBUTED POWERBUILDER EXAMPLE

Step 1   Open and compile the PBServer and PBConsol applications. This can be done in machine code, or in standard p-code without altering the effect of the example.

Step 2   Open the TCP/IP services file. This file is a text file that will most likely be found in your Windows directory and should be named 'Services.' You can open this file with notepad. Instructions for how to format your entries are contained in comments at the top of the file. We are going to add a new service to this file that will allow PowerBuilder to communicate with the distributed object. This service will have the following characteristics:

Service Name: DEMOSERVER
Port ID: 11001
Protocol: tcp
Comment: PB Book Demo
Your entry in the services file should look like:
DEMOSERVER   11001/tcp   #PB Book Demo

Step 3   Open the client application. This application object is in the PBClient.PBL library. You can either compile this application, or you can run it in the development environment directly.

Step 4   Start the PowerBuilder Demo DB V5 (THIS IS CRITICAL TO DO BEFORE STARTING THE DISTRIBUTED APPLICATION).

Step 5   Start the PB Server and PBConsol applications. Use the Run option or double click on the .EXE from explorer.

Step 6   Run the PB Client application.

Step 7   Connect to the distributed PowerBuilder application using the PB Server Connect command button.

Step 8   Connect to the SQLAnywhere database using the **DB Server Connect** command-button.

Step 9   Test the connectivity with the **Test DB Server** command button.

6   *Advanced PowerBuilder 5.0*

If you want to actually place the distributed applications on your server, follow the same steps but place the PBConsole and PBServer compiled applications on the server with the appropriate PB deployment kit libraries. Then you must set up the appropriate port on the server and define that port in your services file for the DEMOSERVER service.

1.4.4 SETTING UP THE OLE AUTOMATION EXAMPLE

Step 1   Register the OLE object. You can register the OLE object by double clicking on ole_obj.reg which will cause the object to be set up in the registry.

1.5 WHAT'S NEXT?

I am certain that we will not be able to get everything that I want to get into this book due to various factors beyond my control. If I was, this book would probably be over 1500 pages and you wouldn't see it for another six months. Maybe there is a Volume Two in the future?

In the interim, I wanted to leave you some information about other places to get information on PowerBuilder and to network with other PowerBuilder users.

The PowerBuilder documentation includes an excellent series of reference manuals including a *Programmers Reference Guide* and other valuable reference books. The on-line help is also very extensive and useful.

Powersoft/Sybase Press will have an excellent line of books covering the entire line of Powersoft/Sybase products that you will want to take advantage of including *Sybase SQLAnywhere Developers Guide* and books on distributed PowerBuilder or Optima ++, Powersoft's new GUI based C++ development environment.

You can go online and find Powersoft and PowerBuilder users on CompuServe (GO PBFORUM) and the Internet (http://www.powersoft.com).

You can also join up with local users groups in your area. If you can't find one, contact Powersoft to find out more details. Once a year Powersoft hosts their International Users Conference (usually in Orlando, Florida) in the late summer which is an excellent opportunity to network with thousands of other PowerBuilder users and learn the latest in advanced techniques.

Last, but not least, there are a number of PowerBuilder books and publications that will help to keep you in the loop about Powersoft and PowerBuilder including the *PowerBuilder Developers Journal (PBDJ)*, the *PowerBuilder Advisor* (check out my column "Into the Looking Glass"), *Powersoft PAD* and others.

PowerBuilder Developers Journal:

Subscription Hotline
(800)513-7111
(201)332-1515
Internet: 73611.756@compuserve.com

PowerBuilder Advisor

Customer Service
(800)336-6060
(619)483-6400
Internet: 70007.1614@compuserve.com

CHAPTER 2

The Development Methodology for Enterprise PowerBuilder

"It is common sense to take a method and try it. If it fails, admit it frankly and try another. But above all, try something."

– Franklin Delano Roosevelt,
Address at Oglethorpe University, Atlanta, Georgia,
May 22, 1932

One of the most inconsistent aspects of developing PowerBuilder applications is the use of a proper development methodology. This is a component of application development which many projects overlook or ignore, often with some particularly undesirable results. For small, ad hoc development, many single developers skip any formal development process, but doing so in the enterprise development environment will quickly lead to missed deadlines and cost overruns.

2.1 THE EVOLUTION OF CLIENT/SERVER DEVELOPMENT METHODOLOGIES

Until recently, there have been two dominant methodologies utilized in client/server development. The first of these is the 'Waterfall' methodology which although still used, is outdated and inappropriate for client/server projects. The second of these I call the 'Seat of the Pants' methodology, or in other words, no methodology at all.

It was quickly apparent to everyone using PowerBuilder to build multi-developer enterprise applications, that a new methodology would need to be devised. Over many different projects, we have evolved a methodology which has proven to be very successful in allowing us to deliver our projects on time and usually under budget.

A complete methodology goes beyond the scope of this book, so we are going to focus on the highlights of the development segment of the Accelerated Client/server Enterprise methodology (ACE).

To best understand ACE, you need to understand the evolution that preceded the current model. The road to developing a development methodology that would be suitable for PowerBuilder applications requires a lot of different approaches to be tested. The best components of each are retained and used in the ACE methodology.

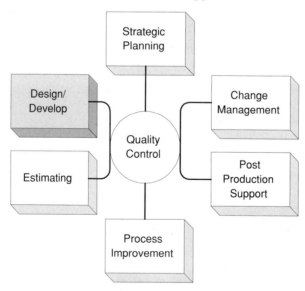

Figure 2.1 The ACE Methodology has been used to deliver many enterprise PowerBuilder applications on time and on or under budget.

2.2 THE WATERFALL RUNS DRY

In the days when we were developing custom enterprise applications in COBOL or FORTRAN we utilized a rigid methodology for structured application development. Many of you will already be familiar with a methodology based upon the waterfall concept.

The waterfall breaks the development cycle down into discrete steps each with a rigid, sequential begin and end date. Each step is to be fully completed before the following step is started. Once a step is finished you never go back to change it.

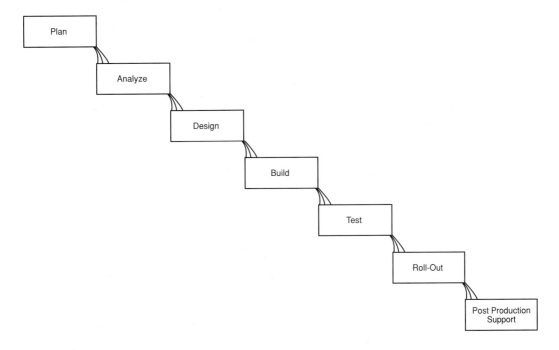

Figure 2.2 *The Waterfall methodology has been used for many years to develop systems based upon structured analysis and design and developed with procedural languages. This methodology proved to be inappropriate for use in client/server development.*

In Figure 2.2, we can see that the first stage in the waterfall is to plan. This encompasses the overall objectives of the system, project timelines, delivery dates and more.

12   *Chapter 2: The Development Methodology for Enterprise PowerBuilder*

Once the planning stage is finished, the outputs from the planning process flow over into the analysis process. In this stage, the users are interviewed, their requirements are analyzed and a document is produced detailing what the users requirements are. Any reengineering or process redesign is incorporated into this step. Functional decomposition diagrams are created to allow the system to be broken down into manageable components.

The outputs from analysis are used to develop a design of the system. Various structured design techniques are used to produce a design specification that will be passed on to the build phase.

In the build phase, the programmers develop the system according to the design. Once complete, the system enters the testing phase where it will be unit tested, string tested, system tested and finally user tested.

Now the system is delivered to the users in the implementation phase. Once implemented the final phase begins, this is known as post-production support.

The waterfall methodology was used by most client/server developers who entered this industry through structured development projects. This was where I first learned the waterfall. In attempting to use the waterfall we found a number of shortcomings:

- The end users of the system were only involved in the very beginning and the very end of the process. As a result, the system that they were given at the end of the development cycle was often not what they originally visualized or thought that they asked for.

- The long development cycle and the shortening of business cycles led to a gap between what was being delivered and what was really needed. You have probably heard the famous end user quote "It's exactly what I asked for, but it's not what I need!." The lack of user involvement between the analysis and the implementation phase resulted in development time and dollars being expended to deploy systems which were no longer appropriate for the current business model.

- We expected our end users to be able to describe in detail what they wanted for a system, before we began to build. This may seem logical to developers, but to end users who haven't used a computer system before and aren't really certain of what can be built, this can be ludicrous. Users usually do not know what they want until they see it and like to be presented with samples to choose from, like buying carpet for your living room!

- When we reached the 'end' of a phase, we found that we really weren't complete, but the methodology required that we press on anyway. In fact, you cannot ever fully complete a phase; there is always more work that can be done. When you think about it, is any system that we deliver ever "completely" finished? Probably not. The methodology we use should take this into consideration and allow us to see the progression between phases and recognize that the preceding phases are not 100% complete.

We quickly learned that the waterfall methodology was going to be woefully inadequate for our client/server development projects. Soon, experts were beginning to publish methodologies based upon other models, many of which were based upon a *cyclical* approach to systems development.

2.3 THE SPIRAL METHODOLOGY

I will generalize here and lump all the first generation cyclical methodologies under the label of 'Spiral' methodologies (this includes 'fountain' based methodologies). These methodologies suggest a process of working from a base and building a system incrementally. Upon reaching the end of each phase, developers would always reexamine the entire structure and revisit each major stage before proceeding to the next phase.

The spiral methodology is represented by drawing the four major phases of systems development, Planning/Analysis, Design, Build and Test into quadrants. The process begins by performing preliminary planning and requirements analysis. Then a design is made for the base components of the system and for the functionality determined in the first step. Next this functionality is constructed and tested. This represents one complete iteration of the spiral.

Having completed this first loop, the users are given the opportunity to examine the system and enhance its functionality. This begins the second iteration of the spiral. The process continues, looping around and around the spiral until the users and developers agree the system is complete and you can proceed to implementation.

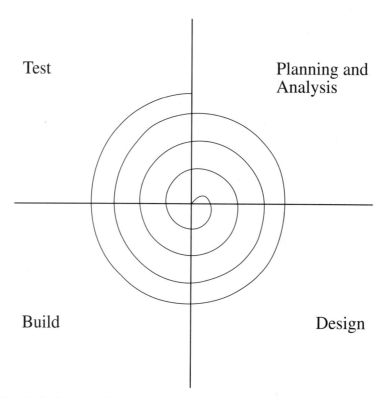

Figure 2.3 *The Spiral methodology allows a system to be built incrementally, revisiting each of the four major phases for each spiral through the development process.*

This methodology was good for ensuring that the users requirements were being adequately addressed and that the users were closely involved with the project. It also allowed for the system to adapt to any changes in business requirements that occurred after the system development was begun. There was one central fatal flaw that made this methodology fail, there was never any firm commitment to implement a working system! You could go round and round the quadrants, never actually bringing a system into production. This brought to mind the image of the way a crocodile kills its prey, it grabs it and then spirals down and down into the water until it is dead. Thus I affectionately call this problem 'The Death Spiral'.

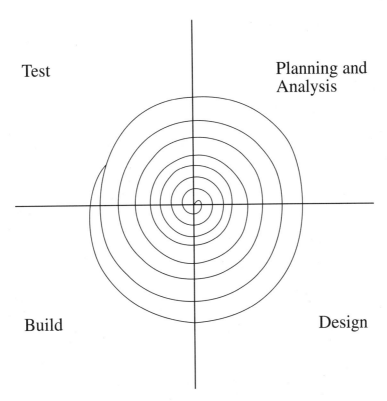

Figure 2.4 *The major shortcoming of the Spiral methodology is that you can continue to add functionality over and over and never actually implement the system. This is a condition that I call 'The Death Spiral' as it will surely kill your project.*

While the Waterfall had proven itself to be too inflexible, the Spiral has demonstrated the exact opposite problem. If we could learn to harness and control the spiral, it would become an effective methodology for PowerBuilder development.

2.4 THE ITERATIVE METHODOLOGY

The Iterative methodology was an enhancement on the spiral. It was intended to force the development team into actually reaching a point where the system would be implemented. The Iterative methodology recognizes that a system is never truly complete, but is instead evolutionary. However, it also realizes that there is a point where the system is close enough to complete to be of value to the end user.

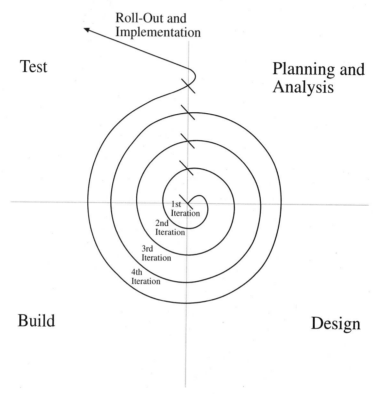

Figure 2.5 *The Iterative methodology is designed to force the project to reach a completion point where a real, live system is implemented.*

The point of implementation is decided upon prior to the start of the system. A certain number of iterations will be specified with goals identified for each iteration. Upon completion of the final iteration, the system will be implemented whatever state it may be in.

To demonstrate this methodology, let's examine the possible iterations involved in developing a system to handle time sheet entry and tracking. The first iteration could be devoted strictly to time entry. First the time entry process is planned, the requirements are determined and processes are modeled. The data elements are mapped to the data model, or if this is a new system, the data elements are created in the appropriate data model entities. Next the windows and objects necessary for the entry process are designed in detail. In the build phase, all the objects are constructed with PowerBuilder and if necessary, the data model entities and elements are created or revised. Then the data entry components are unit tested and, where applicable, string tested. This would end the first iteration of our cycle.

The second iteration could focus on maintenance and modification of our time details. The third would implement reporting and the fourth would develop system maintenance functions. A final fifth iteration would deal with any final changes and add a security layer to the application.

All in all we went through five complete iterations of the system. In the final stage, complete string testing and user testing would need to occur as part of the implementation process.

This methodology worked reasonably well, and is still used in a number of PowerBuilder development shops today. Where we found limitations in this methodology was that it was not a strong mechanism for addressing changing business needs during the development cycle as completed iterations are not usually revisited in future iterations. The other significant drawback to this methodology was that the time to delivery of a system was usually much longer than one would expect even though we are using a tool set that supports rapid application development and delivery.

This led to our development of the flattened spiral approach, which is the methodology that we utilize today.

2.5 THE FLATTENED SPIRAL METHODOLOGY

The flattened spiral approach is the current evolutionary stage of the ACE methodology. I would fully expect that as we learn more, this model will continue to be refined, but for now, it has proven to perform very well in a variety of circumstances.

This approach allows you to break down the system into modules and components, like in the waterfall. It incorporates the ability to cycle through the elements of the system and revisit and improve them, like in the spiral. It has the control and built in limits of the iterative methodology. It also has more.

The flattened spiral incorporates prototyping as a key element of its early stages to provide better feedback to the user and allow the organization to make a go/no-go decision early in the system process before investing large amounts of time and resources into a system.

Chapter 2: The Development Methodology for Enterprise PowerBuilder

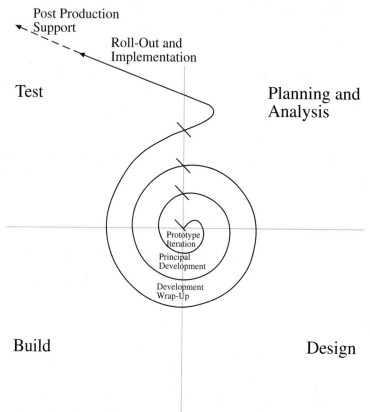

Figure 2.6 *The Flattened Spiral Methodology takes some of the best features of its predecessors and combines them into a functional and effective development methodology.*

When diagrammed, the flattened spiral has a look very much like the spiral and iterative methodologies. You will still use the four major quadrants and work your way through each of them for each iteration of development. However, each iteration is very clearly defined and there are exactly three iterations to be performed, no more, no less.

In the remainder of this chapter, we will focus on the development of a system using this methodology. The data model, if it does not already exist, should be developed in it's own spiral which is separate from the development spiral, but is tied to it in a parallel fashion. Most systems being developed in the enterprise client/server arena today are utilizing a data warehouse concept. This means that the data model should have a life which extends well beyond the current system being developed. In the interests of remaining focused on PowerBuilder enterprise development, we will not be dealing with data modeling in this book.

2.5.1 THE FIRST ITERATION

The first iteration of development should occur within a very quick time frame. For most systems, the complete iteration should be wrapped up in four weeks. If you are taking longer than this, you are moving beyond what should be done in iteration one and are trying to perform segments of the second iteration.

2.5.1.1 Planning and Analysis

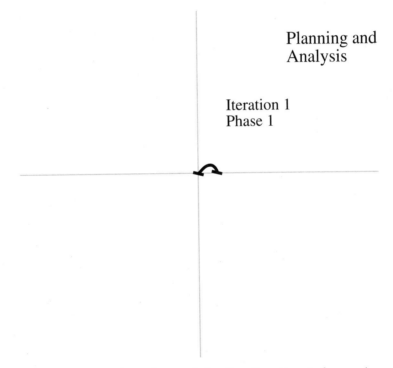

Figure 2.7 *The first phase of the first iteration is focused on determining functionality.*

In this first phase the objective is to deliver a preliminary functional decomposition diagram and functional specifications. This can be done using a variety of techniques, but one of the most effective is to hold a Joint Application Design (JAD) session. Six or eight of the key users of the system are included in the session. An experienced JAD facilitator and scribe are also key to success. A representative from the development team is also important to ensure that the planning and analysis has a firm grounding in what can be practically accomplished. The JAD facilitator may double up and carry out this role if they have the background to do so. These sessions are very effective for driving out the details of the processes and functions involved in the system and in obtaining consensus from the users on what the system must accomplish.

Inputs: system objectives (from your strategic plan), user input
Deliverables: Functional Decomposition Diagram, Functional Specifications
Tools Used: variable, tools for drawing functional decomposition (many case tools provide this functionality, or Visio is one that I like)
Time to Complete: 1 week

2.5.1.2 Design

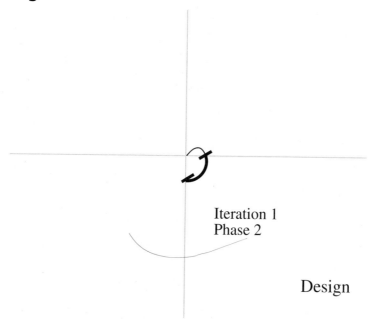

Figure 2.8 *The second phase of the first iteration is focused on designing front end mock ups which support the business processes.*

In this second phase the objective is to design some screen mock ups that can be presented to the user group to demonstrate a possible user interface for the system. These mock ups must be based upon the business processes that the system is intended to deliver. Business processes that are involved can often be identified here but may not be fully developed until the second iteration. These screen designs must incorporate the design and user interface standards for the organization (which implies that they have already been developed).

This phase is not usually as formally documented as other phases. If your developers are also your business systems analysts (BSA) then you may choose to have the developers mock up the screens directly in PowerBuilder. If your BSAs are somewhat PowerBuilder literate, then the same thing can be done. If your BSAs and your development team are two separate groups, the analysts can simply sketch the user interfaces on paper and pass these to the development team. There are tools on the market specifically designed for analysts in this phase, however, I feel that they are a waste of money as you can either use the manual process above, or use PowerBuilder as your screen building tool.

You don't need to spend too much time and effort here, remember that one of the goals of the first iteration is to complete it quickly and produce an online prototype at the end.

Inputs: Functional Decomposition (from Phase 1, Step 1), Functional Specifications (from Phase 1, Step 1), development and user interface standards (from organizational standards, if they don't exist, they must be created). Logical data model (from organizational data model, or as a result of a database design subproject).

Deliverables: quick and dirty screen designs for the user interface

Tools used: optional: PowerBuilder or case tool for screen mockups (not essential)

Time to Complete: 1 week

2.5.1.3 Build

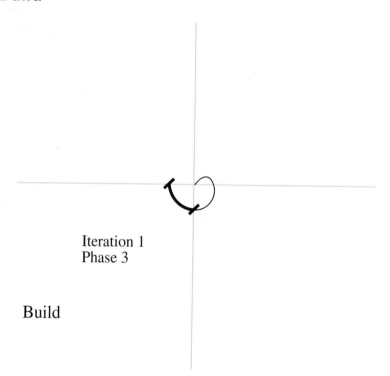

Figure 2.9 *Now we can create the windows and objects for the prototype.*

In the build phase the screen designs from the previous step are turned into real windows and objects in PowerBuilder. If the data model exists then DataWindow objects can also be created where applicable. This is preferable because you are maximizing the reusability of the prototype for the second phase of the system. If the data model is not yet created, then the DataWindows will have to be created in an external format for the prototype and recreated in iteration two when the data model does exist.

None of the business functionality is built into the prototype, just the look and feel of the user interface is created.

Inputs: screen designs for the user interface (from Phase 1, Step 2)
Deliverables: completed user interface online mock up
Tools used: PowerBuilder, optional: class library and framework
Time to Complete: 1 week

2.5.1.4 Test

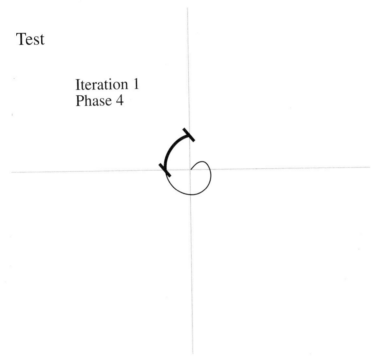

Figure 2.10 *The interface should be tested before being presented to the user.*

The phase in PowerBuilder application development most often skipped or ignored by development teams is the testing phase. Most of the applications being rolled out today have not been adequately tested and this results in a high level of bugs and user dissatisfaction with the system.

The implementation of software quality assurance techniques is critical and needs to be taken more seriously. At this stage, the quality assurance process involves ensuring that the designs of the prototypes adhere to the design standards that have been implemented in the organization. It also involves ensuring that all the functions indicated in the decomposition

24 *Chapter 2: The Development Methodology for Enterprise PowerBuilder*

and specifications are addressed in the prototype. Any links to navigate through the proto-type which have been installed must also be tested.

There are a number of automated testing tools that can help you with improving the quality of the software that you deliver to your end users. I highly recommend checking them out and taking advantage of the improvements they can make to your quality processes. Of course, testing can all be done manually, but this can become a slow and tedious phase if everything is done by hand.

The testing becomes more and more exhaustive with each iteration. The first iteration testing is fairly simple and straightforward, but be prepared for it to get far more intensive in iterations two and three.

Inputs: online system mock up (from Phase 1, Step 3)
Deliverables: Test Results Document (expected results versus actual), bug list
Tools: PowerBuilder, optional: automated testing tool
Time to Complete: 1 week

2.5.2 THE SECOND ITERATION

The second iteration of the methodology is where the bulk of development of the business processes and functionality should occur. The time frame for this iteration is more variable and depends upon the scope of the system being developed. As a rough guideline, it will probably range from 8 weeks to 10 months. If you expect that your second iteration will take longer than this, you may want to reexamine the scope of your system and see if it can be better modularized and approached one module at a time.

2.5.2.1 Planing and Analysis

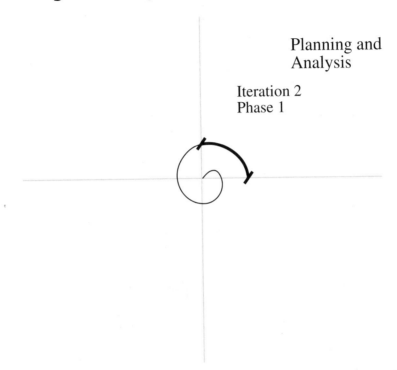

Figure 2.11 *The first phase of the second iteration allows the users to determine a design that will meet all the functional requirements of the system.*

The objective of the first phase of the second iteration is to obtain user consensus on the design and final functionality of the system. At the end of this stage, 90% of the functionality of the system should be fully analyzed.

Again we will utilize the JAD session, but modified to perform a review of the prototype and solicit feedback from the users. Having a prototype to review is of tremendous value. Often end users have difficulty in determining what kind of interface would be best for their application until they are presented with some examples on which to base their feedback.

Inputs: tested prototype (from Phase 1, Step 4), user input
Deliverables: Revised Functional Decomposition and Specifications, interface enhancement requests.

Tools Used: variable, tools for drawing functional decomposition (many case tools provide this functionality, or Visio is one that I like)

Time to Complete: variable: 2 days to 12 days depending on scope

2.5.2.2 Design

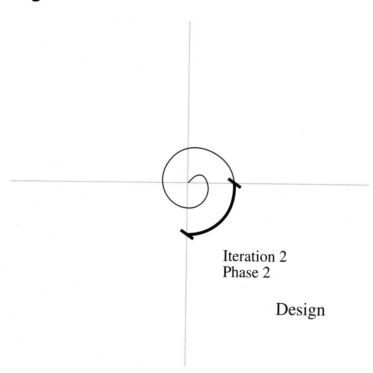

Figure 2.12 *The second phase of the first iteration will develop detailed design specifications.*

In this second phase the objective is to develop detailed design specifications for each object to be built by the design team, both visual and non-visual. These designs are very detailed and include: a description of the object (covering the purpose of the object), a screen shot of the object (if applicable), how the user navigates to the object (where it is used in the system), a detailed description of all objects and controls used on the object and also any business rules or security issues associated with the object.

2.5 The Flattened Spiral Methodology

For each object and control placed on the first level (primary) object, a detailed description is also required. This description will include the relevant attributes and their values, and any interactions with other objects or the data model. If the object is a DataWindow, or data interaction object, the design should detail each data element that is involved and discuss any client based validation rules, edit masks, acceptable values and other specific information relating to the field.

The amount of detail required here will depend upon the business experience of the development team and if your BSAs are also your developers. User sign off of the design should be obtained at the end of this phase.

Inputs: Revised Functional Decomposition and Specifications (from Phase 2, Step 1), development and user interface standards (from organizational standards). Physical data model (from organizational data model or from data base subproject).
Deliverables: Detailed Design Specifications
Tools used: word processor of choice
Time to Complete: variable: 2–10 weeks

2.5.2.3 Build

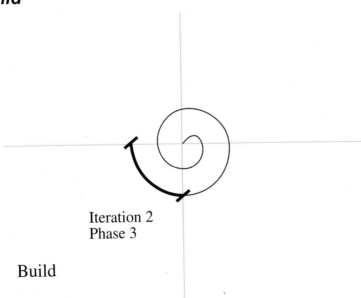

Figure 2.13 *Now the real development begins as we create all the objects for the system.*

In the build phase the detailed designs are transformed into real objects in PowerBuilder (or in a multi-tiered architecture into service objects, RPCs or stored procedures. See Chapter 3 for more details). The business logic is all put into place. All the necessary data fields have been mapped to their physical data model data elements. Each object should be unit tested by the developer before being deemed to be completed.

This is the longest phase of the whole development life cycle as each object must be carefully constructed and unit tested.

Inputs: Detailed Design Specifications, physical data model
Deliverables: completed functional system
Tools used: PowerBuilder, optional: class library and framework, version control software, other third party add ins.
Time to Complete: variable: 6 weeks to 8 months based upon scope of application

2.5.2.4 Test

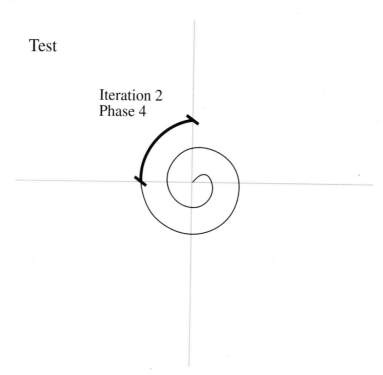

Figure 2.14 *Full unit and string tests are executed to ensure the robustness of the application.*

The test phase will focus on performing complete unit and string testing of the application. Regression tests should be developed to allow future revisions and changes to the system to be fully tested. A documented test plan should be developed and carried out.

Inputs: functional system
Deliverables: Test Results Document (expected results versus actual), bug list
Tools: PowerBuilder, optional: automated testing tool
Time to Complete: variable: 1 week to 1 month

2.5.3 THE THIRD (AND FINAL) ITERATION

The third iteration will be the final iteration of the methodology. Here, any business changes that occurred during system development can be determined and the system adapted. This will eliminate the "It's exactly what I asked for, but not what I want!" reaction from the users. The system will be reviewed and any change requests, either functional or cosmetic are documented.

Any final layered functionality is incorporated here. This is defined as functionality which is important to the functioning of the system, but is not necessarily an integral part of the business processes. The most common element to include here is security. The time frame for this iteration is variable but is generally brief. As a rough guideline, it will probably range from 4 weeks to 10 weeks.

2.5.3.1 Planing and Analysis

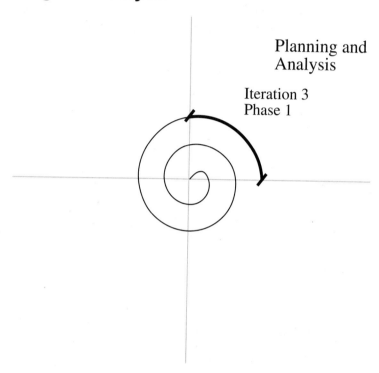

Figure 2.15 *The first phase of the final iteration allows us to determine any business requirements that may have changed during development and to incorporate any layered functionality such as security.*

The objective of the first phase of the third iteration is to discover if any of the functionality in the system has changed or is incorrect. We also want to determine how to incorporate any layered functionality such as security. This is the final opportunity for user input prior to implementation.

Like before we will utilize the JAD session modified to perform a review of the functional system and solicit feedback from the users. Users will be asked to specifically watch for places where the business functionality may have changed since the last user review. Users will also be asked to confirm the security requirements of the system that have been previously worked out by the BSAs.

Inputs: tested functional system, user input, Security Requirements Document
Deliverables: system enhancement/change requests, final Security Requirements Document
Tools Used: variable, word processor
Time to Complete: variable: 2 days to 12 days depending on scope

2.5.3.2 Design

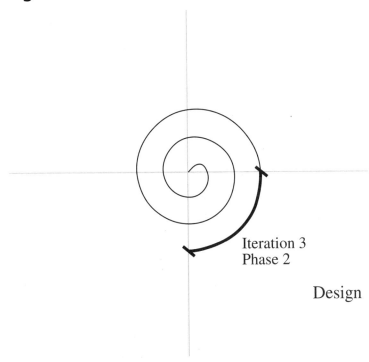

Figure 2.16 *The second phase of the final iteration will develop detailed design specifications for any approved enhancements, changes and layered functionality.*

In this second phase the objective is to develop or revise the existing detailed design specifications for all approved enhancements, changes and for any layered functionality to be incorporated.

Inputs: system enhancement/change requests, Security Requirements Document
Deliverables: revised Detailed Design Specifications

Tools used: word processor of choice
Time to Complete: variable: 2–6 weeks

2.5.3.3 Build

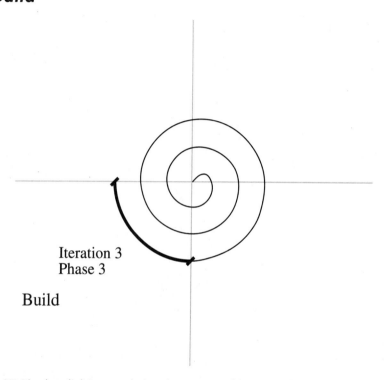

Figure 2.17 *Final polishing and development of layered functionality occurs in the third phase of the final iteration.*

In the build phase any changes to the objects a specified in the detailed design specifications are incorporated. All layered functionality is implemented. Layered functionality can often be incorporated through the use of third party tools. There are a number of good third party security tools on the market for PowerBuilder applications. If your class library does not already have a security mechanism in it, I recommend you investigate these.

Inputs: revised Detailed Design Specifications
Deliverables: final functional system

2.5 The Flattened Spiral Methodology

Tools used: PowerBuilder, optional: class library and framework, version control software, other third party add ins.

Time to Complete: variable: 2 to 8 weeks based upon scope of application and volume of changes

2.5.3.4 Test

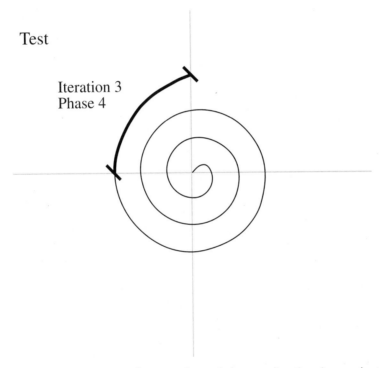

Figure 2.18 *Final complete testing of the application is conducted, including full user testing.*

The final test phase will be the most extensive testing effort yet. All previous tests should be reexecuted and full regression testing performed. A documented test plan should be developed and carried out.

Upon completion of these tests, user testing should begin. Results of user testing should be incorporated into the Test Results Document.

34 *Chapter 2: The Development Methodology for Enterprise PowerBuilder*

Inputs: final system
Deliverables: Test Results Document (expected results versus actual), bug list
Tools: PowerBuilder, optional: automated testing tool
Time to Complete: variable: 2 weeks to 6 weeks

2.5.4 IMPLEMENTATION

The iterations are over, the system is built and tested, now it is time to deliver it to the end users. This section of the methodology is not radically different from others you may be familiar with. All the basic requirements are the same. Now you must prepare the documentation, train the users and roll out the system to their workspaces.

2.5.4.1 Documentation

Documentation consists of two components, user and system.

2.5.4.1.1 User Documentation

The user documentation phase can actually begin earlier than this stage. The assigned technical writer can begin developing the user manuals and the online help in the build phase of the second iteration as the system begins to take shape. The documentation can not be truly completed however until the final testing of the third iteration is complete and the system is done.

Manuals can be developed using your favorite word processing tool. To generate the online help, I strongly recommend using a help authoring tool. Anyone who has tried to develop online help using only the Windows SDK can testify that it is not a pleasant experience. There are many currently available commercial help authoring tools which are excellent. Many shops no longer produce paper manuals, but build only online help. This is for a variety of reasons including cost, ease of updating and environmental friendliness.

I would strongly recommend producing quick reference cards for your end users where possible. Print these on a thick card stock paper and fold it in such a way that they can stand it up like a café menu beside their monitors (this way is doesn't get lost in the stacks of paper that we all collect on our desks!)

Inputs: final system
Deliverables: User Manuals, Online help, optional: Quick Reference Cards
Tools: Word Processor, Help Authoring Tool
Time to Complete: variable: 2 weeks to 6 weeks

2.5.4.1.2 System Documentation

The purpose of system documentation is to provide the information necessary to allow the system to be maintained and repaired in the future. It also provides a paper trail that details how and why the system was designed the way it was.

All documentation produced during the system development life cycle should be gathered into one place. This includes all functional specifications, decomposition diagrams, process models, detailed design specifications, physical and logical data models and technical print outs of all objects incorporated into the system.

Inputs: all system documentation
Deliverables: unified System Documentation binder(s)
Time to Complete: variable: 1 to 2 weeks

2.5.4.2 Training

The training phase of implementation involves developing a training plan and carrying it out. Depending on the number of users, the magnitude of this task varies. Users could be trained directly by one of the BSAs, or in groups, or user trainer representatives could be trained in a 'Train the Trainer' session. These representatives would then return to their user base and perform all the training for their users.

Inputs: final system and User Documentation
Deliverables: Training Plan, end user training, optional: training manuals
Time to Complete: variable: 1–8 weeks

2.5.4.3 Roll-out

The process of rolling out an application has a lot of the same procedures as before, but there are a few new twists. A staging plan needs to be prepared for all hardware that needs to be installed. The physical networks must be established and tested. Servers need to be installed and tested. All relevant supporting software must be installed and tested. And so on...

Depending on how you have decided to roll out your client application, either to each individual workstation, networked on the server, or using a multi-tiered architecture, this will affect your planned roll out.

Inputs: final system, Enterprise Architecture Plan (if available), organizational hardware and network standards

36   *Chapter 2: The Development Methodology for Enterprise PowerBuilder*

Deliverables: Enterprise Architecture Plan, System Roll Out Plan
Time to Complete: variable

2.5.4.4 Post Production Support (Help Desk)

Once the system is out and in the hands of the users. This is when the post production support phase begins. You need to detail how user issues and system issues will be handled. Will a help desk or support line be established? Is there one already? How can a user request a change to the system? Who approves changes? And so on…

Just because a system is installed, doesn't mean the process is finished. To be complete, and to ensure the long term viability of the system the above questions and more must be answered. A Post Production Support Plan should be developed to document and establish the mechanisms to manage the system now and in the future.

Inputs: live production system
Deliverables: Post Production Support Plan
Time to Complete: variable: 1–3 weeks

2.6 WHERE TO GO FROM HERE

"Our ideas are only intellectual instruments which we use to break into phenomena; we must change them when they have served their purpose, as we must change a blunt lancet that we have used long enough."

–Claude Bernard

The world that we exist in changes faster than we can believe. The ACE methodology outlined above must be considered a work in progress. Take this work and use it as best you can. Change it when part of it does not apply to your situation or your world. I would be very pleased to hear any changes that you have been successful in implementing that have improved the above model.

CHAPTER 3

Architectures for Development

"The physician can bury his mistakes, but the architect can only advise his client to plant vines."

– Frank Lloyd Wright, October 4, 1953, New York Times Magazine

rchitecture plays a very important role in the success of client/server applications. When we discuss the architecture of an application we are referring to the manner in which components of the applications and functions of all the systems are stored, where they are stored and how and where they are executed.

When developing applications using PowerBuilder, you have the flexibility to implement a variety of different types of architectures depending on your specific application or enterprise requirements. Selecting the appropriate architecture can reap substantial rewards for both the developers of the system and the users. These rewards can include a reduced development time and effort, increased application consistency, improved scalability, faster application performance and easier maintenance.

A variety of different types of architectures can be considered, and architects are coming up with more every day. The most commonly utilized architectures today are the two-tiered architecture, the three and N-tiered architectures and the service based architecture.

In this chapter we will review these architectures at a high level, and will tie them in to different techniques in later chapters. To see how to build a basic distributed object, turn to Chapter 7 New PowerBuilder 5.0 Features, section 7.2 Distributed Objects.

3.1 TWO-TIERED ARCHITECTURES

Most PowerBuilder applications developed to date have been implemented using a two-tiered architecture. This architecture divides the application into two components, the *client* and the *data server*. Multiple client applications can access a single data repository on a shared database server.

The client is the component where the user interface resides. It manages the interface with the end user of the system. You may have heard this component referred to as the presentation layer. In PowerBuilder this includes of all the visual objects such as windows, window controls and DataWindows.

The data server is where all the data that the application will access and manipulate is stored. This is usually contained within some kind of a relational database (RDBMS). Obviously there are other kinds of servers such as print servers, file servers, image servers and so on, but for the purposes of this example, the only server that matters is the database server.

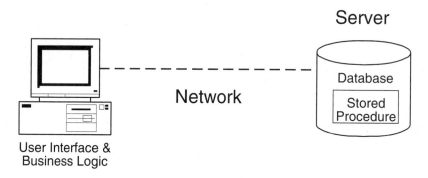

Figure 3.1 *The two-tiered architecture places the user interface on the client, the data on a data server and the business rules can be programmed into either the client front end, or in stored procedures on the data server.*

The business logic is programmed into the client front end, as part of the PowerBuilder code, or as stored procedures on the server database. Most existing PowerBuilder enterprise applications are a combination of both, but usually much more heavily weighted towards having the business rules coded into the PowerBuilder application. It is very rare to see a PowerBuilder application where all the business rules reside on the server, although this would help to eliminate most of the drawbacks of a two tiered architecture discussed below.

Two-tiered architectures are particularly good for developing what we call "One Of" or "One Off" applications. These are applications where the objects involved are not likely to be reused and the business logic is not transportable across many different applications. These types of applications typically do not take advantage of any pre-built or existing business objects.

A two-tiered application can often be put together very quickly as less preparation is required to separate out the potential business logic and service objects. These objects are built right into the user interface or the relational database.

We have come to realize, after the industry has built thousands of two-tiered client/server applications, that although quick to design and build, there are some distinct limitations to this architecture. One drawback is that the business rules are all coded into either the client or the server. This means that if you select a new best of breed technology to replace one of these tiers (for example, you decide to replace your Visual Basic application with a PowerBuilder application) you will very likely have to rebuild the entire application, including your business logic.

Of even greater impact is the potential maintenance problem. If a basic business rule changes, you have to find every spot in the PowerBuilder application where that rule applies, change it, recompile the application and redistribute it to the users.

There is one other primary disadvantage to the two-tiered architecture: scalability. If you are rolling out your application to a lower number of concurrent users (the number is relative and we cannot be specific, but a rule of thumb I have heard is under 200 concurrent users), the two-tiered architecture functions adequately, however, once crossing over this dynamic threshold (the 200 user 'line in the sand') application performance begins to suffer. With all the business logic on the client, these applications tend to make many small calls to the server to help them process the user input. The server gets overloaded trying to respond to all the user requests. The network tends to also slow down as the amount of data being shuffled from the server to the clients increases. This has been discussed as the 'fat-client' syndrome and has plagued client centered development environments like PowerBuilder for some time.

You may encounter the term 'partitioning' in your client/server documentation and training. Partitioning refers to the separation of the presentation, process/business rules and the data into three distinct and isolated units. Partitioning can be rolled out in a two-tier or multi-tier environment by selecting the location of the business logic. In PowerBuilder you can separate these components by building non-visual user objects that contain these rules. This can be a very valuable preliminary step to migrating your application from a two-tier to a multi-tier model.

3.2 THREE-TIERED ARCHITECTURES

To help overcome some of the inherent limitations of the two-tiered architecture, the concept of the three-tiered architecture was devised. In this architecture, the business logic is removed from both the client and the server and located on some other third layer. This third layer acts as a middleman, providing services to the user interface on the client and consolidating and managing transactions for the data server (or servers).

Note: I should point out that only in the theoretical world is all the logic removed from the client and server. Usually some of the logic still resides in these objects.

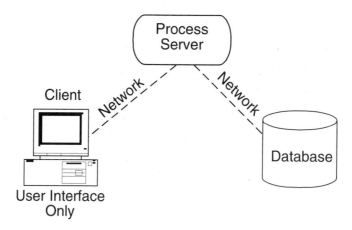

Figure 3.2 *The three-tiered architecture removes the business logic from both the client and the server and places it in some other third layer which could reside and execute on a physically separate machine from the client and the server.*

With this model, if you decide to change the front end tool for your application, you should be able to do so (if your third tier was developed in a non-proprietary format). In theory, any application development tool and any relational database should be able to be used with the business rule objects stored on remote servers. This theory holds up if your objects are built to be DCE (Distributed Computing Environment), CORBA (Common Object Request Broker Architecture) or OLE (Object Linking and Embedding) compliant. As these standards are still evolving, most of the three tiered applications in production today are still proprietary in nature.

With a three-tiered architecture, maintaining your business rules becomes easier as they are all maintained in one place (in theory, although in practice, many three-tiered applications will still place some business rules on the server and/or client). Many different applications can access the same business rule objects. Through centralization of objects focused on specific purposes, the burdens on the network and the database server may be able to be better managed.

Although a three-tiered architecture was conceived of to overcome some of the limitations of a two-tiered architecture, it also comes with its own disadvantages. There is a lot more up front work to be done. The investment in time and also the hardware for the third tier is no pittance. While you could still utilize many of the traditional structured development techniques to build applications with PowerBuilder, to build true three tiered architectures requires that you perform proper object oriented analysis and design. These techniques have their own substantial learning curve.

A second issue with three tiered architectures is that they become quite complex to manage and maintain. Although it becomes easy to alter an application if something like a business rule changes (all you have to do is change the appropriate business rule object on the third tier), you now find that your objects and your business logic is scattered throughout your architecture. Objects can be become lost and controlling them becomes difficult. The theory of moving parts also begins to come into play: The more moving parts, the more likely a machine is to break down.

As I mentioned earlier, many of the three tiered PowerBuilder solutions in production today rely upon sophisticated (some would say 'complicated') third party products such as Novell's Tuxedo, Open Environment's Entera, IBM CICS, or Transarc Corporation's Encina. These tools, although providing some of the benefits of the three tier architecture, quickly fall victim to inflexibility and complexity.

3.3 N-TIERED ARCHITECTURES

The n-tiered architecture is the next level beyond the three-tier architecture. In the n-tier environment, your objects could reside almost anywhere in your overall architecture. You won't have one specific piece of hardware dedicated as the 'process object server.' Instead, your objects will be placed onto the servers where their functions are most appropriate. Through careful planning and design you will be able to reduce load on the network. Data stores inside these distributed objects can help to reduce load on the servers. This is the type of architecture which will truly allow you to scale your applications.

Like the three-tiered architecture, to be effective, an n-tiered architecture requires extensive up front planning and design effort, but they also have similar drawbacks, including the complexity factor.

3.4 SERVICE-BASED ARCHITECTURES

In traditional discussions of multi-tiered architectures, the distributed objects that are usually discussed are based upon logical business entities or processes. For example, an HMO (Health Management Organization) may develop two distributed objects, one called a doctor, and the other a patient. Each would contain the methods and properties of their relevant business entities and could be stored and executed on a remote server.

In contrast, a service based architecture is based upon taking common services that many applications require and separating them out as distributed objects. Many of these services are common amongst multiple systems and include such items as e-mail, faxing, printing, error handling, security management and EDI (Electronic Data Interchange) to use a few of the more common examples. Services can also be driven down to a lower level and may include items like DataWindow row selection (single, multi or other), messaging and error handling/logging in your PowerBuilder applications.

You can begin to imagine some of the possibilities this architecture could provide. Think of an e-mail service. You could build an e-mail object that would reside and execute on a remote server. When any of your internal applications need to send or work with your e-mail system, they connect through the standard interface you have constructed into the distributed object. The CPU cycles that the mail server requires are taken on the server and not on your client machine.

3.4 Service Based Architectures 43

Developers Tip: In PowerBuilder we usually offer services at one of three levels:

- **Instance Service—when only one instance of an object in the client can use the service at a time. A separate instance of the service object would be created for each instance of a client object that requires the service.**

- **Class Service—when a single instance of the service object can be used to provide services to multiple instances of a given class of client object. A separate instance of the service object would be created for other classes requiring this service.**

- **Application Service—when a single instance of the service object can be used to provide services to all instances of all classes of client objects in the application.**

There is another added benefit to this architecture. If you have five applications that all utilize e-mail, and then your organization switches from MS-Mail you could be faced with a challenge that may have an adverse impact upon your systems. If you use a standard MAPI (Messaging Application Program Interface—from Microsoft) compatible mail system you can take advantage of the built in MAPI functions that PowerBuilder supports. Then, if you decide to switch to cc:Mail which is based upon VIM (Vendor Independent Messaging—from Lotus) you will face some potentially difficult integration challenges as PowerBuilder does not have built in support for VIM. If you had used anything other than a service based architecture, you would need to modify every object that has a method that uses e-mail one at a time. Through the service based architecture, you only need to make the changes in the one object and have it take effect for all your current and future applications. The improved maintenance and the productivity gains realized across multiple applications is tremendous.

One potential disadvantage to a pure service-based architecture is that the business logic can end up spread amongst a number of unrelated objects and this can become a maintenance problem.

3.5 SELECTING THE RIGHT ARCHITECTURE

When you were about halfway through the above subsection, you were probably thinking to yourself "But if I combine the n-tiered architecture with the services architecture, couldn't I get the best of both worlds?" and you would be absolutely correct. However, I would caution you that you are again increasing the complexity of the environment you work in and creating more "moving parts."

You cannot point at one architecture or another and say "This is the best architecture to use all the time." You must examine your corporate requirements and determine the appropriate architecture for your needs. You may be able to combine a number of the above architectures into one that works for your particular enterprise.

If you have a small company with only a dozen users and just two or three systems it might make sense to combine a two-tiered and a service-based architecture. There is not a lot of opportunity to implement large scale reuse and scalability is not really an issue. The speed of development and cost effectiveness is likely to appeal to you, yet you can benefit from services which all the applications need, like providing fax services.

On the other hand, if you are a large scale corporation with dozens of custom applications of all shapes and sizes you would likely benefit from an n-tier architecture integrated with a solid foundation of distributed services.

If this is your first application with this environment and tool set, I would discourage you from trying to build a fully integrated n-tier and service based architecture. You have to learn to walk before you can run. The more complex you make the first application you approach, the greater the risk of failure. Corporate n-tier architectures should be approached by experienced personnel and professional consultant mentors if those skills are not available in house.

As a closing note when dealing with distributed PowerBuilder applications, remember that you have to expand your thinking to imagine your local and distributed objects as one big application with some of the parts scattered around your architecture and placed where they can be more effective and useful to you!

CHAPTER 4

Designing a PowerBuilder Application

*D*esigning your PowerBuilder application correctly is a critical stage in the success of *enterprise PowerBuilder systems. In this chapter I hope to give you an overview of the considerations involved in creating a good application design. The principals are substantial enough that they could be the subject for their own book, so we will address some of the most important areas here.*

There are three central components involved in building PowerBuilder applications; the data model (data server), the user interface (client) and the business processes (process server/object request broker).

4.1 THE DATA MODEL

If you are one of the fortunate, your organization may already have a robust corporate data model. If not, you may be saddled with small islands of data stored in a multitude of different formats throughout your organization. Or perhaps this is the first system in your organization, and if so, what a terrific opportunity for you to build the foundation for an open corporate data model and data warehouse!

Having a well constructed data model provides you with the key to building a robust and effective PowerBuilder application. Creation of a conceptual data model is essential for starting the design of a system on the right foot. Having the physical data model in the design process is not an absolute requirement, but I would strongly recommend it before proceeding with the low level detailed design.

We will not discuss how to build a data model here, as this is one of those topics well covered by many other books. The point I wish to emphasize is that in a non-enterprise application you may be able to get away with building the data model at the same time as you build the application. For developing larger scale or enterprise systems this is not acceptable and will result in a lot of unnecessary redevelopment. For any enterprise project the data model MUST be constructed before you design the application. I'm not implying that it has to be 100% rock solid (although it would be nice!), but it should be at least 80% stable or better.

4.2 THE USER INTERFACE

Many elements combine together to make up the design of the user interface. This is an area where getting the users involved is critical. I would also recommend that you read a book by Don Norman entitled *The Design of Everyday Things*. It is a book you will find in the 'architecture' section of your local book store and does not relate specifically to GUI or application design, but many of the issues that are raised in the book should be forefront in your mind when you are designing applications for your users.

4.2.1 USER CENTRIC DESIGN

In traditional systems development, we tended to focus development of the system around the business process we were working on. We assumed that the users would have to adapt to whatever system we gave them, instead of adapting the system to the users. In traditional development the real critical factor was that the system was able to fulfill the requirements of the process.

This is obviously no longer the case. We have come around 180 degrees in our thinking in this area. We are now developing our applications centered around the needs of the users. There are many reasons for this, including a paradigm shift that has occurred in information systems development. In the past, many of the systems we developed were tactical in nature. They addressed a specific business process, such as billing. Now the systems we develop tend to be more strategic in nature and they address the management of entities and data rather than being designed around a single primary process.

It is critical in all PowerBuilder development projects to center your application design around the users. You need to get them involved in the initial analysis and design, and then keep them involved throughout the entire process until they actually take delivery of the completed system. This requires a great deal of bi-directional communication, but this is one of those factors that will increase the likelihood of project success by several orders of magnitude. Users must be continually updated on system development progress and be provided with regular opportunities to provide feedback on the system.

PowerBuilder is an event driven tool and follows the user centric model very well. The environment allows you to provide unambiguous feedback to the user during execution, and when necessary, to hold their hand through various processes through the creation of what have become known as 'wizards.' The flexibility and strength of PowerBuilder allow you to build a system that fits the user instead of trying to make the user fit the system.

4.2.2 THE OVERALL DESIGN

The overall design of your application is a task of equal, if not greater, importance on an enterprise project than the actual application coding. If you have a bad design (or no design), then it doesn't matter how good your skills are with your chosen tool set, you will have a bad application.

You must make decisions about the overall look and feel of your application. This includes using your corporate GUI design guidelines, or if you don't have any, developing some (refer to Thomson's 'Web Extra' site at http://www.itcpmedia.com for more details on Design Guidelines and Standard) that will apply to this project and across the enterprise in the future. Many published standards in this arena are incomplete and inconsistent. You may be able to use them as a foundation, but you must be sure to adapt them to your requirements and evolve them as your environment changes.

The design of your application must also take into account your conceptual and physical architecture. Your design will vary if you are using a two tier versus a three tier architecture (refer to *Chapter 3—Architectures for Development* for more details). On the physical side, you must take into consideration the kinds of hardware involved. If your clients are running Intel based 386 PC's with 8 Mb of memory, you will design a much lighter and less processing intensive interface than if they will have Pentium 166 workstations with 32 Mb of memory. Similar considerations will have to come into play based upon the network and the server that are being used.

4.2.3 User Analysis Matrix

Part of building an application that is truly user centric is the process of analyzing the users themselves. You must evaluate their skills and abilities in order to be able to design an application that will provide the best interface for them.

I will use an example based upon an actual enterprise PowerBuilder application that I was involved with to demonstrate the use of a user analysis matrix. My role on this project was to help mentor the team in the use of client/server development concepts on PowerBuilder applications. The system was intended to help store and process student insurance policies (policies for accident, sickness and death). The primary users of the system were defined as being the people in the claims department who would take and process insurance claims from their customers. Had they been the only user group, the system would have been quite straightforward, however, they were not. We realized there was a secondary user group who represented the executive in the company. They wanted to be able to use the system to obtain high level reports and statistics. Then we realized there was a third group, for three months of the year, they hired a number of temporary personnel who would come in and enter the new insurance policies into the system. So we had three user groups who all required access to the same system. We had to decide what kind of an interface to build.

We assembled the three groups of users into a user requirements matrix such as the one in Figure 4.1.

CATEGORIES / USER GROUPS	Business Knowledge	Computer Expertise	Frequency of Use
Claims Personnel			
Executive			
Data Entry Temps			

Figure 4.1 *A User Requirements Matrix contains the major user groups on the left side and has the categories of analysis across the top.*

The user groups are listed down the left column, while we have the three analysis categories across the top; business knowledge, computer expertise and frequency of use.

We look at each group individually and rank them in each category as High (3), Medium (2) and Low (1). The claims people have a high business knowledge, medium computer expertise and a low frequency of use (the number of claims processed per day is quite low). The executive also have a high business knowledge, very low computer expertise and a low frequency of use. The data entry temps have a very low business knowledge, high computer expertise and high frequency of use. This results in values in our matrix as we see in Figure 4.2.

CATEGORIES	Business Knowledge	Computer Expertise	Frequency of Use
USER GROUPS			
Claims Personnel	3	2	1
Executive	3	1	1
Data Entry Temps	1	3	3

Figure 4.2 *The results of our user requirements matrix for the insurance example.*

When we look at the numbers in the matrix, we can see that there are really two different groups of users with two very different types of interface needs. The claims personnel and the executive both have high business knowledge, low frequency of use and relatively low computer expertise. This is sharply contrasted by the temporary data entry personnel who have very little business knowledge but high computer expertise and frequency of use. If we build an interface that is very GUI-oriented, with a lot of mouse controls and push buttons, this would benefit the claims personnel and the executive who don't use the system all day long, who understand the business and are after an intuitive interface. This style of interface would reduce the amount of time that they would need to spend in training and the amount of system detail they would need to memorize. It would also help to reduce the quantity of errors they would incur when using the system. This kind of interface would be the kiss of death to the temporary data entry people as it forces them to remove their hands from the keyboard to use the mouse thus slowing their productivity dramatically. This group requires

50   *Chapter 4: Designing a PowerBuilder Application*

an interface that allows them to enter as much data as possible as quickly as possible without having to take their fingers off the keyboard. Heavily GUI oriented interfaces which require a lot of mousing around would severely impact the productivity of this group. They require a heads down data entry display designed to move smoothly from one data entry task to the next. In fact, this was the solution that was built. The same application was constructed with two different user interfaces, one for the users with extensive business knowledge and low frequency of use, and one for the data entry personnel who had little business knowledge, but used the system all day long.

Developers Note: If you are thinking, 'This would be an ideal situation to take advantage of application partitioning!', you are absolutely correct! The business processes could be built into a set of non-visual business objects allowing us to build two completely different user interfaces with the exact same business logic and rules.

Performing this kind of an analysis on your project will help you to determine the appropriate kind of interface for your user group and to see if any conflicting requirements exist among the different users. It may also force you to think outside the bounds of normal system design. It is unusual for most designers to contemplate rolling out more than one user interface for the same system.

A word of warning: Developing the correct user interface is a thankless task. If you do your job correctly, the interface will be almost transparent to the users and they will likely not give it a second thought. However, if you do it wrong, every user will be letting you know!

4.2.4 MDI OR SDI?

When developing an application in PowerBuilder, you will have to decide if the application would be best developed as a Multiple Document Interface (MDI) application or as a Single Document Interface (SDI) application. Most business oriented software available in the traditional windows platform is MDI in design. This means that you have one primary window, the MDI Frame, and virtually all the other windows in the application are opened inside the MDI Frame. The MDI Frame acts as the desktop or workspace for the application.

Most commercial windows applications are MDI based. Some examples include Microsoft Word and Excel and even PowerBuilder itself! The advantage of choosing to build your application as an MDI application is that you can contain very diverse functionality all within the context of the same application. For example, one major university that I worked with has constructed their entire admissions system in PowerBuilder. One problem that was identified with the old system was that if someone in the Registrar's office was working on one student admission and they receive a call from a second student asking about their status, they would have to back all the way out of the student they were working on to look up the new student. With the PowerBuilder system that was developed, they used an MDI approach and now the people working on the system can have multiple students open at the same time.

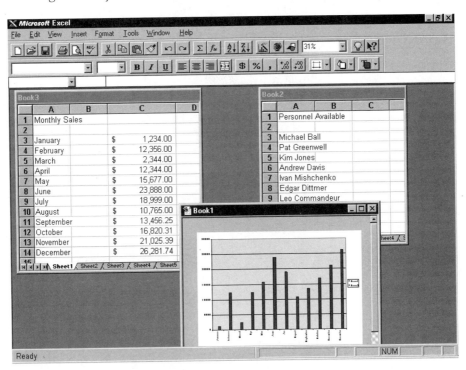

Figure 4.3 *An MDI application like Excel allows you to have multiple tasks going at the same time. In this example we have two spreadsheets and a graph all open at the same time.*

MDI based applications can be further subdivided into single function MDI and multiple function MDI. A single function MDI usually performs only one relatively focused primary task. Microsoft Word is an example of a single function MDI, although you can have multiple documents open, all it really does is create and modify documents (a relatively narrow primary task). PowerBuilder, on the other hand, is an example of a multiple function MDI.

Each painter develops a completely different type of object and other painters perform completely different functions such as source code management or table creation.

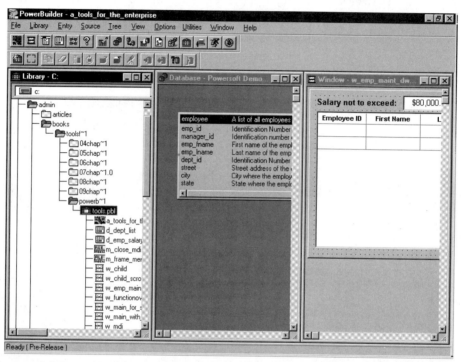

Figure 4.4 *PowerBuilder is an example of a multiple function MDI application.*

Within an SDI application, the functionality of the application is usually much more limited. Many windows can be opened simultaneously, but not having a container like the MDI Frame to help manage them makes keeping them all under control substantially more difficult. I think it is important to point out however, that the new 32 bit operating systems like Windows 95 and Windows NT seem to be slowly trending away from MDI and developing applications as complex SDI systems.

At present, most enterprise applications being developed in the windows environment are still being developed using MDI standards. From a user perspective, I feel that the MDI interface is beneficial in unifying the interface and keeping confusion to a minimum.

> **Developer Tip:** In many business applications today there is a distinct trend towards the use of tab folder based interfaces. These are interfaces that use the real world metaphor of file folders to allow the user to access different subsets of information within a given window. This type of interface can be observed in many common commercial applications like the Microsoft Word Options dialog window shown in Figure 4.4b.

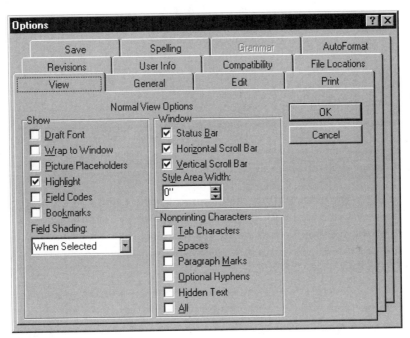

Figure 4.4b *The tabbed interface is becoming increasingly common in today's applications. This is fully supported in PowerBuilder 5.0 and can be used in both MDI and SDI type applications.*

In previous versions of PowerBuilder, we had to use third party user objects, or write our own, in order to implement tab folders. This functionality is now supported natively in PowerBuilder 5.0. (refer to *Chapter 7—What's New In PowerBuilder 5.0* for details on the tab folder object).

Tab folder implementations in applications can occur in either MDI or SDI formats.

4.2.5 CHOOSING THE CORRECT WINDOW TYPE

Using the correct types of windows in your applications is very important. It is important to remember that the window is your primary means of interfacing with your user. The way that your chosen window will appear and behave is critical to your overall system success.

4.2.5.1 The Foundation Window

Every application has a *foundation window* or primary window. This is the main window of your application and reflects where the user will be spending most of their time. For most enterprise applications this will be the MDI frame. The MDI frame is very strong as a foundation window because it already come pre-equipped with a mechanism for managing sheets (main windows opened within the frame), displaying a toolbar with the menu and providing feedback to the user through the MicroHelp or Status Bar.

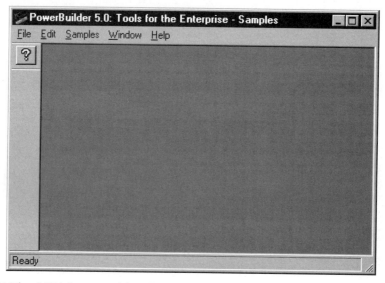

Figure 4.5 *The MDI Frame with MicroHelp is the most commonly used foundation window in enterprise applications.*

If your requirements fit appropriately, you may decide to build a SDI application. This would mean that you are creating your foundation window from a Main window. These are particularly useful for systems with a single function which are relatively simple and straightforward. For example, an amortization calculator for mortgages which you want to roll out to all the employees in a bank as a simple pop-up application would be a good use for SDI.

4.2.5.2 The Main Window

The main window type in PowerBuilder is most often used in enterprise level applications as sheets within the MDI frame. Sheets are intended to be extremely flexible. This means, among other things, that they are *modeless* and allow the user to move from sheet to sheet within the application at will. We are not forcing them down a specific route when we use main windows.

> **PowerBuilder 4.0 to 5.0:** In PowerBuilder 4.0, sheets on an MDI frame were always resizeable, regardless of whether the Resizeable property was set to true or not. In PowerBuilder 5.0, if the Resizeable property is set to False, then the window cannot be resized by the user.

The main window is relatively independent. If attached to an MDI frame, it will close with the MDI frame, and if minimized, its icon will appear inside the MDI client area. If the main window is not part of an MDI application, it will only be closed when the user directly closes it, and if minimized, it will appear as its own icon in the program manager. If you are building an SDI application, your foundation window will most likely be a main window.

4.2.5.3 The Child Window

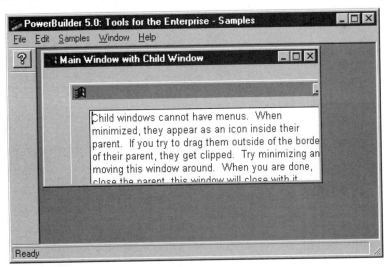

Figure 4.6 *A child window is completely dependent upon its parent. If moved beyond the borders of its parent, its edges get clipped off. This window type also never receives the activate event.*

56   *Chapter 4: Designing a PowerBuilder Application*

The child window is a very interesting object. You will likely not use them very often due to some of their particular characteristics. The child window is completely dependent upon its parent. If you move a child window beyond the borders of its parent, the edges of the window get clipped off. If you minimize a child window, its icon appears within its parent. If you close the parent, the child closes also. The child never receives the activate event. If you click on the child window when the parent is deactivated, the parent receives the Activate event.

Development Tip: You can capture the activation of a child window through declaring an undefined system event for the window and capturing the "pbm_childactivate" event id. Refer to Chapter 8 - Advanced Development Concepts for more information on setting up undefined system events.

This last characteristic is the one which makes it difficult to pass information to and from a child window. These windows do not find their way into enterprise applications often, but I have seen them used in some very creative situations. One example where I have seen it used was where we had a main window, and we wanted to place a number of small DataWindows on the main window. The DataWindow controls provided side by side drill down capability. The left most DataWindow control showed a list of countries, when a country was selected, the DataWindow next to it would show a list of states/provinces within that country. Upon selecting a state, the DataWindow to its right would show a list of counties and so on until you had drilled down to the lowest reasonable level. This could potentially involve up to eight side by side master detail DataWindows. As the window was only wide enough to display four of these at a time, the user wanted to see a scroll bar beneath the DataWindows and have the ability to scroll back and forth. There were also other controls on the window that we didn't want to scroll. In order to resolve this conflict, we placed a child window upon the main window and all the DataWindows were placed upon the child. The child was set to display no border or title bar, but would display a horizontal scroll bar. This gave us a fairly straightforward solution to what would have otherwise been a technically challenging problem.

4.2 The User Interface   57

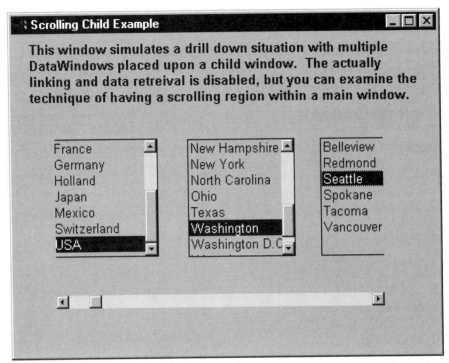

Figure 4.7 *A child window was used in a production application to allow the scrolling of multiple DataWindows from side to side within a main window. This is a screen shot from the application on the companion CD.*

A simulation of this solution can be found on the companion CD. The data selection logic is not there, but you can examine how the scrolling child was used.

4.2.5.4 The Popup Window

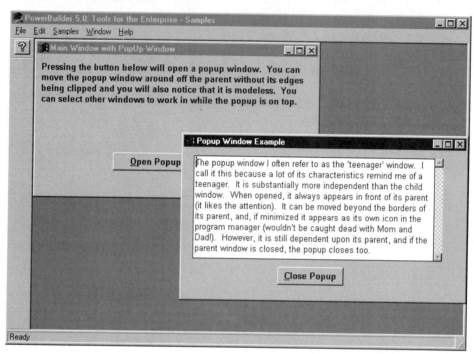

Figure 4.8 *The popup window is more independent than the child and can be moved outside its parent and minimized in the program manager.*

The popup window I often refer to as the 'teenager' window. I call it this because a lot of its characteristics remind me of a teenager. It is substantially more independent than the child window. When opened, it always appears in front of its parent (it likes the attention). It can be moved beyond the borders of its parent, and, if minimized it appears as its own icon in the program manager (wouldn't be caught dead with Mom and Dad!). However, it is still dependent upon its parent, and if the parent window is closed, the popup closes too.

The popup is modeless, so you still have the ability to move from the popup to the parent and to other windows in the application, but every time you look, active or not, that popup is on top of the heap trying to get your attention!

Popup windows are used frequently in enterprise applications. You might find them used to present detail information about something in a main window. For example, a main window may contain a list of orders and double-clicking on a row would cause a popup window to be opened with the details of that specific order. You could double-click on multiple rows and see many detail windows on your screen. You should note that when a popup window is opened in an SDI application, its parent is the currently active window unless otherwise specified. This means that the script

```
Open(w_p_one)
Open(w_p_two)
```

would result in the main window being the parent of w_p_one, but w_p_one would become the parent of w_p_two. This could be resolved by specifying the parent window as the second argument in the Open function:

```
Open(w_p_one, w_parent_name)
Open(w_p_two, w_parent_name)
// If applicable, the reserved word PARENT or THIS can be
// substituted for w_parent_name.
// This would result in a more generic use of the function.
```

The example pictured in Figure 4.8 is a shot from the sample application that comes on the companion CD.

4.2.5.5 The Response Window

All of the windows that we have discussed so far are modeless windows. The user can move back and forth from window to window within the application whenever they choose. For the most part, this is an admirable accomplishment, however, sometimes we need to restrict the user from moving throughout the application and give us the answer we require now so we can continue. To do this we use a window called a response window. These windows are application modal and when opened, the user can only work within that window. Attempting to move to any other window within the same application results in a chastising beep from windows. You can jump to a different application, but the application you were working in will not proceed until the response window is dealt with.

You normally want to be careful to minimize the use of this type of window because of their modal nature and the restrictions this places on the user. In many enterprise applications being built today, there is a user requirement for 'wizard' like technology. Wizards are a series of response windows which lead the user by the hand (or by the nose) through the creation of some entity or process. Response windows are ideal for this type of application as

60   *Chapter 4: Designing a PowerBuilder Application*

opening one response window from another causes a chain to be formed and requires that to close the wizard, all the response windows must be closed in order.

You will find a sample of opening a response window in the demonstration application on the companion CD.

4.2.6 PROVIDING FEEDBACK TO THE USER

Many users feel uncomfortable when the system 'goes away' and does processing while the user waits for the task to finish. Often they are not even aware of what task it is that the system is trying to accomplish. It is imperative that during execution of the application you keep your user informed of what the system is doing, and what their options are. This can be accomplished through any combination of visual and auditory cues.

4.2.6.1 Visual Cues

Visual cues are mechanisms for providing information to the user through the GUI interface. This can be done through a combination of visual objects, colors, fonts and so on. For example, when the mouse passes over a column where the user is not allowed to enter data, the pointer can be made to turn into a 'no-entry' symbol. You should be certain to ensure that all possible visual cues are designed into your application.

PowerBuilder has a number of features built into the standard objects for enterprise development that can assist you with the visual cues. One of these is *MicroHelp*. MicroHelp is the text that appears in the status bar at the bottom of an MDI frame. PowerBuilder will automatically use it to display information about the various options in the current menu. You can also make use of it to display information to the user about what your application is doing, such as "Connecting to the database…One moment please…"

A second mechanism for providing visual feedback is through PowerTips, PowerBuilder's version of Microsoft's balloon help. Microsoft first introduced the concept of balloon help around two and half years ago. Balloon help is a popup message that appears when your mouse stops moving over a toolbar button. You can provide this same functionality in your PowerBuilder application. This text is set in the menu painter on the toolbar tab of the properties sheet. You can enter a short text and a long text. The short text appears before the comma, and is the text that appears under the button when the ShowText for the toolbar is set to true. The long text appears after the comma. If you don't enter any long text, then the short text will be used for the balloon help, but, since you can provide a better cue, you should.

4.2 The User Interface

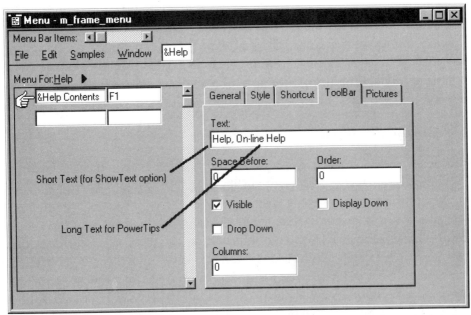

Figure 4.9 *In PowerBuilder you can have PowerTips (a.k.a. balloon help) show up for each toolbar item by entering it after the short text in the toolbar page of the menu properties page.*

Developers Tip: The new Tab Folder object in PowerBuilder 5.0 allows you to define PowerTips for each tab. When the user rests the mouse over the tab text, the balloon help box will pop up.

Color is the third mechanism you can use to provide feedback to your users. It is important to keep in mind however that a substantial proportion of the general population has difficulty discerning color differences and this should never be the primary mechanism for communicating information. You can use color to send a message to the user, just be certain that there is also another way that the user can receive the same information that is not dependent upon color. Many successful enterprise systems do use color to enhance the communication of data such as status of a record. For example, you can flag rows in a DataWindow by changing the background color for rows with a status of active to green and inactive to red. By also displaying a field saying 'Active' or 'Inactive' we are eliminating the dependence upon color as the primary communications mechanism.

4.2.6.2 Audible Cues

You can also provide audible feedback to your users in the form of beeps or .WAV files. This also is not recommended as a primary means of communication as it would preclude deaf or hard of hearing people from using your system. Sound can still be used as a user interface enhancement.

4.2.6.3 System Delays

I would strongly recommend that you be sure to provide feedback to the users whenever the system is occupied with a task. The users will appreciate being informed of progress and will be more tolerant when your system is busy. For any processes that cause a short delay (such as the opening of a window, or a short retrieval) change the pointer from the arrow to the hourglass using the SetPointer(Hourglass!) function. As the delay gets longer, the users will begin to wonder if the system has locked up. You can place a message in the MicroHelp area to inform them of what task the system is doing, and change the message as the task progresses, if applicable. For substantial delays (to be arbitrary, let's say 15 seconds) you should display some sort of a progress meter so that the user is able to see that the system is really still running and is doing something productive.

4.3 PROCESS OBJECTS

Whether you are building a two tier or an n-tier application, you must remember that your design needs to include not only the user interface, but also the business processes that are involved in developing the system. This may involve designing non-visual objects and service based objects, or building the business logic into the appropriate visual objects if you are using a two tier architecture.

4.3.1 APPLICATION SECURITY

Security is one of those issues which has been severely neglected in PowerBuilder applications, and in fact, I would say in client/server applications in general. There has been a tendency in the past to rely on the database to provide security for an application. For more complex enterprise applications this is simply not sufficient.

When designing your application, you need to establish categories of users and what permissions the different categories of users can have. Permissions are simply a matter of who can do what. From a design perspective, you must be able to identify which functions and options will be visible and available to different security levels and include this in your detailed design.

There are two traditional approaches most enterprise projects take to application security. The first is to build your own non-visual security management object which would ride herd over each of your applications. The second option available to you is to purchase one of the third party security management libraries for PowerBuilder. They are gaining a lot of ground in the PowerBuilder arena and by most reports are convenient and effective.

With the release of version 5.0, the PowerBuilder Foundation Class library contains a complete set of security processes and objects. Although, given the youth of version 5.0, I have not used this in a production application yet, it appears to be quite strong.

The important thing to remember when deciding on which approach to security you will implement is that it must be easy to administer and maintain, or it will slowly degrade until it is not effective. Users are notorious for developing their own workarounds when they find a system is awkward to use or doesn't meet their real requirements.

4.3.2 OTHER PROCESS OBJECTS

The possibilities for types of process objects that you might create are endless. For your specific industry alone there are probably dozens of potential process objects. For example, if you were developing systems for a hotel reservation system, you may have a process object for a guest. This object would have methods such as CheckIn, CheckOut, RoomService, GenerateBill and so on. You could also have process objects for a room with methods for Clean, Classify and Reserve. You could extend this model to all the entities that are involved in the reservation system, or the hotel industry (if you wanted to grow the system).

You may decide to build service based objects for managing system services such as faxing, printing or e-Mail. If you isolate these services into their own objects it will make your maintenance much easier in the future. It will also provide you with the flexibility of possibly distributing these objects onto a process server (3 and 'n' tier architectures) so that multiple applications can use them (refer to Chapter 7 for more information on using distributed objects).

64   *Chapter 4: Designing a PowerBuilder Application*

4.4 ONLINE HELP

I have seen many enterprise development projects that move forward, always telling themselves that they will write the online help at the end of the development cycle when they have time. Guess what? It never gets written.

online help needs to be taken more seriously and properly integrated into the project plan. Windows should be designed to be able to provide context sensitive help to users. One of the goals of the GUI interface is to reduce the cost of end user training. If users can look in the help file when they need more information, it will go a long way towards achieving this goal. Every major function in your functional decomposition should have a segment in the online help.

Writing windows help is now easier than ever before. You no longer have to get down in the mud with the Windows SDK to produce a help file, now we can use one of the many excellent third party tools like RoboHelp or Doc-2-Help to use our standard word processor to create fully functional help files including hot-links, screen captures and some even support video clip playback.

The help files should be written by an experienced technical writer. Any enterprise project should be able to incorporate a person with this skill set into the project team. A technical writer has the skill and background to help communicate online help information in a format that the end user will be able to understand.

4.5 SUMMARY

Designing a solid PowerBuilder application is still part science and part art. You must be sure when you design your application that you center the design around the users and keep them involved throughout the system development process.

Be thorough in your design, including plans for non-visual, process and service objects where appropriate. Be sure to include your plans for security implementation, online help and all processes which you otherwise might be tempted to leave to the end. The most successful enterprise PowerBuilder applications were built upon the foundation of a solid and thorough initial design.

CHAPTER 5

Object-Oriented PowerBuilder

PowerBuilder is considered a flexible object oriented development tool in that it allows you to be as object oriented, or non-object oriented as you choose. It was intended to allow developers who were unfamiliar with object orientation to adjust to the new concepts slowly, without having their arm twisted behind their backs. This may have been a good concept, however, one serious implication of this is that now thousands of PowerBuilder enterprise level production applications exist with code that is half OO (pronounced 'oh-oh') and half not. This means that the applications become a nightmare to maintain and are not as efficient with the system resources as they should be. They are probably also somewhat unstable and GPF (Global Protection Fault—but I am sure you are probably very familiar with that!) more regularly than a proper object-oriented application.

If you are already familiar with object orientation, you can skip this chapter and move on to the next, however, if you are new to OO or only have a fundamental grasp, I would recommend spending some time with this chapter. We will address some of the foundation concepts of OO including objects, classes, inheritance, encapsulation and polymorphism. We will relate these concepts to the PowerBuilder enterprise development environment and will look at some sample objects to see how these concepts are used.

5.1 WHAT DOES USING OO MEAN?

There are many potential benefits to using object-oriented design and development techniques, however, in order to realize them, the techniques must be understood and applied correctly. These techniques are particularly useful to an enterprise application developer.

It would be nice if I could tell you that OO makes it easier to develop applications, unfortunately, that is not necessarily true. It can help to make a developer more productive and to produce better quality applications that are easier to maintain, but it requires just as much, in fact probably more skill and effort, than traditional environments.

The developer who will be successful with object-oriented technology is the one who can make the paradigm shift to the object oriented concepts and grasp which components provide a practical benefit versus those that are more theoretical in nature. The successful OO developer cannot just focus on the details of the section of the application they are currently assigned, they must be able to see and comprehend how the area they are currently working on fits into the big picture. This requires keeping your finger on the pulse of all the development going on throughout the project (no small task on an enterprise project!).

Although PowerBuilder gives the impression that you can tear the shrink wrap off and begin building slick applications immediately, if you do this in the enterprise environment, you will fail. To build a successful OO PowerBuilder application requires a very substantial investment in up front planning and design and no small amount of self-discipline from the development team. The quality of your up front planning will make or break your project.

There are a wealth of Object-Oriented Analysis (OOA) and Object-Oriented Design (OOD) tools and concepts on the market, which all advocate different methods and procedures. Peter Coad and Ed Yourdon are often spoken of as significant contributors to the world of object oriented analysis and design. Their books *Object-Oriented Analysis* and *Object-Oriented Design* (often referred to in OO circles as "the yellow book" and "the blue book" respectively because of the colors of their covers) are a must read for any object oriented analyst and programmer. However, in the modern arena, it is difficult to point to one OO methodology and say "This is the one you should use!" If I was to make a recommendation, I would check out the results of the joined forces of three OO powerhouses, Grady Booch James Rumbaugh and Ivor Jacobsen. Their new object modeling methodology called "Unified Method" seems to be getting a warm reception from the OO community.

The tools, though important, are not nearly as important as the skill and mindset of the project team. The team must be able to identify and build a system around the fundamental entities of that system, instead of trying to build it around the processes or data. This means being able to identify properties and methods of entities and model them into the structure of the object that represents that entity.

To begin to apply the concepts of OO, it is important to understand the terminology and how it relates to PowerBuilder. Some of the concepts we will discuss here are not 100% in line with purist object oriented philosophy. This is because PowerBuilder bends some of the purist views a little. For the purist approach, check out the books in the bibliography relating to OO.

5.2 WHY USE OO WITH POWERBUILDER?

As we stated earlier, PowerBuilder does not require you to use OO to develop software, and depending on what you are trying to develop, it may not even be worthwhile, however, for most enterprise projects, there are considerable advantages.

Don't be confused between object orientation and client/server. When client/server first became the rage, all the advocates said that it would reduce development times and costs. We all know that that simply isn't true. Client/server is another architecture different from mainframe computing architectures, but that doesn't make it faster, or necessarily cheaper. Now OO is promising the same things and the skeptics are saying, "We heard the same story about client/server." Client/server and OO are not the same animal, although they are often found together, one does not necessarily imply the other, and OO does live up to many of its promises (when implemented correctly!).

Your organization may be able to realize significant productivity gains through the adoption of object oriented project techniques for their PowerBuilder systems development. The first project you build with OO technology will be a genuine struggle and you will not deliver the system any faster than with traditional methods, in fact, it will probably take you longer. You will be trying to define and create objects that are generic enough that they can be used in other applications in the future. The real improvements in productivity will come with your second, third and fourth applications when you can begin to reuse all the functionality that you developed for your first application, and these gains can be substantial. On one client site, it took four months of intensive effort to deliver their first, medium scope application. After that, we were able to deliver the next 6 applications in less than half the time normally allotted for systems of their scope.

68 *Chapter 5: Object-Oriented PowerBuilder*

These productivity gains, when realized, will translate directly into dollars and reduced cost, although you should be prepared to invest substantially in your first project to ensure that the results will provide the benefits that you expect. Failing to provide the proper training, tools and mentoring for an inexperienced team will be the downfall of an enterprise project.

Maintenance of OO applications is substantially easier than with traditional systems. If implemented correctly, maintenance will cost less and be easier to perform. In traditional systems, changing one part of an application often results in unexpected failures throughout other parts of the application. This chain reaction is often called the "snowball effect." Anyone with any history in this industry has experienced this phenomenon. OO helps to eliminate this by reducing the coupling between the elements of the system and keeps a change in one area from rippling out and affecting any others.

Application execution speed and effective use of system resources can be enhanced through OO. But be warned that improper use of OO, or OO implemented without proper planning can reduce execution speed and pirate system resources and not return them unless you reboot your hardware!

Given the benefits, I would strongly advocate utilizing OO for any enterprise development where the architecture is stable and the commitment exists from the organization to ensure it is performed properly. What follows is a discussion of some of these essential concepts and how they relate to PowerBuilder.

5.3 OBJECTS

It was once explained to me some time ago that an object is merely a "thing." Since then I have used the term "thing" to describe objects to hundreds of my students. By this, I mean that an object is any thing that can be identified and named. For example, a person is an object, a car is an object and windows (either in an application or in your home) are also objects.

When business analysts are trying to determine what the fundamental entities are in an organization, they can often begin discovering objects by extracting nouns from comments, interviews, JAD sessions or available documentation.

PowerBuilder stretches the definition of objects a little. Everything you create is called an object. Every window, DataWindow, structure and so on is called an object, but one fundamental concept that defines an object is that they all have *methods* and *properties*, and not all PowerBuilder objects do (i.e. function 'objects' have no properties). Also, the distinction between *classes* and *instances* is not as clear in PowerBuilder. This difference is discussed in the relevant sections below.

> **PowerBuilder 4.0 to 5.0:** You may have heard properties referred to as *attributes* in PowerBuilder 4.0, or other OO documentation. Attributes is also correct nomenclature. In PowerBuilder 5.0 we have switched to using properties to be consistent with the Windows 95 and NT terminology. You may see references to both properties and methods in this book. Both terms refer to the same concept and are used interchangeably.

I will use the example of a house as our object. This example will serve us well as we describe some of the other fundamental concepts around object orientation in PowerBuilder.

Figure 5.1 *A house is a conceptual example of an object. It is a tangible "thing" that we can identify and name.*

5.4 PROPERTIES

All objects have properties. Properties define the appearance and behavior of an object. In PowerBuilder they are like variables that belong to the object and define it. Properties include things like the width, height and color of an object.

For our house, properties would include its color, its size, how many bedrooms it has and so on. In PowerBuilder, the properties on an object such as a window include its title, color and position.

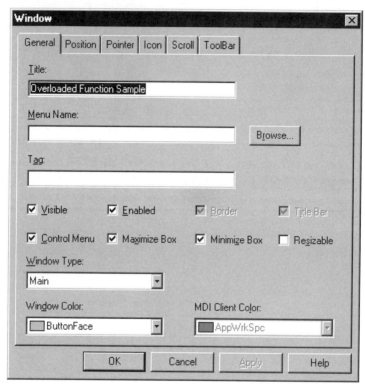

Figure 5.2 *Properties define the look and behavior of an object. Opening the properties page of any object in the PowerBuilder environment will give you access to all the properties you can modify.*

Developers Note: When you define your own classes of objects in PowerBuilder using the user object painter (discussed in Chapter 12) you can add your own properties to these objects by defining instance variables within the user object painter. You can also use instance variables to add to the properties of an application, menu or window class.

5.5 METHODS

The same colleague who provided me with the definition of an object as a 'thing' explained to me that a method is as simple as 'things do stuff.' To be a little more precise, a method is a process that is attached to an object. A PowerBuilder window, for example, has a method attached to it called Resize. When this method is called, we can alter the size of the window to a new width and height that we specify as parameters for the method. Objects usually have many methods, and they also have access to all the methods of their ancestors.

When you write a *function* or an *event script* for a PowerBuilder object, you are creating a method for that object. Global functions, which can be created in PowerBuilder, are one of those objects that are not very object oriented, for they are a method which is not attached to any object, which in a purist OO world, cannot exist.

5.6 CLASSES

As people begin to learn about and study OO concepts, the difference between a class and an instance is often a little confusing. You can think of a class as a more abstract definition for a group of objects, like a blueprint or template.

Let's look at our house example. I live in a house at 123 Main Street. My house is an object, but in order to have this object, someone created a blueprint that has a definition of a house. This definition says that a house has four walls and a roof and one door. My house is a little different from the house next door, they are different objects, but they both fall into the class of house which is defined as having a roof, four walls and one door.

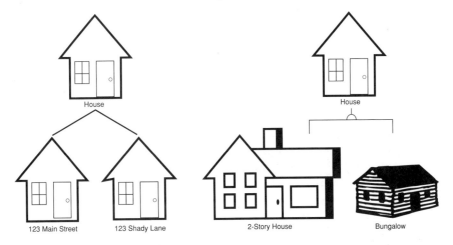

Figure 5.3 *A class is a blueprint or template for an object. This blueprint can be used to create specific objects (i.e. my house at 123 Main Street) or as a template for other classes. The general class 'house' is the abstract class for the object two story and also the abstract class for a bungalow, two different objects.*

Chapter 5: Object-Oriented PowerBuilder

When you create an object in a PowerBuilder painter, you are creating an object which is somewhere between the purist definition of a class and an instance, but it fits best into the definition of a class. In the purist world, a class has no values associated with its properties, for example a house has four walls and a roof, but we don't know their length, width or height, whereas an instance has values for its properties. When we paint a window in PowerBuilder, we define a PowerBuilder class with properties (the window has a width and a height), but we also assign them values (we set a standard width and height for the object). When we actually open the window, we can override these values and set different values for its properties in the open event. You can see where the overlap in definitions is. The PowerBuilder objects are somewhere between a class and an instance.

> **Developers Note:** When you compile an application and distribute the .EXE, .PBD and .DLL files, you are providing the end user with your library of class definitions. At runtime, these 'blueprints' will be used to create the objects that the user requires.

Classes of objects are often described in relation to other classes. For example, we can have a class of object called 'shelter.' Shelter is related to the classes 'house,' 'hotel' and 'tent,' all of which are types of shelter. Shelter is a *superclass* and house, hotel and tent are all *subclasses* of shelter. The diagram can be continued in both directions, adding superclasses and subclasses as appropriate. We can turn house into a superclass by adding 'two story,' 'bungalow' and 'ranch' as subclasses of house. In PowerBuilder these relationships are formed through the use of inheritance.

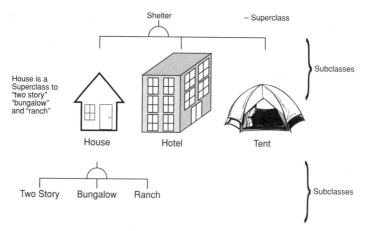

Figure 5.4 *Classes are related to each other through a superclass/subclass association. In PowerBuilder, these associations are achieved through inheritance.*

Every descendant in PowerBuilder contains all the methods and properties of its ancestor. The properties can be overridden in descendant classes. Methods can be left as they are, extended or overridden. These principles are discussed further when we discuss inheritance below.

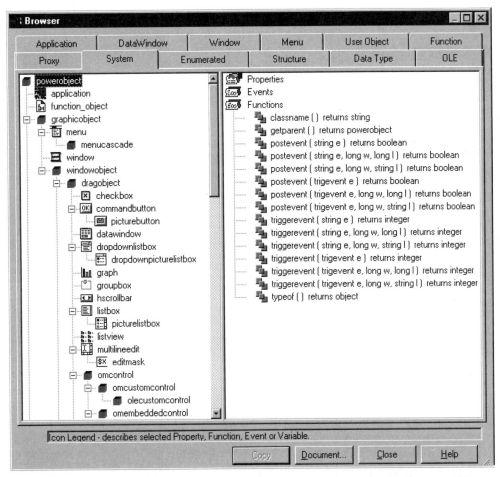

Figure 5.5 *The PowerBuilder object hierarchy contains both PowerBuilder superclass objects and all the objects that you have created.*

All objects in PowerBuilder exist within a hierarchy of classes/objects. You can examine this hierarchy through the Object Browser. The technique for accessing the hierarchy is not very straightforward. First you must select the System tab. Once in the system, you must click on the text of the PowerObject class in the class list on the left side. This will display a popup menu. Select the option Show Hierarchy. This will load and display the entire object hierarchy. Some of it will be hidden inside lower levels. To get the entire hierarchy visible at the same time, click again with the right mouse button on PowerObject and select Expand All (if you do it in any other order you won't see the entire hierarchy).

5.7 INSTANCE

When you build an object in a painter in PowerBuilder, its definition is stored in your library as an object class. When you issue a command that causes that object to be created in memory (and, if visual, displayed on the screen) you have created an instance of that object. The class definition (your 'blueprint') still exists in the library, and if you require, a second instance can be created from the same class definition. All object instances will have values defined for their properties. The instantiation of an object is the physical creation of the object.

With our house example, the blueprints used to create my home at 123 Main Street could be used to create an identical home next door. Now we have two instances of the same class of home. Each house is individual and can be customized. I could paint my house green and my neighbors could paint their home blue.

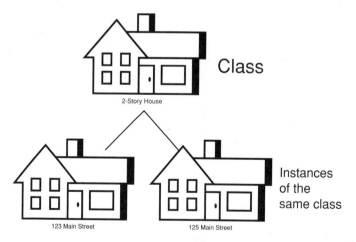

Figure 5.6 *An instance is the physical implementation of an object. A specific class of house could have multiple instances.*

This example translates to the PowerBuilder world as the creation of the same object many times. The most obvious example is the creation of multiple instances of the same window. You might have multiple sales order entry windows open at the same time in your order entry system.

5.8 CONTROLS

In PowerBuilder, we often use objects in the construction of other objects. Some objects are intended to be building blocks for other objects, whereas others are intended to be containers. The objects that are container type objects are those that are stored independently in the library painter. We can refer to these objects as *first level objects* or *primary objects*. The Window and the User Object are examples of first level objects. When I place an object on a window, this object is referred to as a *control*. An example of a control would be a command button. These objects can also be referred to as *second level* or *secondary objects* as they are not stored in the library painter by themselves, but rather are only stored when they are part of a first level object.

5.9 INHERITANCE

The colloquial definition that I was provided with for inheritance is "I look just like Dad!" The allegory holds quite true. Inheritance is a process whereby a new object is created with the properties and methods from another object, just like you might inherit your fathers nose or eyes. This means that instead of building a new window from scratch you could inherit from a previously defined window, which becomes the ancestor. The new window, which is called the descendant, begins with all of the same methods and properties (including values for the properties) of the ancestor.

The concept of inheritance implies that, for the most part, descendant objects are only instantiated with the properties and methods that are different for each instance. Any commonality will remain in the ancestor class to be called when required. This prevents the duplication of a lot of superfluous code and allows for a more efficient use of system resources. With PowerBuilder we have the ability to either extend or override the methods in an ancestor. Methods are implemented either as scripts in events, or as object level functions.

76 *Chapter 5: Object-Oriented PowerBuilder*

The relationships that form between ancestor and descendant objects is referred to as a class hierarchy. An OO tool like PowerBuilder allows us to make changes to ancestor objects and those changes will automatically flow through to the descendant objects. You must be very cautious however when removing objects or making changes in an ancestor as those objects and values may be referenced in a descendant.

You gain some specific advantages through the use of inheritance. The code you place into an object can be reused by its descendants. This reduces the amount of code that a descendant class contains and the amount of time a developer has to spend creating the object.

Maintenance can be made easier by ensuring that code for a specific set of functionality is located in one place. If the need to make a change to that code arises, you need only change it in one place and any other objects that use that functionality are automatically aware of the change. No more hunting around for all the places where the functionality exists and no chance for having the alteration made differently in different locations.

Your applications will also look and behave more consistently when they draw upon a base set of objects which share a common appearance and set of functionality.

Other terms you should be familiar with when working with inheritance are *abstract* and *concrete classes*. Abstract classes are objects that are used only as ancestors. They are never physically instantiated. They are used purely as repositories to store common methods and properties for their descendant classes. This prevents the duplication of these properties and methods across multiple objects. OO designers and developers also speak of *abstraction* which is the technique of searching out common properties and methods among objects of similar classes and developing an abstract class to act as an ancestor to all those classes.

Concrete classes, on the other hand, are classes of objects that are physically instantiated. These classes will inherit all their common properties and methods from an ancestor class. They will layer their own additional functionality and properties on top of that which is received from their ancestor. Note that although concrete classes get instantiated, they can still serve as ancestors for other concrete or abstract classes.

One of the myths of inheritance is that using it makes an application run slower. This can be true if the inheritance is not well designed. Many experts have run empirical tests to measure this and have proven repeatedly that a solid OO application in PowerBuilder will actually improve both performance and memory efficiency.

> **Developers Tip: If you are using inheritance and find that object creation is taking too long at runtime, you could instantiate the ancestor classes in memory (in a non-visual format) so that when the descendants are opened, PowerBuilder does not have to search for and instantiate all the ancestors.**
>
> **This is accomplished by declaring a reference variable of the appropriate scope (perhaps an instance variable in the application service object) and calling:**
>
> ```
> iw_reference_window = CREATE w_ancestor_window
> ```
>
> **This window would not be visible to the users, but by creating it in memory will speed up instantiation of descendant classes. This technique should only be used when the client PCs have ample memory available as this object will consume resources while it is instantiated.**

One other caution when it comes to using inheritance is to be careful with the complexity of your inheritance tree. Creating haphazard inheritance will make it difficult to determine where code is located and when a maintenance issue comes along you will be challenged to make the change effectively, especially if you weren't the original author of the object. Be careful to create logical and carefully layered objects and to document all objects clearly.

5.10 ENCAPSULATION

As we continue with our plain English definitions, encapsulation would be "My insides are none of your business!" Encapsulation is the process of incorporating all the properties and methods that relate to an object inside the object itself. All the functionality and data you would care to know about the object is all contained within. These inner workings are hidden from the users, and the only way a user can interact with the properties and methods of the object is through a well defined public interface. You may hear encapsulation referred to as 'information hiding' because the effect of encapsulation is to hide information from the user of the object and shield them from the object's inner complexities.

The effect of proper encapsulation is that every object can stand independently. It has no need for anything outside of itself. For example, a well encapsulated object could not depend on a value from a global variable, because if that object was used in an application where the

78   *Chapter 5: Object-Oriented PowerBuilder*

global variable did not exist, the object would fail. These kinds of external dependencies are what create the snowball effect of changing one process or value and having that change affect many other areas.

You can begin to see how encapsulation promotes code modularity and can have a significant positive impact on the maintainability of your system. If you had a need to alter a process inside a well encapsulated object, the rest of the application would be completely unaffected assuming that the public interfaces that you built into the object remain unchanged.

A simple example of encapsulation in PowerBuilder would be the Command Button from the window painter. When you use a Command Button in your application, you automatically expect, that when it is pressed by the user it will appear to be pressed in and then released. You did not have to build this functionality into the Command Button, it was already there, encapsulated inside. You also don't have access to this process as it is hidden from you, and to use the button effectively, you have no need to access or understand the process that is involved.

Let's look at an example of encapsulation using an object that we might create for an application. We have a non-visual object called Customer. Inside this non-visual object is a process called CreateCustomer. The process is defined as a pubic object level function. When someone inside our application wants to create a new customer, they instantiate a Customer object and call the CreateCustomer function, passing the relevant details like customer name, address and phone number. Inside the object, hidden from view of the user of the object, is a process that inserts a customer into the customer table and sets up a credit limit in the credit table of $500.00. Now, if the business rules change and it is decided that new customers will not automatically receive a $500.00 credit limit, instead, they will be given a credit status of 'pending' and a flag must be placed on the record so that when the credit department logs on, they will see that they have a new credit application to approve. This process can be changed internal to the non-visual Customer object, but as long as the CreateCustomer function still accepts the same parameters and returns the same value, nothing else in the application is affected.

There is a lot more thought that must be put into designing a well encapsulated object. I would feel quite safe right now making a bet that probably 80% of the current production PowerBuilder applications in an enterprise environment are not well encapsulated. I hope this percentage will decrease substantially as more groups realize the benefits of OO.

When designing an encapsulated object, you want to be sure to insulate the methods and properties inside the object so that they cannot possibly be accessed from external objects or processes. This reduces the temptation to violate the object orientation of the system. How do we do that? We have the ability to create all our user defined properties (instance variables) and methods (object functions) as being either public, private or protected.

Public means that these instance variables and functions can be called and referenced by objects and functions outside of this object. This is our publicly defined interface. By default, all instance variables and functions will be declared as public. For good encapsulation, instance variables should never be public, and only those functions that you want to publish as being the proper method for accessing this object should be public.

Private instance variables and functions can only be called and referenced by processes within that object. All private variables and functions are completely hidden from external processes. This includes keeping them hidden from any objects inherited from this object. Even the descendants cannot use these variables and functions.

Protected is a little more flexible. External objects and processes cannot use protected variables and functions, but descendants of this class will have access to them and be able to call and reference them when required.

You are probably familiar with how to declare an object function as public, private or protected. This is accomplished through the function definition window. The access level can only be set for object level functions, global functions are always public by definition.

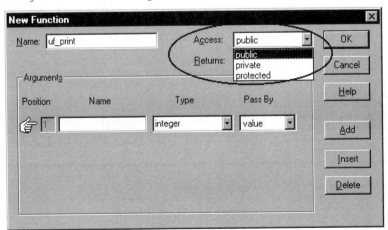

Figure 5.7 *The function declaration window for an object allows you to define the function as being either Public, Private or Protected.*

What you may not be familiar with is how to change the access level of an instance variable. In this past this has been a well kept secret, but it is time that you know how it is done. In the Declare Instance Variables window you can set up three different sections simply by entering a label at the top of each section saying "PUBLIC:", "PRIVATE:" and "PROTECTED:." All variables that you declare under each of these labels will have that access level. Figure 5.8 shows an example of a public, private and protected instance variable.

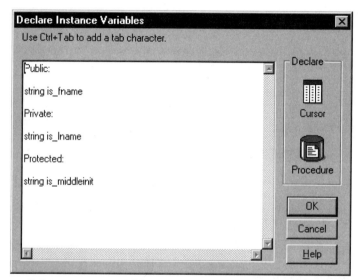

Figure 5.8 *Instance variables can also be declared as either Public, Private or Protected by declaring them within subsection of the Declare Instance Variables window.*

PowerBuilder 4.0 to 5.0: In PowerBuilder 5.0, by using the keyword READONLY when declaring an instance variable we can make the variable PUBLIC for reading, but PRIVATE for writing.

READONLY long il_counter

As a general rule of thumb, your instance variables should never be public. The way you allow the outside world to modify the properties of your object is through the declaration of a public function that will change the property. You are probably thinking, "That's a lot of work when they could just access the property directly and change it when required." It is a lot more work to build a function for any property that you want to provide access to change, but when the time comes to perform maintenance and you make a change to the internal structure of the object, if that property changes in any way, you have now created the snowball effect and will have to hunt through the other objects in the application to find where the variable was referenced. With the public function as the interface, everything is internalized and encapsulated inside the object and you can make modifications without fear of being hit by a big snowball!

You will likely use the protected access level more than the private as you will want to ensure that the descendants of your object class will have access to the data and processes that they need to operate effectively.

Although we suggest that you make all your user defined instance variables either private or protected, remember that PowerBuilder's system attributes and events are all public.

Strong encapsulation is a critical element to the success of PowerBuilder and OO projects in general. Be sure that your objects are well thought out and planned in advance. This is not something which can be accomplished effectively by the seat of your pants method!

5.11 POLYMORPHISM

When I think of polymorphism, the title of Frank Sinatra's famous song "[I Did It] My Way" comes to mind. Polymorphism is really the ability to call the same function on different objects, and have each object respond to the function call in a way that is specific to their requirements.

Let's look at the example of our house one more time. My house has a method called WaterLawn. If we call the method of watering the lawn on my home, it involves bring the hoses out of the shed, attaching them to the faucet, turning on the faucet, monitoring the process and shutting off the faucet at a specific time. However, watering the lawn on the bungalow across the street involves setting the timer on the underground sprinkler system which will automatically control the deployment of the sprinklers and the duration of the watering cycle. We are both watering our lawn, but our processes are different.

A good example of this in the PowerBuilder world would be the declaration of a function uf_Print() on all objects. The objective of having a general print method is straightforward: we want to be able to print the contents of the object as appropriate. Each object however is going to have different information inside of it and a different way that it might want to print

82 *Chapter 5: Object-Oriented PowerBuilder*

it. Each object can have their own uf_Print() function declared with the specific method of executing that print method encapsulated inside the object. All we need to know is that if the user indicates they wish to print, we call the uf_Print() function on the current object.

Polymorphism can be implemented not only across multiple objects, but also within an object. This is accomplished through *function overloading*. Function overloading means establishing two or more functions with the same name, but different sets of parameters within the same object. At execution time, when the function is called, PowerBuilder will match the argument list for the function against the appropriate function definition and select which process that it will execute.

Developers Tip: You can overload a function by specifying different argument sets, but you cannot overload a function by specifying a different return data type.

Let's use our example of uf_Print. Let's say that we want to have two variations of uf_Print. One takes no parameters and does a screen dump of the window. The second takes one parameter, asking if you want to show a print dialog box, and will print the contents of the window. The function list for this example is shown in Figure 5.9.

The companion disk contains an example of a window with two overloaded functions, both named uf_Print. One has no parameters, one has a single string parameter. You can execute the sample and then examine the code behind the window to see how it was constructed.

This powerful feature of OO languages is not always obvious to the new OO developer, however, as you begin to design and build your application you will begin to see the value this adds. In previous versions of PowerBuilder, the only way to overload a function was to use a different level of inheritance for each function variation because you weren't allowed to declare two functions with the same name at the same level. I am very pleased to announce that this is no longer the case in PowerBuilder 5.0. You can now declare all your overloaded functions at the same level simply by assigning them different argument sets or return values.

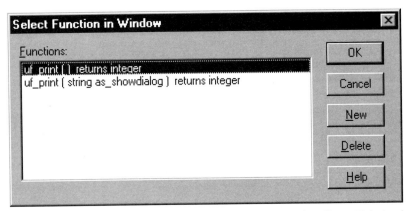

Figure 5.9 *PowerBuilder supports function overloading. This is the definition of multiple functions on the same object with the same name, but with different parameter sets.*

5.12 SUMMARY

The concepts of OO, when implemented properly, lead to a system that is very easy to maintain. Across all your projects, you may be able to realize substantial productivity improvements and cost savings. The systems you build will be more flexible, and may even run faster and consume fewer system resources than the same system in a non-OO environment. Notice that I said 'may' run faster. This is a very important point that is debated amongst PowerBuilder experts and OO experts in general. You will find arguments to support the argument that proper OO can improve the speed of an application and others that say it can't. The most important factors to remember is the increase in developer productivity and ease of maintenance.

OO is apparent throughout the PowerBuilder environment. You can take advantage of it when you build any object in PowerBuilder. A critical element to integrating your OO and architecture strategies will be the use of non-visual user objects. These are discussed in *Chapter 12—User Objects.*

CHAPTER 6

Class Libraries and Frameworks

"Libraries are not made; they grow."
– Augustine Birrell, 1850-1933, Obiter Dicta. Book Buying

Now there is a fundamental truth if I ever heard one! (Okay, he was referring to books, but I think it is equally applicable to PowerBuilder libraries.) The one basic concept that is imperative for me to impart to you in this chapter is that a library of PowerBuilder objects and classes should always be considered a work in progress. You must be prepared to continually evolve and improve the contents, adding new objects and improving processes wherever possible. Any library which never changes, quickly grows stagnant and becomes obsolete.

So what are libraries and frameworks and why would I want them? Good question! A framework provides a library of objects that allow you to develop your applications much more quickly, with a higher degree of robustness and improved application consistency. They accomplish this through the power of inheritance, encapsulation and polymorphism as we discussed in the last chapter. A solid framework will provide a standard set of base objects which contain many of your commonly used processes and application logic. This can then be reused without having to recode the functionality. With this chore out of the way, you can focus on the business solution without having to worry about many of the low level programming details such as set-

86   *Chapter 6: Class Libraries and Frameworks*

ting up every single DataWindow control in your application to either single select or multi select the rows it contains.

Objects in a framework tend to all be necessary parts of a whole. They represent all the required elements and foundation upon which you can build your application. You can take advantage of all the existing functionality and support that the framework provides. Often, however, when it comes to a framework, you must take all of it, or nothing. This can sometimes result in you having to bring a lot of excess baggage into your application that you weren't planning on including.

Object libraries are a little different from frameworks (although many third party vendors use the two terms interchangeably). Object libraries, like frameworks, also have a great deal of logic and functionality built into their components that you can reuse or inherit. The fundamental difference is that each object in an object library stands on its own. It does not require the framework or any other objects to be in existence in order for it to function correctly. You don't have the excess baggage problem because you only use what you need. Object libraries are good for specific techniques or problems, but remember that the object library does not provide the general foundation that every good enterprise application requires. That is where the framework comes in.

So which one should I have? A framework or an object library? You should probably have both. The framework is going to provide you with the solid foundation that will help to make your project a success, and the object library will enhance the tools that you have available to accomplish your business objectives.

6.1 A SINGLE LIBRARY SHOULD SUPPORT ALL YOUR ENTERPRISE APPLICATIONS

When you create or purchase a library of objects and a framework for your organization, be sure to think beyond the current project. The library should be general enough to support all the applications that the organization uses. Each application can have its own library which contains any objects which are particular to just this application, or are customized versions of objects from the corporate library.

6.2 The Build Versus Buy Dilemma

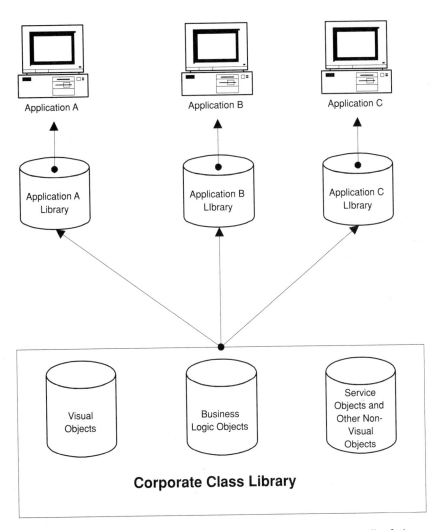

Figure 6.1 *A single corporate class library should service all of the PowerBuilder applications in your organization.*

Your object library's configuration will depend upon what architecture your organization uses. Most corporate environments should be working on attempting to isolate their business processes into business objects, and standard services into non-visual service objects. This would result in a corporate class library which contains three primary libraries, one for each class of object, like in Figure 6.1. More details on these libraries is available in section 6.5.

88 *Chapter 6: Class Libraries and Frameworks*

6.2 THE BUILD VERSUS BUY DILEMMA

When an organization first acquires PowerBuilder, or launches their first significant project, they are faced with the dilemma "Should I buy a class library or build my own?". There is no right or wrong answer here. Which way is correct for you depends on a variety of factors.

How tight are the project timelines? Short timelines might suggest that buying an existing library may help accelerate your development cycle. You have to remember to factor in sufficient time to come up the learning curve on the new library. If you are under no time pressure to deliver (not likely, but it happens once in a while…a long while…) then you may have a significant window to develop a strong class library, or if you have the ability to factor the time into the project schedule.

How much skill and experience does your team have? If your team is really green when it comes to PowerBuilder, buying an object library might be an inexpensive way to put some expertise on your side. On the other hand, if your team has strong PowerBuilder skills, building a robust object library would probably be a very useful and productive exercise.

What is the cost? You must weigh the cost of third party libraries against the cost of developing it internally (usually measured in time). Many third party libraries have hundreds of person hours of development time behind them.

There are many other factors to consider such as the complexity of your applications, the environment they are operating within and so on. You have to consider all the factors and then make the decision that is right for your organization.

6.3 BUILDING YOUR OWN

The primary goal when designing the class library is to maximize reusability and reduce the amount of coding required to deliver an application to your users. This requires a great deal of planning and forethought.

Be aware that simply building your own class library is not quite as simple as it sounds. Most of the class libraries in use in the corporate environment are the result of a tremendous investment of development time and a great deal of work and rework by some very dedicated personnel.

Probably the biggest single advantage to building your own class library is that you understand every object that is inside. You know how it all works because you built it. Many of the commercial class libraries which you can purchase have become so complicated that learning to use them is like learning a whole new language and programming tool (not to mention, marrying yourself to that firm for upgrades as new releases of PowerBuilder become available).

When you build it yourself you can also be reasonably certain that you are not bringing along any functionality that you don't need ('excess baggage'). A lot of the libraries that you can purchase try to solve 80% of your problems before you incur them. As a result, 50% of the code that is in the object, is almost never used, but eats up system resources anyway!

The other final significant factor to building your own custom class library is that you have the opportunity to make it truly custom for your organization's business requirements, instead of implementing a relatively generic third party product.

With PowerBuilder 5.0, Powersoft has given you a tremendous leg up when it comes to developing your own class library. The PowerBuilder Foundation Class (PFC) contains a set of base objects that form the basis of a very solid class library. The PFC is quite comprehensive in its scope and is built using up to date development techniques. I would highly recommend using it as your starting point if you are going to develop your own class library. See *Chapter 7, New 5.0 Features* for more details on the PFC.

There are a number of potential gains to building your own class library and with the new PFC on your side, doing so is now easier than ever before. You should still keep in mind that many of the third party libraries have been built by experts with a great deal of experience and talent.

6.4 PURCHASING THIRD PARTY

So you have decided to purchase a class library. Now you have to wade out into the jungle and fend for yourself among the wild animals all trying to sell you their 'state of the art' class library. I don't mean to scare you off, but the maxim for consumers in the PowerBuilder library market is 'caveat emptor'—let the buyer beware.

There are hundreds of class libraries available for sale, they range in price from $99.00 to $40,000.00 (no kidding!). The average price for a class library is somewhere between $800.00 to $3,000.00 per developer (run time licenses are usually free). The ratio of good libraries to poor libraries is quite extreme. Be very careful when investing in one of these. Be sure to get an evaluation copy and to take it apart and examine it closely. If you are new to PowerBuilder, hire a seasoned expert to help you evaluate them.

90   *Chapter 6: Class Libraries and Frameworks*

When you look at the manuals for the library, it should read like PowerScript. Don't buy it if the manual looks like you are getting into a whole new language. You didn't decide to use PowerBuilder because you wanted to layer another language on top of it!

Don't buy libraries which have every conceivable option either. Look for ones that have functionality you will use 80% of the time. If the bulk of the functionality you think you would never use, then that library is probably not appropriate for you. You would just end up wasting your available system resources.

Look for consistent and correct use of GUI and development standards. The library should also have a published set of standards that you can follow for your application development. Along with the standards should be complete documentation of the objects and samples of how they are used.

Never buy an object library unless you get the source code with it! Although it is not advisable to go modifying a commercial class library (instead you should have an inherited layer that you can modify) you will still want full access to the code so you can break an object down and understand how it functions. Having the source code also eliminates your dependence on the vendor if you require something to be changed, or if the vendor goes out of business!

You should try to find a class library that contains a solid security methodology and a good set of independent object classes. This is critical in enterprise application development. Many of the major vendors now have security libraries that they sell separate from their class libraries. If you decide to build your own class library, you may still want to consider one of these third party security libraries to help safeguard your applications (check out the security functionality of the new PFC also!).

Developer Tip: Many of the third party class libraries on the market are based upon concepts from PowerBuilder 3.0 (or even 2.0) and have much of the functionality attached to the window objects, or other places where it doesn't really belong. Be aware of this if you are evaluating libraries to purchase.

PowerBuilder 5.0 is still quite new to the market at the time that I am writing this, but I expect to see quite a few third party libraries come to market that are extensions of the PowerBuilder Foundation Class library. These are definitely worth checking out if you are in the market to purchase a pre-built library.

6.5 WHAT KINDS OF OBJECTS SHOULD A LIBRARY HAVE?

Whether you buy or build your object library, there are some standard objects that should be part of it. These fall into one of three general classes; visual objects, business objects and service/non-visual objects.

6.5.1 Visual Objects

The visual objects are those that make up the user interface of your application. They contain standard logic that is common throughout most applications. Examples of these objects include various types of windows such as sheets, response windows, MDI Frames, query windows, pick lists, login windows, single-row updates, multi-row updates and so on. Other visual objects include menus, OLE objects and user objects.

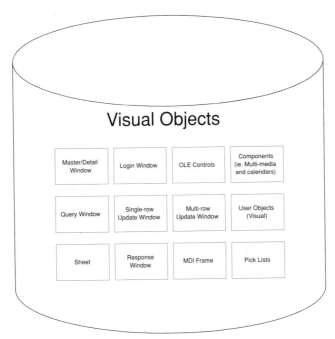

Figure 6.2 *Visual objects are used to develop the user interface of your application.*

There is an increasing supply of third party objects that fill specific niches. You can now obtain multi-media objects, calendars, spreadsheets, word processors and internet access objects.

6.5.2 BUSINESS OBJECTS

Your library should contain objects that contain the business logic that is applicable to your organization. These may be difficult to purchase from third party vendors unless your industry is one of those which has been well serviced by the third party software development houses, like the oil and gas industry (which seems to be well serviced by everyone!).

If you are using a two tiered architecture, you will likely not be developing business logic, but instead rolling your business logic into your visual objects. If you are developing under a three or n-tiered architecture then this area will develop over time and become more complete as you roll out more applications.

The kinds of objects you find here will relate to the primary entities which house business logic. If you are building a system for an education center, you may have a business object for a student, one for a company and another for a course.

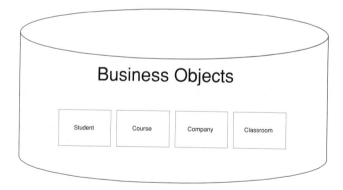

Figure 6.3 *Business objects are used in three and n-tiered applications to contain methods and properties for specific business objects.*

6.5.3 Service/Non-Visual Objects

This library will contain any non-visual and service objects that you will use in your applications. The service objects include things like e-mail objects, fax objects, modem controllers and security objects. Non-visual objects could include things like sheet managers.

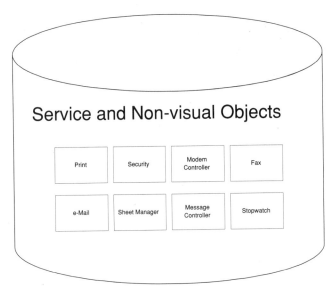

Figure 6.4 *Service and non-visual objects libraries are used to contain objects that provide application services as described in Chapter 3—Architectures for Development.*

6.6 CONCLUSION

Using a robust class library is a key factor in the success of any enterprise development project. Whether you decide to buy or build you should ensure that you factor in the appropriate time to integrate the class library into your project. The combined benefits of reduced development time, improved robustness and the ease of post implementation maintenance make the use of a class library a hands down winner for all projects.

Whether you choose to buy or build your libraries, be sure to check out the functionality of the new PowerBuilder Foundation Class library. It is well constructed and provides a great deal of your essential functionality.

CHAPTER 7

What's New In PowerBuilder 5.0

*P*owerBuilder 5.0 is full of new and exciting features to help you develop better applications with greater efficiency. If you are already familiar with PowerBuilder 4.0, this is a good place to start in order to discover the new and improved version 5.0 features and how to use them.

7.1 NATIVE COMPILED CODE

One of the most common complaints that I have heard about PowerBuilder applications over the years has been "My applications run too slow!" Many of the trade magazines and industry experts regularly put down the 4GL tools because of their interpreted code and the resulting overhead in the execution of enterprise applications.

In PowerBuilder 5.0, we now have the option of compiling our applications in machine code to improve the performance. We can still generate p-code executables, but when we are ready for production, we can have PowerBuilder generate C code which is passed to the embedded Watcom compiler and compiled into a machine code executable.

Chapter 7: What's New In PowerBuilder 5.0

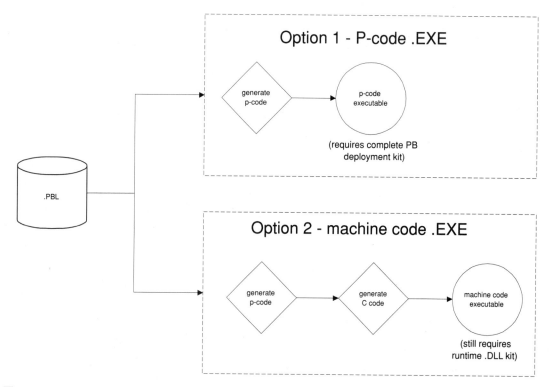

Figure 7.0 *You can generate either p-code or machine code executables with PowerBuilder 5.0. When you generate a machine code executable, PowerBuilder first generates C code which is then passed into the compiler. The C code generation is all behind the scenes and cannot be accessed by the developer.*

Developers Tip: Generating a machine code executable can take an extremely long time, even for a small application. It is not unusual for compile times to be several hours or more. Compile to p-code until you are fairly close to your final product to avoid wasting time waiting for compiles.

The magnitude of performance improvement you will see from machine code compilation will vary tremendously depending on your application. The compiling will improve the performance of your PowerScript which formerly was interpreted. It will not improve the speed with which your windows open or your data is retrieved from your data base. Specifically within your scripts you should see improved performance in the areas of:

7.1 Native Compiled Code   97

- Access to variables

- Execution of operations such as assignments, string concatenation and general math

- Flow of control statements such as IF/THEN and CHOOSE CASE statements

- Calling functions

The ability to generate machine code is available in the Windows 95 and Windows NT versions of PowerBuilder 5.0. The 16 bit version of PowerBuilder 5.0 for Windows 3.11 can only generate p-code executables. The objects from any version of PowerBuilder 5.0 can be recompiled in the 95 or NT versions and 16 bit machine code executables can be produced for Windows 3.11 from either of the 32 bit environments (although registry functions work differently in 16 and 32 bit environments—refer to the Registry Functions section later in this chapter).

When you compile your application into machine code, the .EXE file becomes a native executable. However, you must still distribute a set of runtime .DLLs that store some of the PowerBuilder functions that you may have called in your application. These could have been rolled into the .EXE, but Powersoft decided that doing so would add too much unnecessary bulk to the EXE. You may notice the machine code EXE is larger than the p-code EXE but that is all right, it will still run faster!

Developers Tip: The processing of compiling a machine code executable can take a significant amount of time. To help to improve the speed of .EXE generation, ensure that you have the maximum amount of RAM available to PowerBuilder by; physically increasing your RAM, changing a temporary swap file to a permanent swap file, and increasing the size of virtual memory when applicable.

Under machine code generation, your PowerBuilder Dynamic Libraries (.PBDs) will become Dynamic Link Libraries (.DLLs). However, these DLLs, unlike the .DLLs that we call in the External Functions (section 8.5.2) examples, cannot be called by external applications.

The process for generating a machine code executable is very straightforward. You enter the project painter where all executable files are generated (in version 5.0 the generation option was removed from the application painter). You will see the window in Figure 7.1.

Chapter 7: What's New In PowerBuilder 5.0

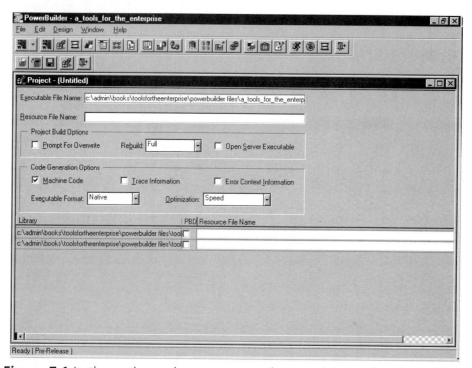

Figure 7.1 *In the project painter you can select machine code executable to allow you to build true compiled code executables.*

You select 'Machine Code' in the Code Generations Options group box. Then you press the Build button in the toolbar. PowerBuilder does the rest! You can choose to optimize your generation for speed, space or no optimization (I can't imagine too many situations where you would optimize for anything but speed).

Development Tip: Local and instance variables will execute faster than global and shared variables. Yet another reason for avoiding these variables!

Development Tip: Do not compile into machine code until you have reached your final stage of testing. If you use the p-code version for testing you can still take advantage of switches like PBTRACE that allow you to shadow the execution of a p-code compiled executable and track where errors are occurring.

7.2 DISTRIBUTED POWERBUILDER

Authors Footnote: I would like to thank Dave Cinderella for the extensive work he has done in engineering the distributed PowerBuilder and OLE Automation sections of this book. His experience with these technologies has been invaluable.

Distributed computing has had its share of the spotlight recently in the information technology (IT) industry. With many companies having completed their "experiments" with client/server and many moving on to enterprise development, a distributed architecture has become a significant part of their IT strategy. Powersoft, realizing the benefit of this architecture, has implemented distributed computing capabilities in PowerBuilder 5.0.

7.2.1 DISTRIBUTED POWERBUILDER CONCEPT

To this point, the PowerBuilder model for application development has been designed with two components; a client application and the database server. The client application contains the user interface, application navigation controls, data validation and editing as well as business logic. The database server may contain some part of the business logic but is primarily used as a data source for PowerBuilder clients.

Figure 7.2 *The 2-tier architecture model with client and server.*

The new model using PowerBuilder 5.0 allows for distributed application development. Non-visual business or service objects can be installed and executed on a physically separate third server. Using a 3-tier model as an example, the components of distributed PowerBuilder applications are the PowerBuilder client application, an application server (or object server), and the database server. In this model the user interface is separated from the business logic.

The PowerBuilder client will control the application navigation, GUI standards, and simple application validation. PowerBuilder objects and functionality that perform critical business processes can be physically moved to the application server. The application server can execute these PowerBuilder objects in a distributed environment through the new *transport* and *connection* objects in PowerBuilder 5.0. The Transport object is used by the server application to process the requests from a PowerBuilder client application. The Connection object specifies the parameters that PowerBuilder uses to connect to a server application.

By locating these business objects on a single distributed server, maintenance for all applications using that object can be centralized. The database server will still act as the data repository.

The advantages of this new distributed PowerBuilder model include:

- ability to 'thin out' the client application ('thin' clients will require fewer resources to run effectively)
- take advantage of server processing and resources
- allows the design to be scalable over time
- business functionality centralized in one location
- centralizes support, maintenance, distribution

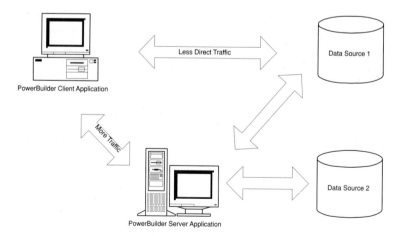

Figure 7.3 *The 3-tier model with client, application server, and database server.*

The distributed model can be further extended into an "n-tier" model by distributing the business functionality to multiple remote servers. The functionality of each server may be different in terms of either implementation or business logic. The multiple application server model may also be used to replicate functionality in the event of a failure on one or more servers. The objects distributed on these application servers can take advantage of the processing power and resources of each individual server platform.

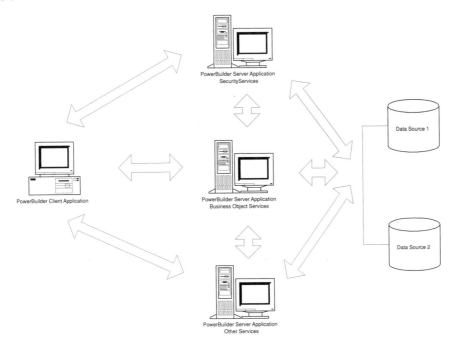

Figure 7.4 *The n-tier model can have multiple application servers that interact with each other and also with multiple databases.*

In order to take advantage of a multi-tiered model, you must first clearly identify the business specific elements of the application. These business entities will be deployed as nonvisual PowerBuilder custom class user objects on one or more application servers. The properties and methods of the user objects will map to the business elements and their associated functionality. The client application can instantiate a copy of the business object (on the application server) and set properties or execute functionality as necessary. The actual execution of the functionality occurs on the server and is communicated back to the client.

102   *Chapter 7: What's New In PowerBuilder 5.0*

These business objects are implemented using familiar PowerBuilder objects and PowerScript code. If you are in the build phase of your application, you can initially design and implement the objects locally on your client. The application can be scaled up to multiple distributed servers as you are ready to roll out, or as you discover an increased need for more throughput or processing power.

Key areas of the design include:

- separation of business and/or service logic from user interface
- partitioning the application
- PowerBuilder client to application server communication
- data flow
- error processing

7.2.2 NEW OBJECTS FOR DISTRIBUTED COMPUTING

Several new PowerBuilder 5.0 classes have been created to allow the new distributed capabilities in PowerBuilder 5.0. The new classes are inherited from either the non-visual object or the structure object.

7.2.2.1 Inherited from the NonVisualObject

7.2.2.1.1 ConnectObject

The ConnectObject is the ancestor object class for both the Connection and Transport objects.

7.2.2.1.1.1 Connection

The Connection object is used to connect a PowerBuilder client to a PowerBuilder server application. Once the connection is established, the client application can call object methods for those remote objects located on the server in the same manner as is it were a local object method. The connection object works in conjunction with the Transport object.

7.2 Distributed PowerBuilder 103

Several properties exist for this object:

ApplicationName(string)—name of the PowerBuilder server application

for the *WinSock* driver this specifies the port on the server machine that contains the application. This can be done either directly, by specifying the port number (i.e. '11000') or indirectly by specifying the service name which is specified in the TCP/IP services file on the client machine. Every server application must have a unique port on the server machine that it 'listens' to.

for the *NamedPipes* driver this specifies the application portion of the pipe name

for the *OpenClientServer* driver this specifies the query service (SQL.INI)

for the *Local* driver this is ignored

ConnectString(string)—application specific text sent to the ConnectionBegin event of the server application object. You can use this to pass parameters to the server application which you can then evaluate in your scripts in the ConnectionBegin event. For example, you could pass the user id and password for a database connection.

Driver(string)—communications driver used between client and server. The valid values for this driver are:

WinSock—use the Windows Sockets driver which provides the interface between Windows and TCP/IP

Named Pipes—interprogram communications method using Application Program Interfaces (API).

OpenClientServer—Sybase middleware which provides interprogram connectivity.

Local—a special driver built into PowerBuilder which allows you to test a distributed application locally without having to get caught up in all the communication protocol issues. PowerBuilder will simulate the remote server for you (thus eliminating, at this level, the need for a transport object—discussed later).

ErrCode(long)—code indicating success or failure of most recent operation. A value of 0 indicates success. Anything greater than 0 indicates failure. Refer to the chart that follows the methods section or your PowerBuilder documentation for a full list of failure codes.

ErrText(string)—text string describing the success or failure of most recent operation. The ErrCode and ErrText attributes function very much like the SQLDBCode and SQLErrText of the database Transaction object.

Location(string)—specifies location of the server application

for the *WinSock* driver specifies the specific server host. This can be done by naming the host (as specified in the TCP/IP hosts file), giving the specific IP address (such as 225.15.15.15), or by using the literal 'LocalHost' which indicates to PowerBuilder that the server application actually resides on the client machine.

for the *NamedPipes* driver specifies the location portion of the pipe name if not specified then a local pipe is constructed using dot (.) as machine name

for the *OpenClientServer* driver this is ignored

for the *Local* driver this is ignored

Options(string)—allows you to specify communication options such as:

BufSize—sets the size of the Windows Sockets buffer (for WinSock only).

MaxRetry—sets the maximum number of times that the client application will try to connect to the server if the server's listening port is busy.

NoDelay—allows you to override the default packet sending delay to send with no delay. This is very specific to your network and should not be used without consulting your network administrator as it could cause significant performance degradation. Use 'NoDelay = 1' to activate this option (for WinSock only).

PacketSize—specifies CTLIB packet size (OpenClientServer only).

RawData—allows you to override the default data passing method of the network (which obscures the data) and pass the data in its raw format. The benefit to this setting is a potential improvement in performance of distributed objects. In order for this to work, the server application must be expecting data in raw format or it will not be able to understand it. Use 'RawData = 1' to activate this option (for WinSock only).

This argument is ignored for NamedPipes and Local drivers. If you want to specify multiple options for this argument, separate them with a comma. For example:

my_connection.Options = 'MaxRetry=4,NoDelay=1'

Password(string)—Server application password. This application specific text is not used by the PowerBuilder client application. It is passed to the ConnectionBegin event of the server application.

Trace(string)—specifies the tracing options for debugging purposes such as

Level—setting 'Level = 1' will turn on the Console, ObjectCalls and ObjectLife trace options.

ObjectLife—allows you to trace each attempt to create/destroy a remote object and its success or failure. This option is set by specifying 'ObjectLife=1'

ObjectCalls—allows you to trace which methods have been invoke and with what parameter types. It will also specify if the method was called successfully. This option is set by specifying 'ObjectCalls=1'

ThreadLife—trace thread life creation/destruction

Log—will specify the file name that will contain the log information. All new information will be appended to this file (not overwritten). Each connection object must have its own specific log file.

Console—enables console logging (Windows 95 and NT only). This is extremely useful for letting you see in a console window all the communication and between the client and server. Activate this option by specifying 'Console=1'.

Userid(string)—User ID of the user who is connecting to the server. This application specific text, like Password, is not used by the PowerBuilder client application, but is passed to the ConnectionBegin event on the server application.

Several methods exist for the Connection object:

ConnectToServer()—connects a client to the application server specified in its arguments above. Returns a 0 if the connection was successful, or one of the distributed error codes (greater than zero) if an error occurred. Refer to the chart below for the full set of error codes.

DisconnectServer()—disconnects a client from the application server it was connected to.

GetServerInfo()—allows a client (with administrative privileges) to retrieve server information. This is done by passing an array of datatype *connectinfo* (described in

106   *Chapter 7: What's New In PowerBuilder 5.0*

detail in a subsequent section). This is a structure specifically created for this purpose. With this the administrative level client can perform such actions as finding out which other clients are connected and could disconnect them with a RemoteStopConnection() function. This method returns a long containing the number of elements in the connectinfo array.

RemoteStopConnection()—allows an administrative level client to disconnect another client by specifying that client's remote id as an argument. The remote id is obtained from the GetServerInfo() method.

RemoteStopListening()—allows an administrative level client to instruct the server to stop listening for client requests

All methods, except GetServerInfo() return long data type with a value of 0 for success and a value greater than zero for an error. The possible errors are:

Code	Description
50	Distributed service error
52	Distributed communications error
53	Requested server is not active
54	Server is not accepting requests
55	Request was terminated abnormally
56	Response to request was incomplete
57	Not connected
62	Server is busy

7.2.2.1.1.2 Transport

The Transport object is a PowerBuilder server side object that enables the server application to listen for clients requests. A method called Listen() enables this process and can be initialized in the same way transaction object is initialized.

Several properties exist for this object many of which are similar to those defined for the connection object:

ApplicationName, **Driver**, **ErrCode**, **ErrText**, **Location** and **Trace** all have the same definition and possible values as specified for the connection object.

Options(string)—specifies communication options but has a different set of options than the connection object:

BufSize, MaxRetry, NoDelay, RawData and PacketSize are the same as for the connection object.

MaxServerConnections—specifies the maximum number of open connections that are allowed on an OpenServer client. (for OpenClientServer only)

MaxServerThreads—specifies the maximum number of threads that the Open Server application can use. (also for OpenClientServer only)

NetBufSize—sets the maximum I/O buffer size of the network for client connections. (OpenClientServer only)

TimeOut—sets the maximum length of time that client applications can be inactive before the server will automatically disconnect that client. If you leave this option unspecified there will be no automatic disconnection of clients.

The methods for the Transport object include:

Listen()—instructs the server to listen for client requests. Returns a 0 if successful or a greater than zero error code as specified in this table:

Code	Description
50	Distributed service error
52	Distributed communications error
55	Request was terminated abnormally
56	Response to request was incomplete

StopListening()—instructs the server to stop listening for client requests. Returns a long of 0 if successful or an error code from the table above if unsuccessful.

7.2.2.1.1.3 RemoteObject

PowerBuilder remote objects are nonvisual objects that exist on the server and can issue any nonvisual PowerBuilder function and/or issue database commands. They may also use the new nonvisual DataStore object which has all the data intelligence functionality of a DataWindow, but without the visual user interface. The remote object is functionally equivalent to a procedure call in the sense that it supports parameter passing and return values for all nonclass or simple PowerBuilder data types. This means that you cannot do functionality such as ShareData() between a remote DataStore and your local DataWindow object. It would be nice, but we don't have it.

108 *Chapter 7: What's New In PowerBuilder 5.0*

Development Tip: Be sure to use only simple data types in your remote object functions. If you use complex or class types these methods will not be allowed in the remote form of your object and the PowerBuilder compiler will flag and remove them.

7.2.2.2 Inherited from the Structure

7.2.2.2.1 ConnectionInfo

The structure connectioninfo holds information that describes the connections in place on the server. The members of the structure are:

> Busy (boolean)—is the connection busy processing
> CallCount (long)—total number of calls made by the client
> ClientId (string)—the Id of the client that has established a connection
> ConnectTime (DateTime)—date and time of client connection
> LastCallTime (DateTime)—date and time of the last client request
> Location (string)—machine where client resides
> UserID (string)—the user id of the client

7.2.2.2.2 ProxyObject

The proxy object is an optional part of the nonvisual user object (NVO). If a proxy name is defined for an NVO, then every time the NVO is saved the proxy is also saved. The proxy is the signature for the NVO. The signature defines the methods and interface for the remote NVO. When we distribute an application by moving the business NVOs to the server, the corresponding proxy objects for those NVOs are left on the client. The calls to the NVOs are replaced with calls to the proxy. The method call is routed through the connection object to the server where it executes. The proxy is similar to the Interface Definition Language (IDL) used by the Distributed Computing Environment (DCE) and Microsoft.

To create a proxy object you would open the remote user object in the user object painter, click on it with the right mouse button and select the **Create Proxy Object**... option from the pop up menu. This object will be placed in the same .PBL as the distributed object. You will need to move it to the appropriate library.

7.2.3 Other Issues

Data sharing issues exist with a distributed application. The server creates separate client context areas for each client connection so data may not be shared across client connections. Within each client context, variable and object scope rules are similar to a standard PowerBuilder application (i.e. global variables are initialized at application startup).

Also keep in mind that the distributed functionality can only be called synchronously. The client will wait for the server to finish a process prior to any other events executing. The application object now has events for ConnectionBegin and ConnectionEnd to signal connection to and disconnection from a PowerBuilder server.

Another area that will take some planning is error processing. The error processing for a distributed PowerBuilder application is that if an error occurs on the server, the error information is populated for the current client thread and sent to the current client. On the client side, an application error will fire and the appropriate logic must be coded. The error can be processed in the Error event of the connection object using one of the 4 new enumerated error types; ExceptionFail!, ExceptionRetry!, Exceptionignore!, or ExceptionSubstituteReturnValue!.

Finally, the server component of PowerBuilder 5.0 has been architected so that a single misbehaved client will not terminate the server. An exception handler within the server will attempt to locate the misbehaved client and terminate the thread gracefully, freeing resources if possible.

7.2.4 Distributed Example

Let's walk through the steps for building a distributed PowerBuilder application.

Step 1 Design the application.

A solid design for an object-oriented client/server application is a critical success factor. The application architect must be aware of the business problem to be solved by the application, the data flow within the application, any external systems to which the application will interface, and importantly differentiating between what the users need and what the users expect from the application.

The design will likely include a number of specifications or models. Some examples would be:

110   *Chapter 7: What's New In PowerBuilder 5.0*

the functional specification
the process model
the data flow diagram
the entity relationship diagram
the object model

The most important aspect of this part of the development cycle is to define and describe the system as clearly as precisely as possible.

The sample application included on the CD illustrates a distributed PowerBuilder application using a centralized security server. The security will be managed by a non-visual user object *n_security* with encapsulated methods for connection and disconnection to the database server.

The application could have security embedded in the login window *w_login*. The problem is that this scenario ties the user interface and the business logic. By separating the security logic from the window, application security can be called from any object in the application. Using the distributed PowerBuilder model allows the centralization of the security processing and allows security to be handled by a different and possibly more powerful machine.

Step 2 Identify business or system logic that can be implemented as custom class user objects.

The distributed PowerBuilder model involves partitioning our applications by removing critical business or service processing from the user interface. This technique allows you to alter either the business processing without requiring changes to the user interface and vice versa. For example, a change from an MDI style of application to a tab folder metaphor would not require us to recode the business functionality. In addition to the business logic, system management functionality such as error processing or security should also be removed where possible from the user interface.

The business processing and systems management functionality should be constructed as non-visual or custom class user objects. These objects support the object oriented principles of inheritance, encapsulation, and polymorphism without a visual interface. Once these objects are designed and coded, they may be moved to the application server where the processing will take place.

In our example, the application security will be designed as a non-visual user object (a custom class object, refer to Chapter 12 for details on constructing these objects) with methods for connection and disconnection to the database and the application server.

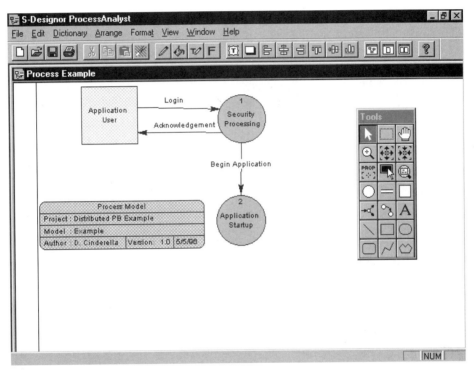

Figure 7.5 *Showing the business and system objects/entities.*

Step 3 Code the application components.

One of the more straightforward steps in the development cycle is the actual coding of the user interface and custom class user objects. We can group these user objects by similar business or systems functionality. The objects will have attributes and methods encapsulated within them. We do not need to expose the user of the object to the specific details of how these methods are implemented. Instead, we provide them with a set of object functions that serve as the application programming interface (API) that will be the object's link to the rest of the system.

112   *Chapter 7: What's New In PowerBuilder 5.0*

The security object *n_security* with have the following methods which can be called:

uf_connect_to_db(as_inifile) returns long

```
// This script will read all the database values from an application .INI file.

// Initialize the transaction object attributes
SQLCA.DBMS = ProfileString(as_inifile,"Database","DBMS","")
SQLCA.Database = ProfileString(as_inifile,"Database","Database","")
SQLCA.UserID = ProfileString(as_inifile,"Database","Userid","")
SQLCA.DBPass = ProfileString(as_inifile,"Database","DatabasePassword","")
SQLCA.DBParm = ProfileString(as_inifile,"Database","DBParm","")

// Connect to the dbms
CONNECT USING SQLCA;

RETURN SQLCA.SQLCode
```

uf_disconnect_from_db() returns long

```
// Disconnect from the dbms
DISCONNECT USING SQLCA;

RETURN SQLCA.SQLCode
```

The client application can connect directly to the database server and/or connect to the application server.

These two methods handle a fairly simple process. You could extend the functionality of this object by adding a method called uf_can_update() which when called with an activity as an argument, will return a TRUE or a FALSE to indicate if the current user has sufficient security access to perform that functionality.

The third method tests the connection status of the example application.

uf_test_db_connection() returns long

```
// Attempt to select the count of the total number of employees which will
// test the validity of the DBMS connection

long ll_NumRows

select count(*) into :ll_NumRows
from employees
```

7.2 Distributed PowerBuilder   113

```
using SQLCA;

Return ll_NumRows
```

Step 4 Test the application logic locally

Of course we need to test our design. The best approach is to revisit the functional specifications and models to prove that the system solves the business problem and conforms to the specifications. The testing process initially should be done using a single client machine. Until this point, we've followed the design, coding, and testing of a typical PowerBuilder application. We have declared an instance variable *iu_security* on the login window and instantiated the user object at the appropriate level with the CREATE function:

```
iu_security = CREATE n_security
```

In our scripts we call the methods on *n_security* with traditional techniques:

```
iu_security.uf_connect_to_db("PBBook.ini")
```

Once we know that the non-visual object works as it is supposed to, we must prepare the application for the distributed model.

Step 5 Declare the connection object reference variable and a proxy for each custom class user object

Once we can prove that the application provides the needed and/or desired functionality, now we must determine which objects in our application can be distributed to one or more application servers.

The actual creation of the server application and the moving of the relevant objects will occur in Step 8. Right now we have to create a special user object called a *proxy* object. A proxy object contains all the names of the methods on the appropriate server object, but doesn't contain any of the functionality. You can think of it as a placeholder or a stub for the distributed object.

To create a proxy object you must open the non-visual user object that you are distributing and click on it with the right mouse button. The popup menu will have an option that reads **Set Proxy Name....** Select this option and provide a name for the proxy object. Don't forget to provide a comment too!

Chapter 7: What's New In PowerBuilder 5.0

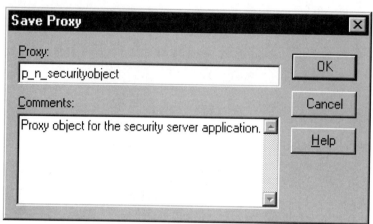

Figure 7.6 *We define a proxy object in the custom class user object painter.*

The proxy object will be created when the user object is saved. It will be saved in the same library as the user object so you may need to relocate it into the library where your client application is stored.

The next step will be to declare a *connection* object at a scope that is appropriate for the term of the connection. If you will need to connect frequently to the server application, you may choose to declare the connection object at a global level. You must remember to issue a CREATE statement to have PowerBuilder actually instantiate the object.

We will be using a standard class user object inherited from the connection object to which we have added two custom functions for connecting and disconnecting with our server application. These methods are explained in the code below.

After creating the connection object, you must specify the name of the server application, where the application can be found and how you will be communicating with it. These are all handled by the application, location and driver properties of the connection object.

The connection to the server application can be made using one of four protocols:

Local, Winsock, Named Pipes, and Open Client/Open Server. The Local protocol is used to test a single combined executable (client and server). The other protocols can be used on a single machine or across a network.

7.2 Distributed PowerBuilder   **115**

Once the necessary properties are set, we can connect to the server application by issuing the ConnectToServer() function call for the connection object. You can check the ErrCode property of the connection object to ensure that your connection was successful and the ErrText property will contain a text string describing the error.

```
// declare a reference variable for the connection object
connect dpb_connect

uf_connect_to_app_server(string as_driver, string as_location, string as_application)
returns long

// set the connection object attributes

THIS.driver = as_driver  // communications driver for TCP/IP
THIS.location = as_location // server location
THIS.application = as_application // server application-service name


// the application server name must defined in the SERVICES file // for your TCP/IP vendor
// connect client to server application
THIS.ConnectToServer()

// Return the error code
RETURN THIS.errcode

uf_disconnect_from_app_server()  returns long

// Disconnect from the application server
THIS.DisconnectServer()

//Return Error code to client
Return THIS.errcode
```

Step 6 Replace calls to the custom class user object methods with calls to the proxy's methods.

Any calls made to the custom class user object methods in your application scripts will need to be altered so that they now reference the proxy object. Once the proxy is connected to the server application, these calls will actual execute the remote object methods on the application server.

We will call the remote object proxy *ro_security*.

116   *Chapter 7: What's New In PowerBuilder 5.0*

The remote object proxy must be declared and instantiated. We will use the application open event.

```
// Instance Variable
ro_security iuo_securitymgr

// Declare a variable to hold function call results
long ll_ReturnCode

// Connect to the Sybase SQL AnyWhere DBMS locally
//iuo_security_mgr = CREATE uo_security
//ll_ReturnCode= iuo_security_mgr.uf_connect_to_db_server("PBBook.ini")
// Connect to the Sybase SQL AnyWhere DBMS using the PowerBuilder // Application Server

iro_security_mgr = CREATE ro_security
iro_security_mgr.SetConnect(i_connection)

ll_ReturnCode = &
iro_security_mgr.uf_connect_to_db_server ("PBBook.ini")

// Set the status of the checkbox to indicate DBMS connection //status
IF ll_ReturnCode =  0 THEN
     cbx_dbserver.Checked = TRUE
     cb_disconnect_db_server.Enabled = TRUE
     cb_test_db_server.Enabled = TRUE
     ib_dbms_connected = TRUE
ELSE
     cbx_dbserver.Checked = FALSE
END IF
```

Step 7 Create the server application using the custom class user object and the transport object.

You must build the non-visual object into a mini application that will run and instantiate the object. This mini application should also have a visual component that allows you to press buttons to start and stop the application. You may choose to add a monitor window to the server application so you can watch what the distributed objects are doing!

The PowerBuilder application on the server is nearly identical to a standard application with the addition of the transport object. The *transport* object specifies the para-

7.2 Distributed PowerBuilder   **117**

meters that PowerBuilder uses to process requests to connect to a server application. It will act as a listener waiting for client requests. The initialization of the transport object includes setting the application, location and driver properties.

The transport is initialized and the listening process is started as demonstrated in the script below. The user object *n_security* now is instantiated in our server application. Any calls to the custom class user object in our client application will now be handled remotely by the server application.

The server application consists of an application object *a_server*, a window object *w_server_console*, and the user object *n_security*.

The application object open event can start listening for client requests and open the *w_server* window. In our example, we will declare a reference variable for the transport object as a instance variable.

```
transport itp_transport
```

```
// Open server application window
Open(w_server_console)
```

The console window will have the code to start the listen process in the start server commandbutton.

```
string ErrText, ErrNo

//      Create a transport object

itp_transport = create transport

//      Specify the communications driver
itp_transport.driver    = ProfileString("PBBook.INI","transport","driver","")

//      Specify the server location
 itp_transport.location   = ProfileString("PBBook.INI","transport","location","")

//      Specify the server application name
 itp_transport.application = ProfileString("PBBook.INI","transport","application","")

// Specify tracing options
 itp_transport.trace    = ProfileString("PBBook.INI","transport","trace","")
```

118   *Chapter 7: What's New In PowerBuilder 5.0*

```
        // Start the server Listen() process - listening for client connections
itp_transport.Listen()

// check the return codes
ErrNo = string(itp_transport.ErrCode)
IF ErrNo <> "0" THEN
        ErrText = itp_transport.ErrText
        MessageBox("Server Start Error", ErrNo + ":" + ErrText)
        Close(parent)
    END IF

// Set the connection status flag
ib_connected = TRUE

// Start the server console messages
TIMER(.14)
```

Note that the server that is running the server application must have the PowerBuilder deployment kit installed in order for the server application to be able to run.

Be sure to code a close event for the server window. In this close event you must be sure to DESTROY any non-visual objects that you have created to avoid causing memory leaks on the server. The listening process is stopped in a Stop Server commandbutton using the function StopListening(). Our window close event would contain:

```
// Destroy the transport object
DESTROY itp_transport
```

It is on the server application where you can take advantage of the two new events in the application object. The *ConnectionBegin* and the *ConnectionEnd* events fire when a client application connects or disconnects from the server application respectively. In these events you could perform processing such as logging the activity on the server to keep track of clients connected and other important statistics. This would also allow someone who is considering shutting down the server application to observe if anyone is connected before doing so. This event contains arguments that include the user_id and password of the person connecting (allowing you to perform security checks when they connect to the object) and also a connect string for other processing.

If you want to control access to the server application you can deny access to the client application by coding:

RETURN NoConnectPrivilege!

This is an enumerated data type which will tell the client application that their connection was refused. Alternative return codes are ConnectPrivilege! for a good connection or ConnectWithAdminPrivilege! to allow the client application full administrative privileges (if applicable).

Developers Tip: Once you have removed the functionality from the client application and placed it on a remote server, the client applications will have no knowledge of the methods and functions that are available on the server application unless you document them! Any server applications must be fully documented and updated as appropriate.

Step 8 Test the application using the distributed model on a local machine.

The application should be tested initially on a single machine. Using either Windows 95 or Windows NT, the client and server applications can be simultaneously run. We can take advantage of this environment to test our application logic before deploying across an enterprise wide network.

Step 9 Test the application using the distributed model using the network (TCP/IP, Named Pipes, etc...).

If the local testing is successful, the last step is to move the server executable to a different machine and use one of the supported communication protocols (Named Pipes, TCP/IP, or OpenClient/Open Server). The only modification necessary is to change the driver with which the connection object establishes the PowerBuilder client—PowerBuilder server conversation.

This simple example demonstrates how distributed computing is performed. Your actual implementation will probably involve more sophisticated objects.

120 *Chapter 7: What's New In PowerBuilder 5.0*

7.3 INBOUND OLE AUTOMATION

Another important technology that integrates with distributed computing is also available in PowerBuilder 5.0. This technology is OLE Automation support. When used with a distributed architecture, OLE Automation and OCX support allows the inclusion of non-PowerBuilder components in a distributed solution.

Microsoft Object Linking and Embedding (OLE) 2.0 further extends application interoperability. The OLE technology is available in PowerBuilder 5.0 allowing both visual and non-visual automation of OLE controls. Using this mechanism, both visual and non-visual PowerBuilder objects may be exposed as In-Process OLE Automation Servers for use by other OLE compliant client tools such as Visual Basic. Likewise, PowerBuilder applications can act as OLE client to other servers such Microsoft Word, Excel, and others.

The OLE Automation technology is also available in the Window object as a control, the DataWindow Object as a presentation style, and through the User Object.

The first flavor of OLE Automation is the placement of an OLE container on the surface of the Window object. The OLE container control is selected and an OLE server or an OLE enabled object (e.g. Excel worksheet) is associated with the control. The user can activate the OLE server or the OLE enabled object by clicking with the mouse. The OLE server will then be executed either InPlace or OffSite. If activated InPlace, the menus, toolbars, and workspace of the PowerBuilder application is replaced by the menus. toolbars, and workspace of the OLE server. When finished, the user closes the OLE server and the interface returns to the familiar PowerBuilder interface. Offsite activation involves the OLE server application being executed separately from the PowerBuilder application.

The second flavor of OLE Automation uses OLE as a presentation style for a DataWindow. This is the industry's first point and click SQL interface to OLE. More details are covered in section 7.5.11.

The third flavor of OLE Automation is the construction of an OLE enabled user object using PowerBuilder. The first step is to design and code the PowerBuilder object. The object must make its properties and functionality known to the Window system through the OLE Registry. Once the PowerBuilder object is registered as an OLE object, the client applications supporting OLE can instantiate the object and access the object's inherent functionality. The PowerBuilder object can be executed in one of two ways either as interpreted p-code or as compiled code using the PowerBuilder runtime engine.

7.3 Inbound OLE Automation

Using this form of OLE Automation requires that a unique OLE identifier and REG (Registration) file be generated by the application. Two object functions encapsulated in the PowerBuilder.Application object GenerateGUID() and GenerateRegFile() are needed to complete the OLE registration process.

The GenerateGUID() function returns a unique global identifier. The GenerateRegFile() function creates a registry file used by other OLE clients to understand the properties and methods of your object. The necessary steps documented for deploying an object as an OLE Automation server object will be presented in the following example.

A sample PowerBuilder script for creating a GUID and then generating a registry file for a pCode object:

```
oleObject        PBObject
string           ls_GUID
long             ll_result

PBObject = create oleObject
// Establish a connection with PowerBuilder.Application
ll_result = PBObject.ConnectToNewObject("PowerBuilder.Application")

ELSE
IF ll_result < 0 THEN
  // handle the error
li_result = PBObject.GenerateGUID(REF ls_GUID)
  IF (li_result < 0) THEN
    // handle the error
  ELSE
     ll_result = PBObject.GenerateRegFile(ls_GUID,"n_classname", &
     "Programmable.Object",1, 0,"OLE Automation Object Release 1.0",&
       "C:\dev\n_class.reg")
  END IF  // GUID created successfully
END IF // Connection to PowerBuilder.Application established successfully
```

To use non-visual PowerBuilder objects as an OLE Automation Server, the custom generated registry (.REG) file is required on the client machine.

The OLE automation using this approach can be made available to any client application that supports OLE. For example, a Visual Basic application could take advantage of the new DataStore capability if exposed as an automated OLE object.

122   *Chapter 7: What's New In PowerBuilder 5.0*

A more sophisticated method is available to utilize PowerBuilder objects in OLE-enabled clients through application automation using the new OLE automation *PowerBuilder.Application* identifier. This new functionality allows an OLE client to access a PowerBuilder runtime application and its objects. It is a registered programmable OLE object that is installed when PowerBuilder is installed. The client application sets the runtime application the LibraryList property and creates instances of non-visual objects with the CreateObject method. The CreateObject method takes a string containing the PowerBuilder class name. This type of OLE Automation requires more effort but in the long run is more flexible as it does not require the pre-registration of the object in the OLE Registry. This allows the PowerBuilder class to be either publicly exposed or private and not exposed to the clients.

The *PowerBuilder.Application* properties include the *library list* which needs to be set before the object is instantiated and the *machine code* attribute which is set to TRUE if compiled or FALSE if p-code.

The steps are as follows:

Step 1 Create a Non-visual PowerBuilder class.

A custom class user object is created using the user object painter. We will use the *n_security* custom class object from the distributed demo application.

Step 2 Define the object's public methods and properties to be exposed through OLE Automation.

The encapsulated functions *uf_connect_to_db()*, *uf_disconnect_from_db()*, and *uf_test_db_conection()* are declared as public. This will allow any OLE-enabled client application to instantiate and use the n_security object.

Step 3 Connect to PowerBuilder.Application OLE automation server.

A call to the ConnectToNewObject() function is needed to connect to the PowerBuilder.Application programmable OLE object.

```
long ll_status
double ld_result
OLEObject PBObject, PBNVObject

PBObject = CREATE OLEObject
ll_status = PBObject.ConnectToNewObject &
("PowerBuilder.Application")
```

Step 4 The library list and machine code properties are set.

Once these properties are set, a call to the CreateObject() function passing the PowerBuilder classname as an argument is executed.

```
IF ll_status = 0 THEN
    // Handle the error
ELSE
    PBObject.LibraryList = "c:\myappl\mylibrary.dll"
    PBObject.MachineCode = TRUE
```

Step 5 Create an instance of your OLE object.

```
PBNVObject = CREATE OLEObject

PBNVObject = PBObject.CreateObject("nvo_myobject")
IF IsNull(PBNVObject) THEN
    // Handle the error
ELSE
    // CALL the NVO methods

END IF
```

Step 6 Destroy the OLE objects.

```
        DESTROY PBNVObject
        PBObject.Disconnect( )
    END IF

    DESTROY PBObject
```

7.4 POWERBUILDER FOUNDATION CLASS LIBRARY

Through the previous versions of PowerBuilder, many third party companies have arisen around the production of class libraries and frameworks. Now Powersoft has decided to throw their hat in the ring and distribute with PowerBuilder a base class library of objects that you can use for your enterprise applications.

124 *Chapter 7: What's New In PowerBuilder 5.0*

You can use the objects in the PowerBuilder Foundation Class (PFC) Library as the underlying layer for your own class library and applications. As a ready to use base, the PFC provides substantially expanded functionality that you can use when you inherit your objects directly from the PFC (via the PFC extension layer). All this functionality can also be rolled into your own class library by using PFC as the foundation upon which your library will be built.

The PFC relies heavily upon a service based architecture (refer to *Chapter 3— Architectures For Development*). There are a large number of non-visual classes of objects which provide services to the visual classes. For example, the non-visual object n_cst_dwsrv_querymode provides the DataWindow control with all the QueryMode functionality (allowing you to use the DataWindow as a processor for ad hoc query criteria entered by the user). By building this functionality into a non-visual object, the DataWindow control only needs to instantiate the object when it wishes to use QueryMode functionality. If it never needs to do this, the non-visual object is never instantiated and as a result, the DataWindow control uses fewer resources and has a smaller overall footprint. The functionality inside of the non-visual can also be accessed by many different DataWindow controls simultaneously.

The PFC covers many bases such as DataWindow functionality, security layers, debugging assistance and much more. After looking at the PFC, I was very pleased and surprised at its quality and usefulness (Powersoft's previous application library in version 4.0 left much to be desired). I believe that the extensive functionality of the PFC will help you to build better applications faster which are easier to maintain. Isn't that what we are all really trying to do?

The PFC consists of many libraries that will need to be added to your library search path in your application object. These libraries can be divided into two groups; the PFC libraries and the extension libraries.

7.4.1 THE PFC LIBRARIES

The PFC libraries contain the core of the PowerBuilder Foundation Class libraries. These libraries all have PFC at the start of their name. You should never change anything in any of these libraries. If you want to make a change to an object in the PFC you should do this in the extension layer PBLs as discussed in section 7.4.2.

There are four different PFC libraries; one for application services, one for DataWindow services, one for window services and a fourth that covers other functionality. The application services PBL contains objects that provide services throughout the application. These services include debugging, security, error handling, log on and other functions. The DataWindow services PBL contains objects for all standard DataWindow services. These services include row selection, filtering, sorting, querymode, resizing, drag and drop and more. The window services PBL contains objects for common window services such as status bar management, menu management and user definable preferences. The final PBL contains any services and objects that didn't fit into the first three PBLs. This includes standard class objects for each window type (MDI frame, main, child, popup, response) and window controls.

7.4.2 THE EXTENSION LAYER LIBRARIES

The extension layer libraries are where you can make your modifications and enhancements to the PFC. These libraries all have the characters PFE at the start of their name. The objects inside the PFE libraries are identical descendant classes of all the objects in the PFC libraries. By making your changes in the PFE libraries instead of the PFC ones you have insulated yourself from future changes in the PFC. When Powersoft releases updated or enhanced versions of the PFC, your simply insert them in the place of the old libraries and the linkages from your customized PFE classes should remain the same.

7.5 DATAWINDOW ENHANCEMENTS

This book will not review every DataWindow presentation style and feature that exists in PowerBuilder. We will assume that if you are reading this book you have a fundamental understanding of the DataWindow. Instead, we want to focus on what is new with the DataWindow. In particular, we will examine the two new presentation styles that are available, we will look at some of the enhancements in the DataWindow painter, see how data is manipulated and what has changed with how you use the DataWindow object and control in your scripts.

7.5.1 Two New DataWindow Object Presentation Styles

Version 5.0 gives us some new toys to play with, both of which are going to provide us with expanded and enhanced functionality. We can now use an OLE 2.0 and a Rich Text Edit (RTE) presentation style.

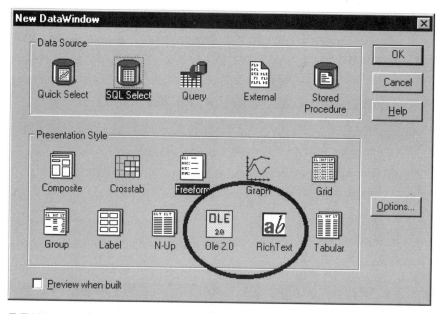

Figure 7.7 *We now have two new DataWindow presentation styles that we can use, OLE 2.0 which acts as a gateway into OLE 2.0 server compliant software, and Rich Text Edit (RTE) which allows us to insert data into an RTE formatted file.*

7.5.1.1 OLE 2.0 Presentation Style

The OLE 2.0 presentation style is a gateway to a world of new and exciting possibilities. What it allows us to do is to take our data from a SQL select statement and pass it to a valid OLE 2.0 server. That server can then be made to perform functions with the data that we pass to it. For example, we could take our result set and pass it to the media player allowing us to integrate the playing of .WAV (sound files) and .AVI (video) files into our DataWindows. Or we could use MS-Graph as an engine for performing some advanced graphing that perhaps PowerBuilder does not support. One industry group I have been heavily involved in where this will be invaluable is in the energy, forestry and natural resource industries where integration with GIS (Geographic Information Systems) is critical. The opportunities are endless and will continue to grow as more and more software becomes OLE 2.0 compliant.

We can link any OLE 2.0 server product into the DataWindow as long as it supports the OLE standard Uniform Data Transfer (UDT). You should be able to learn if the application supports this from the vendor documentation, and you can learn what data is expected to be passed.

For our example, let's use Microsoft Graph as our OLE 2.0 server. This is an application that is installed with the Microsoft Office suite of tools, if you don't have it, you won't be able run this sample from the companion CD.

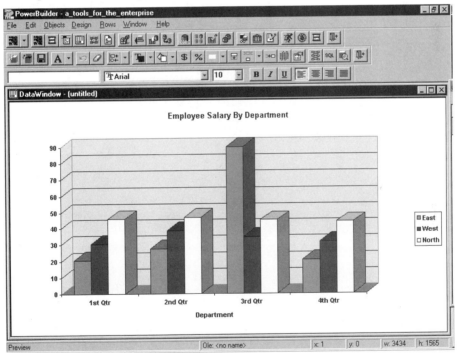

Figure 7.8 *The OLE 2.0 presentation style can use any OLE 2.0 server that supports UDT (Uniform Data Transfer) to display data from the database. In our example, we will use Microsoft Graph as an OLE 2.0 server within a DataWindow object.*

7.5.1.1.1 Creating A Microsoft Graph OLE 2.0 DataWindow

Step 1 Start the DataWindow painter and select **New....** Select **SQLSelect** as your data source (or other as appropriate) and **OLE 2.0** as your presentation style. Notice that the **Options...** button is disabled as the display of the data will be handled by the OLE 2.0 server and not by PowerBuilder. Select the **OK** button.

Step 2 Select the appropriate tables and columns for your data source. In our example we selected the employee and department tables.

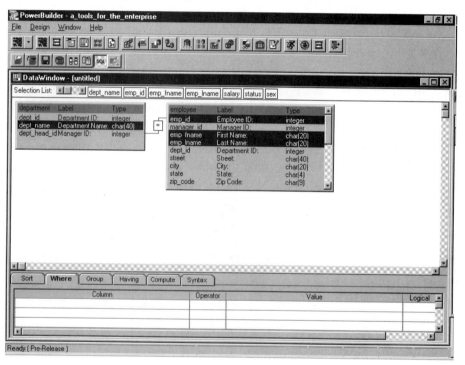

Figure 7.9 *Select the data columns you wish to pass to the OLE 2.0 server.*

Step 3 Note that to move from the SQL Painter to the Design window inside the DataWindow painter, you no longer push the Design button. Now you select the **SQL** button, which is a push on/ push off button that will bring you in and out of the SQL painter. Do this now to move from the SQL Painter to the Designer.

Step 4 When moving into the designer, PowerBuilder will need to know what OLE 2.0 server you will be using. It opens the window in Figure 7.13 to ask you to select one (alternatively you could open an .OCX control as the container for the data). In our example, we are selecting Microsoft Graph 5.0. Selecting the **Browse...** command button will take you to the Object Browser where you can examine the inside of your selected OLE 2.0 server. You will see options such as where the server is physically located, which .DLL it uses, and so on.

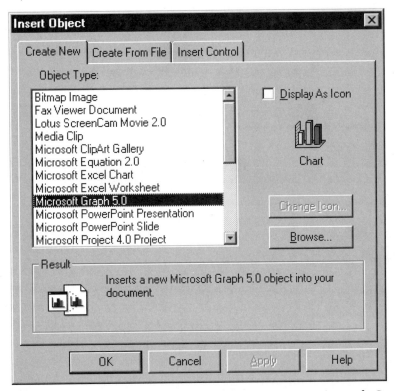

Figure 7.10 Select the OLE 2.0 server. We are using Microsoft Graph.

Step 5 You will return now to the DataWindow designer. The OLE 2.0 server will be visible and selected in the middle of the DataWindow painter. Notice that the toolbar at the top of the painter is actually the tool bar for Microsoft Graph. While the OLE 2.0 server object is selected, you have access to all the functions and features of MS-Graph. If you click outside the OLE 2.0 object, on the blank area of the DataWindow, you will revert back to the PowerBuilder DataWindow toolbar. To go back to MS-

Chapter 7: What's New In PowerBuilder 5.0

Graph, click on the OLE 2.0 server object at any time you are in the designer. Click outside the OLE server now.

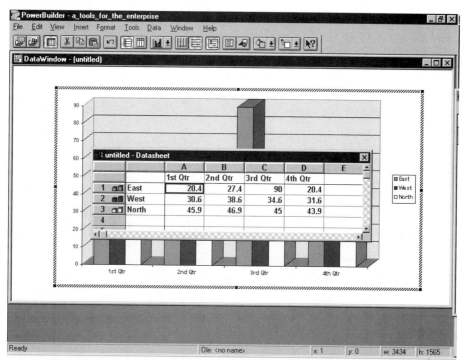

Figure 7.11 *When you enter the designer, you will notice that the OLE server object is selected. When selected, the menu for MS-Graph appears in the toolbar. You have access to all the features of MS-Graph.*

Step 6 When you clicked outside the OLE server object in step 5, you returned to the normal DataWindow painter designer. Then, a dialog window appeared asking you to define the object as in Figure 7.11. Specifically, the object needs to know what data it is receiving.

7.5 DataWindow Enhancements

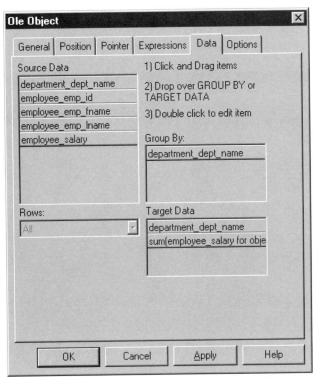

Figure 7.12 *The OLE server now needs to know what data we are passing it.*

In this window we have to specify which data we are sending to the OLE 2.0 server and how we are grouping it. We do this using drag and drop. First, let's drag the column **department_department_name** into the Group By box. This specifies that we are going to group by the department name. Next, drag the same column into the Target Data box, indicating that we are going to pass the department name to the OLE server. Then drag the column **employee_salary** to the Target Data box. Notice that the field in the target data box changes to **sum(employee_salary by object)**. PowerBuilder makes the guess that you want to graph this data by the sums of salaries within a department. If this is true you can leave it, if you want to change the expression, you can double click on the column in the Target Data box and it will take you to the expression editor dialog window. For our purposes, this is the correct value, so we do not need to alter it.

There are other tabs on the window for modifying the attributes of the OLE server object including expressions, OLE options, which pointer to use and where to display the object. We will look at these later, for now, just select **OK**.

132 *Chapter 7: What's New In PowerBuilder 5.0*

Step 7 Now we are in the DataWindow painter. Let's preview our data. Select the Preview button from the DataWindow painterbar. Your DataWindow should appear similar to the one you see in Figure 7.13.

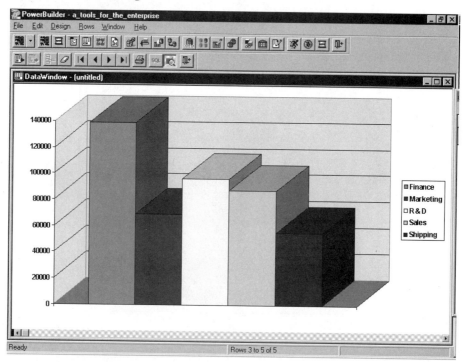

Figure 7.13 *Your data should appear something like this.*

By double-clicking on the object the end user will be able to bring up the MS-Graph server and begin changing the properties of the graph. If you want to provide this kind of functionality to the user, then you can just leave the settings as they are. Some of the benefits of leaving this functionality in place is that the user now has a high degree of control over the data they are being presented with. They have the ability in our example to change the graph type, colors, and formatting, or view the data sheet, or almost any other functionality that MS-Graph provides. The drawback is that you also cannot limit that functionality. If there are some features of MS-Graph that you don't want the to have access to, like importing an external chart, that functionality comes along with the package and you cannot selectively restrict the user. It

7.5 DataWindow Enhancements 133

also increases the complexity of the user interface, and depending on your user group (remember Chapter 4 when we talked about analyzing your users) you may want to keep the interface as straightforward as possible.

If you want to override the double clicked functionality which activates the OLE server, this can be accomplished on the tabbed window where we specified the data. If you started up the MS-Graph server, switch back to the DataWindow by clicking on the white space outside the OLE object. Now press the preview button again (it is another push on/push off button) to return to the designer. Within the designer, if you click on the OLE object with the right mouse button you will get a popup menu. Select the **Properties...** menu item. This will open up the OLE properties dialog window again. Select the **Options** tab. On this tab, change the Activation setting to Manual. Now the user cannot start up the MS-Graph server. Although launching the server application is disabled for the user, you can still start it up through your script.

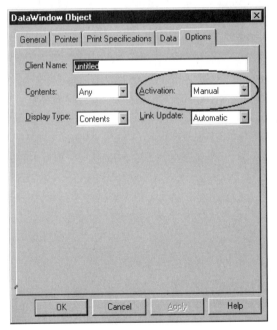

Figure 7.14 *You can deny the user access to the functionality of your OLE server by overriding the activation setting and changing it from DoubleClicked to Manual.*

Step 8 Let's enhance our graph by adding some labels. Double-click on the OLE server object. This will start up the MS-Graph server inside our DataWindow painter (alternatively, to start up MS-Graph outside of our DataWindow painter, click on the server object with the right mouse button and select **Open...** off the popup menu). Click with the right mouse button inside the graph. This will bring up a popup menu. Select the **Insert Titles...** option. You will then be given the option of attaching a title to the entire chart, or to the axes. The options are check boxes, so you can select whichever ones you desire. Choose Chart and Value Axis.

Figure 7.15 *The Insert Titles dialog from MS-Graph allows us to customize our OLE object.*

Now you can select the titles in the graph and enter new text for them. Like in PowerBuilder, you can select an object and then with the right mouse button, you can change it's properties. Change the properties of the Value Axis label by clicking with the right mouse button and adjusting the font alignment to display the text vertically. Now let's move the legend to the bottom of the window. Do this by selecting the legend, clicking with the right mouse button and selecting **Format Legend...** from the popup menu. On the Format Legend dialog window, you can go to the Placement tab and change the position to the bottom of the window. Now return to the DataWindow painter by clicking outside the OLE object and let's preview our work. Your DataWindow should look similar to the one in Figure 7.16.

7.5 DataWindow Enhancements   135

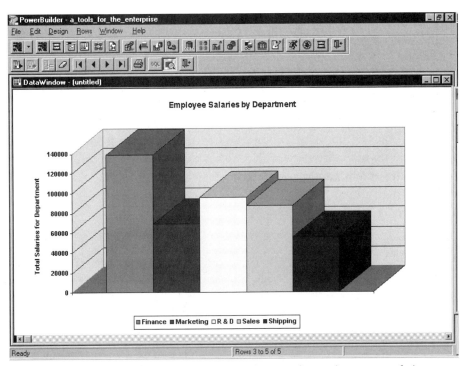

Figure 7.16 *Our enhanced OLE object takes advantage of the functionality of the OLE server.*

To see the completed version of the above example, examine the sample application on the companion CD.

In the spring of 1996, Sybase (the new owner of Powersoft) acquired a company called Visual Components which manufactures, among other things, .OCXs that you can use for your OLE 2.0 presentation style.

7.5.1.2 Rich Text Edit Presentation Style

If you have ever had to produce a report or DataWindow object that involved substantial amounts of text and the need to embed information into the text, you will be very pleased to learn about the new Rich Text Edit presentation style. It will allow you to mix text and images of any shape, size and color you desire. This particular format is extremely valuable for document generation and creation of form letters.

Enterprise applications are often called upon to generate form letters. In the past, we have accomplished this through a variety of means including the generation of a mail merge file and then using DDE to command Microsoft Word or WordPerfect to perform a mail merge with some predefined template. Now we have the ability to generate these documents directly in PowerBuilder.

We can provide the end user with the ability to edit and modify these letters at runtime. All this functionality is encapsulated within the RTF presentation style, all you have to do is turn it on! The end user can also be provided with a popup menu that will allow them to take their modified letter and cut and paste it into their word processor of choice to manipulate. We have the ability to add headers and footers to our text, mix fonts and perform automatic word wrapping and column sliding.

Let's create a sample RTF DataWindow object using data from our Customer table in the PowerBuilder sample database. We want to send out a letter to all customers in a particular state informing them that there is a special sale coming up which is custom tailored to customers from their state!

Step 1 Launch the DataWindow painter and select SQL Select as the data source and RichText as the presentation style (notice that the **Options...** button is disabled).

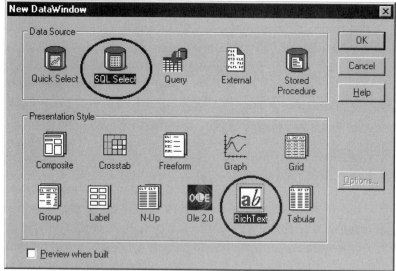

Figure 7.17 *Launch the DataWindow painter and select SQL Select as the data source and Rich Text as the presentation style.*

7.5 DataWindow Enhancements 137

Step 2 You will enter the standard SQL Select painter. Let's select the Customer table. From this table, select all the columns except ID and Phone.

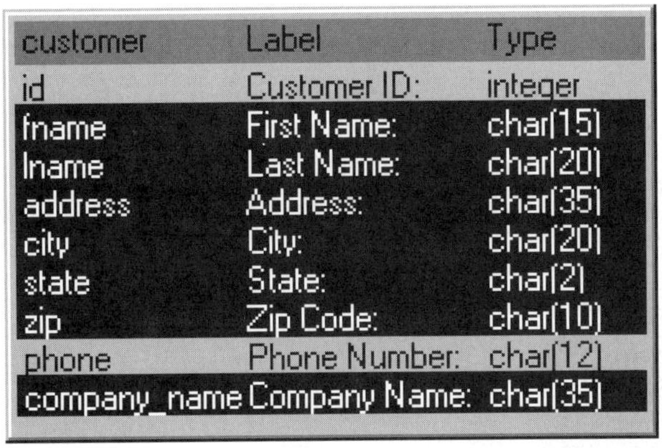

Figure 7.18 Open the Customer table and select all the rows except ID and Phone.

Step 3 Define a retrieval argument for the State. From the **Design** menu bar item, select **Retrieval Arguments...**. This will open up the Retrieval Arguments Dialog window as shown in Figure 7.19. Here, define one string argument called as_state.

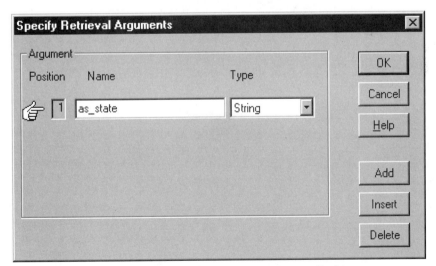

Figure 7.19 Define one string argument called as_state.

Step 4 Declare a where clause in the SQL Toolbox at the bottom of the SQL Painter. Set the column "customers"."state" to be equal to your retrieval argument defined in Step 3.

"customers"."state" = :as_state

Note: Remember that the colon (":") in front of the argument name denotes it as a host variable.

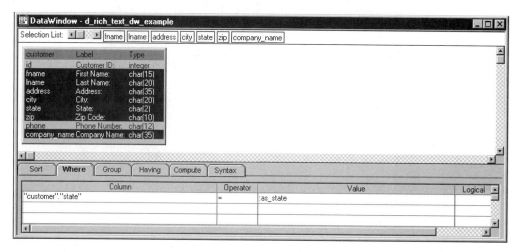

Figure 7.20 *Declare a where clause in the SQL Toolbox.*

Step 5 Return to the Designer by clicking on the SQL button in the toolbar and turning the SQL painter off.

Step 6 Before the designer appears, you will be asked to fill in the details of the properties for this RTF object. The Rich Text Definition dialog will appear. We want to deselect Header/Footer as we won't be requiring these for our letter. We want to enable Word Wrap so that our text will wrap to fit the page as appropriate. Under the Rich Text Bars group we have the option of providing the user with a toolbar, tab bar and ruler at runtime with which they can edit the RTF DataWindow. We want to provide the user with the RTF Tool Bar.

The Popup menu option enables the menu that allows the users to cut, copy and paste text from the RTF DataWindow. It also allows them to access the properties page and alter the properties settings for the object, turning toolbars on and off, enabling viewing options, and so on.

7.5 DataWindow Enhancements

You can also make the DataWindow Display Only. This means that the user cannot alter the text inside your document. In the area of presentation, you can choose to show embedded characters for returns, tabs and spaces. This is very similar to a feature that most major word processors have. The colors for the background of the DataWindow and the embedded fields can be selected here.

Another major option that can be selected is the option of using a RTF file that you have built prior to the creation of the DataWindow. To do this you indicate Use File and then specify the file you with to include.

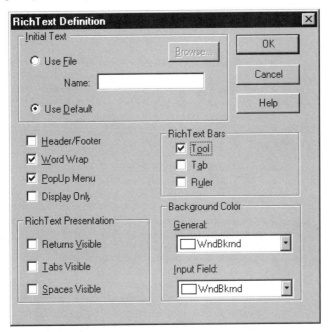

Figure 7.21 *The Rich Text Definition dialog allows you to select options for your RTF DataWindow object.*

Step 7 Within the designer you will see all the fields that you selected in the SQL Painter. These fields are enclosed in braces to indicate that they are RTF fields. Before each field is the traditional DataWindow label. We don't want these labels in our letter, so we are going to remove them. Delete these labels from view now.

140 Chapter 7: What's New In PowerBuilder 5.0

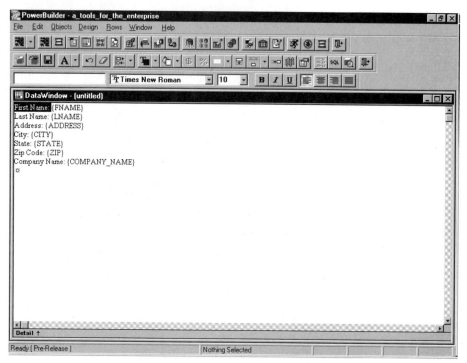

Figure 7.22 *All the fields selected in the SQL painter will appear enclosed in braces to show that they are RTF fields. Remove the labels from these fields as they are not necessary for our letter.*

Step 8   Now that the labels are gone, rearrange the fields so that Last Name comes after First Name (separate them with a space) and that State comes after City (separate these with a comma and a space). Move Company Name to the line below the customers name.

Now we want to insert a date field at the top. Move the cursor to the top and insert two blank lines. To insert a computed field, select **Computed Field...** from the **Objects** menu bar item. Then click where you want the computed field to appear, at the top of the page. Now you have to define the computed field in the . Give the computed field the name of Date_String and define it as:

String(Today(),"MMM DD,YYYY")

7.5 DataWindow Enhancements 141

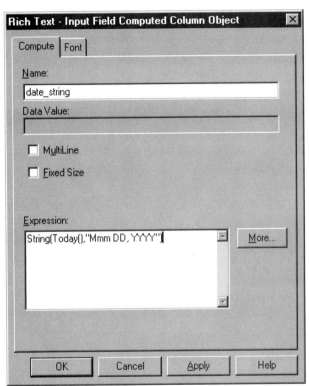

Figure 7.23 *The Rich Text Input Computed Column Object dialog window allows you to define your own computed column. We will use it to show the current date formatted as Mmm DD, YYYY.*

Step 9 Now we enter the body of the text. On the first line we want to enter "Dear" and then follow that with the first name of the customer again. To do this, we have to make the same column appear twice. Select the **Column** menu item from the **Objects** menu bar item. Then select where you want the column to appear (click after the text "Dear"). You will be given a window with all the columns in it as shown in Figure 7.24. Select the 'fname' column. This field will now appear after your text. Follow it up with a comma.

142   Chapter 7: What's New In PowerBuilder 5.0

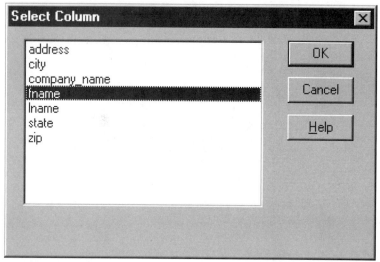

Figure 7.24 The Select Column dialog window is used for insert fields into our RTF DataWindow.

Use this same technique to insert the name of the city into the body of your text You can make the body of your text anything you want. Our sample uses:

Dear {FNAME},

I just wanted to take a moment to thank you for your continued support over the years. We recognize that our success in the pet products market is due to our loyal customers like yourself. We would like to express our gratitude by inviting your to participate in our **V.I.P. Sale**, coming soon to your local Janice's Pet Emporium in {CITY}. We will have special deals on all our pet supplies and food. Just show your V.I.P. card to the clerk.

Once again, thank you for your continued support and for letting us earn your business!

Sincerely,

Janice Wolf
President

For some finishing touches, we bold the name of the sale and underline the name of the store and the customer's city. Then we add at the very top of the page some letterhead like text. We could also, if we desired, insert a bitmap with the president's signature at the bottom in the signature area, and maybe add a bitmap logo to the top of the letter.

Step 10 Now save your RTF DataWindow before previewing. This is just being cautious, but I believe in saving these objects regularly. After saving, preview your object by selecting the Preview button on the toolbar. Enter a valid state (I will use 'CA'). You should see all your letters appearing in your DataWindow. Along with viewing these letters, you can print them too! Note that if you scroll up and down in the DataWindow using the vertical scroll bar, it will only scroll within the existing page and will not take you to the next page. To page forwards and backwards you must use the toolbar buttons or the PAGE UP and PAGE DOWN keys on your keyboard. Keep this in mind when you build your applications as you may want to provide 'forward' and 'backward' buttons to your users.

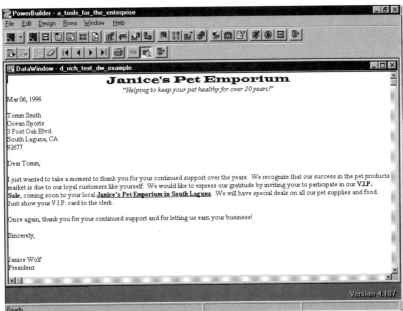

Figure 7.25 *Our finished RTF DataWindow object can be incorporated into an application.*

7.5.2 CHANGES TO THE DATAWINDOW PAINTER

Aside from the two new presentation styles, you will also notice a number of other changes in the DataWindow painter. You will see some new icons with new ways of using them and some usability enhancements in the overall interface.

7.5.2.1 New Toolbars and Icons

One of the first things you will notice when looking at the DataWindow painter in PowerBuilder 5.0 is that the icon on the PowerBar is different. The icon is similar, but sports blue coloring rather than the red in previous versions of PowerBuilder. Why did Powersoft do this? I don't know. I guess that they wanted to make their interface more aesthetically pleasing.

Inside the SQL Painter, there are some new icons, some of the old icons, and some old icons with facelifts. You will notice that the Colorbar, which we old timers have become quite accustomed to, has now disappeared to be replaced with drop down toolbar color selectors which are discussed below. The painterbar in Figure 7.26 shows the current line up of icons in the SQL Painter.

Figure 7.26 *The painterbar in the SQL Painter has some new icons, some old icons, and some old icons with new pictures (painterbar is displayed with ShowText set to true).*

The functionality of the icons from left to right is as follows:

New—NEW ICON: This icon will clear your current query and allow you to start over again from scratch.

Open—NEW ICON: Allows you to open a query object and load it as your SQL data source.

Save—NEW ICON: Allows you to save the current SQL query as a query object.

Tables—OLD ICON: This icon has the same picture and functionality as in PowerBuilder 4.0. It allows you to open another table or tables for your SQL query.

Join—OLD ICON: This icon also has the same picture and functionality as in earlier PB versions. It will allow you to select columns that you wish to join in your SQL query. This icon now has push on/push off functionality.

Toolbox—OLD ICON: Although this icon was around in version 4.0, you may not have used it before. What it does is turn the SQL Toolbox at the bottom of the SQL painter on and off.

SQL Select—OLD ICON/NEW PICTURE: This is the button that you use to toggle back and forth between the SQL painter and the DataWindow designer. The hard to read blue SQL picture has been replaced by a clear, black on gray SQL. The button also appears as a 'push on/push off' type button.

Preview—OLD ICON/NEWPICTURE: The preview button will be disabled when you are in the SQL painter for the DataWindow object. It becomes enabled when you move back to the designer. The icon has been changed from the ambiguous blue shape from PB 4 to the slightly less ambiguous box with a magnifying glass. I think it is somewhat of an improvement as the magnifying glass does signify looking for more information, and the box has been used to indicate the SQL query on other buttons. (I often give software vendors a hard time about their icons, but Powersoft is getting better, and it is hard to come up with good icons when you only have a 16x16 bitmap to work with).

One improvement that I applaud regarding the icons on the toolbar is the proper enabling and disabling of their functionality. When there is no query to be saved, the Save toolbar button is non-functional and also appears visually to be grayed out. This is a nice improvement over previous versions of PowerBuilder.

The toolbar in the DataWindow designer has also been revised. You can see the new icons and layout in Figure 7.27.

Chapter 7: What's New In PowerBuilder 5.0

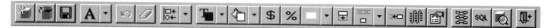

Figure 7.27 *The painterbar for the DataWindow designer has also been revised with some new icons and functionality.*

The icons in the toolbar include (from left to right):

New—NEW ICON: You will recognize this icon from the SQL painter, but the functionality is slightly different. In the designer, it will open up a new DataWindow object.

Open—NEW ICON: This icon you will also recognize from the SQL painter. Like New, the functionality of the Open icon in the designer is to open an existing DataWindow object.

Save—OLD ICON: This icon will save the current DataWindow object.

DataWindow Object Drop Down Toolbar—NEW TOOLBAR: The drop down toolbar is an entirely new object in PowerBuilder 5.0. It was created to save space on the toolbars and allow you greater flexibility in your customization of the PowerBuilder development environment. Selecting the drop down arrow allows you to change the current object selected from the object palette. The current object is displayed to the left of the arrow. If you would like to use the current object, just select the icon representing the object to the arrow's left.

Figure 7.28 *The DataWindow object drop down toolbar allows you to select a DataWindow 'control' to place on your current DataWindow.*

Most of the icons that appear in the palette should be familiar to you. From left to right/top to bottom they are:

- the object selector (arrow)
- text object
- picture object
- line
- oval
- rectangle
- round rectangle
- column (for pasting in a column from the result set)
- computed field (note the new icon)
- graph
- nested report
- OLE object
- OLE Large Binary (BLOB) object
- average (creates a computed field calculating the average of the currently selected column)
- count (creates a computed field calculating the count of the currently selected column)
- page (creates a computed field that shows page numbering)
- sum (creates a computed field that calculated the sum of the currently selected column)
- today (creates a computed field that shows the current date).

Undo—OLD ICON: Undoes the last action you initiated.

Delete—OLD ICON: Deletes the currently selected object.

148   *Chapter 7: What's New In PowerBuilder 5.0*

Alignment Drop Down Toolbar—NEW ICON: Like the other drop down toolbars, selecting the arrow allows you to select from a palette which offers the opportunity to align the selected objects to the right, left, top, bottom, center horizontal or center vertical. There are also icons on this palette for resizing the selected objects.

Remember that when aligning or sizing multiple objects, PowerBuilder will always align or size all the selected objects to the first object selected.

Foreground/Text Color Drop Down Toolbar—NEW ICON: This drop down toolbar allows you to select the foreground or text color for your currently selected object or objects. This replaces the left mouse button functionality on the Colorbar from previous versions.

Background Color Drop Down Toolbar—NEW ICON: This drop down toolbar allows you to select the background color for your currently selected object or objects. This replaces the right mouse button functionality on the Colorbar from previous PowerBuilder versions.

Currency Format—OLD ICON: This is the same icon with the same functionality you are used to. It will change the display format of the currently selected column(s) to display in a standard currency format with a dollar sign, comma separators for the thousands and two decimal places.

Percent Format—OLD ICON: This is also the same icon with the same functionality you are accustomed to. It will change the display format of the currently selected column(s) to display in a percentage format.

Border Drop Down Toolbar—NEW ICON: This drop down toolbar allows you to select the border you desire for the currently selected object or objects. You can choose from:

- no border
- underlined
- box
- shadow box
- 3D lowered
- 3D raised
- resizeable (if applicable)

7.5 DataWindow Enhancements **149**

Autosize Height—NEW ICON: This button is a 'push on/push off' button that is used to toggle the Autosize Height property of a column on or off.

Slide Above Drop Down Toolbar—NEW ICON: This drop down toolbar allows you to select the appropriate Slide Above property for an object or set of objects. (refer to Chapter 10—Advanced DataWindow Techniques for details on sliding columns). You can select between:

- no slide above (the column will not slide up, even if the field directly above it is empty)

- slide all above (the column will slide up if all the fields on the row above it are empty)

- slide directly above (the column will slide up if the fields directly above the current field are empty)

Slide Left—NEW ICON: This button is a 'push on/push off' button that is used to toggle the Slide Left property of a column. If the Slide Left property is set on (TRUE) then if the column or columns to the left of the current column are empty, the current column will slide to the left to take up the available space (refer to Chapter 10—Advanced DataWindow Techniques for details on sliding columns).

Newspaper Columns—NEW ICON: This button is also a 'push on/push off' button. It is used to toggle the Newspaper Column property of the DataWindow object. This will cause the DataWindow object to display with multiple columns, if applicable, when in Print Preview mode. (Refer to Chapter 10—Advanced DataWindow Techniques for details on building Newspaper Column DataWindows.)

Properties—NEW ICON: Opens the Properties page for the currently selected object. If no object is currently selected, the Properties page for the DataWindow object will open. The Properties page is discussed in the following section.

Tab Sequence—NEW ICON: This button places the DataWindow painter in tab sequence mode. In this mode a red number appears above each table object in the DataWindow indicating the sequence. You can alter these sequences and then use the Tab Sequence button to return to regular design mode. This is a 'push on/push off' button.

SQL Select—OLD ICON/NEW PICTURE: This 'push on/push off' button toggles you between design mode and the SQL painter.

Preview—OLD ICON/NEW PICTURE: This 'push on/push off' button places the current DataWindow into/out of preview mode where you can see what your DataWindow object will look like with real data in it.

Exit—OLD ICON: This button will exit you from the DataWindow painter.

7.5.2.2 DataWindow Painter Properties Page

In keeping with the changes in the other painters, we now have a Properties page which we use to maintain the properties of the DataWindow and objects that we place on it (columns, text fields, pictures, etc.). The Properties page can be opened by double clicking on a specific object, by selecting the object and pressing the properties icon in the toolbar, or clicking on the object with the right mouse button and selecting **Properties...** from the popup menu. If no object is currently selected, the properties page for the DataWindow object itself will open.

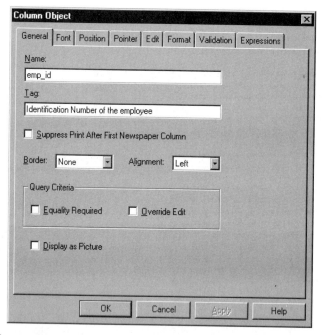

Figure 7.29 *The Properties page for the DataWindow object, and objects on the DataWindow object, is accessed by double-clicking the appropriate object, or pressing the properties icon on the toolbar.*

The tabs that are available in the properties page will vary depending on the type of object that you have selected. Selecting a column for example will give you access to pages for maintain the font, position, pointer, edit style, display format, validation rule, property expressions and other general properties. You will recognize these tabs as being the options that in previous versions of PowerBuilder you selected with the right mouse button. Clicking the right mouse button in PowerBuilder 5.0 will give you a substantially different menu with an abbreviated set of options. It is expected that you will perform the bulk of your maintenance from the properties page.

Having said that, I need to point out one shortcoming of the properties page. It is modal (yuck!). That means that if you want to change properties on a number of objects, you must select the first object, open the Properties page, make your change, close the page, select the next object, open the Properties page, and so on and so on. It would be much better if the page was modeless and allowed you to keep it open while you selected the different objects on the DataWindow. This would be far more intuitive and easier to work with. And if you select multiple objects, you cannot open the Properties page. In this situation, I would expect the properties page to display any properties that are common between the objects and give you the opportunities to change properties that will affect all the selected objects. Let's hope Powersoft puts this high on the priorities list for PowerBuilder 6.0!

7.5.2.3 SQL Formatting

When you are working with SQL in the syntax mode as opposed to the graphical mode, there are some distinct improvements over previous versions of PowerBuilder. One of the biggest annoyances when working in syntax mode in PowerBuilder 4.0, was that if you left the SQL painter and then came back to it, all the formatting of your statement was gone. Instead, it was strung out across your screen in one long physical line. In PowerBuilder 5.0, the SQL painter will retain the formatting of the syntax when you move in and out of the SQL painter.

You will also notice that when in syntax mode, the SQL script is color coded like the PowerScript painter to make it easier for you to work with.

7.5.2.4 Automatic Scrolling

In PowerBuilder 4.0, if you wanted to move an object in the DataWindow designer to an area that was not currently visible in your screen you had to do a lot of unnecessary work. This involved picking the object up, dragging it to the edge of the visible area, going down to the

152   *Chapter 7: What's New In PowerBuilder 5.0*

scroll bar, scrolling over, picking up the object before it disappeared of the side of the screen, dragging it over and so on until you reached your final destination. In PowerBuilder 5.0 you can do it all in one smooth step! You select your object and drag it in the direction that you want to move, when you hit the edge of your visible area, the designer will automatically scroll to the edge that you are pressing against for as long as you continue to press against it (or you hit the edge of a reasonable amount of working space).

This functionality also works when you are using the lasso to select multiple objects or if you are resizing an object and want to extend its border beyond the visible area.

7.5.2.5 New Column Types

PowerBuilder 5.0 has provided three new data types that you can use for your columns in the DataWindow painter. These data types are LONG, ULONG (unsigned long) and REAL. By adding these data types, the PowerBuilder DataWindow can make more effective use of memory space which could lead to performance improvements in your application (it saves memory space because we don't have to 'over allocate' and select a data type that is designed to hold more information than we are going to use).

7.5.2.6 Expression Enhancements

Our ability to dynamically modify the properties of objects on a DataWindow has steadily increased with each release of PowerBuilder. In version 3.0 we could set a salary column to dynamically change its background color depending on the value it contained. This was accomplished through the use of a complex dwModify() function. dwModify() considered, at that time, to be the most complex PowerBuilder function to master and was generally left alone by most developers.

To make it easier for all developers to access the functionality of the dwModify() function, in version 4.0 Powersoft provided us with access to a window called the Attributes dialog window. On this window, we were given the ability to write expressions that would execute at runtime and dynamically modify any of the conditionally modifiable attributes for any object on the DataWindow. Many of the attributes are conditionally modifiable, but not all. Some you will have to modify using the traditional scripting technique.

With the latest release of PowerBuilder we are once again provided with increased functionality in this area. The attributes dialog has been placed onto the Properties page (refer to section 7.5.2.2 above) and has been given its own tab called the Expressions tab as shown in Figure 7.30.

7.5 DataWindow Enhancements   153

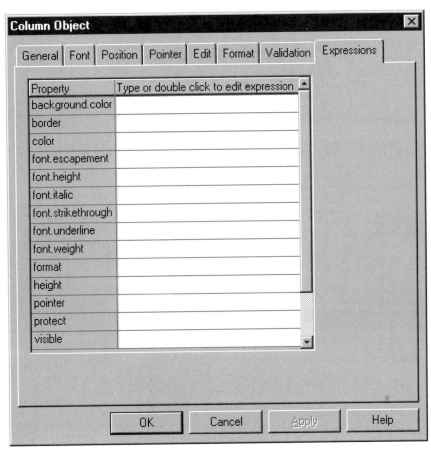

Figure 7.30 *We can dynamically modify any modifiable attribute of any object on a DataWindow through the development of an expression that we enter on the Expressions tab of the Properties page.*

All of the modifiable properties for the current selected object are visible. You can enter an expression next to the property that you wish to modify. Double-clicking on an entry field with take you to the Modify Expression dialog box (shown in Figure 7.31) where you have access to all the functions and columns that you can cut and paste into your expression.

Chapter 7: What's New In PowerBuilder 5.0

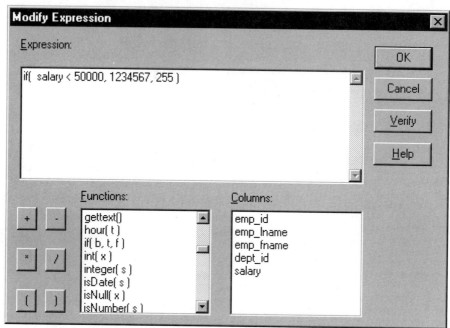

Figure 7.31 *The Modify Expression dialog box is accessed by double-clicking on an entry field. From here you can cut and paste functions and columns into your expression.*

The expressions you define can include conditional statements that allow you to change the value based upon some value in the row. An example of this is shown above in Figure 7.31. We are changing the background color of a column (background.color) based upon the value that is in the salary column. If the salary is below $50,000, then we set the background to the color represented by the long 1234567 (which happens to be a pale lime green). If the salary is over this amount, then we change the background color to the long represented by 255 (which is red). A sample of this can be found on the companion CD in the DW Expressions - CurrentRow() example where we have modified the salary column as we discuss here.

Expressions are also used in other places in our DataWindow. We use them when we define DataWindow settings such as filters and graphing criteria.

Keeping with tradition, Powersoft has given us expanded functionality in this area for version 5.0. We have some new functions and flow of control statements that we can take advantage of in our expression definitions.

7.5 DataWindow Enhancements **155**

7.5.2.6.1 CurrentRow() Function

The first new function that we can add to our expression is CurrentRow(). This function will return the row number of the DataWindow control current row. This function returns a different value than the GetRow() function which will return the row number for the row in which that object is existing.

The sample on the companion CD uses a simple example to demonstrate the difference between these two functions. We define two computed fields; one with the function **GetRow()**, the other with the function **CurrentRow()**. As you click or scroll to different rows, you will see that the GetRow() computed column does not change, but the CurrentRow() completed column does.

To demonstrate a practical application for this information, we have set the **font.italic** properties of each of the fields to contain the following expression:

If(GetRow() = CurrentRow(),1,0)

This results in the current row always having its text converted to italics.

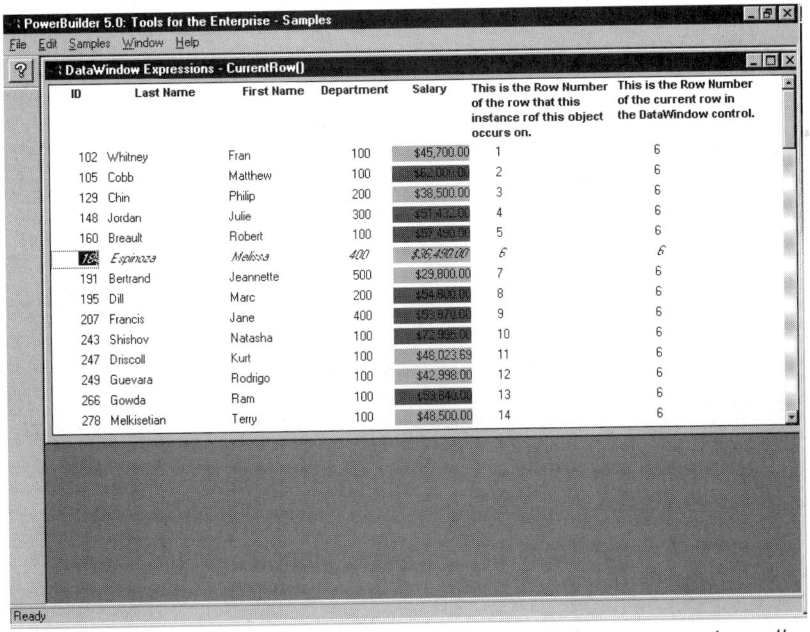

Figure 7.32 *The CurrentRow() function in a DataWindow expression allows us to determine which row in the DataWindow control is the current row. This is a value that will change within each row whereas the GetRow() function would remain static.*

156 *Chapter 7: What's New In PowerBuilder 5.0*

7.5.2.6.2 Choose Case Support

In the past, if we wanted to define an expression that evaluated anything more that a simple IF THEN statement, we had to define some particularly complex nested IF THEN ELSE expressions, which could become quite challenging. Now we can take advantage of the CHOOSE CASE style flow of control statement in our expressions. Flow of control statements in expressions are executed as functions. The IF THEN statement uses the If() function and the CHOOSE CASE uses the Case() function.

Like the IF THEN flow of control statement, the syntax for a CHOOSE CASE statement is different in an expression than it is in PowerScript. When you paste the Case() function into an expression it looks like:

case(x WHEN a THEN b WHEN c THEN d... ELSE e)

where 'x' is the expression that you are evaluating. WHEN is a reserved word indicating a specific case. 'a' is the value for the first case. THEN is also a reserved word that separates the value for evaluation of the condition from the value that the expression should equate to if the condition is true. This is then followed by as many WHEN and THEN expressions as are necessary to complete the evaluation of 'x.' If you like, you can add an ELSE condition at the end to catch any conditions of 'x' that do not equate to any of the supplied expressions.

When added to your expression dialog, these case statements can become difficult to read, particularly if you begin to embed other expressions inside your Case() function. I would recommend that you apply similar code formatting guidelines as you use in your scripts. You can spread your statement over as many lines as you like. New lines can be created by pressing the CTRL and ENTER keys together. Here is an example of a Case() function that is used in an expression to change the background color of the salary column to red if the salary is less than $10,000, to green if between $10,000 and $50,000 and to blue if greater than $50,000.

```
case( salary
  when is < 10000 then 255
  when is  < 50000 then RGB(0,255,0)
  else RGB (0,0,255)
  )
```

The above example demonstrates embedding another function within the Case() function. We embed the RGB() function to make it easier to define the colors we want.

7.5.2.6.3 RGB() Function

PowerBuilder developers have been plagued with having to use long color definitions in our expressions. Long color values were combinations of a quantity of red (1* (0 to 255)) plus a quantity of green (255*(0 to 255) plus a quantity of blue (255*255*(0 to 255). The number that we received was a result of this complex calculation. If you simply wanted to make something white we would have to pull out our calculator and figure:

$$\text{white} = (1*255) + (255*(255)+(255*255*(255))$$
$$= 255 + 65025 + 16581375$$
$$= 16646655$$

and use this number in our expression. Now we have the ability to embed an RGB() function into our expressions. This function works exactly the same as the RGB() function in PowerScript. This function takes three arguments:

RGB(red, green, blue)

Each argument contains the amount of that color you want to factor in from 0 to 255. Making something white would then be a matter of embedding RBG(255,255,255) into your expression.

Unfortunately, it does not make it any easier to figure out how much red, green and blue there is in that special yellow you use for your manila folder window, but if you are using colors like black, white, red, green and blue, things are now much simpler. Some values for the RGB function have been included in the Developer's Tip for this section.

Developers Tip: Use the following quick reference chart for determining RGB() function settings for some standard colors.

Color	Red	Green	Blue
Black	0	0	0
White	255	255	255
Light Gray	192	192	192
Dark Gray	128	128	128
Red	255	0	0
Dark Red	128	0	0
Green	0	255	0
Dark Green	0	128	0
Blue	0	0	255
Dark Blue	0	0	128
Magenta	255	0	255
Dark Magenta	128	0	128
Cyan	0	255	255
Dark Cyan	0	128	128
Yellow	255	255	0
Brown	128	128	0

7.5.2.6.4 Pseudo SQL Operators

We now have the ability to include in our expressions comparison operators LIKE, BETWEEN and EQUAL. The functionality of these operators is the same as it is in SQL. This will allow you to modify your expressions and use fuzzy search and evaluation techniques.

For example, we could define a filter for our employee list that only shows those employees whose last names begin with 'B' as follows:

```
emp_lname like 'B%'
```

If we wanted to expand this to include all employees who have a 'b' anywhere in there last name we could define our filter as:

```
lower(emp_lname) like '%b%'
```

The percent operator within the string acts like a wildcard and allows any valid string match. We have to use the Lower() function as otherwise it would only find those people who have a lower case 'b' in their name and exclude any that contained an upper case 'B.'

We can use the BETWEEN in a filter as follows:

emp_id BETWEEN 0 and 150

The NOT operator can be used with all these pseudo SQL operators such as:

emp_id NOT BETWEEN 0 and 150

7.5.3 DATAWINDOW CONTROL SCRIPTING CHANGES

There have been some drastic changes in PowerBuilder 5.0 in the way that we manipulate data and objects on the DataWindow from within our scripts. The interface for working with DataWindow objects is much less cryptic and works in a very similar fashion to other objects in the PowerBuilder environment.

7.5.3.1 Direct Manipulation of Object Properties

We now have a new way of dealing with DataWindow properties partially replacing the Modify() function which has been both our best friend and worst enemy over the past few years. Now when we need to make a dynamic change to our DataWindow at runtime we can access all its properties and the properties of all objects on the DataWindow directly. This brings the DataWindow a little more in sync with the other objects that we work with in the PowerBuilder environment.

When we wanted to change a property of an object at runtime in PowerBuilder 4.0, we would issue a modify function such as:

dw_employee.Modify("emp_lname.visible = 1")

One of the problems with this was that the Modify() function accepted only one argument, and it was a string. You could not determine if you had coded an error until runtime when the function either would work, or would do nothing, but not produce an error message.

160   *Chapter 7: What's New In PowerBuilder 5.0*

Developers Tip: You may already be familiar with the program DWSyntax which has shipped with previous PowerBuilder versions. This application has been upgraded for version 5.0 and allows you to build syntax for direct manipulation of DataWindow object properties. You can also compare the 'old' modify and describe syntax to the new direct manipulation syntax. You will find the icon for this utility in the program group.

The syntax that we use for PowerBuilder 5.0 allows us to reference everything in the DataWindow directly:

```
dw_employee.Object.emp_lname.visible = 1 // Sets column to visible
          // Replaces the modify function

li_vis = dw_employee.Object.emp_lname.visible // Stores visible
          // status of column in variable. Replaces Describe()
          // function.
```

We use the standard hierarchical dot notation to drill down within the DataWindow control. After naming the DataWindow control we insert the reserved word Object which indicates that we are referencing the dataobject associated with the DataWindow control. This is immediately followed by the name of the object (such as a column) that you wish to read or alter.

To reference or change a property of the DataWindow object itself we would use similar notation but would replace the column name with the reserved word 'DataWindow':

```
// Set the number of copies to print to 2
dw_employee.Object.DataWindow.print.copies = 2
```

This method for referencing DataWindow object properties is much more user friendly and in line with how we work with other objects. Be aware, however, that you may think it is checking the syntax of your attributes but it is not. The compiler will only check the syntax until it finds the keyword 'Object.' At this point, the compiler stops checking. If you have made any mistakes, they will show up as a runtime error.

At the beginning of this section I mentioned that this would replace only part of the functionality of the Modify() function. We will still use the Modify() and function for some other DataWindow modifications, like the creation of new objects on the DataWindow, destruction of objects on the window and modifying an object on the DataWindow that you don't know

7.5 DataWindow Enhancements   **161**

the name of until runtime (this dynamic column determination will also save the Describe() function from extinction).

7.5.3.2 Direct Manipulation of Data

Direct manipulation of data has made inroads into the realm of the GetItemx() and SetItem() functions. These functions will still work if you are migrating from an earlier version of PowerBuilder, but they are not necessary for reading and updating data if you know the name of the column you want the data from. These functions, however, are still the easiest way to extract from or set data in a column whose name cannot be determined until runtime.

We can read a single value from our DataWindow, or we can select an entire range of values to be returned. To get data from a data window we can access it directly using this syntax:

variable = dw_control.object.data[row,column{,to_row, to_column}]

variable—The variable into which you are storing the data must be of the correct data type, or of type *any* which can contain any type of data (if you are using the optional arguments to_row and to_column your variable must be an array capable of containing the returned result set.

dw_control—The name of the DataWindow control which contains the DataWindow object you want to read the data from.

object—This is a reserved word that is required to access the data for the DataWindow (this may be a little counter intuitive, but its the way it works)

data—This is also a reserved word meaning that you are accessing the data property of the object.

row—The row number that you want to get the data from (a row value of 0 requests a data set consisting of all the rows).

column—The column number that you want to get the data from. This must be a number, you cannot use the column name as we did in PowerBuilder 4.0 (see the next Developer's Tip).

to_row—OPTIONAL: specifies that you want to return a range of values starting from the row number specified in row and ending in the row number specified in this argument.

Chapter 7: What's New In PowerBuilder 5.0

to_column—OPTIONAL: specifies that you want to return a range of values starting from the column number specified in column and ending in the column number specified in this argument.

To perform the reverse operation and set a value in the buffer you would use syntax like:

```
dw_control.object.data[row,column{,to_row, to_column}] = value
```

When using this syntax, you must use integers to specify the rows and columns that you are reading or setting. If you want to use direct manipulation to access a value for a column you would specify the column name instead of using the 'data' reserved word:

```
dw_control.object.emp_id[row {,to_row}] = value
```

or use the similar syntax to read a value from that specific row. Remember that using this syntax assumes that you know the name of the column when you are writing the script. If you won't know the name of the column until runtime you will probably still want to use the GetItem() and SetItem() functions.

The syntax that we have seen so far assumes that you are accessing the primary buffer where the current values for the DataWindow are stored. The primary buffer is the default buffer that is accessed, but there are also other buffers that you may wish to access including:

- Original—contains the original values as last read from or updated to the database. This is the buffer that PowerBuilder uses to determine how it should send updates to the database.

- Filtered—contains all rows that have brought to the client but filtered out of the Primary buffer through the DataWindow filter (these rows are not visible to the end user).

- Deleted—contains all rows that have been removed from the Primary buffer with the DeleteRow() function. These rows are queued up to be deleted in the database upon execution of the next Update() function.

To access these buffers we add an extra piece of information after the 'data' keyword or the column name (but before the row identifier) in our script such as:

```
dw_control.object.data.original[row,column]
dw_control.object.emp_id.filtered[row]
dw_control.object.data.deleted[row,column]
```

7.5.3.3 Generalized Retrieve Functions

When we write object-oriented PowerBuilder applications, we usually try to make our script as generic as possible. This increases our reusability and our ability to move common code into our ancestor objects.

One area where this has been difficult in the past is with Retrieve() functions on DataWindow controls. These functions would only accept the exact list of parameters that was defined for the currently associated DataWindow object. If you wanted to build a generic ancestor object whose descendants could have many different DataWindow objects associated with them, or if you wanted to dynamically change the DataWindow object at runtime, you were severely limited in where you could code the Retrieve(). Along with this, often the code you had to write was tightly coupled to the DataWindow object and had very low reusability.

PowerBuilder 5.0 will now allow you to pass more arguments in your Retrieve() function than the currently associated DataWindow object requires. This allows you to write retrieve scripts in generic ancestors without having to couple the Retrieve() to a specific DataWindow object. To use this feature will require that you plan your inheritance structure and build the retrieval arguments in your DataWindows in such a manner as to support this.

7.5.3.4 DataWindow Events and Parameters

In PowerBuilder 5.0, we now have the ability to define user events which are not mapped to any underlying windows message. Events also can receive arguments that are passed to them at runtime, very much like a function. Also like a function, events have the ability to return a value when they end. This return value is used in the system defined events to control and alter the behavior of PowerBuilder as was formerly done with the SetActionCode() function. This need for the SetActionCode() function has been completely eliminated.

Events and parameters are discussed in depth in Chapter 8—Advanced Development Concepts.

7.5.4 PERFORMANCE ENHANCEMENTS

PowerBuilder 5.0 promises us better performance through the native code compiling option discussed in section 7.1. This only addresses one of the bottlenecks that we encounter in

164 *Chapter 7: What's New In PowerBuilder 5.0*

PowerBuilder. One of the common sections where many production applications seem to run slowly is in the retrieval of data. To try and alleviate this pressure, PowerBuilder 5.0 has provided two new features that give you more control over how retrieves are managed and where the data is buffered.

7.5.4.1 Static Binding

In prior versions of PowerBuilder, whenever you issued a Retrieve() function, the DataWindow object would request a result set description from the database server before retrieving any data. This naturally added additional overhead to the retrieve. As developers, we now have control over this through the process of *static binding*. Static binding a retrieval is sometimes referred to as a "describeless retrieve" because it skips the step of asking the database server to describe the result set.

You control the static binding process by setting a value in the DBParm attribute of your transaction object. By default PowerBuilder 5.0 will set StaticBind to 1 (for 'Yes') and will perform a describeless retrieve. If you wish to change this you can override the behavior and set StaticBind = 0 (for 'No').

Developers Tip: At the time of this writing, the StaticBind feature is only available for Oracle, Sybase and ODBC databases. This may change by the time you read this. Please consult your Connecting To Your Database manual that comes with PowerBuilder to see if this feature is supported in your environment.

7.5.4.2 Buffering Rows in Temporary Files

When you find that accessing the database is your primary bottleneck in your application you may want to buffer your frequently used result sets elsewhere. A common technique in PowerBuilder 4.0 was to buffer these result sets in client memory. The trouble with this was that is could quickly sap the available memory in the client.

Some adventurous individuals wrote custom objects and routines to buffer the data in temporary files on your local disk. Now in PowerBuilder 5.0, you have the option to have PB automatically buffer the data in a DataWindow to disk for you. This will provide you with faster access next time you want to use the data. This can be used in exactly the same manner as buffering a result set in memory without using up your precious active memory. The drawback of course is slightly higher overhead as it will take longer to read the rows from disk that to get them from active memory, but it may be faster than waiting for your database to return the result set! This technique is discussed further in Chapter 10—Advanced DataWindow Techniques as part of dealing with large result sets.

Developers Note: This feature is only available in the 32-bit environments.

7.6 POWERSCRIPT PAINTER

For those of you who have secretly coveted the color coded Visual Basic or Delphi script editor, you can come out of the closet! PowerBuilder now has an enhanced script painter that has all the vivid colors of the rainbow. You can select custom colors to represent data types, functions, flow of control statements, comments and literals.

Along with custom colors you also now have the ability to have the script painter auto indent, perform multiple levels of Undo, change fonts more easily (we could do this in earlier versions, but it wasn't exactly user friendly) and customize which drop down options you would like to have appear at the top of the painter.

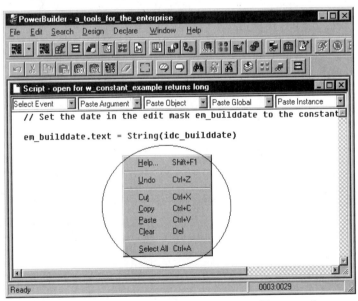

Figure 7.33 *Clicking with the right mouse button will now give you access to a menu of functions for undoing, using the clipboard or accessing help. To alter the properties of the script painter you must select the* **Options...** *menu item from the design menu.*

166 *Chapter 7: What's New In PowerBuilder 5.0*

To access all this customization, PowerBuilder has added right mouse button access in the script painter. In previous versions of PowerBuilder, clicking the right mouse button in the script painter did nothing unless you purchased one of the third party tools like PBToolkit. Now, right clicking will give you a menu with options including undo, clipboard function and access to help information.

> **Release Note:** Although in beta versions of PowerBuilder 5.0 you could access the properties page for the script painter through the popup right mouse button menu, the release version doesn't have this feature anymore. Now you must select *Options...* from the *Design* menu to access this functionality.

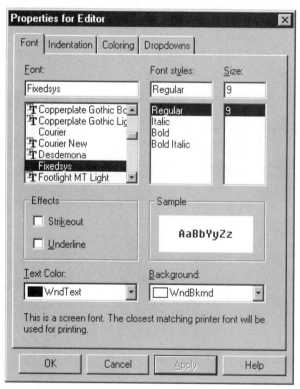

Figure 7.34 The Properties page allows you to customize the script. The Font tab allows you to alter the font that the script is displayed in.

The Font tab of the properties page allows you to adjust the font that the script in the editor displays in. This can be useful if you have good eyes and want to make the script smaller so you can see more, or perhaps the reverse, your eyes are poor (or your screen is small) and you want to make the font larger and easier to read.

Another advantage to changing the font is that it also affects your printer. In version 4.0, all print outs of your code came out in that daisy wheel reminiscent Fixedsys font. If you change the font or font size, you may be able to print more text on your printer (again trading off size for readability).

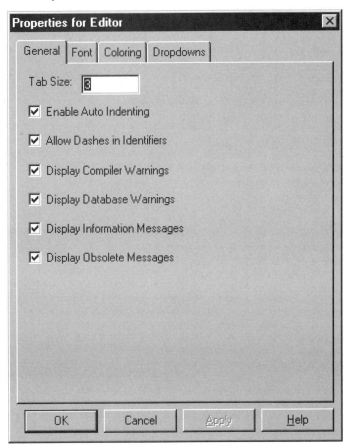

Figure 7.35 *The General tab allows you to adjust the size of a tab indentation and if you want the system to automatically manage your indents for flow of control statements.*

168 *Chapter 7: What's New In PowerBuilder 5.0*

The General tab is where you will adjust the size of a tab indentation and can turn auto indenting on or off. If auto indent is set to on, when you enter a flow of control statement, PowerBuilder will automatically indent the next line one tab stop. Subsequent to that, if you enter a reserved word from the flow of control statement, for example, 'ELSE', then it will automatically remove the indent for that line and keep all the statements blocked appropriately.

This seems like a nice idea, but I am not sold on it yet. Having developed PowerBuilder code for many years, it has become habitual for me to automatically insert tab stops and do indenting. The auto indenting actually slows me down as I have to continuously remove the extra tabs that I insert by habit (although I am certain I will unlearn this habit). If you are not a habitual indenter now, then this feature will probably be good for your, but if you are like me, it will be an obstacle (at least initially!).

This tab will also allow you to control other aspects of the script painter including:

- do you want to allow variables in your identifier names? I strongly discourage this practice.

- do you want to display compiler and database warnings? This is generally a good idea. It helps you to ensure that your code correctly written.

- do you want to display information messages? These are messages that aren't necessarily errors but the system is just letting you know something that may be useful. I would recommend leaving these on.

- do you want to display 'obsolete' messages? These messages will appear when you use a function that is considered obsolete in version 5.0. This isn't a bad idea for those of us who have been working with PowerBuilder 4.0 and earlier versions. It will help to correct our habitual usage of functions which may not be relevant now, like 'SetActionCode.'

7.6 PowerScript Painter 169

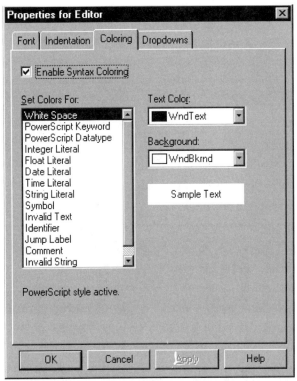

Figure 7.36 *The coloring tab is where you can customize the colors that PowerBuilder uses to represent the different types of text in the script editor.*

One nice thing about the color coding is that it is user customizable. If you really don't like one, or any of the colors that are provided by default, you simply select the type of object that you want to change the color on and select your preferred color choice.

If you want to really make something stand out, you can change not only the color of the font, but the color of the background also. For items like Invalid Text or Invalid String, having the color invert would really make those incomplete or syntactically incorrect strings stand out. It is also nice to have your invalid text show up immediately, whereas version 4.0 didn't point out invalid text until you compiled or tried to exit the script painter.

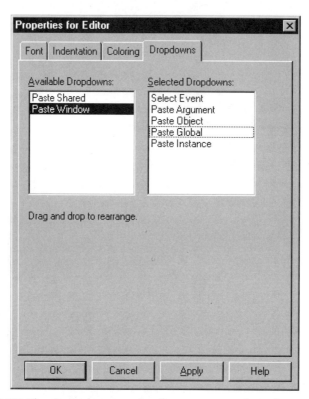

Figure 7.37 *The Dropdowns tab allows you to alter the script editor by selecting which of the available drop down lists you would like to display at the top of the editor.*

As a final method of customization, the Dropdowns tab on the properties page allows you to select which drop down lists you would like to display at the top of the editor. You are given several to choose from. The available set will change in each instance of the painter as appropriate. For example, the Window painter allows you to display any combination of Select Event, Paste Argument, Paste Instance, Paste Global, Paste Window, Paste Shared and Paste Argument.

The version 5.0 script painter has one other functional enhancement worth mentioning. It now supports drag and drop for cutting and pasting blocks of code. You can select a block of code, then drag it to a new location within your script. The initially selected block will be deleted and inserted into the new cursor location.

Overall, I am very pleased with the changes of the script editor. And all those secret Visual Basic code editor lovers can now have the same warm fuzzy feelings about their PowerBuilder editor.

7.7 POWERSCRIPT CODE ENHANCEMENTS

In version 5.0 Powersoft has made quite a few changes and enhancements to PowerScript. We have some new functionality, and some of our existing functionality has changed.

7.7.1 KEYWORDS

There have been a number of changes to the use of keywords in PowerBuilder 5.0

7.7.1.1 CONSTANT

This keyword is used to modify a variable declaration so that it will be turned into a constant value at compile time. For variable values that do not change, this has the effect of increasing application performance. This can be used with variables of any scope.

The following is an example of how this would be used. You can enter the keyword CONSTANT before a variable declaration. The compiler will then go through the script and anywhere that it finds that variable it will replace it with a constant value.

```
CONSTANT lic_daysinweek = 7

w_demo.text = ii_totaldays/lic_daysinweek
```

The second expression would evaluate the variable total days (an instance variable) and divide it by the constant value of 7.

Figure 7.38 shows an instance constant declaration for the build date of the object. As this is determined at compile time, this date will always show the date the object was last compiled or regenerated. This example is available in the demonstration application on the companion CD.

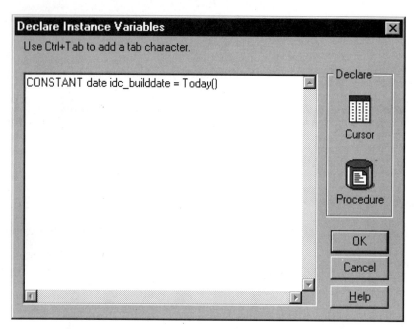

Figure 7.38 *Declaring an instance level constant.*

7.7.1.2 '::' For Global Variable Access

This topic relates to an issue you should hopefully never encounter except in very exceptional circumstances. In the event that you have a variable (of any scope) with the same name as a global variable, the keyword :: (double colon) when placed in front of the variable will tell the script to access the global variable instead of accessing the local, shared or instance variable. The reason I say that you should never encounter this is that if you follow proper naming conventions for your variables, you would never have two variables of different scopes with the same name!

In the event you do encounter the above problem, when you try to exit your script, the compiler will notify you that you have a conflict between the name of a global variable and your local, shared or instance variable. This is an informational message and not an error, so you can ignore it and proceed if you choose.

7.7.2 VARIABLE DECLARATION

In PowerBuilder 5.0, you can now use functions to determine the initial value of a variable during declaration. For example, you could declare a local variable containing the RGB value for green like this:

LONG ll_green = RGB(0,255,0)

This would have given you a syntax error in PowerBuilder 4.0.

7.7.3 READ ONLY FUNCTION ARGUMENTS

When you created arguments for user defined functions in PowerBuilder, you have always had the option to select if you wanted to pass the arguments by value or by reference. Now you can also choose to pass your arguments in a 'read only' format. This format passes the argument by reference, but does not allow the function to modify the passed argument in any way.

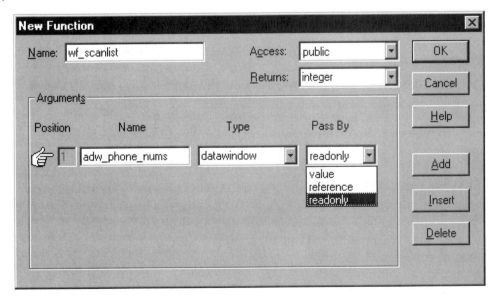

Figure 7.39 We now have the ability to pass user defined function arguments in a 'read only' fashion. This means that the argument is passed by reference but the function cannot alter the argument in any way.

174   *Chapter 7: What's New In PowerBuilder 5.0*

7.7.4 GetParent Function

To determine the parent of an object, we have traditionally used the keyword PARENT. This keyword limited us to only being able to see one level up our hierarchy. I have been asked by students innumerable times, how can I do a PARENT.PARENT to get at the parent of the current parent. Until now, this was extremely difficult. With the GetParent() function, we now have this ability. This value in this function becomes particularly relevant with controls that will be placed upon a tab page where the tab page is the parent to the control, the tab object is the parent to the tab page, and the window is parent to them all.

The following script is on the **Show Parents Parent** command button from the sample application w_getparent_example window:

```
PowerObject lpo_parent

// Get the parent of the current object
lpo_parent = THIS.GetParent()

// Show the class name of the parent of the parent of this object
MessageBox("Parent",classname(lpo_parent.GetParent()))
```

The companion CD contains an example of using the GetParent() function in the way described above. Examine the window w_getparent_example and look at the scripts behind the command buttons to see a live example of how the GetParent() works.

7.7.5 Registry Functions

Instead of using initialization files (.INI files) to store startup and other details in a DOS file, Windows 95 and NT use something called the system registry. If you use one of these platforms, you will be familiar with this. The registry contains an entry for each piece of software registered with the operating system (usually they are registered upon installation).

This registry is arranged as a treed hierarchy of keys. A key represents a single branch in the tree. Each key can have subkeys, and each of those can have further subkeys, and so on. There are four root keys in the registry; HKEY_CLASSES_ROOT, HKEY_LOCAL_MACHINE, HKEY_USERS, and HKEY_CURRENT_USER.

7.7 PowerScript Code Enhancements   **175**

Developers Note: If you are going to use the registry functions in a Windows 3.1 environment, they will work, because there is a registry in Windows 3.1. The registry, however, only has one root key, HKEY_CLASS-ES_ROOT and each key can only have a single value name which is actually unnamed. This is not usually used in Windows 3.1 deployed PowerBuilder applications.

Keys operate very much like the old DOS directory structure. Each subdirectory or in our case, subkey, is separated from its parent by using a backslash ('\').

If you are going to roll out your application in either Windows 95 or NT, you can use this registry as a repository for information very similar to the .INI file. The functions that we use to access the registry include RegistryValues(), RegistryGet(), RegistrySet(), RegistryKeys() and RegistryDelete().

Developers Tip: All the registry functions return a value of 1 if the function was successful and a -1 if the function failed.

7.7.5.1 RegistryValues()

The RegistryValues() function will allow you to query the registry and find out the names of all the value fields within a particular key. The syntax for this function is:

```
RegistryValues ( key, valuename[ ])
```

where

key—contains the name of the key for which you want to get the names of all the value fields. This is a string variable.

valuename[ ]—is a reference array of strings that will contain an entry for each value field within the key. If this is a variable size array, then calling the UpperBound() function will tell you how many values are contained within the key. If this is a fixed array, you must ensure that it is large enough to contain all the values.

With the information from this function, you can use the other registry functions to extract the actual value for a specific registry value name. The following example allows us to extract all the registry value names for the Microsoft Schedule application:

176   *Chapter 7: What's New In PowerBuilder 5.0*

```
string ls_valuename[]

RegistryValues(& "HKEY_LOCAL_MACHINE\SOFTWARE\Microsoft\Schedule+\Application",&
ls_valuename)
```

7.7.5.2 RegistryGet()

Once you have the list of value names (which you may have gotten using the RegistryValues() function) you can obtain the specific value for a value name using the RegistryGet() function. The syntax for this function is:

```
RegistryGet ( key, valuename, value )
```

where

key—contains the name of the key for which you want to get the value for the value name specified.

valuename—contains the name of the value name in the registry you want the value for. If you specify an empty string, it will return the value for the 'default' or 'unnamed' value. A single unnamed value exists for each key in the registry. A registry does exist for windows 3.1, but it only supports unnamed values and is limited in its functionality.

value—a reference variable of type string which will contain the value for the value name specified if the function is successful.

This example will get the 'MailPath' value for the Microsoft Schedule+ application and store it in a string variable:

```
string ls_mailpath
RegistryGet( &
"HKEY_LOCAL_MACHINE\SOFTWARE\Microsoft\Schedule+\Application",&
"MailPath", ls_mailpath)
```

7.7.5.3 RegistrySet()

The RegistrySet() function works exactly the same as the RegistryGet() function but in reverse. It allows you to set the value for a specific value name in a specific field. The syntax is identical except for the last parameter which will contain either a literal or variable with the value that you want to set for the value name. For example, to set the mail path for Microsoft Schedule+ we would code:

```
string ls_mailpath
ls_mailpath = "C:\Notes\mailbox"

RegistrySet( &
  "HKEY_LOCAL_MACHINE\SOFTWARE\Microsoft\Schedule+\Application",&
  "MailPath", ls_mailpath)
```

7.7.5.4 RegistryKeys()

This function will obtain a list of the subkeys for a specified key. The syntax for this function is:

```
RegistryKey ( key , subkey[ ])
```

where

key—contains the name of the key for which you want to get the list of subkeys. This is a string variable.

subkey[ ]—is a reference array of strings that will contain an entry for each subkey within the key. If this is a variable size array, then calling the UpperBound() function will tell you how many subkeys are contained within the key. If this is a fixed array, you must ensure that it is large enough to contain all the keys.

The following example would return a list of all the subkeys in the key value Microsoft:

```
string ls_subkey[]
RegistryValues("HKEY_LOCAL_MACHINE\SOFTWARE\Microsoft", ls_subkey)
```

7.7.5.5 RegistryDelete()

The RegistryDelete() function allows you to remove a value name or an entire key from the registry. The syntax for this function is:

```
RegistryDelete( key , valuename )
```

where

key—contains the name of the key for which you want to delete a value name or delete the entire key. This is a string variable.

valuename—contains the name of the value that you want to remove from this key. If you wish to remove the entire key, specify an empty string ("") for this argument.

For example, to remove all reference to Microsoft Schedule+ from our registry we would code:

RegistryDelete ("HKEY_LOCAL_MACHINE\SOFTWARE\Microsoft\Schedule+","")

7.8 WINDOW PAINTER

With version 5.0, Powersoft continues its efforts to make the PowerBuilder environment easier to use, yet also more powerful. We can see examples of both of these seemingly contradictory goals in the changes in the PowerBuilder 5.0 window painter.

The tools that we use have been made more accessible through changes in the toolbars. All the properties for our objects and controls can now be found in one place, the Properties page. The latest and most widely used controls have now been incorporated into the standard PowerBuilder control offering. I held a short funeral for my object library 'tab' and 'tree' controls and jumped right into using the new ones that Powersoft has provided.

7.8.1 NEW TOOLBARS AND ICONS

The functionality of the toolbar has increased dramatically in version 5.0. The toolbar is not nearly as cluttered as it was in version 4.0, and the icons no longer extend off the edge of your screen.

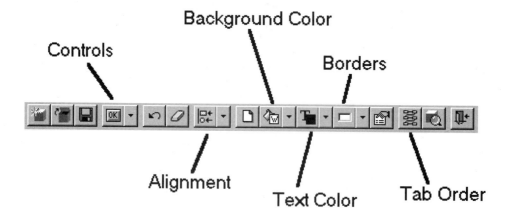

Figure 7.40 *The new default Window painter toolbar.*

The new Window painter toolbar contains a drop down toolbar that will allow you to access the individual controls instead of having them all laid out individually (although you can customize the toolbar and add your most frequently used controls if you desire).

The alignment, background color, text color and border icons will allow you to change this property for an individual item, or for all the items you currently have selected. This is how you can perform a mass change in your painter since this is not possible on the properties page!

Notice also the icon for tab order. You can press this icon to toggle the tab order mode on and off (you still can't change anything else when tab order mode is enabled).

7.8.2 PROPERTY SHEETS

Developers will be happy to find that all the properties of a control or object can be accessed in one central place called the Properties page. No more double-clicking on the object to get one set of attributes and then right mouse clicking to get at the ones that you couldn't access through double-clicking!

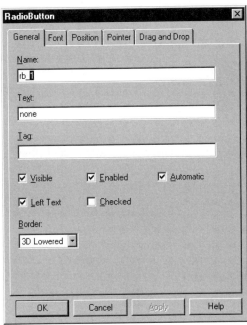

Figure 7.41 The Properties page provides a unified place to change the attributes and properties of an object.

180 *Chapter 7: What's New In PowerBuilder 5.0*

The window uses the now familiar tab control to allow you to access all the properties of the currently selected window object or control. The general attributes for the object appear on the first page and the other pages will vary depending on which type of control or object you select. Most controls have tab pages for Font, Position, Pointer and Drag and Drop.

The Properties page is used throughout the PowerBuilder painters and provides a common interface to maintaining the properties of a variety of objects. The usage and shortcomings of the Properties page are discussed in more detail above in section 7.5.2.2— DataWindow Properties Page.

7.8.3 NEW CONTROLS

It is always nice when you have been working with a tool to find that a new release contains new objects and controls. It is like Christmas when you get to unwrap your gifts and find out what is inside. PowerBuilder 5.0 contains controls to allow us to add tab folders, rich text editing, drop down toolbars, tree views, list views and drop down picture list box controls to our applications.

Developers Tip: To really understand these new controls, I strongly recommend that you closely examine them in the Sample Application on the companion CD. Use this application as an environment where you can play with and test the controls.

7.8.3.1 Tab Control

To most GUI developers, the tab control is not really a new object. Many commercial applications use these controls to take advantage of a 'real world metaphor' that most end users are familiar with, the standard file folder. Most of us in the PowerBuilder arena have written our own tab folder object that we have implemented in our version 4.0 applications. Almost all commercially available class libraries for version 4.0 had tab folder objects in them. These controls were extremely valuable, but often had some very distinct limitations. Most were difficult to use as you had to use substantial amounts of PowerScript code to hide and show all the appropriate controls that were supposed to appear on each tab. From a development perspective, this often made our windows very difficult to work with as they became littered with controls. Some of the third party tab folders required that each tab have a separate child window on it which meant having to open and close a lot of windows, not to mention a rapidly expanding .PBL!

PowerBuilder 5.0 has removed a lot of the pain associated with tab controls. They have provided us with a fully encapsulated tab control native to PowerBuilder. You can place as many tabs on the folder as you like and in the window painter, it will only show the objects that are placed on the currently selected page of the control. As you move from tab to tab in the development environment, the PowerBuilder tab control automatically hides and shows the appropriate objects.

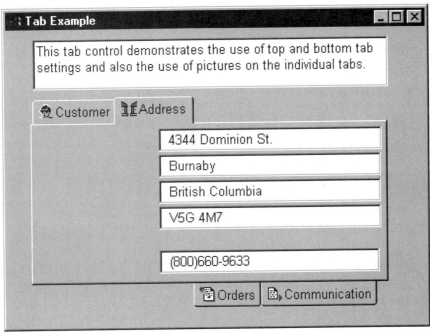

Figure 7.42 *The new tab control will replace the many custom versions of tab folders currently in use in hundreds of PowerBuilder applications.*

The tab control contains multiple pages. Each page is like its own child window. It can contain its own controls, objects and events. When you paint a tab control onto your window, it appears with only a single tab page. Through the popup menu that appears when you click with the right mouse button, you can add more pages to the control. Along with the standard pages, you can also create custom visual user objects (refer to *Chapter 12—User Objects* for details on creating custom visual user objects.) which can be inserted as their own page in the tab control. When you use the custom visual user object as a tab page, no other objects can be added to that page.

182 *Chapter 7: What's New In PowerBuilder 5.0*

Each individual tab page acts like a child window within the tab control. Each page comes equipped with its own set of attributes such as the label text, the picture on the tab and an independently controllable background color.

The tab control is full of very useful functionality. The tabs on the control can be arranged in almost any conceivable fashion. You can have them appear in multiple lines across the top, bottom, left or right sides. You can select between perpendicular or horizontal labels, individual PowerTips for each tab, stretch to fit resizing of tabs, individual pictures for each tab page and more. Another interesting feature is the ability to have the tabs appear on opposing sides at the same time (top and bottom or left and right) like in a spiral notebook. The sample in Figure 7.42 demonstrates this.

Using the Tab Control

Tab controls not only behave in a similar fashion to child windows, they also must be referenced and dealt with in a similar way. To access something on a tab page from a script or function on the window, you must work your way through the hierarchy. For example, to enable a command button called **cb_delete** on the tab page called **tp_address** of the tab object **tab_employee** we would use the syntax:

tab_employee.tp_address.cb_delete.Enabled = TRUE

You should try and take advantage of pronouns such as **PARENT** as much as possible. **PARENT** can be used to reference one level up in the hierarchy. For example, the parent of **cb_delete** would be the tab page **tp_address**. The function, GetParent() can also be used to dynamically obtain the parent from any level within the hierarchy.

PowerBuilder is very particular about where you place a windows control when painting the window. A control must be placed directly onto a tab page in order to become part of the tab page. A control placed on the window and then dragged onto a tab page will continue to think of the window as its parent and will not hide and show when the tab pages are switched. In certain situations, this may be the behavior you desire. For example, if you had a series of tab pages, one with each letter of the alphabet, and then you had a single DataWindow object that you wanted to filter based upon which tab page was selected, then you would place the DataWindow control on the window, not on the tab control, because you would always want it to appear on top of the tab control regardless of which tab page was selected!

7.8 Window Painter   **183**

At this point, I won't describe every property, event and function of the tab control as there are many of them and the online help and PowerBuilder documentation do an excellent job of describing them all and showing you how to use them.

7.8.3.2 Rich Text Edit Control

The number of applications that take advantage of document generation is actually much smaller that the number that should. In the past this was largely because the techniques for doing so were not intuitive and the documents themselves were very difficult to maintain or modify.

The new Rich Text Edit (RTE) control will be a huge asset to anyone who has ever tried, or will try, to incorporate document generation into their PowerBuilder applications. Through this control and its brother, the Rich Text DataWindow (discussed in section 7.5.1.2 above) you will now find it easier than ever to incorporate high quality document generation in your application.

The RTE allows you to create or display a document stored as a Rich Text Format (RTF) file. This document can be linked through a DataSource() function to a DataWindow (almost like a mail merge). This function is very similar to the ShareData() function of a DataWindow control except that data is shared to the RTE control, but if you make changes to the data within the RTE control these changes will not be reflected in the DataWindow data. The columns for the DataWindow that match the input fields in the RTF control will appear inside the document. You will get a separate instance of the document in the control for each row of data in the shared DataWindow.

This control and the Rich Text Edit DataWindow were personally very exciting for me to discover. I have been involved in applications where the RTE functionality would have saved many hundreds of hours of work. The RTE DataWindow presentation style and the RTE control will likely be the medium used to produce letters, documents and forms based upon data in the database.

Again, I will refer you to the on-line help and PowerBuilder documentation to review all the properties, events and functions of the RTE control.

7.8.3.3 Tree View Control

Another object which you may have seen in many of the commercial object libraries on the market is the Tree View control. These controls allow you to view a hierarchical tree of data.

Some examples of the kinds of data people put in their trees includes files and directories, drill down hierarchies in your database and other parent/child relationships.

This control is relatively easy to manage and work with. You can build a customized hierarchical tree that has the ability to expand and collapse nodes. You can associate a different bitmap for each item in the tree.

From the user perspective, every element in the tree can be independently edited to allow them to change the name of each item, or to cut, paste, insert and delete items. You can also implement drag and drop functionality like what you see in the Windows 95 Explorer.

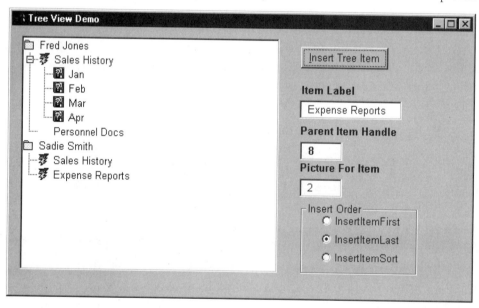

Figure 7.43 *The Tree View control allows you to view and manipulate a hierarchical tree of information. This figure is from the sample application on the companion CD.*

The tree view demo on the companion CD has some of the basic functionality that you can see working in practice. You can insert items into the tree by specifying a label, and a picture by its number(in the sample there are four predefined pictures). By default any items that you insert will be inserted at the root level of the tree. Each item as it is inserted will announce its 'handle.' The handle uniquely identifies each item in the tree. To insert an item as a subitem of another you must specify the handle of the parent item.

The group box at the bottom will allow you to control if the item to be inserted is inserted at the beginning of the list (within its group), the end of the list, or sorted into the list as appropriate. This actually causes the script behind the Insert button to select between one of three tree view functions; InsertItemFirst(), InsertItemLast() and InsertItemSort().

If you want to use a tree view in your application, you will need to use these three functions to add each item individually to your tree.

7.8.3.4 List View Control

The List View control exists to allow you to display a list of items, along with bitmaps to represent the individual items. This is a flexible control that provides you with a variety of ways to display your item list. There are four different ways that the data in a list view can be presented:

- Large Icon view—each item in the list is displayed as a large icon. The user can drag and drop the icons to any position within the control in an unstructured format.

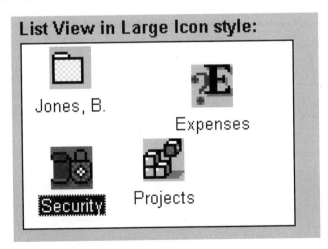

Figure 7.44 *The Large Icon view of a List View control.*

- Small Icon view—same as the large icon view but with smaller icons.

Figure 7.45 *The Small Icon view of a List View control.*

- List view—each item in the list is displayed with the name and a small icon displayed in a tabular list format.

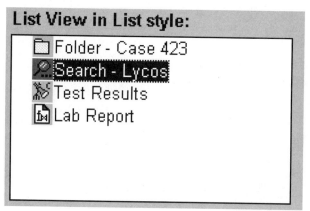

Figure 7.46 *The List view of a List View control.*

- Report view—each item is the list is displayed by name in a tabular report format. Other information about the item can also be displayed.

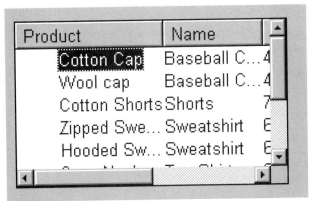

Figure 7.47 *The Report view of a List View control.*

The items in your list can be used in many different ways. You can select an item and double-click on it to launch into the detail for that item. You could use drag and drop to select an item and perform some processing on it (the Sample Application that comes with PowerBuilder has an example of using a List View to drag a product onto an order form).

7.8.3.5 Drop Down Picture ListBox

The Drop Down Picture ListBox (DDPLB) functions essentially the same as the regular drop down listbox in PowerBuilder, except that you can assign pictures to each item in the list box.

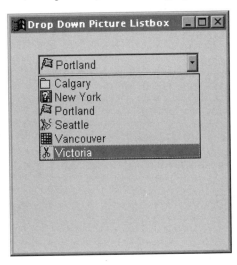

Figure 7.48 *The Drop Down Picture List Box has the same functionality as a regular Drop Down List Box but you can add a picture to each item in the list.*

188 Chapter 7: What's New In PowerBuilder 5.0

The two tabs from the Properties page that are different from a standard DDLB are the Pictures and Items tabs. The Pictures tab allows you to specify which pictures you want to use in the DDPLB. Each picture is assigned a unique index number. You can select the picture from the set of stock picture icons shown in the picture listbox, or you can enter the name of a bitmap image that you wish to use (if you don't know the name, you can press the **Browse...** button to go to a search window). You can select the color of the picture mask (default is transparent) and the width and height that you want the bitmaps to display in.

Developers Note: If you enter a name for a bitmap, but PowerBuilder can't find it, it won't tell you! In the event that it cannot resolve the bitmap reference (meaning that it can't find the bitmap file) it will display the default red X picture.

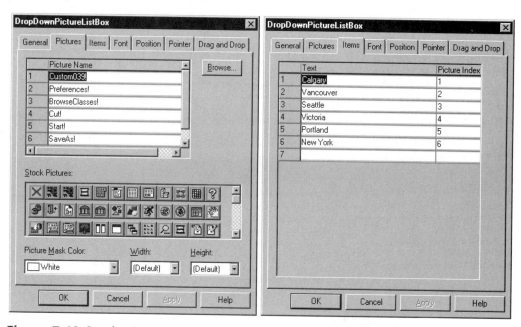

Figure 7.49 *On the Properties page, you have a new tab, Pictures, where you define which pictures will be used in the DDPBL, and you have an enhanced Items tab where you can assign a picture to each item in the listbox.*

On the Items tab you will enter the items for the listbox, but you will also assign each item a picture index as defined on the Pictures tab.

7.8.3.6 Picture ListBox

The Picture ListBox control for PowerBuilder 5.0 is exactly what you expect. It is a listbox version of the DDPLB. You assign all the properties exactly the same way that you did in the previous section. The difference with a listbox is that all the options are always shown and the user has the ability to select multiple items in a picture listbox, whereas a DDPLB can only have one item selected at a time.

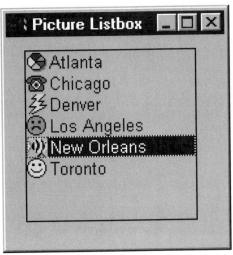

Figure 7.50 *The Picture ListBox is the listbox version of a DDPLB.*

7.9 MENU PAINTER ENHANCEMENTS

The interface that you will work with to build your menus in PowerBuilder has been changed to keep it consistent with the tab folder interfaces used in the rest of the properties pages. All the same properties that you are accustomed to in version 4.0 of PowerBuilder are still here, just moved around a little. We will just have to adjust to the new interface, even though it means more clicking around with the mouse to construct our menu items.

The one new characteristic of the menu that we can apply to our applications is the Drop Down Toolbar.

7.9.1 DROP DOWN TOOLBAR

The Drop Down Toolbar is the icon that you can see in the PowerBuilder development environment for the controls in the Window painter, or the different painters in the PowerBar. It appears as a single icon with a drop down arrow next to it. When you select it, a listbox full of icons drops down. You can then select the icon you want. The last selected icon is the one that will appear beside the drop down arrow in the toolbar.

You can use this kind of functionality in your toolbars. The sample application contains a drop down toolbar for the Edit menu item. Let's walk through how it was constructed.

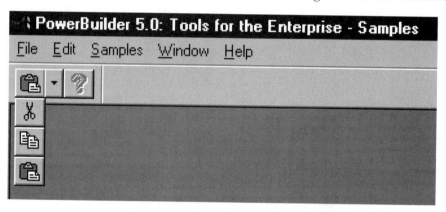

Figure 7.51 *The sample application contains a Drop Down Toolbar for the Edit menu bar option.*

Step 1 Build your menu. Build your menu as you normally would, with all menu items, cascades and toolbar icons.

Step 2 Define the MenuCascade. Every menu item has a new property called MenuCascade. When this property is set, all menu items with toolbar icons contained within that item will appear as a drop down toolbar. This property is set on the Toolbar tab of the menu painter for the parent menu item (in this case, the Edit item).

7.9 Menu Painter Enhancements 191

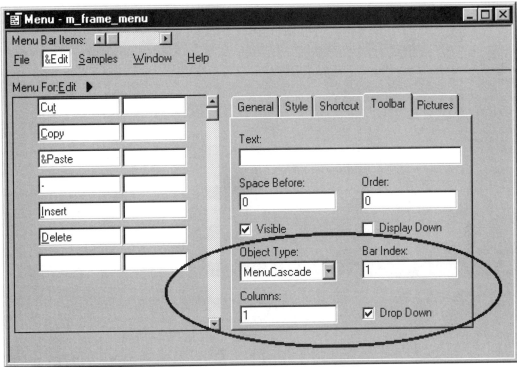

Figure 7.52 *The menu painter now has a series of properties that allow us to define drop down toolbars. These properties are found on the Toolbar tab.*

Set the Object Type drop down list box to MenuCascade. The Drop Down checkbox must also be checked (which it is by default). If you uncheck this listbox, the toolbar items will appear in their normal format.

Step 3 Define the number of columns. We can select how many columns we want our pictures to display in when the drop down area appears. This is set in the Columns field on the Toolbar tab. The default value is 1 column.

Step 4 Save and preview. You can run the window containing this menu to examine its functionality. Note that any menu items within the drop down toolbar which are defined as MenuCascade will not be contained within the drop down toolbar of the parent.

7.9.2 Creating Multiple Docking Toolbars

PowerBuilder 5.0 also allows us to create multiple toolbars in our applications and our development environment. You do not define multiple menus for the window, but rather split the toolbar itself into multiple sections.

To define multiple toolbars for your application is very easy. On the Toolbar tab of a menu item there is a field called Bar Index. In this field you can specify a toolbar number that you wish this particular toolbar item to appear on. PowerBuilder will automatically instantiate as many toolbars as you specify. You can have up to eight toolbars on a sheet and four on an MDI frame. Using this technique effectively allows you to split a single toolbar into many toolbars. This would allow you to show and hide different toolbars as you wish to reveal different sets of functionality.

7.10 APPLICATION PAINTER

There are three significant changes to the application painter in version 5.0. The first of these is the painterbar. In version 4.0, the painterbar has an icon for each of the properties of an application object that you might change, the fonts, the icon, the library search path, and so on. In version 5.0 all of these have been grouped into one properties page. The functionality is all the same, it is merely a different interface that is more consistent with the overall properties orientation that marks version 5.0.

The second change is that you no longer generate your executables from the application painter. Up until version 4.0, this was the only place to do it. In version 4.0, we were introduced to the Project painter and given a second place to generate our executables. At first, people were reluctant to use the Project painter because of some reported bugs that made the executable produced by the project painter larger than the executable created in the application painter. You don't need to worry however, as that bug has long since been fixed. Now you are required to generate your executables from the project painter. I view this as a very positive thing as it requires us to generate all our executables in a more consistent fashion.

The third change to the application painter is the addition of two new events, ConnectionBegin and ConnectionEnd which are used specifically for distributed computing. ConnectionBegin is triggered in a server application when a client attempts to connect to it. ConnectionEnd is triggered in a server application when a client disconnects from it. For further details, see section 7.2—Distributed PowerBuilder.

7.11 TABLE PAINTER

The table painter appears at first to be a new painter, but it is really an enhanced form of the table definition window from the database painter. It has been created so that it can stand alone and provide easier access for the development and maintenance of tables.

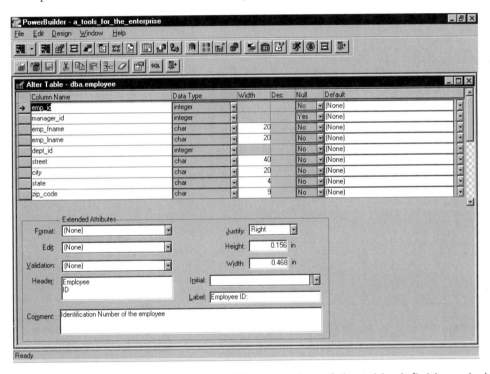

Figure 7.53 *The table painter is a standalone version of the table definition window we are accustomed to. The intention is to provide easier access for creation of new tables and maintaining existing ones.*

One of the nice features of this painter is that it is modeless. You can have multiple tables open at the same time, and they even support cutting, copying and pasting column definitions from one table to another. When you cut/copy and paste, you get everything, the name, the data type, the size, the default and all the extended attributes.

7.12 PIPELINE PAINTER

The pipeline painter in version 5.0 functions essentially the same as it did in version 4.0. There are two things that have changed, however. We can now select from any of four data sources, the Quick Select, the SQL Select, a Query object or a stored procedure.

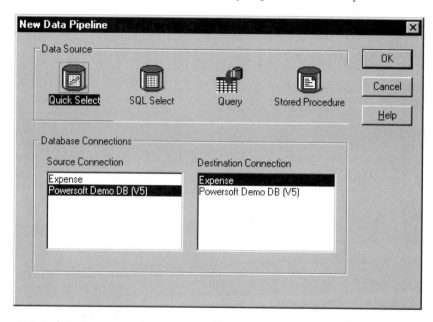

Figure 7.54 *The pipeline painter now allows us to select from four possible data sources; QuickSelect, SQL Select, Query object or stored procedure.*

The pipeline painter now also supports the piping of BLOBS, which was not supported in version 4.0.

7.13 DEBUGGER

The debugger in version 4.0 has been a two edged sword. It has been extremely helpful in allowing us to walk through our code, but when you wanted to check that overloaded function, or look for an instance variable in the parent object, it was not so easy.

I would like to say that version 5.0 has resolved all this, but it hasn't. You still have to hunt around a little for instance variables, but they have made some improvements. The debugger now supports function overloading very nicely.

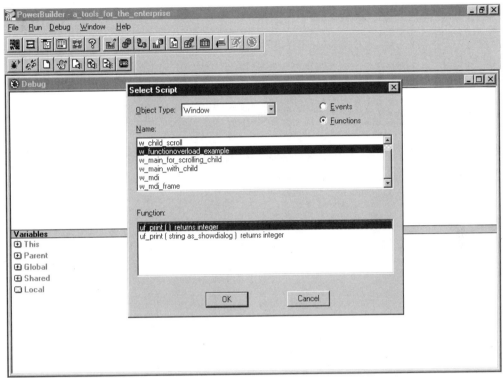

Figure 7.55 *The debugger in version 5.0 has been upgraded to support full function overloading and access to THIS and PARENT objects.*

Although the instance variables aren't nicely laid out like the local, shared and global, by having access to the THIS and PARENT objects, we can begin to find them a little easier.

You can still elect to shut down the debugger during execution, which is sheer suicide. PowerBuilder supplies the message "Warning, shutting down the debugger can cause your system to become unstable." I think they should change this message to "Do you want to hang your system?" as this is truly the inevitable consequence ninety percent of the time.

So we haven't got it all yet, but hey, we have to leave them something to fix in version 6.0!

7.14 OBJECT BROWSER

The object browser has been completely replaced with a new and improved version in PowerBuilder 5.0. The new browser is fully integrated and utilizes the new tab dialog to access every object within the PowerBuilder environment. This includes all the system objects, enumerated data types, OLE objects, distributed proxy objects, data types, application, DataWindow, window, menu, structures, user objects, and functions.

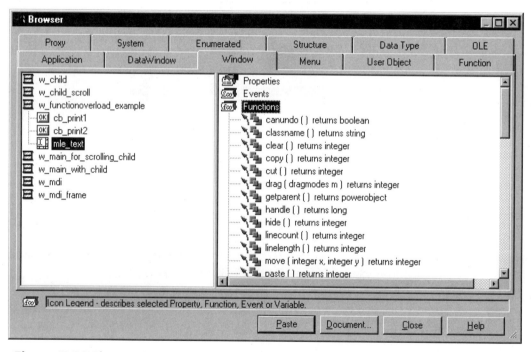

Figure 7.56 *The Version 5.0 Object Browser allows easy access to all the objects in the PowerBuilder environment. Inside an object you can see all the controls or other components that are part of that class. On the right side you can examine the selected object's properties, functions, events, variables and structures.*

You can select the type of object you wish to browse from the tabs on the top of the page. The objects will appear in the left list box. Double-clicking on the object will expand the object so you can see the components that are part of it.

7.14 Object Browser   197

The list box on the right side of the browser will allow you to browse the properties, functions, events, variables and structures (local) in the object. Some items, like functions, can be selected and pasted back into your script painter, like in the version 4.0 browser.

This new browser also has a feature to help you prepare documentation for your objects (something all enterprise projects should ensure is done). If you select an object on the left list box and then press the **Documentation...** button at the bottom, it will open the PowerBuilder documentation window. This window produces a rich text edit with all the details of the object inside. You can save this out as an RTF file and import it into a word processor document, or you could cut and paste it into the clipboard.

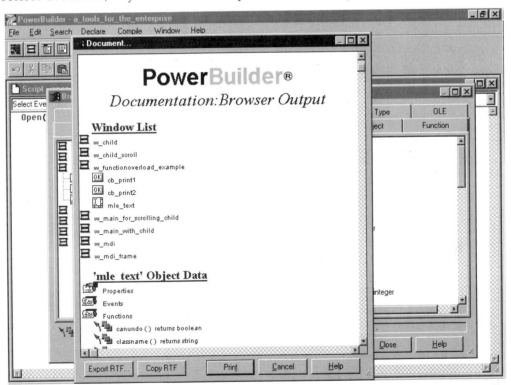

Figure 7.57 The documentation feature of the 5.0 object browser will make it easier to document your objects for enterprise applications.

198 *Chapter 7: What's New In PowerBuilder 5.0*

7.15 OBJECT-ORIENTED ENHANCEMENTS

PowerBuilder has often been bandied about by the press as the world tries to decide if it is really object-oriented or not. Much of PowerBuilder conforms to the standards of object orientation, but does not enforce the rules. Other parts of PowerBuilder are not really object-oriented at all. With each new release, Powersoft makes PowerBuilder just a little more object-oriented. With version 5.0, they are continuing the trend.

7.15.1 FUNCTION OVERLOADING

The concept of function overloading was discussed in *Chapter 5, Object-Oriented PowerBuilder*, but in case you skipped that chapter and turned to this one first (and who could blame you?) here is the summary. Function overloading is a mechanism for providing a variety of polymorphism within an object. Two functions with the same names, but different parameter sets or return value data types are declared within an object. At execution time, when the function is called, PowerBuilder will match the argument list for the function against the appropriate function definition and select which process that it will execute.

We were able to do this in previous versions of PowerBuilder, but since we weren't allowed to declare two functions with the same name in any given object, we tricked PowerBuilder and implemented it by declaring the function once at each level of inheritance. This wasn't a very solid work around.

Now in PowerBuilder 5.0, we can implement function overloading simply by declaring the functions in the objects where they are needed. We no longer have the restriction of not being able to declare two functions with the same name.

7.15.2 EVENT PARAMETERS AND FUNCTION POSTING

We have always referred to event scripts and functions as ways that methods are implemented in PowerBuilder. Each had it own purpose, advantages and disadvantages. In PowerBuilder 5.0, the differences between functions and events is slowly dissolving away. Now you can pass arguments to user defined events, like we have always done with user defined functions. And user defined functions, which in previous versions of PowerBuilder would always execute immediately when called, can now be posted to a queue instead of being immediately triggered.

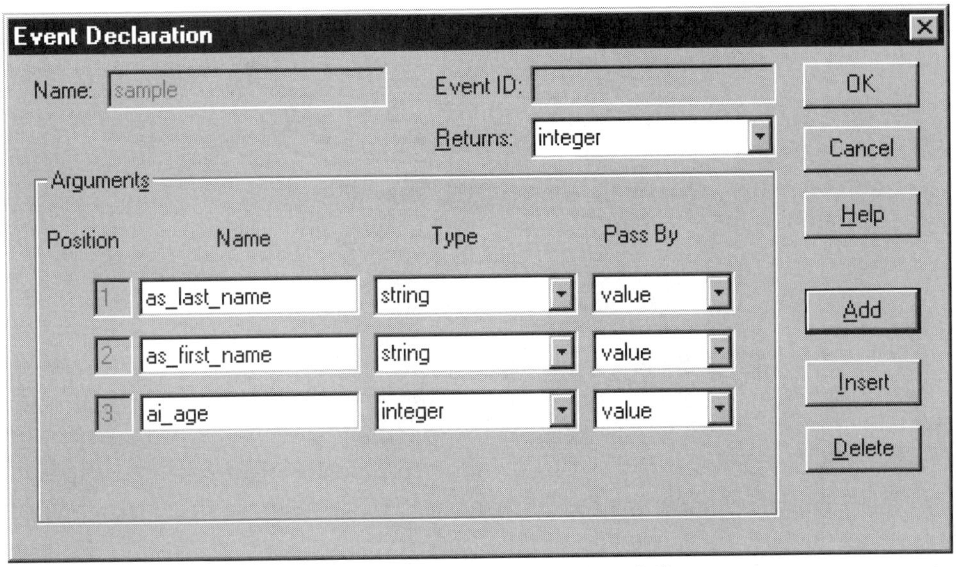

7.15 Object-Oriented Enhancements   **199**

Figure 7.58 *All events in PowerBuilder now have the ability to accept arguments and utilize a return value to alter standard DataWindow actions. The differences between event scripts and functions are slowly eroding away.*

All events now have arguments and return values that you can use. Arguments will replace many of the functions that were used in your scripts to determine system information, like the location of the pointer or the current row in a DataWindow (formerly provided by PointerX(), PointerY() and GetRow() functions). The return code allows you to alter the default system processing that occurs when the event ends. This will replace all the functionality of the SetActionCode() function that we used in the DataWindow control, and will also affect other events where we returned information to the system. The CloseQuery event, for example, in PowerBuilder 4.0 required setting a value of

Message.ReturnValue = 1

to stop the window from closing, in PowerBuilder 5.0 we no longer have to do this. Instead, this is managed by the return value. A value of 0 allows the window to close whereas a value of 1 stops the window from closing.

For most events, the arguments and return values cannot be altered by the developer, but now in PowerBuilder 5.0 you can create an event on an object, and by leaving the event id

200   *Chapter 7: What's New In PowerBuilder 5.0*

blank, it allows you to specify any arguments that you would like. You will notice in figure 7.58 that the window for defining event arguments looks suspiciously like the function definition window.

There are four different types of events; predefined system events, undefined system events, custom events and user defined events. Predefined system events are the ones that you see listed in the event box when you enter the script painter. These are the events that Powersoft has selected as being the ones most often required for the standard object sets. The arguments and return types of these events are already predefined and cannot be changed.

An example of a predefined system event would be the clicked event for a DataWindow control. This event has four predefined arguments that replace some traditional PowerBuilder 4.0 functions. Instead of using the GetClickedRow() function, now the current row is stored in an argument. You can also access the X and Y coordinates of the pointer (replacing the PointerX() and PointerY() functions) and you have a generic reference argument named dwo that represents the specific object within the DataWindow that was clicked on (for example, which column, text field, bitmap or other object that was clicked).

Undefined system events are object events that are caused by the system, but are not part of the predefined set of events that PowerBuilder has pre-declared. You can still add them to your list of events easily. These events, like the predefined events, have a static set of arguments and a predefined list of return codes.

Custom events are those that are defined by you, and are assigned event ids pbm_custom01 through pbm_custom75. In previous versions of PowerBuilder, these were referred to as 'user defined events', now we call them 'custom events.' This is because we are assigning user defined events as the label for those events that we give a name, but don't assign any event id to. On this type of event we can define our arguments and return value in any combination we like.

Full examples of all of these event declarations and how to use them can be found in Chapter 8 along with example of how to trigger and post functions.

7.16 DATABASE ENHANCEMENTS

The world of client/server keeps improving as the databases that we use become more sophisticated and versatile. With each release PowerBuilder tries to accommodate the new features and functions of the database vendors.

> **Developers Note: Note that if you are operating in Windows 95 or NT, native driver support no longer exists for Oracle 6.0 or 7.0. Oracle 7.1 and 7.2 are still supported.**

7.16.1 NATIVE ENHANCEMENTS

There are two primary enhancements to the native database drivers in PowerBuilder 5.0. PB 5 now has native support for Oracle 7.1 under NT (PB 4.0 now has this support also, but didn't initially). This will be relief to all those shops running Oracle NT 7.1 and having to connect through ODBC.

The second enhancement is for people who are accessing Microsoft SQL Server 6.0. You can now choose to access the integrated security of Window NT when accessing SQL Server. You can do this by coding the following statement in your DBParm attribute:

```
sqlca.dpbarm="secure= {'Yes' or 'No'}"
```

where secure will be equal to either 'yes' (or 'true' or 1) or 'no' (or 'false' or 0). Yes indicates that the integrated NT security will be used, overriding any of the logon values in the transaction object. The default setting is 'no.'

7.16.2 ODBC ENHANCEMENTS

Powersoft has tried to improve the performance and functionality of their ODBC interface in PowerBuilder 5.0. They have added support for clustered indexes and blocked fetch support. These features must also be able to be supported in the ODBC driver that you are using to connect to your data source.

When using blocked fetch support, PowerBuilder will support a maximum blocking factor of 100 for a table list, of 25 for a column list and 10 for an index list.

202 *Chapter 7: What's New In PowerBuilder 5.0*

7.17 INTERNATIONALIZATION

For those of you who need to have your PowerBuilder application work in other countries and other languages, Powersoft has added international characters, double byte characters and right to left cursor movement to PowerBuilder 5.0.

7.18 COMPONENT LIBRARY

You will notice an extra directory of objects that is installed with PowerBuilder 5.0. This directory is called the Component Gallery. The gallery contains a number of OLE .OCX controls that you can include in your applications (and distribute royalty free). You can use these controls in the standard OLE 2.0 window control or in the new OLE DataWindow. You should be aware however that these controls are generally limited in functionality and they are intended to tease you into buying the full blown version (some are from Visual Components, the company that Sybase acquired recently, and others are from other third party vendors like Gamesman and Novell.).

Most of the objects are 32 bit objects, so if you are installing or planning to roll out in a 16 bit environment, be sure that there is a 16 bit version of the .OCX that you can obtain. The gallery contains:

- a spreadsheet type control.

- an Internet spreadsheet plug in for use in conjunction with Netscape.

- a very sophisticated graphing/charting tool that provides full 3D rendering of your charts.

- an integrated spelling checker (useful for things like the Rich Text Edit controls and DataWindows!).

- a calendar with full keyboard and multi-language support.

- a clock which can display system time. A real valuable use for the clock is that you can set alarms, and the clock will trigger an 'alarm' event when the appropriate time hits. You can use this as a scheduling tool or to kick off batch processes at certain times.

- a progress meter, slider and spin controls.

- a picture clip control. This type of a control allows you to view a portion of a bitmap and can be used for simple animation purposes by containing all the frames of the animation within the bitmap image.

- a set of controls to help you access Novell's NDS (Network Directory Services) if you are using a Novell network.

7.19 SUMMARY

The new features of PowerBuilder 5.0 will be very beneficial to enterprise developers. There are many new features that will allow us to build applications that are more robust, scalable, better performing and with better user interfaces. I am looking forward to seeing some very sophisticated enterprise applications rolling out on PowerBuilder 5.0 in 1996 and 1997.

Not every new feature in PowerBuilder 5.0 is discussed in this chapter. Some of the smaller changes have been addressed in the relevant sections of this book.

CHAPTER 8

Advanced Development Concepts

*D*espite some of the claims of Powersoft, there is a considerable leap to be made to move *from being a PowerBuilder beginner to being an intermediate or expert developer. Experience and networking have been two of the ways that we have been required to learn in order to become better developers. These are still excellent learning tools and will never be replaced, but we hope to provide you with many of these advanced skills in this chapter and the ones that follow.*

These skills relate to almost all areas of PowerBuilder. In this chapter we will address concepts that relate to objects in general. In the following chapters we will address specific subjects including the DataWindow object, reporting and more.

8.1 SETTING UP OBJECT EVENTS

PowerBuilder works within an event driven model. The objects that we create respond to messages sent by the operating system and we build our code into the events to allow our program to carry out its purpose. Every PowerBuilder OO object comes with a set of predefined events. Beyond those we have the ability to define other system events, define custom events or our own user defined events.

Chapter 8: Advanced Development Concepts

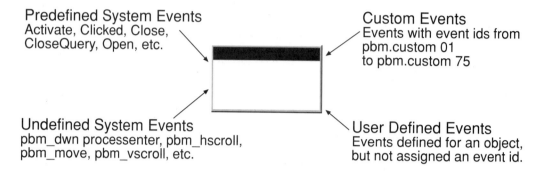

Figure 8.1 *PowerBuilder operates within an event driven model. Predefined system events are built into all OO objects. We also have the ability to define other system events, define custom events or our own user defined events.*

8.1.1 PREDEFINED SYSTEM EVENTS

In the Windows environment, there are literally hundreds of messages that an object could listen and respond to. To provide access to all those objects would make the PowerBuilder programming environment far more difficult to use, and having all those stubs could affect the performance of our objects. To avoid these problems, Powersoft has selected the system events that you are most likely to need for each object and built stubs into those objects to allow you easy access to events for inserting your application code.

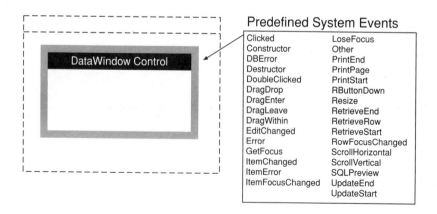

Figure 8.2 *Every PowerBuilder OO Object has its own set of predefined system events. These are the events that Powersoft has determined that developers will require most often.*

The predefined system events are the ones that you have used a lot in the past. What is new in PowerBuilder 5.0, as discussed in Chapter 7, is the ability to pass arguments into an event. In the system defined events, these arguments replace many of the functions which you are accustomed to. For example, in the ItemChanged event for a DataWindow control, you no longer call GetText() to find out what data the user has entered, it is now obtained through an event argument called *data*.

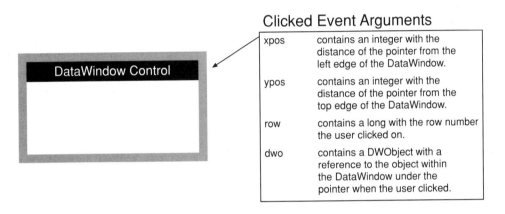

Figure 8.3 *Arguments within a predefined system event can be used to provide system specific information. They are static and cannot be changed.*

Arguments can be used in your scripts for a great deal of the system specific information you need to know during execution such as what row was clicked on and the X and Y coordinates of the pointer in the Clicked event of a DataWindow control. This replaces the ClickedRow(), PointerX() and PointerY() functions used in previous versions of PowerBuilder.

Developers Tip: If you use a TriggerEvent() or PostEvent() function to trigger any system event (predefined or one you define yourself) the arguments that are provided will be empty. Be aware of this when you write scripts for these events and be careful when forcing a system event to fire.

Chapter 8: Advanced Development Concepts

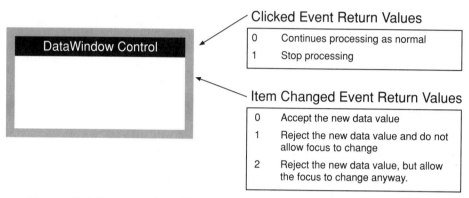

Figure 8.4 *Return values for system defined events allow you to alter the default system processing that would occur when an event ends. These are static and cannot be changed.*

The return value allows you to change the default system processing that would occur when an event ends. In earlier versions of PowerBuilder this was accomplished through either a function, as in the case of SetActionCode() in the DataWindow control, or through setting the ReturnValue in the Message object (i.e. Message.ReturnValue = 1 in the CloseQuery event of a window would stop the window from closing).

Here is an example of a script in the ItemChanged event of a DataWindow control. You can see the use of the argument *data* for this event to allow us to validate the value, and the use of the return code to tell the system whether we wish to accept the data or not. This script is from the demonstration application on the companion CD and can be found in the DataWindow control dw_employee_list on the window w_emp_maint_dw_events.

Sample Note: In the sample application on the companion CD (and in the script example below) only one column is updateable by the end user, the Salary column. This means that we don't need to check in the script which column is being validated. In a situation with a DataWindow where there are multiple updateable columns, you will need to do a CHOOSE CASE statement to determine which column was clicked on and execute the appropriate valiation rule.

As a second note, many experts recommend that the error message be displayed in the ItemError event and I agree. This is because it is possible for

8.1 Setting Up Object Events   **209**

the DataWindow to have encountered an error and triggered the ItemError event before reaching the ItemChanged event. The inclusion of all messaging in the ItemError event helps to properly encapsulate your object. The error is included in this event for the purpose of clarity.

```
// Validates entry to ensure that employee salary has not been increased
// above limit in em_max_salary

DECIMAL ldec_max_salary

IF em_max_salary.GetData(ldec_max_salary) < 1 THEN
        // Invalid value in edit mask
        MessageBox("Invalid Maximum Salary","Maximum Salary does not"+&
        "contain a valid value, please correct before changing"+&
        " salaries")

        // Reject value, but allow the focus to change
        RETURN 2
ELSE
        // Validate new data
        IF IsNumber(data) THEN
                // Valid number entered
                IF Dec(data) > ldec_max_salary THEN
                        // Salary exceeds maximum limit
                        MessageBox("Salary Too High","The salary entered is"+&
" above the allowable maximum")
                        // Reject value, but do not allow the focus to change
                        RETURN 1
                ELSE
                        // Accept the new value
                        RETURN 0
                END IF
        ELSE
                // Invalid number entered
                MessageBox("Invalid Salary","The salary you entered "+&
                "is not valid.")
                RETURN 1
        END IF
END IF
```

8.1.2 UNDEFINED SYSTEM EVENTS

The predefined system events will probably meet 90% of your system event requirements. To allow you to fulfill the other 10%, we have the ability to define our own events that can be linked to any of the currently undefined system events.

> **Developers Note:** In some of the PowerBuilder documentation and educational materials predefined and undefined system events are referred to as 'mapped events'

These undefined system events all have a unique event id. PowerBuilder filters these event ids so they do not appear precisely as they will in your Microsoft Windows SDK or other windows programming manual. Instead you will see them prefixed with a "pbm" identifier (for **P**ower**B**uilder **M**essage) and there will be some events that you won't find listed in your windows guide because they are unique to PowerBuilder (specifically, those that relate to DataWindows). This also allows PowerBuilder applications to use the same objects across multiple platforms as the message from the relevant operating system will be translated to a PowerBuilder Message.

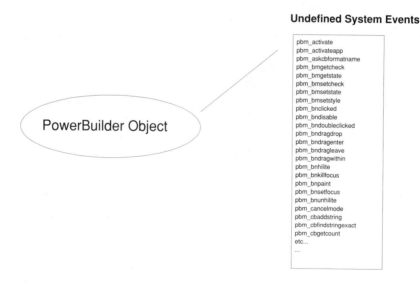

Figure 8.5 *Undefined system events are those events that respond to system messages, but do not have stubs predefined in the object. All undefined system events have unique event ids, all prefixed with "pbm."*

If you are going to be working in the windows environment, most messages still retain the same name and can be looked up in your windows guide to determine their function. If you don't have a windows programming guide, or the Microsoft SDK, and you hope to utilize undefined system events, or other underlying windows functionality, I strongly recommend you acquire one.

To incorporate the undefined system events into your application, you must first open or select the object for which you want to define a new system event. Once opened/selected you will select the **User Events...** menu item from the **Define** option on the menu bar. This will cause the window in Figure 8.6 to open.

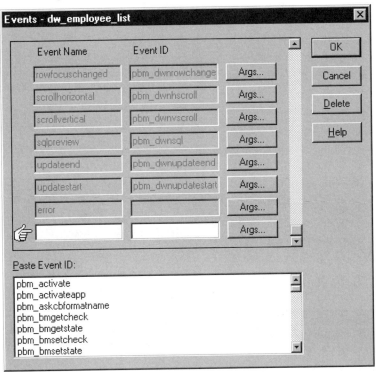

Figure 8.6 *The events window lists all the events currently defined for an object and their respective event ids. You can enter new events here, but you cannot alter events that have been defined at a higher level within the object hierarchy.*

212   *Chapter 8: Advanced Development Concepts*

From this window, you can see all the existing predefined system events. They are the ones that are grayed out and you do not have access to them (any undefined system events, custom events, or user events that you have incorporated into ancestor objects will also be grayed out).

To add an undefined system event to the event list, you must move to the bottom of the existing list and enter a name for the new event. The name for the event should have a prefix that allows you to identify it as an event that you have defined. In previous versions of PowerBuilder, many people named these events with a 'ue_' prefix for 'user event'. With the significant difference between the different types of user events, I would recommend different naming standards for each type. For user defined system events, I would stick with the standard naming that Powersoft has used for the predefined system events. For example, if defining an event for pbm_mousemove, call the event MouseMove. I don't feel there is a need to add a prefix to this event type as they are essentially predefined events that simply weren't predefined. If you are more comfortable adding a prefix to the name of the event then use 'se_' for 'system event'. For the other user defined events, I would recommend using 'ce_' for the custom events, 'ee_' for the external events (pbm_uonexternal01 to 25), for the visual basic events (pbm_vbxevent01 to 50) 'vbx_' and for other user events 'ue_'.

This is an increase in complexity in the naming of user events, but it will allow the developer to discern at a glance what kind of stimulus would trigger a particular event.

Next, to create a previously undefined system event you must select the appropriate event id from the event list. In figure 8.7 we have created an undefined system event pbm_rbuttondblclk and given it the name 'RButtonDblClick.' This event will now appear in the event list for this object and all objects inherited from this object. It will be triggered when the user double clicks the right mouse button on this window.

PowerBuilder 4.0 to 5.0: Notice that the event list is now sorted alphabetically in PowerBuilder 5.0. Your user defined events will be placed within the list in their alphabetical location, not just slotted at the end as they were in PB 4.0.

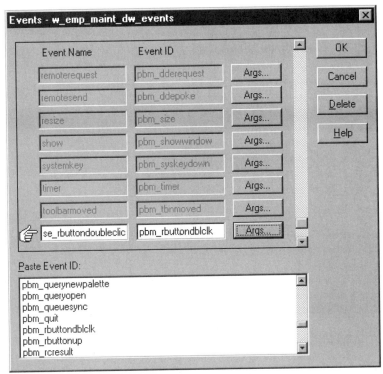

Figure 8.7 *An example of creating a previously undefined system event pbm_rbuttondblclk and assigning it the name 'RButtonDblClick.' This event will be triggered when the user double clicks the right mouse button on this window.*

Like the predefined system events, these events have arguments predefined for them. You can view these arguments by pressing the **Args...** button, but you cannot alter them. Each system event will have a different set of arguments.

8.1.3 CUSTOM EVENTS

The next type of event you might decide to create in an object would be a custom event. In previous versions of PowerBuilder these were referred to as user events. They were given event ids ranging from pbm_custom01 to pbm_custom75. The intention of these events was that the user could call them when they were required using the TriggerEvent() and PostEvent() functions.

214   *Chapter 8: Advanced Development Concepts*

There were two problems with these events. First, there were only 75 stubs (placeholders for custom events). For most PowerBuilder developers this was plenty, but for some of the really involved applications, or the really hefty class libraries, this was not quite enough room. The second problem was that although these were supposed to be user events, they could actually be triggered by certain system messages. Some third party object developers would use these events (quite correctly) to pass messages into the PowerBuilder application from their object. This became a problem if the third party developer passed a message pbm_custom32 and you had defined a different event to occur on that message than the third party software developer had intended. Suddenly your user defined events became system events.

For this reason, the class of event called a user event was created. See the following section for details on how to use these events.

You may still want to use custom events. If you are migrating an application up from a third party class library developed under version 4.0, you will definitely still be using them. If, on the other hand, you are developing a completely new application in PowerBuilder 5.0, you will probably want to not use the custom event unless you do desire the event to be triggered by some external party. For purely internal events, use the user event.

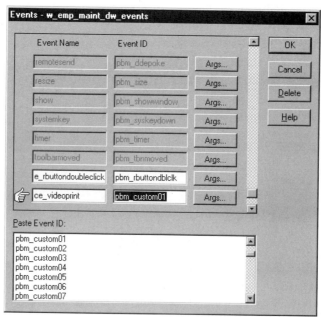

Figure 8.8 *The custom event is an event that you create and is given an event id between pbm_custom01 to pbm_custom75.*

All the custom events have two arguments predefined for them, *wparam* which is an unsigned long and *lparam* which is a normal long. You may recognize these from the Message.WordParm and Message.LongParm attributes that we used to use in PowerBuilder 4.0 to pass parameters to events. You cannot change or alter these arguments. This ensures reverse compatibility with previous versions of PowerBuilder.

8.1.4 User Defined Events

The name user defined event has been around for a long time, but as we discussed above, in PowerBuilder 5.0 it means something new. This name now refers to a very special class of event that has a name, but is not linked to a specific system event id. These events are specifically intended to allow you to attach your own methods to an object and then have them triggered only when you call a TriggerEvent() or PostEvent() function.

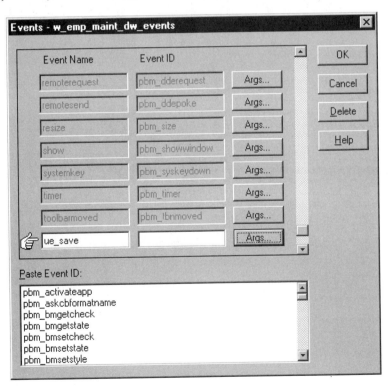

Figure 8.9 *To create a user event you simply give the event a name and leave the event id blank.*

To create one of these events is very straightforward. You simply give the event a name and leave the event id blank. If you choose you can define arguments and a return value for the event by pressing the **Args...** button.

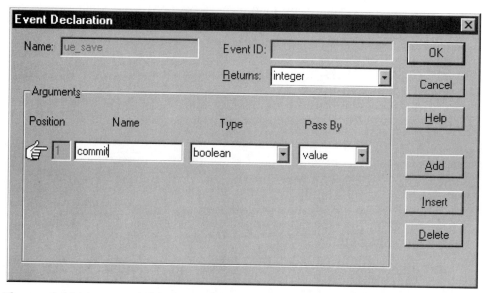

Figure 8.10 *You can define arguments for the events in the Event Declaration window, like you would in the Function Declaration window.*

8.2 FUNCTIONING WITH FUNCTIONS

Functions are an essential part of any development tool. PowerBuilder comes equipped with a very substantial set of built in PowerBuilder functions (at last count I think it was somewhere between 500 to 700) and also supports functions that are defined by the user and functions defined external to the PowerBuilder environment and saved as .DLLs.

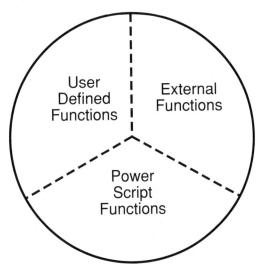

Figure 8.11 There are three primary classes of functions in PowerBuilder, PowerScript functions, user defined functions and external functions.

Each of the classes of functions are important for providing the functionality and flexibility of PowerBuilder.

8.2.1 POWERSCRIPT FUNCTIONS

PowerBuilder's built in PowerScript functions will fulfill the bulk of your requirements for your processing related development efforts. There are functions for manipulating variables and arrays, functions for opening and closing objects, functions for communicating with the user and more.

Two types of PowerScript functions exist; global and object level. Global PowerScript functions are not attached to any specific objects. They can be used anywhere in your application. They include functions such as Open(), Close(), Today(), Now() and so on. Object level functions are functions which are encapsulated within a specific object class. These functions are only applicable to that class to which they belong. For example, the DataWindow control has functions for Retrieve() and SetRow() that are only of use on the DataWindow control. These functions would serve no purpose on an object such as a command button.

Like all other functions, PowerScript functions accept arguments and return values to the script that called them. Precise explanations of all the PowerScript functions can be found in your PowerBuilder Function Reference Manual or your on-line help.

8.2.2 USER DEFINED FUNCTIONS

There is always some business process, system process or other functionality that won't exist in the tool and language you decide to work in. PowerBuilder allows you to develop your own user defined functions as required. These functions can accepts arguments, perform processing and return a value just like any PowerScript function.

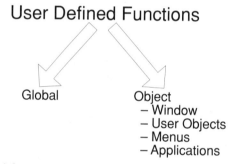

Figure 8.12 *User defined functions can exist at two possible levels, global or object (in the form of functions attached to windows, user objects and menus).*

Functions in PowerBuilder can exist at two possible levels, global or object. Object functions can only be declared for windows, user objects, application objects and menus.

8.2.2.1 Global

The global function has been created to allow you to develop methods that you want to have accessible anywhere in your application. These objects are not really considered OO for two reasons; they exist at a global level which is contradictory to the rules of encapsulation, and they are processes with no substance. A function has a method, but has no properties.

Global functions are declared from the main PowerBar. This icon looks like the script painter icon, a piece of paper with the corner folded over, except that the function painter icon has an 'F(x)' symbol on it. This painter exists solely for the purpose of creating global functions, object level functions are created in the painter of the object for which they are created.

8.2 Functioning with Functions

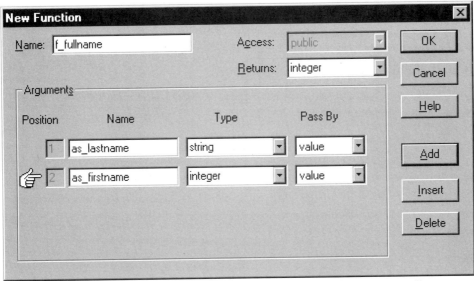

Figure 8.13 *The function declaration window for a global function allows you to define the name, arguments and return values of the function.*

In the function declaration window for a global function, you must provide the function with a unique name. This name serves a dual purpose, it is the name that the function object will be saved under in the library, and it is the name that you will use to call the function in your scripts. The name can be up to forty characters in length and is not case sensitive. You can use alphanumerics, underscores, dashes, pound characters (#) and percent characters (%) in the function name although these last three are not recommended (see the Development Tip below).

Development Tip: Although the name of a function can include dashes, pound, and percent characters, you should not use them in the naming of your functions. These characters can have special meanings and this can be confusing for developers. Consider this example: If you have a variable named A and a variable named B. If you have another variable named A-B it is hard to differentiate from A minus B (A - B).

The access level of a global function is always public. This is necessary as the purpose of this kind of a function is to allow the process to be called from anywhere in the application.

220 *Chapter 8: Advanced Development Concepts*

The return type of a global function can be anything in your class hierarchy. The default return value is integer, but you could return a string, a DataWindow, a structure, a window, or any other object anywhere in your class hierarchy (including classes that you have defined with the PowerBuilder painters).

Optionally, you could choose a return type of '(None).' This means that the function will not return a value to the script that called it. This type of function is commonly referred to as a *subroutine*.

You can declare as many arguments for a function as you like (or you could declare none at all). To declare an argument you must decide upon a name for the argument (I recommend prefixing all arguments with **a{datatype}_**, such as **as_lastname**). The name conforms to standard PowerScript identifier rules. You must also assign the argument a data type. Any data type from within the class hierarchy is acceptable, including any classes that you have defined.

The final element that must be defined is how the argument is to be passed. You have a choice of passing the argument by value, reference, or read only. Passing an argument by *value* means that when the argument is used in the function, you are using a copy of the original value. If you make any changes to the argument the original value from the calling script is not affected.

Passing an argument by *reference* is the exact opposite. What is passed when an argument is sent by reference is not a value, but rather a pointer to where the value can be found. This means that when you use the argument in the function, if you make any changes to the argument these changes will affect the variable which contained the argument in the calling script.

Anything other that a simple datatype (i.e. string, integer, long, etc) is always passed by reference (even if you specify value). This includes objects like DataWindows, windows, menus and so on. If you want to ensure that any object passed by reference cannot be changed in the function you are declaring, you can declare the arguments as *read only*. Any attempt to change the argument or pass it to another function or event will cause a compile time error.

8.2 Functioning with Functions

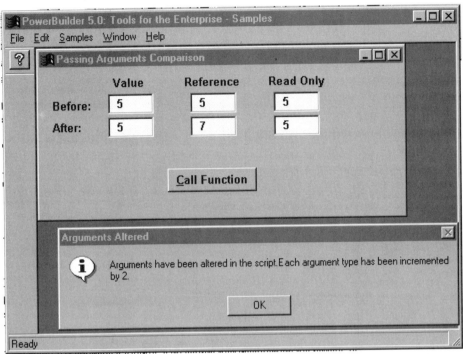

Figure 8.14 *The companion CD contains a window with scripts that demonstrate the passing of arguments of all three types.*

On the companion CD we have an example which demonstrates the passing of arguments of all three types. You can open the window **w_passing_arguments** to observe the above scenarios. In the Clicked event for the command button Call Function we have three local variables declared: **ll_value**, **ll_reference** and **ll_readonly**.

Each of these local variables is set to a value of 5. The values of each are displayed in a set of single line edit controls, one for each category. Then the function is called and each of the variables is passed in their respective positions. When the function is over the values of the variables are displayed in a separate set of single line edits so that you can compare the differences.

222   *Chapter 8: Advanced Development Concepts*

Script for Clicked Event of cb_callfunction on w_passing_arguments:

```
long ll_value, ll_reference, ll_readonly

// Set Before Values

ll_value = 5
ll_reference = 5
ll_readonly = 5

sle_value_before.text = String(ll_value)
sle_reference_before.text = String(ll_reference)
sle_readonly_before.text = String(ll_readonly)

// Call function
wf_arguments(ll_value,ll_reference,ll_readonly)

// Set After Values
sle_value_after.text = String(ll_value)
sle_reference_after.text = String(ll_reference)
sle_readonly_after.text = String(ll_readonly)
```

Within the function wf_arguments the script tries to increment each argument by two. The script compiles for the value and reference types, but does not compile for the read only type. If you wish to see the error message, remove the comments from the line that tries to modify the read only argument. The function concludes by sending a message to the user indicating that the arguments have all been incremented.

Function wf_arguments for w_passing_arguments:

```
// All three arguments will be received. They will all be altered by adding 2 to each.

al_value=al_value + 2
al_reference = al_reference + 2
//al_readonly = al_readonly + 2    This statement is not valid.
//                        Trying to execute it would result
//                                        in an error at compile time

RETURN MessageBox("Arguments Altered",&
"Arguments have been altered in the script."+&
         "Each argument type has been incremented by 2.")
```

Your application should not require many global functions. Most functions that we would have written as global functions in earlier versions of PowerBuilder should now be included as methods attached to objects (often non-visual).

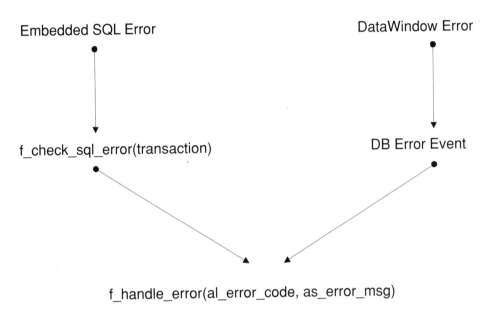

Figure 8.15 *Global functions have often been used in enterprise systems in areas that cross over many boundaries such as error handling.*

An example of where global functions have been often used in enterprise systems is in the area of error handling. Figure 8.15 shows a diagram detailing how database errors have often been funneled through our system. A database error can occur in one of two places, after embedded SQL or in a DataWindow. The embedded SQL has often been trapped by a global function like f_check_sql_error(transaction). This function determines the error code (i.e. SQLCA.SQLDBCode) and error message (i.e. SQLCA.SQLErrText) and passes them to f_handle_error(error code, error message) to handle. The DataWindow error causes a DBErrorEvent to be fired. In this event the error code and message are determined by using the DataWindow functions DBErrorCode() and DBErrorMessage(). These are also passed to f_handle_error(error code, error message). The function f_handle_error would then be responsible for tasks such as managing the error, communicating with the user and informing systems support.

224 Chapter 8: Advanced Development Concepts

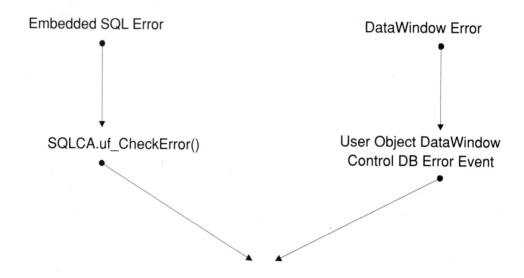

Figure 8.16 *In the PowerBuilder applications we build today, methods that may have otherwise become global functions are now being located inside non-visual objects.*

All these functions would now be located in different places in today's enterprise development environment. The global function for error checking would be built into the transaction or error object. This is more in line with the rules of encapsulation. All the methods that belong to the transaction object should be contained within the object. The DBErrorEvent script is contained inside of a user object DataWindow control that serves as the ancestor for all required DataWindow controls. These two methods still call a common error handling routine, but this routine instead of being global is now a part of the non-visual standard Error class that you have modified (refer to Chapter 12 for specific details on how to modify and use the standard class objects).

8.2.2.2 Object Level

Object level functions are used a great deal in any OO PowerBuilder application. These functions are the mechanism that we use to attach methods to specific objects. We also use this level of function extensively in user object method definition and to build the public interface for any user objects (further discussion on this can be found in *Chapter 12—User Objects*).

Defining an object level function is very similar to defining a global function. Where it is defined is quite different. You do not use the function painter to create an object level function, instead you use the painter for the object for which you wish to create the function. Under the **Declare** option on the menu for the Window, Menu, Application and User Object painters you will see an option that says **Window Functions...**, **User Object Functions...**, **Application Functions...** or **Menu Functions...** as appropriate. Selecting this option will open a similar window to the global function selection window. The one that opens will display all the existing user defined functions for this object. You can open one of the listed functions or create a new one by pressing the **New...** command button.

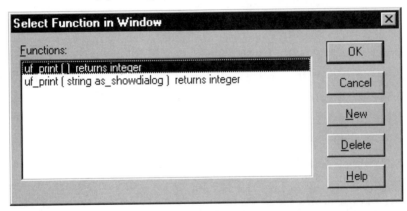

Figure 8.17 *The user function selection window for an object level function displays all the functions for the current object.*

Developers Tip: Although it has never been well documented, you can create object level functions in the Application painter for the application object. These are almost global in scope because the application object exists as long as the application is running, but this is a better solution as the rules are at least encapsulated within the application object.

If you select new, you will be taken to the user function declaration window. This window is identical to the one for global user function declarations except that you can now change the access level of your function. You can select from Public, Private or Protected. A *public* access level means that this function is visible and can be called by other objects outside of the current object. For example, from a script on the window for the event ue_retrieve, we can call:

226 *Chapter 8: Advanced Development Concepts*

dw_employee.Retrieve()

This is because Retrieve() is a public function of a DataWindow control. If the function was private or protected, the above script would cause a compile error in the script painter.

Being able to declare a function as private or protected is essential to the concept of encapsulation. It is this process of hiding the functionality within an object that has led to the colloquial definition of encapsulation as 'information hiding.'

Declaring a function as *private* will limit its access to only those scripts actually contained within that object, or on controls on that object. Even descendants of this object will not be given access to the function. An example of this would be a window with a 'flashwindow' function that causes the background color of the window to change at regular intervals. This function could be declared private, and as such could only be called from other scripts and functions on the window or from events on controls on that window. Scripts on controls on a descendant of the window (i.e. a command button clicked script for a command button placed on a window inherited from this window) could not access this function.

To allow descendant classes to access the functions in an object, you would declare your function as *protected*. All the same rules apply as the private access level, but now we are going to be generous and share the functionality with our descendant classes.

In a strong OO application, you should have a substantial quantity of private and protected functions.

The other difference that you will find in an object level function is that you have access to all the same variables, properties and objects that the window event scripts do. You can directly access the window's instance variables, the attributes of a control on the window and so on. Calling functions on controls or on the object directly is not considered negative with regards to OO because the control and the function exist on the same class of object. That means these references are not coupling two independent classes together which violates the rules of OO.

8.2.3 External Functions

External functions allow you to integrate functions written in other languages like C, C++, MicroFocus COBOL and Object Pascal into your PowerBuilder applications. In fact, PowerBuilder external functions can access standard windows compliant .DLLs (Dynamic

8.2 Functioning with Functions   **227**

Link Libraries) written by any other language (as long as they have been declared with the standard pascal calling sequence).

There are three primary reasons why you might choose to incorporate external functions into your application:

- The functionality does not exist in native PowerScript (i.e. playing a .WAV file or connecting to an external device)

- The performance of a native language .DLL will exceed the performance that we can obtain out of PowerBuilder. For example, while working on a project with a large telecommunications firm, we needed to calculate the resistance of a standard copper telephone cable. The calculations were quite complex, and although they could be performed in PowerScript, writing them into a C .DLL would result in much faster execution. This was the solution we implemented.

- There are .DLL's already written which will provide the functionality that you require without you having to reinvent the wheel.

Like user defined functions, external functions can be either local or global in scope. Global external functions can be declared in any painter, but are stored in the application object. These functions can be called from anywhere in your application. Local external functions are declared in the painter for the object that you wish to define them for and can only be called by referencing that object first using the traditional 'dot' notation. Like user defined functions, local external functions can be given access levels of public, private or protected.

To declare an external function, you will select either **Global External Function…** or **Local External Function…** from the **Declare** menu item. That will open the window shown in Figure 8.18. The window appears the same for both global and external declarations with the exception of the title. The locally declared function will be stored as part of the definition of the object you are currently in whereas the global external will be stored as part of the application object for the current application.

Chapter 8: Advanced Development Concepts

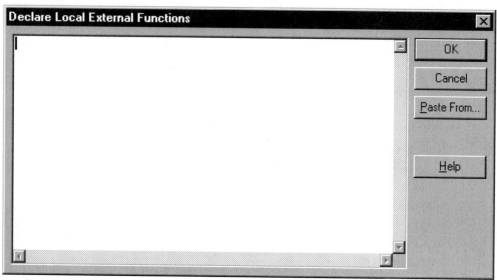

Figure 8.18 *The Declare Local External Functions allows you to declare local functions for the current object that are written outside of PowerBuilder. These functions are stored in a .DLL and could be written in C, C++, Object Pascal or another language.*

In this window, you must declare all the different components of the external function. The syntax is as follows:

{*access* - PUBLIC, PRIVATE or PROTECTED - only applicable for Local declarations} FUNCTION *return_type function_name* ({*{passed_by* - REF or empty} *argument1_datatype argument1_name, {passed by} argument2_datatype argument2_name, ...}* LIBRARY *library_name* {ALIAS FOR *extension_name*}

This may look a little complicated, but it really isn't once you get a handle on the different variables:

access   This is the access level for the function. If you don't declare this, it will assume it is public. Global external functions can only be public. Local external functions can be declared as public, private or protected. This argument is optional.

return_type   This is the data type of the value that the function will return to you.

function_name   This is the name of the function within the .DLL that you are accessing. If the function name in the .DLL is not a valid PowerBuilder name, you

8.2 Functioning with Functions   **229**

can use an alias for the function name. This requires appending the ALIAS FOR keywords at the end of the function (see below).

passed_by This argument is used to define each of the function arguments as being passed either by reference or by value. Many windows API calls utilize variables passed by reference. To indicate a variable passed by reference, enter REF, for all others leave this argument out.

argument_datatype This is the data type of the argument that you are passing into the function. There will be one of these for every argument that is being passed in.

argument_name This is the name of the argument that you are passing into the function. You will also need one of these for each argument that the function requires.

LIBRARY library_name This is the name of the .DLL that contains the function (enclosed in quotations as the data type is string). This .DLL must also be available in your executable environment. LIBRARY is a keyword and must be included before the library name.

ALIAS FOR extension_name This variable contains the name of the function within the .DLL. This is an optional argument and is only used if you want to use a different name as the function name to call this function, or if the name of the function is not a valid PowerBuilder name. The extension name must be passed within quotation marks (i.e. "sndPlaySndA"). ALIAS FOR are keywords that must precede the extension name variable. You can see the ALIAS for in use in the sample application contained on the companion CD.

An example of declaring a local external function might look like this:

```
PUBLIC FUNCTION uint GetModuleHandle(string ModuleName) LIBRARY "kernel.exe"
```

You call this function with the syntax

```
integer li_handle

// Determine if MS-Word is running
```

230 *Chapter 8: Advanced Development Concepts*

```
li_handle = THIS.GetModuleHandle("word.exe")

IF li_handle <> 0 THEN
     MessageBox("Found It!","Word is currently running.")
ELSE
     Run("word.exe")
END IF
```

This script uses the external function to determine if Microsoft Word is running already, and if not, it starts it. Two examples of using external functions follow this section, one can be used for playing wave (.WAV) files and the other can be used for altering the system menu on a window.

Developers Tip: Much of the documentation for third party .DLLs that you may want to integrate will describe the arguments in terms of C data types. Here is a conversion chart for these data types to standard PowerBuilder data types:

C Data Type	PB Data Type	Description
UNSIGNED	UINT	16 bit unsigned integer
LONG	LONG	32 bit unsigned integer
BYTE,CHAR	CHAR	8 bit unsigned character
BOOL	BOOLEAN	16 bit signed integer
WORD	UINT	16 bit unsigned integer
DWORD	ULONG	32 bit unsigned integer
LPSTR	STRING	32 bit far pointer to a char string
LPBYTE	STRING	32 bit far pointer to a char string
LPINT	STRING	32 bit far pointer to a character
LPWORD	STRING	32 bit far pointer to an unsigned integer
LPLONG	STRING	32 bit far pointer to a long
LPDWORD	STRING	32 bit far pointer to a double word
LPVOID	STRING	32 bit far pointer to any data type
HANDLE	UINT	16 bit handle to a window object
PSTR_NPSTR	not supported	

Along with external functions, we also have external subroutines. External subroutines use very similar syntax, but do not return a value. The syntax for an external subroutine is:

8.2 Functioning with Functions   231

{*access* - PUBLIC, PRIVATE or PROTECTED - only applicable for Local declarations} SUBROUTINE   *function_name* ({{*passed_by* - REF or empty} *argument1_datatype argument1_name*, {*passed by*} *argument2_datatype argument2_name*, ...} LIBRARY *library_name* {ALIAS FOR *extension_name*}

As you can see, the only difference is the keyword SUBROUTINE instead of FUNCTION and the elimination of the return_datatype parameter.

8.2.3.1 Example—Playing a Wave File

You might decide that you want to provide the ability to play sound bites to your user from time to time. We can use an external function to provide this functionality. I can recall one PowerBuilder application where the ancestor window played the sound effect of opening doors on Star Trek (that distinctive "shoop" sound) when the window opened and then played the sound of the same doors closing when you exited from the window.

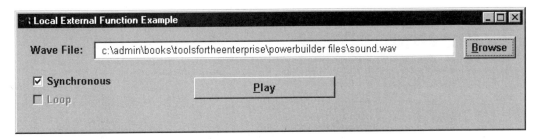

Figure 8.19 The Companion CD example application contains a window which will call a local external function to play a wave (.WAV) file.

To make this work, we need to declare two local external functions. You can follow this example along by examining the object w_local_external_function in the sample application that comes on the companion CD.

The declaration for these local external functions is as follows (the declaration shows both the 32 bit and 16 bit variations):

```
// This set of functions is declared for 32 bit operating environments.
// If you have a 16 bit environment, please comment out the lines below
// and uncomment the section labeled "16 bit local external functions"

FUNCTION boolean sndPlaySoundA(string SoundName, uint Flags)&
     LIBRARY "WINMM.DLL"
```

Chapter 8: Advanced Development Concepts

```
FUNCTION uint waveOutGetNumDevs () LIBRARY "WINMM.DLL"

//16 bit local external functions

//FUNCTION boolean sndPlaySound (string SoundName, uint Flags)&
        LIBRARY "mmsystem.dll"
//FUNCTION uint waveOutGetNumDevs () LIBRARY "mmsystem.dll"
```

The WaveOutGetNumDevs() function is used to determine if we have a valid device for playing .WAV files. If we have a valid device, it will return a number greater than zero. If no device exists, then it will return a zero.

The sndPlaySoundA() function actually passes the name of a wave file to an external API which takes care of the process of playing it. By setting the flags parameter, you can alter if it plays synchronously, asynchronously, loop the sound until you tell it to stop, and other options.

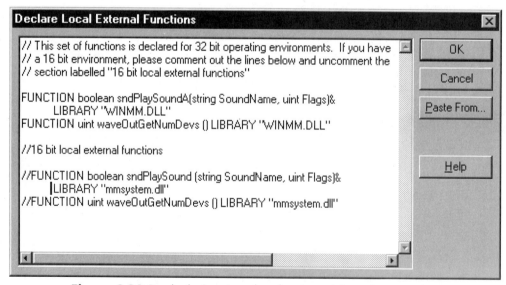

Figure 8.20 *By declaring two local external functions as they appear here, we are sound enabling our object.*

The names of these functions can be a little cryptic, so we can take advantage of the ALIAS FOR keyword to simplify our interface with the external functions. The new declaration looks like this:

8.2 Functioning with Functions   233

```
FUNCTION boolean PlayWave(string SoundName, uint Flags) &
     LIBRARY "WINMM.DLL" ALIAS FOR "sndPlaySoundA"
FUNCTION uint  GetWaveDevice() &
     LIBRARY "WINMM.DLL" ALIAS FOR "waveOutGetNumDevs"

//16 bit local external functions
//FUNCTION boolean  PlayWave(string SoundName, uint Flags) &
//     LIBRARY "mmsystem.dll" ALIAS FOR "sndPlaySound"
//FUNCTION uint GetWaveDevice()
//     LIBRARY "mmsystem.dll" ALIAS FOR "waveOutGetNumDevs"
```

The script we call in the Clicked event of our Play command button looks like this:

```
// Options for playing sound with the windows API.
// These values can be added together to achieve the desired
// combination.
// (i.e. asynchronous sound with looping would be 1+8 = 9)

//SND_SYNC     Value: 0 // play sound synchronously (default)
//SND_ASYNC     Value: 1 // play sound asynchronously
//SND_NODEFAULT Value: 2 // don't use default sound
//SND_MEMORY   Value: 4 // lpszSoundName (the first argument) points //
                    to a memory file
//SND_LOOP     Value: 8 // loop the sound until next sndPlaySoundA
//                                          function call
//SND_NOSTOP   Value:10 // don't stop any currently playing sound

uint lui_numdevs
integer li_options=0

// Set synchronous option
IF NOT cbx_sync.checked THEN li_options = li_options + 1
// Set Loop option
IF cbx_loop.checked THEN li_options = li_options + 8

SetPointer(Hourglass!)
lui_numdevs = GetWaveDevice()
IF lui_numdevs > 0 THEN
        PlayWave(sle_filename.text,li_options)
```

234 *Chapter 8: Advanced Development Concepts*

```
ELSE
        MessageBox("Wave Failure","Cannot play requested .WAV file."&
                    +"No device available.")
END IF
```

Now you can have fun adding sound to your PowerBuilder applications! (remember not to use sound as a primary means of communicating with the user as this would not be a good interface for people who are hearing impaired. Use sound purely as a secondary means of communications).

8.2.3.2 Things to Remember

If you are planning on rolling your application out across both 16 and 32 bit platforms, you will need to be careful. Most .DLLs that you might want to access are different in the 16 and 32 bit environments. You will need to keep separate versions of any objects that use external functions like that.

Remember that when rolling your application out to your end user, any .DLLs being accessed must be available in the Windows directory, the current directory or somewhere in the library search path. They will not be rolled into the .EXE that you are creating.

8.3 CALLING EVENTS AND FUNCTIONS FROM SCRIPTS

You have a choice in how you would like to call your functions and events within your scripts. In previous versions of PowerBuilder, we would call global functions simply by naming them:

```
f_check_sql_error(SQLCA)
```

and we could either Post or Trigger an event using the PostEvent() and TriggerEvent() functions such as:

```
w_employees.TriggerEvent(Clicked!)
```

or

```
dw_employees.PostEvent("ue_save")
```

8.3 Calling Events and Functions from Scripts 235

Triggering an event caused it to be executed immediately, whereas posting an event meant that it was placed in the queue to be processed after the current script was complete. You can still call your function and trigger or post your events with this syntax, however, for PowerBuilder 5.0 we have expanded functionality available to us, and in order to take advantage of it, we need to use the updated syntax.

We now have the capability of not only choosing between post and trigger for events, but now also for functions. The syntax has been standardized so that we can use the same format for both.

> {objectname.}{type - FUNCTION or EVENT}{call_type - STATIC or DYNAMIC}{when - TRIGGER or POST} method_name ({argument1, argument2, ...})

The components that make up this syntax are:

objectname This is the name for the object which the method (function or event) exists on. If this is a global function, then objectname would be excluded from the above syntax. If used, objectname must be followed by a period ("."). This is the dot notation separator.

type Contains a keyword which indicates if you are calling a FUNCTION or an EVENT. If you leave out this optional parameter, it will assume that you are calling a FUNCTION.

call_type By default, PowerBuilder will confirm the existence of the function or event you are calling and its correct syntax. In certain situations, such as using abstract classes of objects, you may want to access a function that does not exist in this object, but may exist in a descendant (this object is never instantiated, but its descendants are). To accomplish this, we must tell PowerBuilder not to check the syntax now, but to check it at runtime. We specify this by using the DYNAMIC key word here. After using this in your script, you will not get a compile error on the method, but you could trigger a runtime error. If you do not specify DYNAMIC, the alternative is STATIC, which is also the default if you do not specify a call type.

when Here is where you decide if you are going to TRIGGER or POST your method. Triggering the method will cause it to execute immediately,

236   *Chapter 8: Advanced Development Concepts*

whereas posting it will cause it to execute when the current script ends. The default if you do not specify a when keyword is to trigger the method.

method_name   The name of the function or event that you will to call. You can use either predefined PowerScript functions and events, or you can use user defined functions and events. The syntax is the same in all cases.

argumentn   (Note: arguments will match the declaration for the object method) The arguments that you are passing to the method. Both functions and events can receive arguments. Refer to the function reference guide or objects and controls manual for details on which arguments are required for the method you are using.

The functions and events within PowerBuilder are becoming more alike with each new release of the product. The *type*, *call_type* and *when* keywords above can be placed in any order and PowerBuilder will be able to understand, just be sure to place them between the dot and the method name.

Here are some examples of the method calling syntax in use.

8.3.1 Triggering an Event

Triggering an event will cause it to be executed immediately. This will cause the user defined event ue_print on the object w_employees to execute:

```
w_employees.EVENT STATIC TRIGGER ue_print("landscape",2)
```

Note that the keywords STATIC and TRIGGER did not need to be included as they would have defaulted if we had entered:

```
w_employees.EVENT ue_print("landscape",2)
```

The event ue_print is set up to accept two arguments. Due to this, we could not use the traditional syntax, TriggerEvent() to call this method as it does not support this type of argument passing.

8.3.2 POSTING AN EVENT

Posting an event will cause it to be placed in the queue of methods waiting to be executed for the current object. This method will run when its turn comes up. We will add a twist to this example, we are declaring this script on the ancestor object w_a_base which never gets instantiated. All the descendants that can print are descendants of w_a_print_base, a direct descentant of w_a_base. We decide to put the call to the print method in the ancestor w_a_base event though it only exists on the descendant.

THIS.EVENT DYNAMIC POST ue_print("landscape",2)

Remember that the keywords can be in any order. We could just as easily have entered:

THIS.DYNAMIC EVENT POST ue_print("landscape",2)

Traditional PostEvent() function syntax does not check for the existence of dynamic user defined events until runtime, but it will check for system defined events if you use enumerated data types to call them. For example:

THIS.PostEvent("ue_print")

would not check for the existence of ue_print until runtime, but

THIS.PostEvent(Clicked!)

will check for a clicked event immediately. Either way, the traditional syntax still could not be used due to the custom arguments being passed.

8.3.3 POSTING FUNCTIONS

For the first time, now you have the ability to make a function execute after the current script has finished running. You can also now define a function to be called dynamically, this means that the function does not need to exist on your current object. Prior to this, functions were always declared statically and if you only wanted to place a function in a descendant, you had to declare the function in the ancestor in order to provide a stub that would allow the function to compile.

238   *Chapter 8: Advanced Development Concepts*

You must use the new syntax to post a function. For example:

```
dw_dept.FUNCTION STATIC POST Retrieve()
```

or

```
dw_dept.FUNCTION DYNAMIC POST wf_update("COMMIT")
```

where wf_update() may not exist on this object, but will definitely exist on the descendant(s) which will use this method.

8.3.4 TRIGGERING FUNCTIONS

Triggering functions is the easiest of all four of these methods. You can use the traditional syntax such as

```
dw_dept.Retrieve()
```

which will cause the function to execute immediately and the function must exist at compile time in order for the above to be syntactically correct.

The same thing could be accomplished with the 5.0 syntax as follows:

```
dw_dept.FUNCTION Retrieve()
```

although using the FUNCTION keyword is redundant as this is the default. You can use the keywords in any order you choose. If I wanted to use a function called ChangeData that does not exist now, but would at runtime (through inheritance) I would call it from my script like:

```
dw_dept.DYNAMIC ChangeData()
```

8.4 IMPLEMENTING DRAG AND DROP

The Graphical User Interface (GUI) has revolutionized the way that people interact with computers in their day to day lives. It has enabled many non-technical people to have regular interactions with information systems. When the GUI revolution arose a number of years back, one of its primary differences was the ability to use the mouse to 'pick up' something and 'drop' it somewhere else. The term that came to describe this is known as *drag and drop*.

8.4.1 WHAT IS DRAG AND DROP?

The concept behind drag and drop is to allow the user to interact with the computer the way they would interact in the real world. When designing applications we call this a *real world metaphor*. An example of a real world metaphor that you are likely already familiar with would be to pick up something (perhaps a file from file manager, or an icon in your Windows 95 desktop) and drag it to a trash can icon (or 'Recycling Bin' in the environmentally conscious Windows 95). When you drop the object/file on the trash can, it deletes it. Just like throwing something into your trash bin in real life.

Another example of drag and drop in an application you are probably familiar with is the Windows 3.11 File Manager, or the Windows 95 Explorer. In these applications, you can copy and move files simply by dragging them and dropping them in their new locations.

8.4.2 HOW SHOULD DRAG AND DROP BE USED?

The end user of your system will initiate a drag and drop by selecting the object they wish to 'pick up' by pressing the left mouse button while the pointer is over the object and holding it down through the drag process. The mouse pointer should now change to an icon that indicates to the user that they have picked up the object. Now the user will move the mouse (still holding down the left mouse button) to the object where they wish to drop what they picked up. Releasing the left mouse button above the object the user wishes to 'drop' on triggers the appropriate action.

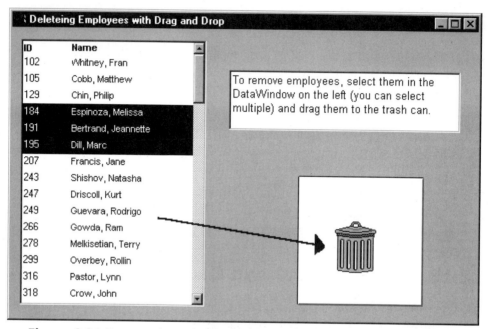

Figure 8.21 *Drag and Drop allows the user to interact with the system in a way that models the way they interact with the real world.*

When you perform the final act of drag and drop, the 'drop,' a variety of actions can occur. There are certain types of business processes to which this techniques lends itself well.

8.4.2.1 Copy and Move Objects or Data

Drag and drop is often used to copy or move selected items from one object into another. This is the type of process being modeled in the Windows Explorer. In a PowerBuilder application, we may have a window with two or more DataWindow objects and we might want to drag and drop rows between them. On the companion CD is a sample window with three DataWindow controls as shown in Figure 8.4.2.2.

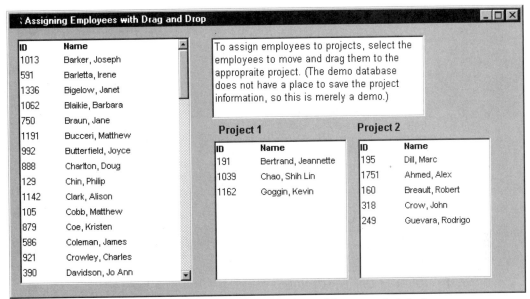

Figure 8.22 *Copying and moving objects and data is a common use for drag and drop.*

You can select personnel from any of the DataWindow controls and drag it to another. You can also select multiple people to move at one time. We will examine the details of these two samples later in this section.

8.4.2.2 Change Properties

Drag and drop is often implemented in situations that allow us to change the properties of the source object or data. On the companion CD there is a window that allows us to see the changing of data for an employee via drag and drop. This is the window pictured in Figure 8.23.

Chapter 8: Advanced Development Concepts

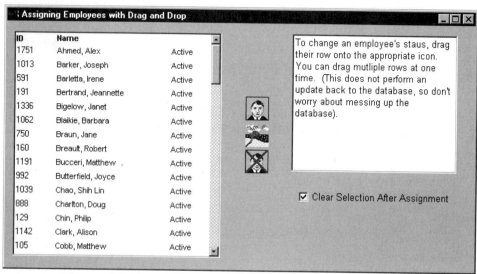

Figure 8.23 *Drag and drop can also be used to change the properties of an object or data.*

In this window we can select an employee, or multiple employees, and drag them onto the picture that represents their current status. This will allow us to perform a mass change of status for any grouping of employees.

8.4.2.3 Process Data

The drag and drop interface can be used to initiate processing on an object or a set of data. In the example in Figure 8.21, we use drag and drop to initiate the DeleteRow() process against any set of employees that we selected.

Another example of this would be taking a document in the Windows 95 desktop and dropping it onto the printer icon or the fax icon. The former would send the document to the printer, the latter to the fax machine. I have worked on an application where a completed order was scheduled for delivery by dragging the order onto a picture of a delivery truck.

8.4.3 How Does Drag and Drop Work?

In order to use drag and drop within your application, you must first identify a *source object* (the object that will be dragged) and a destination or *target object* (where the source object can be dropped). You may have many source and many target objects, but both must exist in order for drag and drop to work.

Figure 8.24 *To use drag and drop you must have at least one source object (to be dragged) and one target object (to be dropped upon).*

All PowerBuilder controls can be dragged with the exception of drawing objects which have no events (lines, ovals, rectangles, round rectangles). The reverse is also true, anything that can be dragged is also a valid target object. Objects can be dragged to any window or object within a PowerBuilder application, but you cannot drag an object to a non-PowerBuilder application (maybe in PowerBuilder 6.0?).

> **Developers Tip:** To obtain a list of objects that can be dragged, go to the Object Browser and select the System tab. Click on DragObject with the right mouse button and select *Show Hierarchy* from the popup menu. Then click again and select *Expand All*. All the objects that appear under DragObject are valid source and target objects. This includes any objects that you create as user objects or descendants of standard windows objects and controls.

8.4.4 The Drag and Drop Events

When an object is being dragged, it will cause certain events to fire in any valid target objects that it comes into contact with.

Chapter 8: Advanced Development Concepts

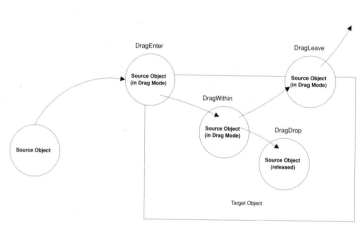

Events:

DragDrop—The source object is dropped on a target object. The left mouse button is released.

DragEnter—The center of the source object crosses over the border into the target object.

DragWithin—The source object is dragged within the border of the target object.

DragLeave—The center of the source object crosses over the border passing outside the target object.

Figure 8.25 *When an object is being dragged, it may initiate DragDrop, DragEnter, DragWithin and DragLeave events on valid target objects it comes into contact with.*

In Figure 8.25 you can see the different events that fire as we drag our source object. When the center of the source object passes over the border of a valid target object, a DragEnter event is triggered on the target object. If you continue dragging the source object inside the target object, a DragWithin event is triggered. If you drag the object all the way through the target object and out again, a DragLeave event is triggered as the center of the source object passes over the border of the target. The most important event that you will want to catch will be the DragDrop event which occurs when the source object is dropped on the target by releasing the left mouse button.

It is up to you to write the scripts for these events that will determine what action will occur when the object is dropped.

8.4 Implementing Drag and Drop **245**

8.4.5 DRAG PROPERTIES

All objects that can be dragged have two properties that relate to the way they appear and behave when they are being dragged:

- DragAuto—This is a Boolean value that determines whether you will be setting drag mode on in your script, of if you want PowerBuilder to do it for you.

- DragIcon—The icon that will display at the pointer for the source object currently being dragged.

8.4.6 DRAG MODE

When an object is being dragged, we say that the object is in *drag mode*. On any given source object we can set the DragAuto attribute to determine if PowerBuilder will automatically place a control into drag mode when a user clickes on it (DragAuto = TRUE), or if you must code a script that will start drag mode (DragAuto = FALSE). A DragAuto value of FALSE (which is the default) means that the drag mode must be initiated using the Drag() function in your script.

You may decide that you like DragAuto for some of your controls to be set to TRUE. As a warning, you need to remember that if DragAuto is TRUE, the clicked event on that object never gets triggered by the system. Instead the object is placed into drag mode. This means that for objects where we do want to deal with the clicked event, such as a DataWindow or a list box, we must use DragAuto = FALSE and manually initiate the drag mode.

246 Chapter 8: Advanced Development Concepts

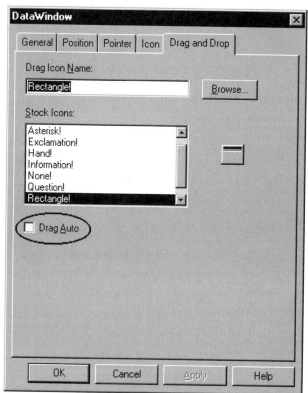

Figure 8.26 *The DragAuto property can be set on the Drag and Drop tab page of the Properties window for any valid source object.*

The DragAuto property can be set on the Drag and Drop tab page of the properties window for any valid source object. This is also where you will set the DragIcon property.

Developers Tip: Always make sure that you do not interfere with the normal behavior of an object or control when you implement drag and drop. For example, setting DragAuto to TRUE in a listbox would result in the user never being able to select an item from the listbox.

Using the Drag() Function

To initiate drag mode manually we will use a function called *Drag()*. This function can be used to both begin and end drag mode, although it is primarily used to begin drag mode and drag mode automatically ends when you drop the source object.

The syntax for the Drag() function is:

objectname.Drag(*dragstatus* - Begin!, End! or Cancel!)

The parameters that compose the syntax are:

objectname   This is the name of the object for which you want to change the drag mode.

Dragstatus   Specifies whether you want to begin, end or cancel drag mode. The values in this parameter are enumerated datatypes: Begin!, End! or Cancel!. Drag mode automatically ends when the user releases the left mouse button. For all but exceptional circumstances, the only drag status you will use is Begin!

So where do I code this function? It should be coded in some event that relates to the mouse, such as Clicked, DoubleClicked, MouseMove, LeftButtonUp and so on. If you code the function in an event which is not related to the mouse, for example, the open event of a window, then the user will be dragging the object without needing to hold down the left mouse button. In order to restore normal functioning of the mouse, the user will need to click on something to cancel the drag mode. This is not standard windows behavior.

Which event you will code the function in is dependent upon the precise functionality you require. The sample application on the companion CD demonstrates the difference between coding the Clicked event and coding the MouseMove or LeftButtonUp events. You can select the option to use one or the other, as indicated in Figure 8.27.

Chapter 8: Advanced Development Concepts

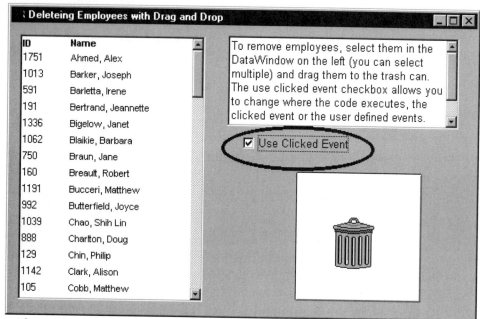

Figure 8.27 *In the sample application, you can choose whether you want to initiate drag mode in the clicked event, or in the user defined events, MouseMove and LeftButtonUp.*

If you use the LeftButtonUp and MouseMove events, the individual rows are not selected or deselected in the process of trying to begin drag mode. If you use the clicked event, they will be. The clicked event script requires less code, but I feel that using the combination of LeftButtonUp and MouseMove provides a better user interface. See section 8.4.8—Looking At The Code to see how the object from the companion CD functions.

The return value of the Drag() function will tell you if the control was successfully placed into drag mode (a return value of 1) or if it failed (a return value of -1). The two reasons that this function might fail are:

- You tried to put a control into drag mode when another control was already in drag mode. Only one control can be in drag mode at a time.

- You tried to cancel drag mode for a control that wasn't currently in drag mode.

8.4.7 SETTING THE DRAG ICON

When you drag an object in a PowerBuilder application, PowerBuilder will show an outline in the shape of the object as the dragged object. This is not always the most visually appealing way of indicating to the user that they are dragging an object. To use a more compact icon you can set the DragIcon property of a control to a custom icon that will appear in place of the standard mouse pointer.

An example of using a drag icon can be seen in the Windows 3.1 File Manager. When you select a file from the listbox, instead of seeing an outline of the entire listbox, you see an icon which shows and arrow and a sheet of paper (representing a file).

You can use the DragIcon attribute to provide a visual cue to the user as to when they can perform certain actions. For example, you can place the object into drag mode and set the drag icon to be a picture of the object (i.e. a file folder if you are moving a file). Then, when the user drags the file over a valid target object, you could use the DragEnter event to change the DragIcon attribute to a different icon (i.e. a round target). It is also useful for indicating areas where the user cannot drop this object by changing the icon to a "no.cur" indicating that dropping on that target is not valid.

Developers Tip: You can create your own icons and cursors using any drawing application that can create .ICO and .CUR files. The Watcom Image Editor which comes with PowerBuilder enterprise can create both of these types of files.

Developers Tip: PowerBuilder will automatically turn the drag icon into a no-drop icon whenever the user moves the pointer to any spot that is an invalid drop zone (such as outside the window or onto the control menu).

8.4.8 LOOKING AT THE CODE—W_DRAG_DROP

In the sample application on the companion CD there are three different drag and drop examples; w_drag_drop, w_drag_drop_2 and w_drag_drop_3. These windows all show the different variations of drag and drop discussed in the sections above.

The key events in w_drag_drop include events on the DataWindow control (se_mousemove and se_lbuttonup) and events on the picture button (dragdrop).

250   *Chapter 8: Advanced Development Concepts*

On the DataWindow control dw_emp_list we have a user defined event 'se_mousemove' which is linked to the windows message pbm_mousemove. This event contains:

```
IF flags = 1 THEN
        THIS.Drag(Begin!)
        ib_drag = TRUE
END IF
```

> **Note: 'flags' is an argument defined for the system event pbm_dwnlbuttonup. At the time of the development of the sample application, this functionality was not working. It is working in the final release. In the actual scripts for mouse move in the sample application you will see Message.WordParm for each instance of 'flags' above.**

This event checks the argument that is passed to the event (flags) to see if the left mouse button is being held down (flags = 1). If it is, it initiates drag mode on this control and sets the Boolean variable ib_drag to TRUE.

Also on the DataWindow control dw_emp_list we have a user defined event 'se_lbuttonup' which is linked to the windows message pbm_dwnlbuttonup. This event contains:

```
IF NOT ib_drag THEN
        THIS.SelectRow(row,NOT THIS.IsSelected(row))
ELSE
        //Set IB_DRAG to FALSE
        ib_drag = FALSE
END IF
```

> **Note: 'row' is an argument defined for the system event pbm_dwnlbuttonup. At the time of the development of the sample application, this functionality was not working. It is working in the final release. In the actual scripts for mouse move in the sample application you will see THIS.GetRow() for each instance of 'row' above.**

This event checks to see if the instance variable ib_drag is set to true, indicating that the control is currently in drag mode. If it is, then set the variable back to FALSE, resetting it for the next use. If the control is not in drag mode, then the script will select or deselect the current row as appropriate.

8.4 Implementing Drag and Drop   251

On the picture button 'pb_trash' we use the predefined system event 'dragdrop' to handle the process we initiate when the user drops the DataWindow control. This event contains:

```
// Declare local variables
long ll_delay, ll_time=12000, ll_selected_row=0
datawindow ldw_source

// Let's check to be sure that the source is really a datawindow
IF source.TypeOf() = DataWindow! THEN

        // Cast the variable into a DataWindow variable
        ldw_source = source

        ll_selected_row = ldw_source.GetSelectedRow(0)

        IF ll_selected_row = 0 THEN
                MessageBox("Nothing Selected",&
                        "No rows were selected to delete.")
                RETURN
        END IF


        DO UNTIL ll_selected_row = 0

                ll_selected_row = ldw_source.GetSelectedRow(0)
                IF ll_selected_row > 0 THEN
                        // We don't want to really discard any
                        // employees, so we'll just remove the rows from
                        // the primary buffer

                        ldw_source.RowsDiscard(ll_selected_row,&
                                ll_selected_row,Primary!)
                        // IF we really wanted to delete the rows, we
                        // would have coded:
                        // ldw_source.DeleteRow(ll_selected_row)
                END IF
        LOOP

// Animate the Icon, just for fun!
THIS.picturename = "Trash4.bmp"
FOR ll_delay = 1 to ll_time
```

252   *Chapter 8: Advanced Development Concepts*

```
      NEXT

      THIS.picturename = "Trash3.bmp"
      FOR ll_delay = 1 to ll_time
      NEXT

      THIS.picturename = "Trash2.bmp"
      FOR ll_delay = 1 to ll_time
      NEXT

      THIS.picturename = "Trash1.bmp"
END IF
```

We use the event argument 'source' to determine what object was dropped on us.

PB 4.0 to 5.0 Tip: The source event argument in the DragDrop event replaces the function DraggedObject() which can still be used in PowerBuilder 5.0

We execute the TypeOf() function on the source argument to determine what class of object the dropped object is. We should be sure that it is a DataWindow before we try to call any DataWindow functions against it.

Once we have confirmed that it is indeed a DataWindow, we cast the generic object 'source' into a specific variable we declared of the class DataWindow (ldw_source).

Now we can begin executing DataWindow control functions against the dropped object. We use the GetSelectedRow() function to determine the first selected row in the source object. If there are no selected rows, we inform the user that they must select rows in order for us to initiate processing. If there are rows selected, we loop through all the selected rows discarding them one by one. If this was a production application, we would be using the DeleteRow() function to initiate the deletion of the rows from the primary buffer and eventually from the database. Instead, we use the RowsDiscard() function to remove them from the buffer without affecting the underlying database.

After completing this, we add in a little icon animation for fun. We show a happy face being placed into the trash can!

Developers Tip: For a more sophisticated DragDrop event where you want to perform different functionality depending on which type of control was dropped on the target you can use the TypeOf() or ClassName() functions embedded inside a CHOOSE CASE flow of control statement as in the following example:

```
// Declare local variables for each class of object involved
SingleLineEdit lsle_dragged
DataWindow ldw_dragged

CHOOSE CASE source.TypeOf()
        CASE SingleLineEdit!
                // Cast the generic object 'source' into
                // its appropriate class variable
                lsle_dragged = source

                // Clear the text out of the SLE
                lsle_dragged.text = ""

        CASE DataWindow!
                // Cast the generic objects source into a
                // DataWindow class variable
                ldw_dragged = source

                // Delete the current row from the DataWindow
                ldw_dragged.DeleteRow(0)
END CHOOSE
```

8.5 SUMMARY

Using these advanced techniques you can go beyond the skills of the beginner and take advantage of the flexibility and versatility of the PowerBuilder environment. Don't be afraid to experiment and push the limits of what you think is possible. That is how you will move from being an intermediate programmer to becoming an expert.

CHAPTER 9

DataWindow Components

A critical part of mastering PowerBuilder is a complete understanding of all the component parts of a DataWindow and the role they play when you are developing applications. In this chapter we will look closer at working with the DataWindow buffers, controlling the updating of DataWindows and how to use the status flags on the rows and columns.

At the end of this chapter we will also take a look at the DataStore and how you can use it in your applications.

9.1 BUFFERS

Behind the scenes of every DataWindow object are a number of buffers that store and manage the data that the DataWindow is responsible for. Four buffers form the foundation of everything that the DataWindow does. These buffers are the primary, filter, delete and original.

Chapter 9: DataWindow Components

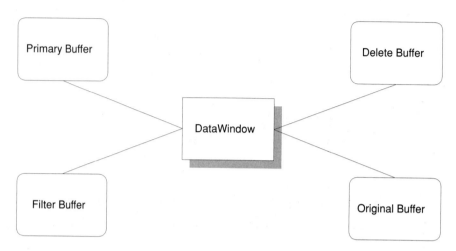

Figure 9.1 *The DataWindow buffers store and manage all the data in the DataWindow.*

9.1.1 PRIMARY

The primary buffer is the one that you will interact with most often. This buffer contains all the currently active data. Active data is defined as data which has not been deleted or filtered out. When the user sees data in a DataWindow control in an application, they are looking at the data that is in the primary buffer.

Data is placed into the primary buffer primarily through the Retrieve() and InsertRow() functions although other functions can also move data into this buffer such as RowsCopy(), RowsMove() and ImportFile().

9.1.2 FILTER

The filter buffer contains data that has been filtered out of the primary buffer though the filter expression of the DataWindow. The filter expression on a DataWindow behaves like a client based WHERE clause that only allows the rows that meet certain criteria to stay in the primary buffer.

9.1.3 DELETE

This buffer contains rows that have been deleted from the primary buffer using the DeleteRow() function, but have not yet been deleted from the database. You can think of the delete buffer as a temporary holding area where rows awaiting deletion are gathered until an Update() function is called. Data could also be placed into this buffer through the RowsMove() function.

9.1.4 ORIGINAL

The original buffer contains a snapshot of all the data values before they were changed. This information is critical to allow PowerBuilder to build the SQL statement where clauses to perform updates against the database. The original buffer is updated when data is first retrieved and also upon a successful DataWindow update.

9.2 MANIPULATING DATA STORED IN BUFFERS

Whenever you are manipulating data in a DataWindow you are effectively working with the buffers. When the user types new data into the edit control and presses the tab key, they are trying to insert data into the primary buffer.

In section 7.5.3.2—Direct Manipulation of Data we examine in detail how we use the new direct DataWindow manipulation to access and manipulate data from the buffers. In this section, we will examine other functions that are available for moving data around in the buffers.

9.2.1 COPYING DATA

Along with the direct manipulation of data from buffer to buffer, we can use the RowsMove(), RowsCopy() and RowsDiscard() functions to shift data around in our buffers.

9.2.1.1 RowsMove()

The RowsMove() function will take a complete set of rows from a specific buffer on one DataWindow and will move them into another buffer on the same DataWindow or onto any

258   *Chapter 9: DataWindow Components*

buffer from another DataWindow with a matching result set. This can be used to move data between DataWindow objects, DataStores and child DataWindows (child DataWindows can have rows moved from them, but cannot have rows moved into them).

When you move rows from one DataWindow to another, the row status (see section 9.3.3 Status Flags below for more details on row status) is changed to NewModified! This will result in the rows being INSERTed into the database table that is updateable for the target DataWindow. When you move rows between buffers within a single DataWindow, PowerBuilder will change the row status as applicable. For example, if I move rows from the primary buffer to the deleted buffer they will be marked for deletion. Doing the reverse would be effectively performing an 'undelete' as the status of the rows in the primary buffer would be returned to NotModified!

The most common uses in production applications for RowsMove() is to perform a mass deletion or to provide 'undelete' functionality.

The syntax for RowsMove() is:

```
dw_control.RowsMove(start_row, end_row, move_from_buffer, dw_target,&
insert_before_row, insert_into_buffer)
```

where

start_row   the first row to move from the source DataWindow control

end_row   the last row to move from the source DataWindow control

move_from_buffer the buffer in the source DataWindow where the rows will be moved from. This is an enumerated data type with possible values of Primary!, Filter! or Delete!

dw_target   the DataWindow control that contains the buffer that will be copied into. This cannot be a child DataWindow.

insert_before_row the row number in the target DataWindow that you want to insert before. A number greater than the number of rows in the target will result in the rows being appended to the end of the selected buffer.

insert_into_buffer the buffer in the target DataWindow into which you want to insert the rows from the source DataWindow. This, like the move from buffer, is an enumerated data type with the same values.

9.2.1.2 RowsCopy()

The RowsCopy() function is almost identical to the RowsMove() function except that rows are not removed from the source DataWindow buffer. This function is particularly useful for copying existing rows of data into the same buffer with a new row status so that they can be modified by the user. This has been used in many production applications and is often referred to as a 'New Using' function. It allows the user to use existing data as a template for new data.

This function can also be used to copy a range of rows to a second temporary DataWindow where they can be printed and then discarded.

The syntax is identical to the RowsMove() function except that we use the RowsCopy() function instead. Please refer to the previous section for descriptions of the function arguments.

9.2.1.3 RowsDiscard()

The RowsDiscard() function allows you to take a row or range of rows from a DataWindow buffer and wipe them out. The effect of this will depend on which buffer you are removing the data from.

If you remove rows from the primary or filter buffer any updates that have not been saved will be lost. These rows are not removed from the database and could be brought back by issuing another retrieve function. The user will see rows disappear from the primary buffer because they are part of the visible data, but rows that are discarded from the filter buffer will not affect the users current view of the data.

If you remove rows from the delete buffer then these rows will not actually be deleted in the database.

The syntax for the RowsDiscard() function is:

dwcontrol.RowsDiscard (start_row, end_row, delete_from_buffer)

The arguments are the same as those from the RowsMove() section above. In an effort to keep the redundant information in this book to a minimum, please refer to that section for descriptions of arguments you are unsure of.

9.2.1.4 Copying Data Directly to a User Object

With the growing usage of non-visual objects to provide services and business rule functions to our applications, we now have an easy way to transfer data from a DataWindow buffer directly into a non-visual (custom class) user object.

To do this you must declare instance variables in the custom class object in the same order and of the same data type as the column data being copied in. For example, if we want to copy a row of data from our bonus table into our nvo_bonus object we would need instance variable declarations like those shown in Figure 9.2.

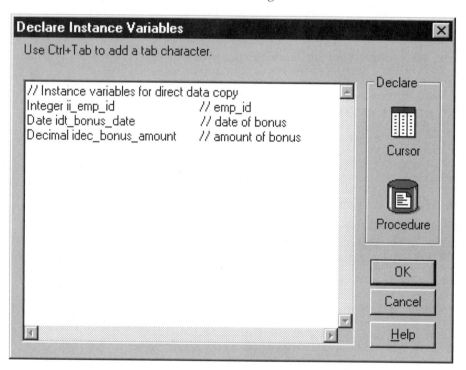

Figure 9.2 *Instance variables in nvo_bonus to allow us to move data directly into the non-visual object.*

To initiate the move of the current row of data from our bonus list DataWindow into our business object we would use the script:

```
invo_bonus = dw_bonus_list.Object.Data[dw_bonus.GetRow()]
```

9.3 Updating DataWindows **261**

These variables are now populated and ready for use in our custom class business object invo_bonus.

9.3 UPDATING DATAWINDOWS

By now you should be familiar with basic usage of the Update() function in PowerBuilder and how to integrate transaction management with COMMIT and ROLLBACK into your applications. In this section we are going to examine some of the more advanced techniques that are involved in performing DataWindow updating including where clause options, the ReselectRow() function, handling autoincrement (identity) columns, coordinating updates between multiple DataWindows and how to use status flags to update multiple tables from a single DataWindow.

9.3.1 ADVANCED UPDATING

To be able to fine tune your DataWindow updating you must be familiar with the where clause options, the ReselectRow() function and how to deal with columns that automatically increment themselves to provide each row of data with a unique identity.

9.3.1.1 Where Clause Options

When we use the Update() function we are taking advantage of the PowerBuilder feature that automatically generates our INSERT, UPDATE and DELETE SQL statements and sends them to the database. To generate these statements, PowerBuilder follows a set of rules. We can alter these rules to control exactly how PowerBuilder puts these statements together. This is accomplished through the Specify Update Properties dialog window shown in Figure 9.3.

Chapter 9: DataWindow Components

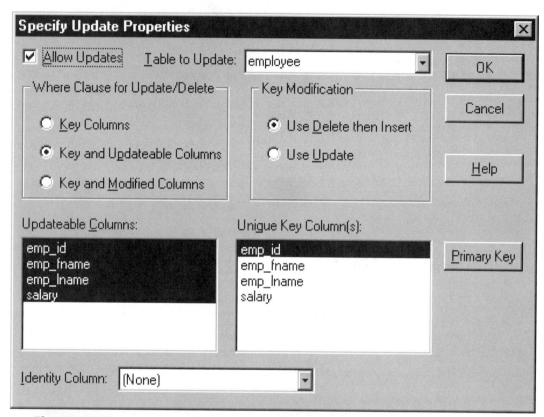

Figure 9.3 *We can control how PowerBuilder generates SQL statements in our application through the Specify Update Properties dialog window.*

In this window we can specify if the DataWindow is updateable at all by selecting the Allow Updates checkbox. By default DataWindows can only update a single table (for a multiple table update process see section 9.3.3.2 later in this chapter). The Table to Update drop down listbox shows the table that is set as the updateable table.

All the columns in the DataWindow are listed in the Updateable Columns listbox. All the columns that you will include in your SQL statement (if appropriate) should be selected. Any columns that are not selected will never be updated in the database even if the user changes them in the DataWindow.

In the Unique Key Column(s) listbox you select the columns in the DataWindow that will uniquely identify one row from another. The vast majority of the time this will be the primary key (which can be automatically selected by pressing the Primary Key command button). The only instances in production where I have had values defined here that were different from the primary key for the table was when I was going to update multiple tables from this DataWindow (which we discuss later).

The Key Modification groupbox allows you to specify what kind of SQL statement that you want PowerBuilder to generate when the user modifies the key columns in a DataWindow. The default option is to have PowerBuilder generate a DELETE statement to remove the initial row and then to perform an INSERT of a new row with the new key. This could have implications if dependent records exist for the row being modified. Depending on how your database is set to handle this, the dependent records could be deleted, updated or orphaned.

The second option for Key Modification is to Use Update. This means that PowerBuilder will generate an UPDATE SQL statement when the user modifies a key value. Which option is appropriate will depend on how you have your referential integrity set up in your database. Your DBA should be able to inform you which option is correct to use.

The final (and most complex) attribute that you can control is how you want PowerBuilder to generate the WHERE clause for the SQL statements it builds. This choice will have some serious impacts on your concurrency and data integrity issues. There are three options; Key Columns, Key and Updateable Columns or Key and Modified Columns. We will look at the positive and negative aspects of each. Note that these example are assuming a minimum of interference from the server database. Some server databases will take control of this aspect of the transaction and make your decision easy.

9.3.1.1.1 Key Columns

With this option, PowerBuilder will use only the columns that you have specified as key columns to uniquely identify a row.

Let's look at an example. We have two users who are going to access our database, User 1 and User 2.

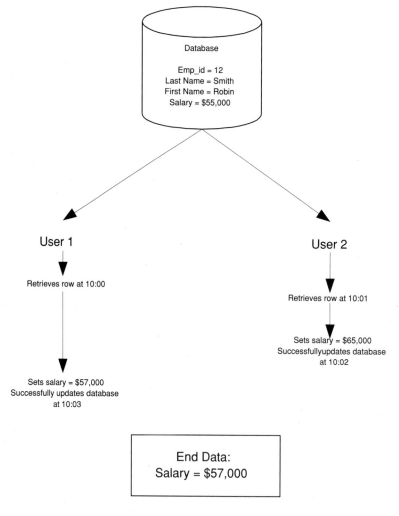

Figure 9.4 Key Updates scenario.

9.3 Updating DataWindows   **265**

User 1 retrieves the row of data (without locking) from the database at 10:00. User 2 retrieves the same row of data at 10:01. User 2 makes a change to the employee's salary, giving them a nice big raise. The SQL statement looks like:

UPDATE employee SET salary = 65000.00 WHERE emp_id = 12

User 2 saves the data to the database successfully. User 1, unaware of what user 2 has done, changes the employee's salary to a small raise and then updates the database at 10:03. This SQL statement looks like:

UPDATE employee SET salary = 57000.00 WHERE emp_id = 12

This statement is also successful as it does not check to see if the data has changed since it was retrieved. The net result is that User 1 has overwritten the work done by user 2 and neither of them knows it!

This option works satisfactorily when you have low concurrency and strict locking in your database, but for high concurrent access systems, this option could result in lost data!

9.3.1.1.2 Key and Updateable Columns

With this option PowerBuilder will build a WHERE clause that includes the key value for the row and all the columns that could be updated in this DataWindow (based upon their original values as stored in the original buffer).

Using our same example from above we can see that the update of User 1 is rejected because the salary has changed.

Chapter 9: DataWindow Components

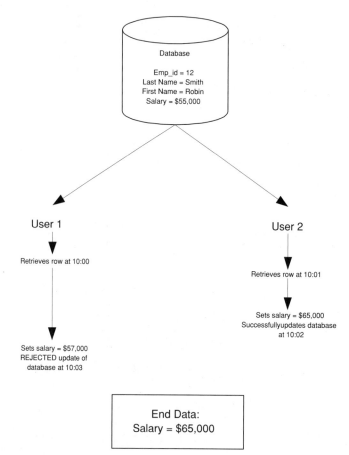

Figure 9.5 *Key and Updateable Columns option would cause the update of User 1 to fail.*

The SQL that is generated by User 2 is:

UPDATE employee **SET** salary = 65000.00 **WHERE** emp_id = 12 **AND** last_name = 'Smith' **AND** first_name = 'Robin' **AND** salary = 55000.00

The SQL that is generated for User 1 is:

UPDATE employee **SET** salary = 57000.00 **WHERE** emp_id = 12 **AND** last_name = 'Smith' **AND** first_name = 'Robin' **AND** salary = 55000.00

This SQL fails because the salary is no longer equal to $55,000.00.

This option will generally ensure the most consistent data in your database. For that reason alone, it is usually my preferred approach. There may be possible update situations that are logically acceptable that could be rejected with this approach. Consider the example in Figure 9.6.

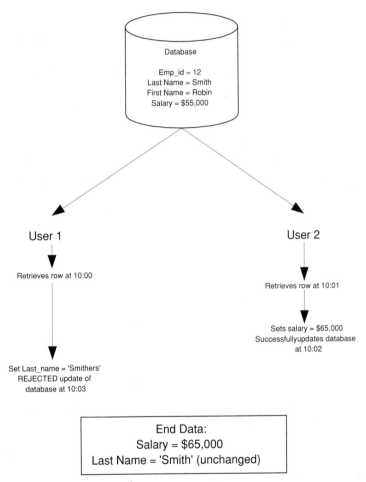

Figure 9.6 *Even though the two users are updating different unrelated data, User 1 will have their update rejected anyway.*

In this example, User 2 updates the employee's salary and User 1 wants to update the employee's name. User 2 succeeds, but User 1 is rejected even though the data being changed is not interdependent.

The benefit here is maximized data consistency, but you may have user transactions that are rejected even though they are logically valid.

9.3.1.1.3 Key and Modified Columns

The final option, Key and Modified Columns, will have PowerBuilder generate a SQL statement that includes the key value and any columns that the user has modified in the WHERE clause. In our example scenario if User 1 tries to update the salary column after User 2 has changed it, the statement would fail. Salary was modified by both, so it was included in the WHERE clause for both.

If we look at the second example where User 2 is changing the salary and User 1 is changing the last name, then our DataWindow would now behave as illustrated in Figure 9.7.

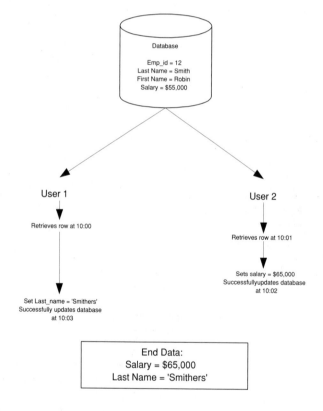

Figure 9.7 *Using Key and Modified Columns as the WHERE clause, both user updates are successful.*

User 2 sends an update statement to the database like:

> UPDATE employee SET salary = 65000.00 WHERE emp_id = 12 AND salary = 55000.00

This update is successful. Then User 1 sends a SQL statement with:

> UPDATE employee SET last_name = 'Smithers' WHERE emp_id = 12 AND last_name = 'Smith'

Both updates would succeed and neither user has interrupted the other. This may seem at first glance to be an ideal solution, but it has one severe limitation. When you have columns with cross column dependencies you can end up with inconsistent data. Let's look at the example in Figure 9.8.

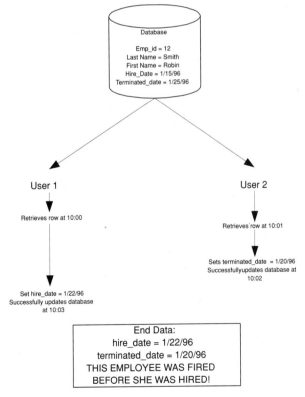

Figure 9.8 *Both updates succeed and we end up with illogical data in our database.*

270   *Chapter 9: DataWindow Components*

In this example, both users make updates that appear valid from their point of view, but when combined the resulting data is illogical. If your database supports triggers and rules this type of inconsistency can be avoided, but from a client perspective this is definitely unacceptable.

9.3.1.2 ReselectRow() Function

If a user attempts to update the database but has their transaction rejected because the data in the database has changed between their retrieve and their update you can use the ReselectRow() function to retrieve the updated data for just that row in the database leaving the rest of the DataWindow buffers intact.

In order to use this function, you must use a database that supports timestamps and the timestamp column must be included in your result set.

The syntax for the ReselectRow() function is:

```
dw_control.ReselectRow(row_number)
```

where

row_number   is the row that you want to reselect the current data for. This can be obtained in the DBError event of a DataWindow control. In this event the *row* argument will tell you which row caused the error.

If the row in the database was deleted by another user or the function was unable to obtain the updated row information this function will return a -1.

9.3.1.3 Autoincrement Columns

Some databases (including Sybase SQLAnywhere) allow you to create columns in your tables that are defined as 'autoincrement.' In these columns the database will automatically generate a unique value for all new rows that are inserted. Autoincrement columns are also known as identity columns and sequences.

PowerBuilder will expect you to specify a key for a DataWindow object if you intend on allowing the object to perform updates. If the key is an autoincrement column this can pose some problems. With autoincrement columns, you cannot include these columns in your INSERT SQL statement, but they must be part of the result set you request from the database. In PowerBuilder 5.0 we can identify autoincrement columns by specifying the column for the updateable table in the Identity Column field in the Specify Update Properties dialog window (refer to Figure 9.3). A table can only have one autoincrement column so only one field is used.

Specifying the autoincrement column will also cause PowerBuilder to refresh the buffer and display the autoincrement value for the newly inserted row after a successful update.

Developers Tip: Although you must include the autoincrement column in your result set for the DataWindow, it does not necessarily have to be shown to the user. If it is shown to the user be sure to identify it as a read only column and protect it from user input.

9.3.2 STATUS FLAGS

As your user works with the data in the DataWindow buffers PowerBuilder assigns flags to the different rows and columns where the user has made changes. There is a single flag on each row. There are four possible row statuses and they are represented by enumerated data types:

New! indicates that the row has just been inserted, but that the user has not yet added any data data to this row. When an Update() function is issued, rows with a status of New! will be ignored.

NewModified! indicates that this is a new row and the user has added data for at least one column in the row. When an Update() function is issued this row will result in an INSERT statement being passed to the database.

NotModified! indicates that this row was retrieved from the database and the user has not modified any of the rows. This row will be skipped in an Update() situation.

DataModified! indicates that this row was retrieved from the database and the user had made modifications to at least one column within the row. When an Update() function is called, this row will result in an UPDATE statement being passed to the database.

The flag on the row identifies to PowerBuilder what rows need to be updated and what kind of statement should be used. PowerBuilder still needs to know which columns in the DataWindow should be included. To this end we also have update flags attached to each column. There is a separate flag for each column of data. These flags have two possible values:

NotModified! indicates to PowerBuilder that this column has nothing new to report and should not be included in any SQL statement being generated.

DataModified! tells PowerBuilder that the user has changed the value in this column and PowerBuilder should build this column into any SQL statement being generated.

Upon a successful Update() function call, all the flags in the buffer are reset and the process begins anew. In a simple update situation, this default behavior is quite acceptable, but in our more complex updating this can cause problems. We will examine some complex updates in the following units.

9.3.2.1 Examining and Changing Status Flags

You can programmatically examine and alter the status flags on a row or column in your DataWindow. You can use this data for a variety of functions. One place that I like to take advantage of this functionality is to define an expression in the DataWindow that will show the user any data in the DataWindow that has not been saved. You can do this by changing the background color of the row. By clicking with the right mouse button on the 'Detail' separator line in the DataWindow painter (the gray bar that you drag up and down to change the size of the detail band) we open up the Properties page dialog for the band. On the Expressions tab we set up an expression like the one in Figure 9.9.

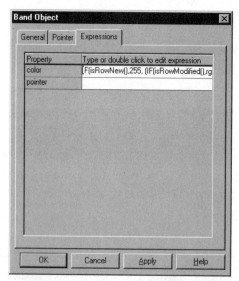

Figure 9.9 *We can use the status flags to define an expression for our DataWindow that will change the color of a row based upon its status.*

The expression that we would enter is:

`IF(isRowNew(),255, (IF(isRowModified(),rgb(0,0,255),rgb(255,255,255))))`

We can also access the status of a row in our scripts using the GetItemStatus() function. The syntax for this function is:

`dw_control.GetItemStatus ( row, column, buffer )`

where

row   is the row number you want the status for

column   is the column that you want the status for. A column value of 0 would return the status for the row. You can use either column number or column name.

buffer   is an enumerated data type specifying which buffer you are getting the item status from. The valid options are Primary!, Filter! or Delete!

The return value for this function is an enumerated data type called dwItemStatus which would evaluate to one of the enumerated data types specified in the valid status types in section 9.3.2.

9.3.2.2 Coordinating Multiple DataWindow Updates

Although the bulk of your DataWindow updates will involve only one DataWindow, you will be faced with a number of situations where you will have two or more DataWindows that must be updated together within the same logical unit of work.

The natural tendency would be to update the first DataWindow and check the return code, update the second DataWindow and check the return code and if they were both successful, commit the transaction to the database. Let's look at an example that will book a ticket for a customer on an airline by recording the ticket in the dw_ticket_issued DataWindow and reserve a seat for them in the dw_seat_res DataWindow.

```
// Update the new ticket and seat selection
IF dw_ticket_issued.Update() = 1 THEN
        // Ticket Update successful, now update the seat selection
        IF dw_seat_res.Update() = 1 THEN
```

```
                    // Both updates successful, commit changes to database
                    COMMIT USING SQLCA;
            ELSE
                    // Seat selection failed, rollback transaction
                    ROLLBACK USING SQLCA;
            END IF
      ELSE
            // Ticket update failed, rollback transaction
            ROLLBACK USING SQLCA;
      END IF
```

This works fine as long as you don't encounter any errors. If the update of the ticket table fails then the transaction rolls back and everything is fine. The user can correct the error and try again. If the seat selection update fails, then we have a different situation.

The ticket DataWindow updates successfully and PowerBuilder clears all the update flags, thinking that everything is fine. The seat selection DataWindow then tries to update and fails. This failure causes a rollback of both the seat selection and the ticket updates. The update flags in the seat selection DataWindow are maintained because that is the DataWindow that failed, but the ticket DataWindow has cleared its flags. Now if the user corrects their error and tries to execute the update again, the DataWindow is out of sync with the database and no changes will be sent to the ticket table. This second attempt will fail.

The obvious solution is that we need to stop PowerBuilder from automatically clearing the update flags and we will manually clear them when we are sure that the transaction has committed successfully.

To accomplish this, we have the ability to pass arguments with the Update() function to alter PowerBuilder's default behavior. The full syntax for the Update() function is:

```
dw_control.Update( accept_text, reset_flags)
```

where

accept_text   this argument controls if PowerBuilder will perform an accept text, validating any data in the edit control and passing it into the primary buffer before executing the update. If the data in the control does not pass validation, the update will abort. The default for this argument is TRUE.

reset_flags   this argument controls whether PowerBuilder will automatically reset the update flags upon a successful update. The default for this argument is true.

To take manual control of the flags we need to use the following syntax for our Update() function:

```
dw_control.Update(TRUE, FALSE)
```

If we look at our previous example, can directly substitute this version of the Update() function for the ones that we were using. Now that we have relieved PowerBuilder of the burden of worrying about the update flags, that task now falls upon our shoulders. If the updates are successful we must issue the **ResetUpdate()** function against all the DataWindows involved. The function must be called for each DataWindow individually using the syntax:

```
dw_control.ResetUpdate()
```

with no arguments.

Our example from earlier would now look like:

```
// Update the new ticket and seat selection
IF dw_ticket_issued.Update(TRUE, FALSE) = 1 THEN
        // Ticket Update successful, now update the seat selection
        IF dw_seat_res.Update(TRUE, FALSE) = 1 THEN
                // Both updates successful, commit changes to database
                COMMIT USING SQLCA;
                IF SQLCA.SQLCode = 0 THEN
                        // Successful commit
                        dw_ticket_issued.ResetUpdate()
                        dw_seat_res.ResetUpdate()
                ELSE
                        // Commit failed, call error handler
                        ROLLBACK USING SQLCA;
                        {insert your error handling code here}
                        // do not reset flags
                END IF
        ELSE
                // Seat selection failed, rollback transaction
                ROLLBACK USING SQLCA;
```

```
            END IF
    ELSE
            // Ticket update failed, rollback transaction
            ROLLBACK USING SQLCA;
    END IF
```

Now if the update encounters errors at any point, the updates will stop, the database will be rolled back to its previous state, and because the update flags are still in place, the user can retry the update after correcting the error.

9.3.2.3 Using Status Flags to Update Multiple Tables from One DataWindow

If I was to try and estimate the ratio of different types of DataWindow updates in an 'average' application, I would say that around 80% of your DataWindows will be simple single DataWindow updates. Another 19% would be coordinated DataWindow updates involving two or more DataWindows. The remaining 1% (or less) would be single DataWindows that, when updated, need to update data in two or more tables on the Database. It is quite rare that I run into this situation, but knowing how to handle it has been has been invaluable on at least a few projects.

Let's examine the hypothetical situation where an employee table is joined to an address table on a one to one basis. We want to see the emp_id, emp_fname and emp_lname columns from the employee table. In our DataWindow, these will be joined to the address table which has an address_id and address_description.

Figure 9.10 *The data model for our example.*

9.3 Updating DataWindows 277

Our DataWindow will consist of a joined set of columns. The select statement would be:

```
SELECT employee.emp_id, employee.emp_lname, employee.emp_fname,
        address.address_id, address.address_description
FROM    employee, address
WHERE employee.address_id = address.address_id
```

We will set up the DataWindow to update the employee table (remember, the DataWindow can only be set to update a single table in the DataWindow painter). We will update the DataWindow, stopping PowerBuilder from resetting the update flags. We can then point the DataWindow towards the address table using Modify() functions, or through direct manipulation. Then you adjust the flags that indicate which columns are updateable, set the key columns and reissue the update. This time, if the update is successful, we will commit and clear the update flags.

The script to do all this would appear like:

```
// Step 1: Update the employee table
IF dw_data.Update(TRUE,FALSE) = 1 THEN
        // Update of the employee table was successful
        // Now we need to alter the characteristics of the columns
        // Step 2: Stop the employee columns from updating.
        dw_data.Object.employee_emp_id.Update = 'No'
        dw_data.Object.employee_emp_lname.Update = 'No'
        dw_data.Object.employee_emp_fname.Update = 'No'
        dw_data.Object.employee_emp_id.Key = 'No'

        // Step 3: Change the updateable table to address
        dw_data.Object.DataWindow.Table.UpdateTable = 'address'

        // Step 4:  Enable updating of address data
        dw_data.Object.address_address_id.Update = 'Yes'
        dw_data.Object.address_address_description.Update = 'Yes'
        dw_data.Object.address_address_id.Key = 'Yes'

        // Step 5:  Update the address table
        IF dw_data.Update(TRUE,FALSE) = 1 THEN
                // Update was successful
                COMMIT USING SQLCA;
                IF SQLCA.SQLCode = 0 THEN
```

Chapter 9: DataWindow Components

```
                                    // Successful commit
                                    dw_data.ResetUpdate()
                        ELSE

                                    // Commit failed, call error handler
                                    ROLLBACK USING SQLCA;
                                    {insert your error handling code here}
                                    // do not reset flags
                        END IF
      ELSE

                        // Update failed, call error handler
                                    ROLLBACK USING SQLCA;
                                    {insert your error handling code here}
                                    // do not reset flags
                        END IF
      ELSE

                        // Update failed, call error handler
                        ROLLBACK USING SQLCA;
                        {insert your error handling code here}
                        // do not reset flags
      END IF

      // Step 6:  Set all the DataWindow characteristics back to the way
      // they were when we started.
      // Enable the updating of employee data
      dw_data.Object.employee_emp_id.Update = 'Yes'
      dw_data.Object.employee_emp_lname.Update = 'Yes'
      dw_data.Object.employee_emp_fname.Update = 'Yes'
      dw_data.Object.employee_emp_id.Key = 'Yes'

      // Change the updateable table to employee
      dw_data.Object.DataWindow.Table.UpdateTable = 'employee'

      // Disable updating of address data
      dw_data.Object.address_address_id.Update = 'No'
      dw_data.Object.address_address_description.Update = 'No'
      dw_data.Object.address_address_id.Key = 'No'
```

9.3.2.4 Using Status Flags to Create Templates

Another useful way of using the status flags in your applications is to use existing data as a template for user input. I have been involved in many applications where the users have indicated that most of the data that they enter is very similar to some data that they have entered previously. They want to identify the row to use as a template and then just change the parts that are different.

To do this, retrieve the row that is being used as a template. Use the SetItemStatus() function to change the status from NotModified! To New!. The syntax for this would appear as follows:

dw_control.SetItemStatus(row, column, buffer, new_status)

where

row is the row number that you want to alter. For our example, this would be the retrieved row.

column is the number of the column whose status you want to alter. In our example we want to change the row status so we would use a column value of 0.

buffer is a enumerated data type with the identity of the buffer that you wish to change status in. Valid values are Primary!, Filter! and Delete!.

new_status this is an enumerated data type indicating the new status that you wish to change the item to.

For our example, the syntax would be:

dw_control.SetItemStatus(1,0,Primary!,New!)

You would then need to alter the key values programmatically, or blank them out and have the user enter them as appropriate. As soon as the user makes any changes to the row (or you do with the SetItem() function) the row status will change to NewModified! and will result in an INSERT statement being generated instead of an UPDATE statement.

9.4 INTRODUCING DATASTORES

In previous versions of PowerBuilder it was very common for developers to use DataWindows in their applications that spent their entire life hidden. We were using these DataWindows as places to store and manipulate data, we never required any of the front end functionality. This caused us to incur excess overhead in our applications because these hidden DataWindows had all the functionality necessary to interact with the user even though we never used it.

280   *Chapter 9: DataWindow Components*

To remove this burden of overhead, in PowerBuilder 5.0 we have a new object called a DataStore which is simply a DataWindow control with no visual component. You can associate a DataWindow object with a DataStore and avoid the overhead incurred by all the visual user interface functionality of a DataWindow control.

All the data manipulation functionality of the DataWindow control is present in the DataStore. You can still call functions such as Retrieve(), InsertRow(), DeleteRow(), RowsCopy() and so on. The functions that you don't have access to anymore are the visually related functions such as SetRowFocusIndicator().

DataStores are non-visual objects. That means that they must be created in the same fashion as other non-visual objects, instantiating them in your scripts with the CREATE function. For example:

```
// Declare DataStore variable
DataStore lds_datastore

// Instantiate DataStore
lds_datastore = CREATE DataStore

// Assign a DataWindow object to the DataStore
lds_datastore.DataObject = 'd_employee'

// Retrieve Data
lds_datastore.SetTransObject(SQLCA)
lds_datastore.Retrieve()
```

DataStores can also be created as standard class user objects (see Chapter 12—User Objects for more details on standard class user objects). Doing this allows you to encapsulate custom business rules or services into a DataStore object and reuse these objects throughout multiple applications.

Developers Tip: Remember that any DataWindow objects that you are going to use with your DataStore are all dynamically referenced objects and must be included in either a .PBD (or .DLL) or brought into the .EXE file with a .PBR (PowerBuilder Resource File).

9.5 SUMMARY

Understanding how to properly set up and manipulate the low level characteristics of your DataWindow objects is critical to building robust enterprise applications in PowerBuilder. Remember that the DataStore will be invaluable to you for manipulating data behind the scenes for thing like data caches or in a distributed environment where data may be held in an object that is not physically located on your client machine.

CHAPTER 10

Advanced DataWindow Techniques

*O*ne of the number one reasons thousands of organizations have selected PowerBuilder as their standard development tool is the DataWindow. This object, recently patented by Powersoft, makes data access from your client/server applications a breeze. There is so much functionality in the DataWindow that in addition to learning the basics of the DataWindow in the FastTrack to PowerBuilder course, Powersoft offers a pair of two day advanced courses which covers nothing but advanced techniques for using DataWindows more effectively.

We will assume that you are already familiar with the fundamentals of using a DataWindow, and we will focus on specific techniques to help you make better use of this powerful object. In this chapter we will examine drop down DataWindows, child DataWindows, sliding columns, edit masks and formats, dynamic DataWindow modification and creation and advanced result set handling.

10.1 DROP DOWN DATAWINDOWS

Drop down DataWindows have been in PowerBuilder since release 3.0. They allow us to insert into a particular column of a DataWindow a drop down list box containing values retrieved from our relational database. Although they are really a subsection of Edit Styles, I have broken them out into their own section because of their high importance and complexity.

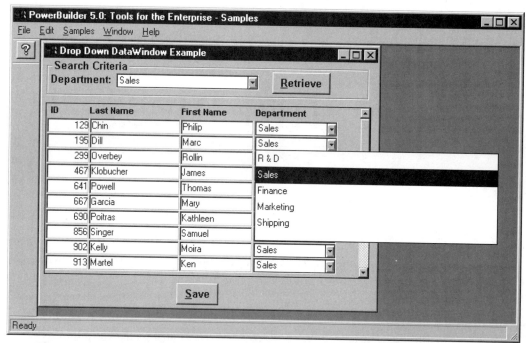

Figure 10.1 *The Drop Down DataWindow allows us to have a column in a DataWindow act like a drop down list box populated with values from our database.*

The drop down DataWindow is like a DataWindow nested inside another DataWindow. It can contain multiple columns and rows and is retrieved when the DataWindow that it is inside (the parent DataWindow) begins a Retrieve() or InsertRow() function. We refer to a DataWindow nested inside another as a child DataWindow. We will refer back to this concept as we progress through this example. This example can be found on the companion CD.

10.1.1 Drop Down DataWindow Example

The first step in building a drop down DataWindow is to build the DataWindow object that will eventually become the child DataWindow (the one nested inside the parent). For our example, we will use the department table as our drop down list. We want to display the list of department names, but store the department number in the field in the parent DataWindow.

Step 1 To start, build a tabular DataWindow selecting the department table as the SQLSelect data source. Select the dept_name and dept_id columns as in Figure 10.2.

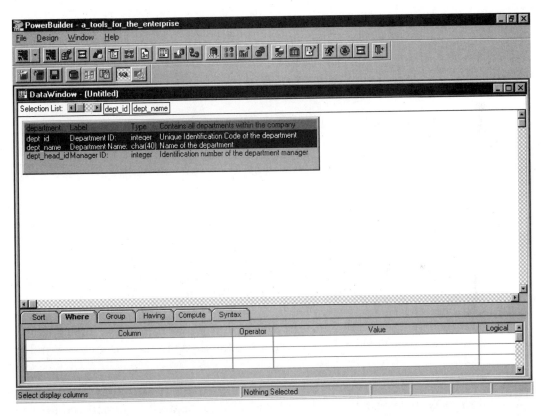

Figure 10.2 *Step 1: Build a tabular DataWindow object with a SQL Select data source. Select the dept_name and dept_id columns from the department table.*

Step 2 In the designer, remove the text fields and delete the dept_id field (it still exists as part of the result set, it just isn't visible). Now rearrange the bands so that everything is neat and clean like in Figure 10.3.

Chapter 10: Advanced DataWindow Techniques

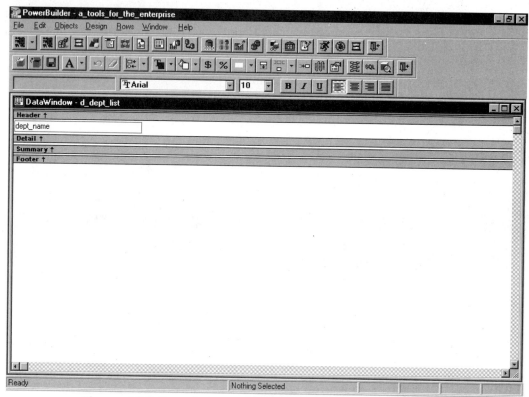

Figure 10.3 *Step 2: Remove the text fields and the dept_id. Then size the band appropriately.*

Step 3   Now save the DataWindow as d_dept_list (don't forget to give it a comment). You now have a DataWindow that you can use as the child in a drop down DataWindow.

Step 4   There are a variety of approaches for the next step depending on where you want to the DDDW to appear. If this object is intended to stand alone (as opposed to being part of a larger DataWindow), you could build a new DataWindow object and insert the child inside it. This technique is discussed in Option A, next. A second approach would be to insert a DDDW into another existing multiple column DataWindow where we want one of the columns to be a DDDW. This is demonstrated in Option B.

10.1 Drop Down DataWindows   287

OPTION A: We need to place the drop down list inside another DataWindow object. Alternatively, you could be recursive and place it inside itself. The method that I prefer for this is to create a new DataWindow object.

Developers Tip: A second common way to implement Option A is to use an External source DataWindow. To do this, replace step 5 below with:

Step 5   Create a new freeform external DataWindow. Define a single column called 'dept_id' with a data type of 'string' and a size of 3.

This will eliminate the excess overhead that you incur creating a DataWindow that originates from a SQL select statement, but it will require you to call the SetTransObject() function in order for your InsertRow() to succeed, even though external DataWindows do not normally require this function.

Step 5   Create a new freeform DataWindow with a SQLSelect data source. Select the department table from the list. Select only the dept_id column. Switch to the designer by pressing the SQL icon on the toolbar. If you enter preview mode, exit and continue to the designer.

Step 6   Change or remove the text label that appears before the column as desired. Make the dept_id column wide enough to accommodate the longest department name plus enough room for the drop down arrow which will appear inside the field.

Step 7   Open the Properties page for the dept_id column (this should be the only column showing).

Chapter 10: Advanced DataWindow Techniques

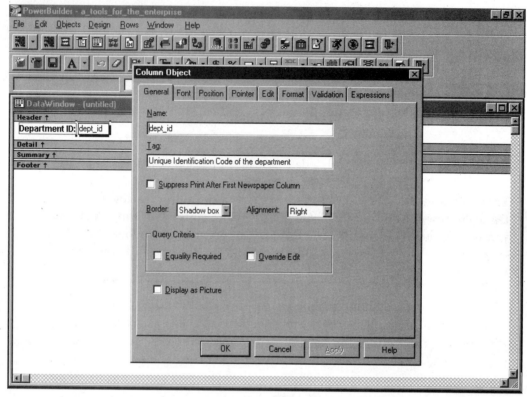

Figure 10.4 Step 7: Open the Properties page for the dept_id column.

Step 8   Switch to the **Edit** tab. Select **Drop Down DW** as the Edit Style.

Step 9   Selecting the DataWindow field in the **Options** group box will open a drop down listbox with a list of all the available DataWindow objects. Select the DataWindow d_dept_list that you created in Step 3 above for your drop down list. Choose the dept_id column as the Data Column and dept_name as the Display Column. Add a vertical scroll bar to your DDDW and select Always Show Arrow.

10.1 Drop Down DataWindows

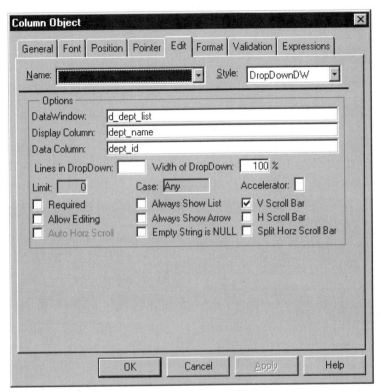

Figure 10.5 *Step 9: You must select the Drop Down DataWindow that will appear inside this field and the columns which you want to represent the data and to display.*

Step 10 Select **OK** to apply your changes.

Step 11 Preview your DataWindow. You will see a separate instance of your DDDW for each row in the Department table. Notice that each one behaves as its own independent DDDW. Now you have a Drop Down DataWindow list of departments that you can use on any of the windows in your application. To use this object in your application you must perform a SetTransObject() function followed by an InsertRow() function to make this object work in your window. This will create a single row where the user can select from the list of departments. See the companion CD for the functioning sample application.

290 Chapter 10: Advanced DataWindow Techniques

OPTION B: We want to insert the DDDW into a column of an existing DataWindow object.

Step 5 Open the DataWindow object that you want to attach your DDDW to. We will use the object on the companion CD called d_emp_list. You can see this object working without the Drop Down DataWindow by running the sample application and selecting Samples > Advanced DataWindows > Drop Down DataWindows from the menu bar. When you select a department, the employees in that department show up. We are going to add a drop down list of departments to the department column in the employee list.

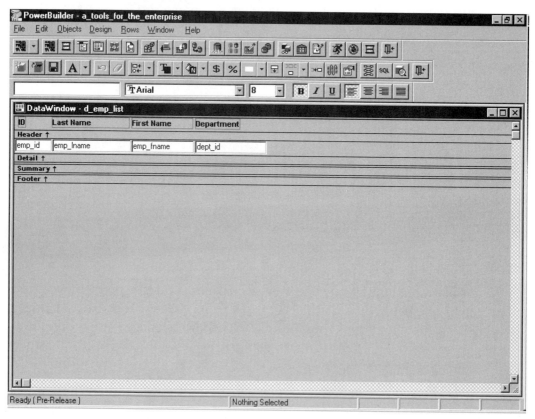

Figure 10.6 Use the object d_emp_list from the companion CD. We will insert a drop down list of departments in the department column.

Step 6 Open the Properties page for the dept_id column as in Figure 10.4 above. Select the Edit tab and make the changes described in Step 9 in Option A.

Step 7 Save the DataWindow object. Run the sample application to see how it behaves.

The above steps can be used to create Drop Down DataWindows and add them to your applications. The DDDWs that we have discussed so far do not accept any retrieval arguments. Sometimes you may want a Drop Down DataWindow to show a different list of options depending on some other outside value. To accomplish this we have to examine the concept of the child DataWindow a little closer.

10.2 CHILD DATAWINDOWS

A child DataWindow is any DataWindow which is nested inside another DataWindow, and therefore dependent upon, another (the parent) DataWindow. Child DataWindows include Drop Down DataWindows, DataWindows inside a nested report and DataWindows placed onto a composite DataWindow.

Child DataWindows have most of the same functionality that their parents do. You can access all the methods and attributes inside the child, but to do so you must first obtain its *handle*. The child doesn't have a name at the window level like 'dw_emp' or 'dw_dept_list' which we can use to reference it. Instead we use a variable to trap the system handle, which uniquely identifies the object and allows us to reference it. We use a PowerScript function called GetChild() to obtain the handle.

10.2.1 USING THE GETCHILD() FUNCTION

The GetChild() function allows us to obtain the handle for a child DataWindow which is nested inside its parent. The syntax for this function is:

> dw_control.GetChild (column_name, child_handle)

where:

dw_control Is the name of the DataWindow control on the window which contains the parent DataWindow object.

292 *Chapter 10: Advanced DataWindow Techniques*

column_name The name of the column or object that contains the child DataWindow.

child_handle A reference variable of type DataWindowChild which is passed by reference. It will contain the handle of the child DataWindow upon successful execution of the function.

The function returns a value of 1 if the execution was successful or a -1 if it failed.

By default, the child DataWindow works in very close conjunction with its parent. It automatically picks up and uses the parent's transaction object and will retrieve its result set from the database when the parent is retrieved or has a blank row inserted into it. You can easily choose to override these defaults yourself.

10.2.1.1 Assigning a Different Transaction Object to a Child DataWindow

Let's say that you want the data in the DataWindow to use the transaction object SQLCA, but the data for the drop down DataWindow is to come from the database specified in the transaction object gtr_DB2TRANS. To make this work, you would have to obtain the handle of the child and then call the SetTransObject() function for the child before retrieving or inserting into the parent. Here is an example:

```
// Declare local variables
DataWindowChild ldwc_current
integer li_return

// Set Transaction object for parent
dw_parent.SetTransObject(SQLCA)

//Obtain handle of child DataWindow in the department column
li_return = dw_parent.GetChild("department",ldwc_current)

IF li_return = 1 THEN
        // Set the child transaction object
        ldwc_current.SetTransObject(gtr_DB2TRANS)
        ldwc_current.Retrieve()
        dw_parent.Retrieve()
ELSE
        MessageBox("DataWindow Error","Unable to obtain child DataWindow handle.")
END IF
```

After setting a different transaction object for the child, you would retrieve the result set for the child and then retrieve the result set for the parent.

10.2.1.2 Populating the Child DataWindow

There are also multiple methods that you could use to retrieve the result set for the child DataWindow. You could let the parent manage all the needs of the child, you could retrieve the result set manually (with or without retrieval arguments), you could share the result set from another DataWindow object or you could create your own result set with the InsertRow() function.

10.2.1.2.1 Letting the Parent Manage the Child

The default process is that the result set for the child is retrieved from the database when the parent window receives a Retrieve() or InsertRow() function. If you have a number of drop down DataWindows in your parent DataWindow, you could incur significant overhead in trying to retrieve the first row of the parent result set because it will also be retrieving all the result sets for the child DataWindows.

For drop down DataWindows where the data is not used very often, the result set is small and the performance implications of the drop down DataWindow default process has minimal impact on the application, use the default process. It takes the least amount of code to manage and is generally very robust.

If you are using the same result set over and over throughout your application, it doesn't make sense to keep retrieving the same result set from the database. Or if you are retrieving a large result set and it has a significant performance impact on the speed of your application, you may want to consider buffering the data on your client workstation. The techniques and implications of this are discussed in section 10.2.1.2.3—Buffering and Sharing a Result Set below.

The default processing method will also not work if you have defined any retrieval arguments for your child DataWindow. You can use retrieval arguments in a child to customize the data that they will show at runtime, but if you let the parent manage the child, the result of a retrieve function on the parent would be to pop up a window that asks the user to specify a retrieval argument *for each row in the parent DataWindow result set*. Obviously not a desirable behavior. To manage this, we must manually retrieve the child result set ourselves. The technique and implications of this are discussed in the next section.

10.2.1.2.2 Manually Retrieving the Result Set

The parent DataWindow will only automatically retrieve the result set of the child if the child does not currently contain a valid result set. You can override the default functionality of the parent, by retrieving the result set into the child manually prior to issuing a Retrieve() or InsertRow() function on the parent. This also allows you to utilize retrieval arguments in the result set for the child DataWindow.

The technique for manually initiating a retrieval is very similar to the technique for manually setting the transaction object. The following example would retrieve a result set for the child that needs to know the security level of the user as a parameter as the child will only show options that are available for that security level.

```
// Declare local variables
DataWindowChild ldwc_current
integer li_return, li_security

// Set Transaction object for parent
dw_parent.SetTransObject(SQLCA)

//Obtain handle of child DataWindow in the "function" column
li_return = dw_parent.GetChild("function",ldwc_current)

IF li_return = 1 THEN
        // Retrieve the child result set, passing the users security
        // level (obtained from security non-visual object
        // on this window).
        li_security = THIS.invo_security.GetAccessLevel()
        ldwc_current.Retrieve(li_security)
        dw_parent.Retrieve()
ELSE
        MessageBox("DataWindow Error","Unable to obtain child DataWindow
handle.")
END IF
```

This is the only option available if you are wanting to use retrieval arguments in your child DataWindows. If you want to simply retrieve the parent window populating the child DataWindow, this can be accomplished by creating a dummy result set for the child. Instead of performing the retrieve in the above example, use InsertRow(0) to insert a single blank row into the child. This is a valid result set, so the parent won't try to retrieve the child when it populates itself.

10.2.1.2.3 Buffering and Sharing a Result Set

A technique becoming more and more common in enterprise applications today is to buffer result sets for DataWindows and share them whenever a child window requires that same result set. For example, if you have a list of states and provinces that you use as a drop down DataWindow in a number of places throughout your application, this is a good candidate to buffer on your client. The result set for this commonly used data set could be retrieved and stored on a non-visual user object with a DataStore (in previous versions of PowerBuilder this functionality was achieved using a hidden window in your application with hidden DataWindows used specifically for storing shared data sets). Then when you use a DataWindow object that has a drop down list of states/provinces inside of it, you can share the result set with your non-visual data store. This will reduce the load on the server and make your application perform faster. For more detail on result set sharing, refer to section 10.9—Sharing Result Sets below.

The important thing to remember when using a shared data store as the source of data for your drop down lists (and other child DataWindows as appropriate) that the data that you are accessing is only as recent as the last retrieval of the data store. This means that this technique is not good for data that changes frequently. Our example of a list of states and provinces above is a good use for this technique because this data is not likely to change within the context of your user session. Data such as inventory for a parts delivery system would probably not be appropriate information to buffer as other users activities will change the information in the database and the data that you have in your buffer may no longer be accurate.

The technique for sharing a result set would be to first of all create a non-visual user object or hidden window in your application which is populated at some convenient time. Usually they are populated as the application starts up. The users would usually prefer to take an initial ten to twenty second performance hit upon startup than to have regular half to one second delays as they are trying to process transactions. Let's assume that we have created a non-visual user object called u_nvo_data_storage. On this object is a DataStore called ds_states. We want to populate the result set for our DataWindow's states column drop down DataWindow by sharing it with the one in u_nvo_data_storage. Here is the code that would let us do this (the non-visual object has been instantiated on this window with the name

296   *Chapter 10: Advanced DataWindow Techniques*

iuo_data_store, although it could easily have been instantiated on the frame, or if necessary, the application object):

```
// Declare local variables
DataWindowChild ldwc_current
integer li_return

// Set Transaction object for parent
dw_parent.SetTransObject(SQLCA)

//Obtain handle of child DataWindow in the "states" column
li_return = dw_parent.GetChild("states",ldwc_current)

IF li_return = 1 THEN
        // Share the result set from the data store for states
        iuo_data_store.ds_states.ShareData(ldwc_current)
        dw_parent.Retrieve()
ELSE
        MessageBox("DataWindow Error","Unable to obtain child DataWindow handle.")
END IF
```

You can make use of filters and sort criteria to alter the display of the data in the result set, but you must remember that altering these criteria alters the primary buffer of the child, the original data store and also any other DataWindows currently sharing that result set! They all point to the same memory location at the same time, so any changes you make are universal.

10.2.1.2.4 Manually Creating a Child Result Set

The result set for a child DataWindow does not necessarily have to come from a relational database. You can create any result set you desire by using the InsertRow() function and then manually setting the values into the new row.

I have often needed to combine the manual retrieval of a result set and the manual insert of new rows to add options to the list that might now otherwise be there. For example, on one project, we wanted to provide a list of products in a drop down DataWindow. This organization had new products that would be produced fairly regularly, so the database may not have always had the newest product in it. Within the list of products, they wanted to add an option called '<NEW PRODUCT>' at the top of the list, and if it was selected, to launch a dialog window that would create the new product in the database.

10.2 Child DataWindows **297**

To accomplish this, we would manually retrieve the list of products and then perform an InsertRow() function adding the '<NEW PRODUCT>' at the top of the list. We would have to check in the item changed event of the DataWindow to see if the user selected this custom option, and if they did, take the appropriate action. The script for doing this was a simple variation of the ones that we have already discussed:

```
// Declare local variables
DataWindowChild ldwc_current
integer li_return

// Set Transaction object for parent
dw_parent.SetTransObject(SQLCA)

//Obtain handle of child DataWindow in the "product" column
li_return = dw_parent.GetChild("product",ldwc_current)

IF li_return = 1 THEN
// Retrieve the child result set
        ldwc_current.Retrieve()

        // Insert a blank row at the top of the child DataWindow
        ldwc_current.InsertRow(1)

        // Populate the row to have a display value of "<NEW PRODUCT>"
        // and a code value of "*NP"
ldwc_current.object.data[1,1] = "<NEW PRODUCT>"
ldwc_current.object.data[1,2] = "*NP"

        dw_parent.Retrieve()
ELSE
        MessageBox("DataWindow Error","Unable to obtain child DataWindow
handle.")
END IF
```

This example uses the new PowerBuilder 5.0 direct data manipulation syntax. You can still use the PowerBuilder 4.0 SetItem() function if you desire. I still find that I am using SetItem quite a bit although this is most likely due to familiarity. If you wish to use the PowerBuilder 4.0 syntax it is:

```
ldwc_current.SetItem(1,"product_name","<NEW PRODUCT>")
ldwc_current.SetItem(1,"product_code","*NP")
```

10.2.1.2.5 Using Other Functions to Populate Your Child

In addition to the techniques we have discussed so far, you could also populate your child DataWindow through the use of ImportFile(), ImportString() or ImportClipboard() functions of a DataWindow. These functions will expect to receive tab delimited data from a file, string or the windows clipboard. Alternatively, ImportFile() can also use dBase (.DBF) file as its data source.

10.2.1.3 Building a Linked Child DataWindow

It is possible to have a child DataWindow within a window that will show a different list of options depending on what value is in a different column in the parent DataWindow. To build this link between the master column in the parent and the child, you should build a function which will adjust the result set displayed in the child.

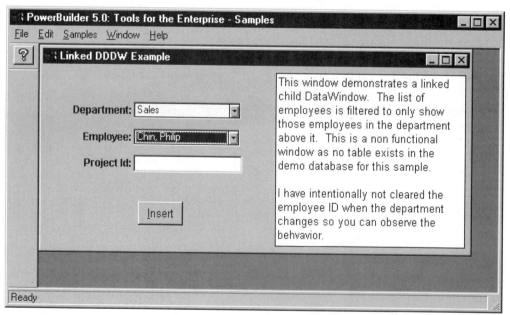

Figure 10.7 *The Employee DDDW in the sample Linked Child DataWindow is linked to the Department field. As the different departments are selected, only those employees in the departments are available for selection.*

The technique for altering the result set will vary depending on many different external factors such as the type of DataWindow presentation style being used. Most commonly, the result set is filtered differently in the ItemChanged event. Alternatively, you could do a ShareData with another data source, or re-retrieve the result set based upon new criteria.

10.3 SLIDING COLUMNS

Individual columns can be set to slide around within the DataWindow to eliminate excess space between columns and/or rows. Look at Figures 10.8A and 10.8B. They show a set of mailing labels without any sliding columns, and then the same labels with the name fields and state field set to slide left and the address fields all set to slide up.

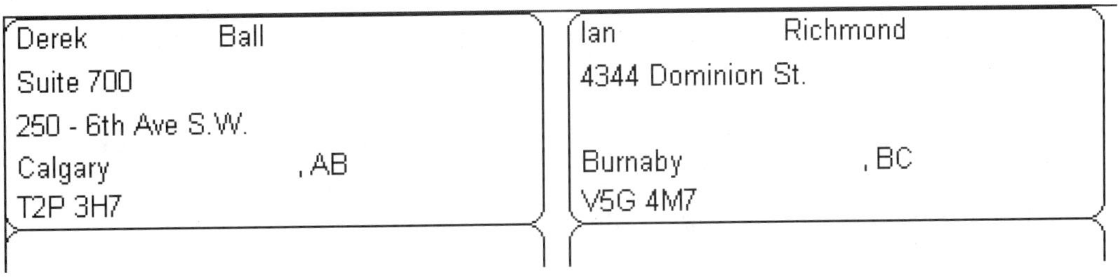

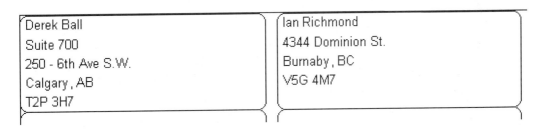

Figure 10.8A *A pair of mailing labels with no sliding. These appear blocked and unprofessional.*

Figure 10.8B *The same mailing labels with the name fields (including the comma) and the state field (also including the comma) set to slide left and the entire address set to slide up where applicable. This looks far more professional.*

Chapter 10: Advanced DataWindow Techniques

The sliding options allow us to build much more flexible DataWindows. They are particularly useful for forms and reports. They also eliminate the need for many of the standard computed fields that we have used in the past, such as combining an individuals full name into a concatenated field.

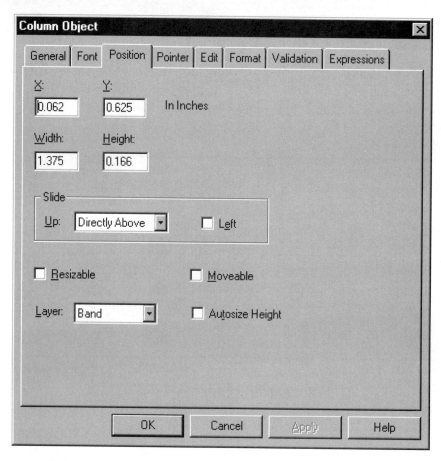

Figure 10.9 *Sliding options can be set on the Position tab of the Properties page for any object on the DataWindow.*

10.3 Sliding Columns

The different sliding options can be set on the Position tab of the Properties page for any object on the DataWindow. There are two properties in the **Slide** group box:

Up   This property defines how you want this object to slide up. Your options are:

None: The object will not slide up

All Above: This object will slide up as long as there are no objects containing data anywhere in the row above it. This includes objects which may be in the row, but not directly over the sliding object.

Directly Above: This object will slide up as long as there are no objects containing data directly above it in the DataWindow. Objects that are in the same physical row above the sliding object but are not positioned directly above it will not affect its slide.

Left   This property can be set to either checked (TRUE) or not-checked (FALSE). When set to true, this object will slide to the left and take up any excess space between it and any object to the left.

If you use the properties page, you can only change these properties for one object at a time. If you want to set the sliding properties for a whole group of objects, you can select the group and then use the toolbar icons to set the properties. There is an icon for slide left shown in Figure 10.10 and a drop down toolbar for the slide up property as shown in Figure 10.11.

Figure 10.10 *A group of objects on a DataWindow can be selected and then all set to slide left by pressing the Slide Left toolbar icon shown here.*

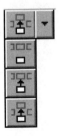

Figure 10.11 *The same principal applies to setting a group of objects to slide up. You can select the appropriate slide up setting from the drop down toolbar shown here.*

302   *Chapter 10: Advanced DataWindow Techniques*

10.4 EDIT STYLES AND DISPLAY FORMATS

The way that the end user views and works with the data in the DataWindow does not necessarily have to reflect how it is stored in the database. The classic example of this is a phone number. When you display a phone number to the user, you probably want it to appear as

(403)265-8335

but you only want to have

4032658335

in the database.

We have two mechanisms available in PowerBuilder to translate the data from what is stored in the database to the interface that the user interacts with. These mechanisms are display formats and edit styles.

10.4.1 DISPLAY FORMATS

Display formats are definitions stored along with a column that specify how the data in the column is to be displayed to the user. These display formats can be different for each column in the DataWindow.

Display formats are *unidirectional* which means that they will only format the data when it is displayed to the user, but when they enter data into a field, they do so in a raw format. For *bidirectional* data formatting, we will use the edit styles discussed below. Unidirectional behavior makes display formats ideally suited for working with two types of data: currencies and percentages.

Let's consider a currency. The standard accounting format for a negative number would place the negative number in parenthesis with all the currency formatting (dollar sign, commas, decimal points) contained within such as:

($1,256.56)

This is great for display purposes, but when it comes to entering data, the user will not enter negative numbers by typing them within parenthesis, the user will enter them by using the minus sign such as:

-1256.56 [ENTER]

10.4 Edit Styles and Display Formats

This is where the unidirectional behavior of the display format is very valuable. As soon as the user hits enter, they indicate to PowerBuilder that they are finished entering the data and PowerBuilder will apply the display format. The user can always enter their numerical information in the raw data mode that they are accustomed to.

10.4.1.1 Defining A Display Format

PowerBuilder has the most commonly used display formats already predefined such as standard currency formatting which inserts dollar signs and commas where required. If the predefined set of formats are not sufficient you can create your own, although very seldom have I every needed to do this.

Display formats can be created in the Database painter and then applied to a column in a table through the extended attributes. Then when this column is used in a DataWindow, that display format is picked up and used automatically. This is the default display format.

Alternatively, in the DataWindow painter you can override the default display format and change it to another format already predefined for defined in the Database painter, or you can make up your own from scratch.

10.4.1.1.1 In the Database Painter

To define an edit style in the Database painter select the **Display Format Maintenance...** from the **Design** menu bar option. This will open the Display Formats window as shown in Figure 10.12.

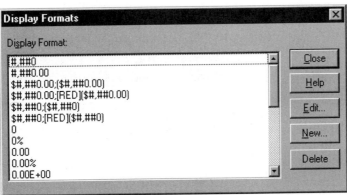

Figure 10.12 The Display Formats window is the entry point into defining display formats in the Database painter. The same window is used for both editing and creating new formats.

304   *Chapter 10: Advanced DataWindow Techniques*

Selecting an existing display format and pressing the **Edit...** or **New...** command button will open the Display Format Definition dialog window as shown in Figure 10.13. This window is used for both editing existing display formats and creating new ones.

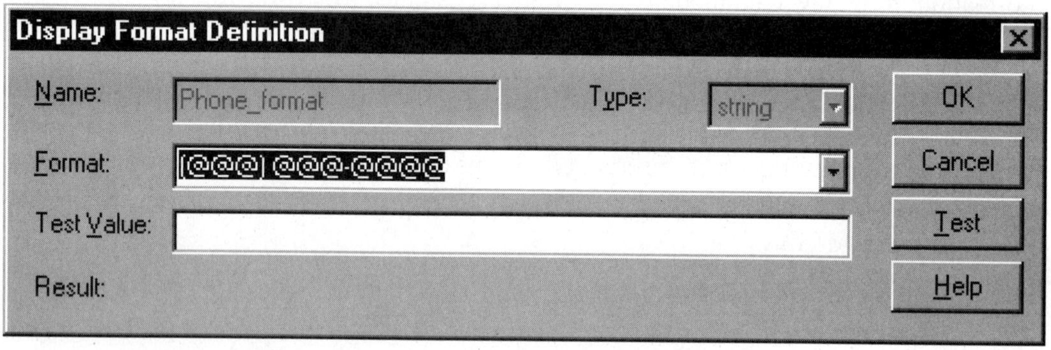

Figure 10.13 *The Display Format Definition window is used for both creating new display formats and editing existing formats.*

When you are editing a display format, you will not be able to change the name or data type of the display format. If this is a new display format you can assign a name up to forty characters long and select a data type of either string, numeric, date, time or datetime.

You will need to create a new definition, or edit the existing definition for the display format. You can enter standard characters that you want to include in the format and special characters such as:

@   to represent any character

to represent numeric characters

mm/dd/yy hh:mm:ss   to deal with date and time formatting components

For example, the definition for a string field containing a phone number would be:

(@@@)@@@-@@@@

which would result in a standard telephone format.

As a second example, we could define a currency format that would display the currency formatted to show a dollar sign, commas between the thousands, two decimal places and display the negative values the same way but in parenthesis and in a red color. The definition would look like:

$#,##0.00;[RED]($#,##0.00)

Once the definition is complete, we can test it to be sure it is working correctly. The test field allows you to enter some raw data, press the **Test...** command button and see how the display format would format the data you entered.

When you have the display format defined correctly, press the **OK** command button to save it. This definition is stored in the database extended attributes tables and can be attached to any column in the database that you choose, or selected at a later time from the DataWindow painter (as will be shown below).

To assign this display format to a specific column, you would open up the table that the column is on in the Database painter and open the table definition by double clicking on the table.

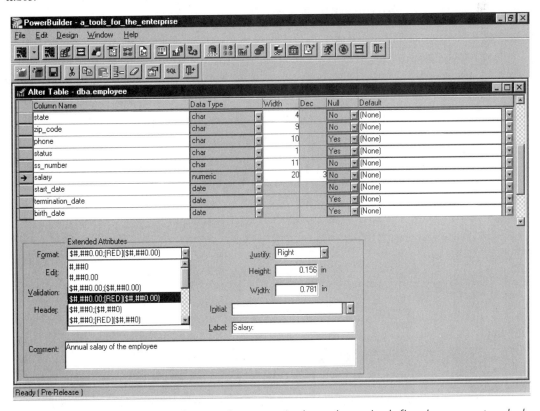

Figure 10.14 *The display format for a particular column is defined as an extended attribute in the table definition window.*

Select the column that you want to set a display format for. The extended attributes section at the bottom of the window only applies to the currently selected column. In the Display field you can drop down the listbox and select from any of the formats listed (only formats that apply to the column data type will be shown) which includes the predefined formats and the ones that you have custom created.

This format will become the default display format for any DataWindows created using this column. Note that this will apply to any DataWindows that will be created in the future. Existing DataWindows using this column will not be affected. If you want to apply this new format to existing DataWindow objects you will need to run the DataWindow Extended Attribute Synchronizer utility which is included in the Advanced PowerBuilder Utilities (APU) installed with PowerBuilder.

10.4.1.1.2 In the DataWindow Painter

When you create a DataWindow object, the display formats for the columns involved will be defaulted to whatever format was defined in the extended attributes. If no format is defined there then the display format for the column will be [General]. You can override the default in the DataWindow painter through the **Format** tab of the Properties page.

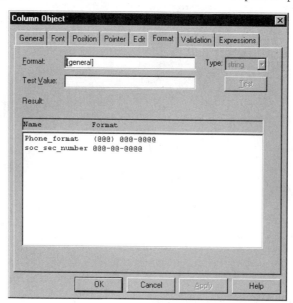

Figure 10.15 In the DataWindow painter we can override the default display format for an object on the **Format** tab of the Properties page.

To change the format for an object, select the object and then open the Properties page. On the **Format** tab you will see the same fields that you saw in the Display Format Definition window in the Database painter. In fact, this window works exactly the same except for the list at the bottom. This list displays all the predefined formats from the database that apply to this column type. You can select any of these format types, or you can define your own for this specific purpose. When you define your own on this tab, you will not be able to reuse this format in another column or DataWindow. To do that you would have to have defined it in the Database painter as discussed earlier.

Pressing the **OK** command button will apply the changes that you have made to the currently selected column.

In the DataWindow designer, you can change a whole range of columns to a standard currency or percentage display format by selecting all the columns that you want to alter and then pressing either the Currency Format or Percent Format icons in the toolbar as shown in Figure 10.16.

Figure 10.16 *You can change the display format of a group of columns together by selecting all the relevant columns and pressing the Currency Format or Percent Format icons in the toolbar.*

10.4.1.2 Dynamically Altering a Display Format

The display format for a column on a DataWindow is stored as a string. This makes it easy for us to read and alter dynamically at runtime. There are two techniques that you can use to do this; using PowerScript functions SetFormat() and GetFormat(), or through direct DataWindow object attribute manipulation.

The GetFormat() and SetFormat() PowerScript functions cross all versions of PowerBuilder and are still supported in PowerBuilder 5.0. GetFormat() returns the current display format of a DataWindow column. The syntax for GetFormat() is:

```
dw_control.GetFormat(column_name)
```

308   *Chapter 10: Advanced DataWindow Techniques*

where

dw_control   is the name of the DataWindow control, DataSource or child DataWindow that contains the column you want the display format of.

column_name   is the name of the column (as a string) that you want to obtain the display format of.

GetFormat() returns a string containing the display format of the column. If there is no currently defined display format, the return value will be NULL. An empty string will be returned if an error occurs.

The syntax for SetFormat() is:

```
dw_control.SetFormat(column_name, format_string)
```

where

dw_control   is the name of the DataWindow control, DataSource or child DataWindow that contains the column you want to alter the display format of.

column_name   is the name of the column (as a string) that you want to alter the display format of.

format_string   is a string containing the new format that you want to apply

To do the same thing through direct manipulation you would use the syntax:

```
string_variable = dw_control.object.proj_id.format
```

String variable is a variable that you have declared to store the returned format string. Of course, you could use this property without having a storage variable by embedding it directly where it is required.

To set the format you would use the reverse syntax:

```
dw_control.object.proj_id.format = string_variable
```

> **Developer Note: The direct manipulation specified above replaces the functionality formerly provided with the Modify() and Describe() functions in PowerBuilder 4.0. You can still use the Modify() and Describe() functions to alter the column display format by using the syntax:**
>
> ```
> string_variable = dw_control.Describe("ColumnName.format")
> dw_control.Modify("ColumnName.format = 'string'")
> ```

I have not encountered the need to dynamically alter the display format very often. Situations where you might include systems where the users have the ability to define their own display formats (for example, if they want to see currencies with decimal places or without) or if you don't know what kind of data a field will be displaying until runtime (for example, your system may hold the e-mail address of an individual which may be formatted differently depending on whether it is an Internet, Compuserve, AOL id or some other format).

One of this books technical reviewers, Oscar Ramirez, provided a second excellent example of dynamically changing a display format. He uses it when working with credit card fields. Different credit cards expect to have the number segments separated in different areas (i.e. American Express has a different format than Visa). He can use this technique to set the correct format for the type of credit card.

The sample application on the companion CD contains an example of dynamically changing the display format of a field. It uses an external DataWindow with a string field. You can experiment with altering its display format. You can choose between using direct manipulation or functions to change the format. Look at the code behind the command buttons to see how the above functions are applied.

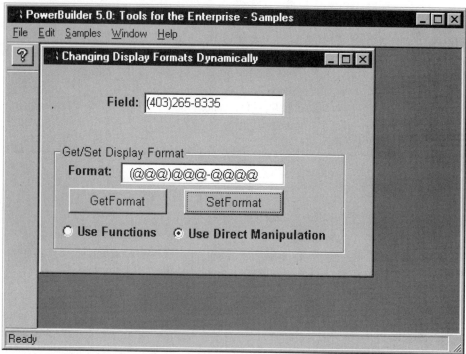

Figure 10.17 *The companion CD contains an example which allows you to dynamically read and alter the display format of a generic field in an external DataWindow.*

10.4.2 EDIT STYLES

The second mechanism that we can use to alter the format and user interface for the data we present to the end user is the edit style. Edit styles differ from display formats in three key areas. First, edit styles are *bidirectional* which means that they affect not only the display of the data to the user, but also are active in formatting the data while the user is entering it. This means that if we were using an edit style to mask a phone number field, PowerBuilder would automatically add the parenthesis around the area code and the dash in the middle as we were typing the characters in, although these formatting characters are still not stored in the database.

The second key difference between an edit style and display format is the variety of edit styles that you have available to use. These styles include; the standard edit box, the edit mask, a drop down listbox, a drop down DataWindow, check boxes or radio buttons. These styles are designed to improve the user interface and make your application more intuitive.

The example that I use most often to describe the functionality of these styles is the storing of gender in a database. Very likely your database will store only M or F instead of 'male' and 'female'. In order to improve the user interface we could define an interface with two radio buttons, one for Male and one for Female. When the user selects the Male radio button, a 'M' is put into the gender column, and when the user selects the Female radio button, an 'F' is placed there. The user interface is improved in a number of ways such as; there is no need to validate the input, the amount of information being stored in the database is minimized, and the radio buttons make the system easier for the user to run.

Like the display format, a default edit style for a column in a DataWindow is established based upon the edit style assigned to the column in the extended attributes section of the Database painter. Also like the display format, there are a number of predefined edit styles that you can use, or you can define your own in the Database painter, or you could create an edit style for a specific instance of a column in the DataWindow painter.

10.4.2.1 Defining an Edit Style

The techniques for defining and edit style are similar to those that we used to define the display formats. You can define edit styles in the Database painter. By doing so, the edit style can be used in multiple places. This is the place to define your edit style if you want to reuse it across multiple columns or if you want to define a default edit style for a column in a table that will be used any time that column is used in a DataWindow.

To create or alter an edit style in the Database painter, you select the **Edit Style Maintenance...** menu option from the **Design** menu. This will open a window listing all the currently defined edit styles—a combination of the predefined PowerBuilder edit styles and any others that you have added.

We can also define edit styles in the DataWindow painter when they will only be used once or we want to override the default edit style assigned in the Database painter. This is done by selecting the column that you want to define the edit style for and opening the Properties page. The **Edit** tab is where the current edit style is defined.

The technique for defining the edit style depends on which edit style type you select. As the technique is the same in both the Database painter and the DataWindow painter, we will address them both at the same time by examining each of the edit style types. The one difference to remember is that once the edit style is defined in the Database painter, you must still apply it to a specific column or columns by defining the extended attributes for that table.

Chapter 10: Advanced DataWindow Techniques

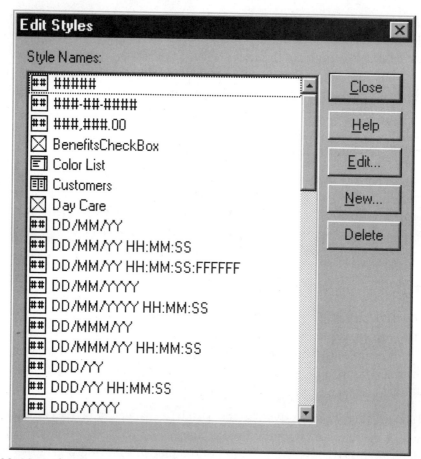

Figure 10.18 *In the Database painter you can edit an existing edit style by selecting it from the list and pressing the **Edit...** command button. Pressing the **New...** command button will allow you to define a new edit style.*

10.4.2.2 Edit

If you don't specify an edit style for a column it will default to a style simply called Edit. It is a standard single line edit box like the ones that you use in the Window painter. It still has a number of properties that you can modify to your needs.

10.4 Edit Styles and Display Formats 313

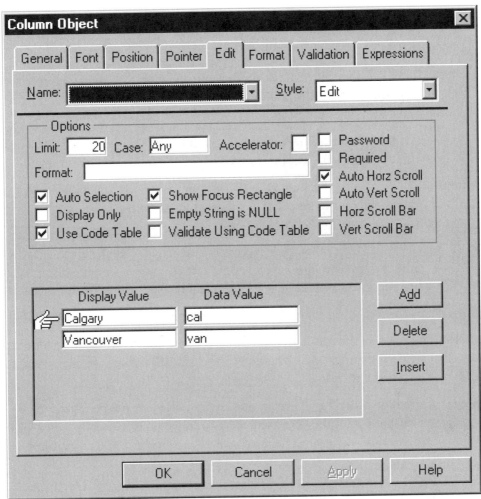

Figure 10.19 The default style for a column is called 'Edit.'

The properties of the Edit style are:

Name (this is the same for all edit styles and won't be repeated in subsequent descriptions) This drop down list box contains the names of all the Edit type edit styles stored in the database (these are the ones defined in the Database painter). If the column has a predefined edit style from its extended attributes, that style will be named here. If you want to use a different previously created style you can select it from the list. If you want to define your own custom version of the Edit style, this will be blank.

314 *Chapter 10: Advanced DataWindow Techniques*

Style	(this is the same for all edit styles and won't be repeated in subsequent descriptions) This is the drop down list box containing all the valid edit styles.
Limit	sets the limit of the total number of characters the user is allowed to enter into the edit field. If the limit is 0, then there is no limit to the number of characters that can be entered.
Case	defines what case the entered text will be in. The options are Any (mixed), Upper or Lower. Text that is entered in the wrong case will be converted.
Accelerator	allows you to specify a letter that is used in conjunction with the ALT key to allow the user to set focus to this field immediately.
Format	this field allows you to define a format that will apply to the value returned by the GetText() function. Normally GetText() will return to you the raw data the user entered into the edit control. If you have a format defined here, this raw data will be formatted as specified.
Password	causes the field to display an asterisk for each character that is entered.
Auto Selection	causes all the text in the field to be selected when the user tabs into the field (when the user types data into the field it will replace the characters that are currently there).
Required	indicates that this is a required field and users are not permitted to tab out of this field until they have entered a valid value. Note that in order for this to take effect the user must have tabbed into the field in the first place.
Empty String is NULL	indicates that if the user enters an empty string in the field (which occurs when you type data into a field, and then decide to use backspace or delete to remove the data) the field is set to NULL.
Auto Horiz(ontal) Scroll	as the user types text into the box and the box fills to its physical capacity, the text will automatically scroll to the left (horizontally) allowing the user to enter more characters. If this attribute is unchecked (FALSE) then the user cannot enter more characters into the field than will fit physically even if this is less than the amount specified in the Limit attribute.

Auto Vert(ical) Scroll works the same as horizontal scroll except that it scrolls the text vertically.

Horiz(ontal) Scroll Bar and Vert(ical) Scroll Bar will cause the appropriate scroll bars to be displayed as needed (when data extends beyond the boundaries).

Display Only prevents the user from entering any data into the field.

Show Focus Rectangle will cause PowerBuilder to display a focus rectangle around the field when it has focus.

Use Code Table indicates that the data that is entered by the end user should be translated by a code table to display something different in the field. In the example in Figure 10.19, the Use Code Table option is checked and a code table has appeared below the options dialog box. In this table we have two values defined with decode values. If the user types 'cal' in the field, this will be translated to 'Calgary' when they tab away from the field, but only 'cal' will be stored in the database. Values in the database that are not part of the code table, or values that the user enters that do not match the code table will be displayed as they are without any translation.

Validate Using Code Table indicates if the data entered by the user will be validated against the code table. This would restrict the user to only be able to enter values that exist in the code table. Values in the database that do not match the values in the code table would still be displayed as they are without any translation. Only user input is validated.

Display Value contains the value that will be displayed in the field when the field value is equal to what is stored in the corresponding Data Value column (only applicable when using a Code Table).

Data Value contains the code value that is the raw data. This code value will be translated to the corresponding Display Value when the field is displayed to the user (only applicable when using a Code Table).

10.4.2.3 Edit Mask

An Edit Mask edit style is used to enforce a specific format on the data that is displayed and entered in a field. It is very similar to the Edit Mask control that you have used in the Window painter. It will automatically insert various formatting characters as required into a field. For example, in the case of a phone number field, it will automatically insert an open bracket, accept three numbers, insert a close bracket, accept three more numbers, insert a dash and then accept four more numbers.

There are two basic subcategories of edit masks; regular edit masks and those that use spin controls.

10.4.2.3.1 Regular Edit Masks

Regular edit masks accept user input in the standard fashion, through the keyboard. One of the most important attributes is the type which defines if this mask applies to a string, numeric, date, time or datetime related field. Because of its importance, I would have preferred it if Powersoft chose to place this field above the Mask and Masks fields as these fields are dependent upon the type, but this is not the case.

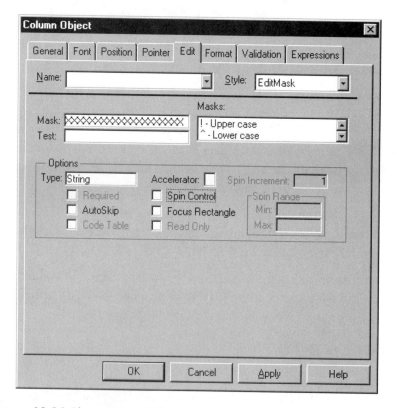

Figure 10.20 *The regular Edit Mask enforces a specific format on the data that is displayed and entered.*

10.4 Edit Styles and Display Formats **317**

The Edit Mask edit style is often used to format strings such as phone numbers or Social Security Numbers. Currencies are often left for display formats because they allow the user to enter data in raw format. Edit masks are also very popular for fields involving dates and times as they require the user to enter valid values.

The properties that you can set for the regular edit mask are:

Type — as mentioned above, this field specifies the data type of the field that this mask is applied to. This is only selectable by you if you are defining an Edit Mask in the Database painter. In the DataWindow painter, the type will be defined by the data type of the column that you are applying the mask to. The valid data types for this field are String, Numeric, Date, Time or DateTime.

Mask — contains the character mask that you will use to format the data in the field. The types of characters that apply depend upon the data type selected in Type. The available mask characters are displayed and can be selected from the Masks field.

Masks — a listbox of all the available mask characters that apply to the selected Type. The characters can be selected and placed in the Mask field at the point of the cursor by clicking on them. Each character listed also has a description as to the type of character it represents (i.e. a '!' is listed as an upper case character). There are also a number of predefined combinations of mask characters such as '###-##-####' for a Social Security Number or 'dd/mm/yyyy' for a standard date field.

Test — allows you to enter characters as if you were entering data into the field in the DataWindow and test to ensure that the mask is working correctly.

Accelerator — allows you to specify a letter that is used in conjunction with the ALT key to allow the user to set focus to this field immediately.

Show Focus Rectangle — will cause PowerBuilder to display a focus rectangle around the field when it has focus.

AutoSkip — when all the characters required by the mask are filled focus will automatically shift to the next field in the tab order.

Spin Control — turns the standard Edit Mask into an Edit Mask with spin boxes that allow the user to click on up or down arrows within the field to change the value (see the following section for further details).

10.4.2.3.2 Edit Mask with Spin Control

The Edit Mask with a spin control attached to it behaves somewhat differently than the standard Edit Mask and it also has additional properties that need to be considered. The Edit Mask will look and behave very similar to the standard Edit Mask until you select the up or down arrow images which are embedded within the field.

The spin control can be applied to any data type, but will behave differently for each one. With a date, time or datetime data type, the spin control will affect the segment where the cursor is currently positioned. For example, if you place the cursor in the day field and click the up arrow, the day number will increase by one, then if you click in the year field and press the down arrow, the year will decrease by one.

With a numeric data type the field will simply increase or decrease the value as specified by the other properties that you must set.

Figure 10.21 *The Edit Mask with a spin control has spin boxes embedded within the field that allow the user to click on the up or down arrows to change the value in the field.*

With a string data type you must define a **Code Table** (which is optional for the other data types). The code table will contain a set of predefined values and as you click on the up or down arrows you will scroll through this table. Code tables can also be used for the other data types when spin controls are enabled.

The other properties that you will need to consider when using spin controls are:

Code Table   as described above, allows you to specify a predefined set of values that will be scrolled through as the user clicks on the up or down arrows.

Read Only   enabled when you are using a code table. This means that the field can only be accessed by scrolling through the fields in the code table. If this is turned off, the user can still enter data directly as if the field had no spin control.

Required   same as the Edit style.

Spin Increment   specifies how much you want the field to increment or decrement each time the user clicks on the up or down arrow. The default value is 1. This property does not apply to string data types.

Spin Range.Min specifies the minimum value that you will not decrement the field below. This property does not apply to string data types.

Spin Range.Max specifies the maximum value that you will not increment the field above. This property does not apply to string data types.

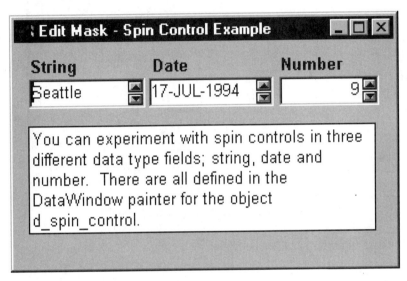

Figure 10.22 *The companion CD contains a window with a spin control edit mask of three different data types; string, date and number.*

10.4.2.4 Radio Button

This edit style is appropriate when you are using a small number of possible values for a field. Each option in the field must be mutually exclusive, for example, employee status of 'active', 'terminated' or 'on-leave' are all mutually exclusive and therefor valid for a Radio Button edit mask. This type of a mask allows users to select their data by selecting one of the available options with the mouse.

Chapter 10: Advanced DataWindow Techniques

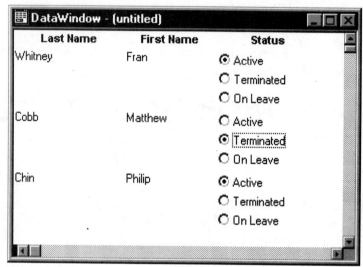

Figure 10.23 *The Radio Button edit mask is useful to select from a small number of mutually exclusive options.*

Radio button edit styles are always driven by a code table which contains a display value and a data value for each item. The properties for radio buttons are quite straightforward:

Columns Across allows you to specify how many columns you want the items to be displayed in. The example shown in Figure 10.23 is displayed in only one column across (the default) but had we specified 3 columns across, all the items would have appeared horizontally.

Left Text causes the text to appear to the left of the radio button when checked, to the right when unchecked.

Scale Circles will cause the radio button circles to be scaled to the size of the font when checked. When unchecked the circles will appear in their default size.

3D Look will cause the radio button to be displayed in 3D.

10.4 Edit Styles and Display Formats

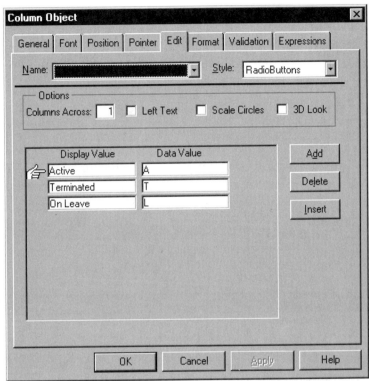

Figure 10.24 Radio button edit masks are always driven by a code table.

You can provide an accelerator key for each display value by placing an ampersand (&) character before the letter in the display that you want to be the accelerator key. When the user presses the ALT key with that letter, that option would be selected.

Developer Tip: You may need to adjust the size of the field in the DataWindow designer to accommodate the radio button edit mask. All the options may appear stacked up on top of each other until you increase the size of the field. The items will spread themselves evenly throughout the available space.

The Radio Button edit style should only be considered if you have six or fewer options that are unlikely to change. If you want to have more than six options, or if you don't have sufficient screen real estate to display all the radio button options, then you should consider using a drop down list box.

322   *Chapter 10: Advanced DataWindow Techniques*

A second consideration when dealing with radio button edit styles is that the values are hard coded into the columns and if you want to alter them you must recompile the object and possibly the application (if your object is contained in the .EXE file). If you want to be able to change the list dynamically at runtime your best option would be to use a drop down DataWindow and load your data from a table.

10.4.2.5 Check Box

We can create a check box as our edit mask for a field. This style fits when the acceptable value is restricted to two values (or three if you include the 'unknown' state option). The most common use for the check box edit mask is for a column that contains either a 'yes' or 'no' value.

The employee table in the sample database has three fields that are defined as having check box edit masks; health insurance, life insurance and day care. Each of these fields is either a yes (they do have this benefit) or no (they don't have this benefit).

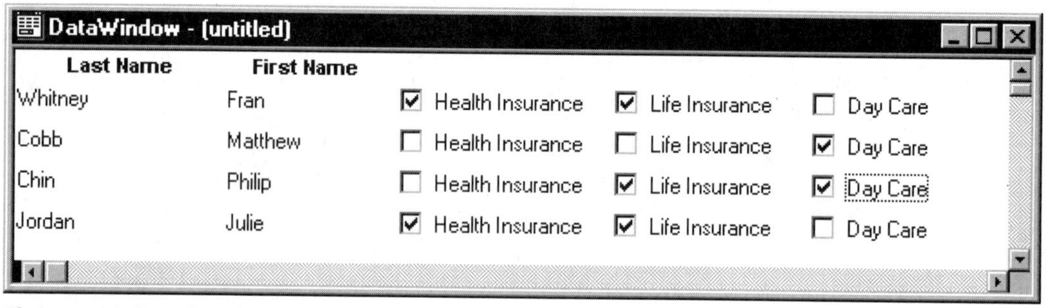

Figure 10.25 *The check box edit style is used for fields that have two possible values.*

If we enable the third state option, we can record if an employee has a benefit, doesn't have a benefit, or we don't know whether they do or don't.

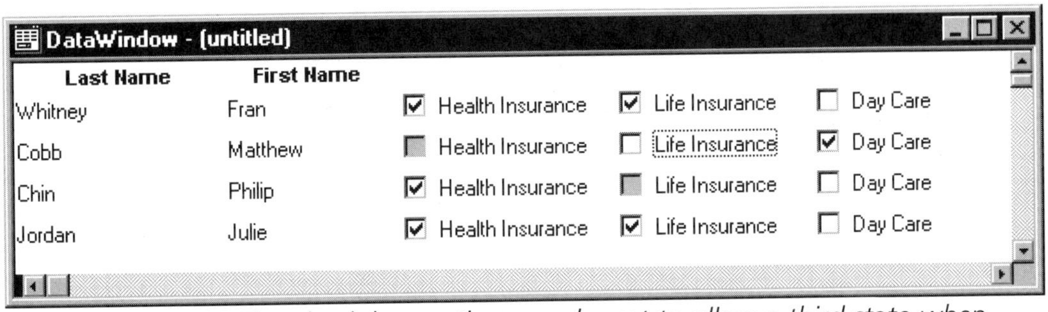

10.4 Edit Styles and Display Formats   **323**

Figure 10.26 *The check box options can be set to allow a third state when applicable. The third state shows by shading the inside of the box gray.*

The properties for the check box edit mask are:

Text   is the text that you want to appear beside the checkbox.

DataValue.On is the value that you want stored in the field when the check box is checked.

DataValue.Off is the value that you want stored in the field when the check box is unchecked.

DataValue.Other (only available when 3State property is true)—is the value that you want stored in the field when the check box is in the third 'unknown' state.

Left Text   controls if the text in the text property is displayed to the left or the right of the box.

Scale   will drawn the box to scale with the font when checked.

3 States   when checked allows the checkbox to be in three possible states; checked, unchecked or unknown.

3D Look   draws the box in 3D.

324   Chapter 10: Advanced DataWindow Techniques

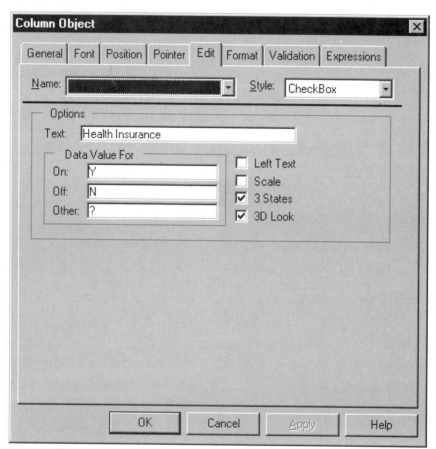

Figure 10.27 *The properties of a check box edit mask.*

10.4.2.6 Drop Down List Box

The drop down list box edit mask allows you to define a selection list for a field and have the user select a single option from the list. The items in the list will need to be relatively static as the values are hard coded into the edit mask and, like the radio button, can only be changed by recompiling the object.

An example of this type of edit style would be a drop down list box with a list of states. The full name of the state is used for the display value, but only the two character abbreviation is stored in the field.

10.5 Creating DataWindows Dynamically

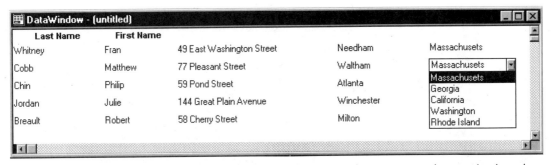

Figure 10.28 *The drop down list box edit style allows the user to select a single value from a list of values in the drop down list.*

The drop down list box edit style relies on a code table, very much like the Radio Button edit mask code table. The properties for this edit style are:

Limit specifies the maximum number of characters that can be entered. A zero indicates no limit. This is only applicable if the field is set to Allow Editing.

Case controls the case of the text in the drop down list box. The choices are Any (mixed), Upper or Lower.

Accelerator specifies a key that will be used in combination with the ALT key to bring the user directly to this field.

Sorted specifies if you want the data in the list sorted or not.

Required same as in other styles.

Allow Edit specifies if the user can type into the field, or if they must select from the list.

Always Show List specifies if you want the list to always be dropped down when the field has focus.

Always Show Arrow specifies if you want the field to always display the drop down list box arrow.

Empty String is Null same as in other styles.

Auto Horiz(ontal) Scroll same as with the edit style.

Vert(ical) Scroll Bar specifies if you want to display a vertical scroll bar within the data list (you should if you have more data than will fit in the drop down window).

326   *Chapter 10: Advanced DataWindow Techniques*

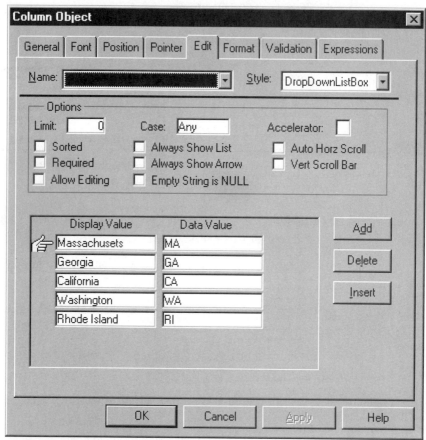

Figure 10.29 *The drop down list box edit mask also relies on a code table to provide display and data values.*

10.4.2.7 Drop Down DataWindow

The drop down DataWindow edit mask is very similar to the drop down list box except that the data is for the display and data values is dynamically loaded at runtime from a table in the database. This edit style is discussed in depth in section 10.1 above.

10.5 CREATING DATAWINDOWS DYNAMICALLY

DataWindow objects can be generated dynamically at runtime. This feature of PowerBuilder is extremely useful when you don't know what information the end user is going to want to deal with until the application is running.

I have used dynamic DataWindows often for two specific types of situations. The first situation is for low level maintenance of tables. If you want to build the ability to select and maintain tables at a low level in your application but you don't want to build and store a separate DataWindow for each table. This would be an efficiency and maintenance nightmare. Instead we read the list of tables from the system table and let the user select the one they want to maintain. Then we dynamically create a DataWindow to allow the user to browse and tweak the data in the table. Obviously this has some limitations, you don't want to allow the user to perform a retrieval on a table with 3 million rows of data!

The second situation where dynamic DataWindows are often used is with user ad-hoc queries. Based upon user input, we can dynamically generate the DataWindow at runtime. I don't recommend going too overboard here and recreating InfoMaker. Use this for simple ad hoc queries. If the users need really powerful ad-hoc querying, you should obtain one of the third party tools on the market specifically designed to do this.

The complete process for dynamically creating a DataWindow object is to:

1. Create a SQL statement

2. Describe the form and style of the DataWindow object

3. Generate the DataWindow object syntax using the SyntaxFromSQL() function.

4. Create the DataWindow object within an existing DataWindow control using the Create() function.

10.5.1 BUILDING THE DATA OBJECT SYNTAX

To build the syntax for the DataWindow object that is to be created, we must have created two strings. One string will contain the SQL statement that will be the data source for the object. The second string will contain the definition for the presentation style for the object.

328 *Chapter 10: Advanced DataWindow Techniques*

We will use an example that will walk us through the process of creating the DataWindow dynamically. To begin, we need to set up our necessary variables:

```
// Declare local variables
string ls_SQL, &            // holds the SQL statement
   ls_presentation, &       // holds the presentation string
   ls_dwsyntax, &           // holds the complete DataWindow syntax
   ls_errormsg              // holds any error returned by generation func.
```

10.5.1.1 The SQL Statement

The first component, the SQL statement could be derived from a variety of formats. You could allow the user to select the table, then the columns to include and then specify the where clause if you desire. To keep our example simple, we will use a SQL statement stored directly in the string variable ls_sql.

```
ls_sql =        "SELECT        company_name," +&
                               "fname," +&
                               "lname," +&
                               "city" + &
                               "FROM customer" +&
                               "WHERE city = 'Boston'"
```

Developers Tip: If you want to dynamically build a DataWindow and then allow the users to use the same SQL statement many times but with different where clauses (very good for what if analysis of ad-hoc queries) build the SQL statement without a where clause and then use the Modify function later to add the where clause.

10.5.1.2 The Presentation Style

The second component that we require is the presentation string. This string is used to define all the details that you would normally have defined in the DataWindow designer. The syntax that we use is the same syntax that you see if you export a DataWindow object from the library painter and examine the text file.

Within the string we must specify a series of key words followed by attributes and values for those attributes in parenthesis such as:

10.5 Creating DataWindows Dynamically **329**

"Style(Type = value)"

For a given keyword, multiple attributes can be set at one time by adding them all within the parenthesis such as:

"Style(Type = value attribute2 = value2 attribute 3 = value3 …)"

The keywords that are valid to use in your syntax are:

- Style
- Column
- Text
- DataWindow
- Group
- Title

There is a huge number of combinations of attributes and keywords that you can use to build your DataWindow. These can get very complex, so PowerBuilder has a tool attached to it to help you build your syntax. It is a separate standalone application that can be found in the PowerBuilder main directory. The name of the application is dwSyntax and should be found as dwsyn050.exe. This useful tool will allow you to browse all the attributes, keywords and values and then cut and paste this into your scripts.

For our example, we are going to define the style of this DataWindow as grid. I would not recommend trying to build extremely complex DataWindows dynamically as this is very labor intensive work and suggests that maybe you should be using a reporting tool. Ad hoc queries are usually relatively simple. The code to set our variable ls_presentation is:

ls_presentation = "style(type = grid)"

If you do not specify a style type, PowerBuilder will default your dynamic DataWindow to be tabular. For other attributes, PowerBuilder will read the defaults from the system catalog. These are the same defaults that you have set up when you create a DataWindow object in the DataWindow painter. You can alter these defaults through the **Options...** command button on the window where you specify your data source and presentation style.

10.5.2 ROLLING IT ALL TOGETHER

Now that we have defined our SQL statement and our presentation string we need to combine them together to form a complete DataWindow syntax definition. To do this we use the function SyntaxFromSQL(). The syntax for this function is:

330 *Chapter 10: Advanced DataWindow Techniques*

string_variable = SyntaxFromSQL(transaction_object, SQL_string,&
presentation_string, error_string)

where

string_variable contains the complete DataWindow syntax string.

transaction_object is the transaction object with the details for the database that this object
will be querying.

SQL_string contains the SQL statement that is the data source for the DataWindow

presentation_string contains the presentation style details for the DataWindow.

error_string is a reference variable that will contain any errors that occurred in the syntax
generation process. If this variable is empty then no errors occurred.

For our example, the code that we will enter is:

ls_dwsyntax = SyntaxFromSQL(SQLCA, ls_SQL, ls_presentation, ls_errmsg)

10.5.3 CREATING THE OBJECT

The final step that we must complete to create this dynamic DataWindow is to call the
Create() function. This function will take the generated syntax string and use it to define a
DataWindow object within an existing DataWindow control.

The syntax for the Create() function is:

dw_control.Create(syntax_string, error_string)

where

dw_control is the name of the existing DataWindow control within which you want to
create the dynamic DataWindow object.

syntax_string is the string that has been created using the SyntaxFromSQL() function.

error_string is a reference variable that will contain any errors that occurred during
DataWindow creation. This variable will be empty if no error occurred.

10.6 Modifying DataWindows Dynamically   **331**

For our example, the script that we will use is:

```
dw_adhoc.Create( ls_dwsyntax, ls_errmsg)
```

Then we want to complete our retrieval process by coding a SetTransObject() and Retrieve() function.

```
dw_adhoc.SetTransObject(SQLCA)
dw_adhoc.Retrieve()
```

We can now perform all regular DataWindow activities upon our dynamically created DataWindow object.

10.5.4 USING A .PBL FOR RUNTIME AD-HOC QUERY STORAGE

You can use a .PBL as a mechanism for storing ad-hoc queries generated by users. Using the LibraryCreate(), LibraryImport() and LibraryExport() functions you can create your own user defined report library!

LibraryCreate() will allow you to create a .PBL dynamically to store your ad hoc reports in. LibraryImport() will allow you to take the object that is currently associated with a DataWindow control (this could be a dynamic DataWindow that you have created) and save it as a DataWindow object in a .PBL. LibraryExport() allows you to export the syntax from a DataWindow object in a .PBL into a string and use the Create() function to dynamically instantiate the object.

10.6 MODIFYING DATAWINDOWS DYNAMICALLY

A critical skill to master when working with PowerBuilder is the ability to dynamically modify a DataWindow object at runtime. In the past this was handled through a pair of functions called Modify() and Describe(). You can still use these functions in PowerBuilder 5.0, but now you can also read and modify all the attributes of the DataWindow through direct referencing. Direct referencing is generally preferable to using the Modify() function because the syntax throughout your scripts would be more uniform. I have heard (although not proven yet)

332 *Chapter 10: Advanced DataWindow Techniques*

that the Modify() function is marginally faster than using direct referencing, although the difference is very small.

Although direct referencing will replace much of the functionality of the Describe() and Modify() functions, it will not eliminate them completely. Using the Modify() function is still the only way to create and destroy objects within a DataWindow object or to alter an expression within a DataWindow attribute.

Let's take a closer look at these two functions.

10.6.1 DESCRIBE

The purpose of Describe() is to return information to you about the various attributes of a DataWindow. For example,

> dw_sample.Describe("DataWindow.Zoom")

would return a string containing an number indicating the current zoom factor of the DataWindow such as '100.'

This function can also be used to return lists of information. I can request a number of complex attributes which will all be concatenated together in the result set. The function call

> dw_sample.Describe("DataWindow.Bands DataWindow.Objects")

would return a string that contains a list of all the bands in the DataWindow separated by a tab character (a '~t'). When the bands are all listed the string will include a new line character (a '~N') to separate the different elements. Then the string will list all the DataWindow objects each separated by a tab character. The string value would be:

> 'header~tdetail~tsummary~tfooter~Nemp_id_t~temp_fname_t~temp_lname_t~tsalary_t
> ~temp_id~temp_fname~temp_lname~tsalary'

I have inserted '~t' for tabs and '~N' for new lines. If you were to take this string and assign it to a multiple line edit you would see actual tabs and carriage returns.

In PowerBuilder 5.0 we can achieve the same result by using direct referencing:

```
mle_1.text = dw_employee_list.object.DataWindow.bands+"~n"+&
             dw_employee_list.object.DataWindow.objects
```

The Describe() function will return the value for the attribute in a string format. If an error occurs the value will return a "!." When you are requesting multiple attributes and an error occurs in a later attribute, the string will contain all the values that were evaluated up to where the error occurred. If an attribute that is requested contains no value the result string would contain a "?."

One other use for the Describe() function which is not possible with direct referencing is the ability to apply an expression to a specific row and column and evaluate the result. This is accomplished through the format:

```
dw_control.Describe("Evaluate('expression','row')")
```

where

Evaluate is a reserved word that activates the evaluate function of the Describe() method.

expression is the expression that you want to apply to the column.

row is the row number that you want to apply the expression to.

An example of the evaluate reserved word would be:

```
dw_control.Describe("Evaluate('If(age < 16 , 1, 0)', 15')")
```

This function would evaluate the age column in row fifteen. If the age is less than 16 then the function will evaluate to '1' otherwise it will evaluate to '0.'

10.6.2 MODIFY

The Modify() function allows us to dynamically modify the properties of a DataWindow object at runtime. This function has been one of the best weapons in a PowerBuilder developers bag of tricks. You can use the Modify() function to create objects within a DataWindow, destroy an object with a DataWindow object, or modify any of the attributes on a DataWindow or any of its objects.

10.6.2.1 Creating DataWindow Objects

To create an object within a DataWindow dynamically you embed the CREATE reserved word at the beginning of the modify string. Next you must add to the string the necessary information to define the minimum requirements for the object. These minimum requirements will vary for each different type of object. This is another situation where the dwSyntax program can be a tremendous asset as it will help you construct your CREATE statement through a point and click interface.

If we wanted to use the Modify() function to add a bitmap in the footer band of our DataWindow we would specify our Modify() function as follows:

```
dw_control.Modify("CREATE bitmap(band=header x='1' y='1' height='125'"+&
     "width='125' filename='c:\trash1.bmp' name=picture)")
```

This would create a 'trash1.bmp' bitmap in the header band at the coordinates 1,1 with a width and height of 125 units and a name of 'picture'.

Refer to the dwSyntax program or the PowerBuilder documentation to see examples for creating other objects dynamically within a DataWindow.

10.6.2.2 Destroying DataWindow Objects

To remove an object dynamically from a DataWindow object we embed the DESTROY reserved word at the beginning of the modify string. This only removes the object from this specific instance of the DataWindow object.

To destroy an object you follow the DESTROY reserved word with the name of the object that you want to destroy. For example,

```
dw_control.Modify("DESTROY picture")
```

would destroy the object that we created in the previous section. This will work for all object types except for columns. When working with columns you can name the column directly or precede the name of the column with the reserved word 'column' such as:

```
dw_control.Modify("DESTROY column emp_salary")
```

10.6 Modifying DataWindows Dynamically **335**

is the same as:

```
dw_control.Modify("DESTROY emp_salary")
```

Destroying cannot be undone, so be sure when you destroy an object that you really don't want it anymore. If you think you may need that object it the future, perhaps you only want to modify its visible attribute so it cannot be seen any more.

10.6.2.3 Changing DataWindow Attributes

The third reason for using the Modify() function is to change the attributes of a DataWindow object or an object within a DataWindow object. This is essentially the reverse of the Describe() function, and for the most part, this capability of the Modify() function has been replaced by direct manipulation of DataWindow attributes.

This variation of the Modify() function is still used if you want to assign an expression to a DataWindow attribute. For example, you want to apply an expression to the Salary.color attribute to be red if the salary is over $50,000 and green otherwise. To do this we would call the following Modify() function:

```
dw_control.Modify("salary.color='"+ string(RGB(255,0,0)) +&
       " ~t IF(salary > 50000, 255,"+ string(RGB(0,255,0)) +&
       ")'")
```

The value that we specify for the attribute is a default value plus a tab (~t) followed by the expression that we want to use, all within quotation marks.

One of the drawbacks of the Modify() function comes when you need to debug a problem with your statement. The only parameter that the Modify() function takes is a string, so whatever you enter in the string is valid as far as the compiler is concerned. You won't know about any errors until runtime. The function returns a string value to you which will be empty if there were no errors encountered in the execution. If something failed to execute inside your Modify() function then the return string will contain an identifier to help you locate the error such as:

```
Line 1 Column 18:incorrect syntax
```

Then you have to go back to your code, and start counting the characters until you find column 18 and find the character that PowerBuilder didn't like. This can be a frustrating task.

336 *Chapter 10: Advanced DataWindow Techniques*

If you are going to perform a large number of modifications to objects in a DataWindow, you could execute multiple Modify() function calls or multiple direct DataWindow manipulation statements. After either of these, the DataWindow will redraw itself. If you are performing a large number of changes this can have a negative performance impact.

There are two possible solutions to this; combine all the statements into a single Modify() function or create a DWObject variable to use in the direct manipulation. If you have a number of Modify() calls to the same DataWindow control, they can all be placed within the same string as long as you separate them with a '~t' character (an embedded tab) such as:

```
dw_control.Modify("emp_lname.visible = '1' ~t "+&
"emp_lname.color = '255'"
```

which would change the emp_lname to be visible and change the text color to red. Because only one Modify() function is called, the DataWindow is only redrawn once.

Alternatively, you could declare a variable of data type DWObject. DWObject can contain any of the component objects of a DataWindow object. You assign the object that you want to modify and alter those elements as desired. For example:

```
DWObject ldwo_modify

ldwo_modify = dw_control.Object.emp_lname
ldwo_modify.Color = 255
ldwo_modify.Visible = 1
DESTROY dwo_modify
```

This would perform the same functionality as the Modify example above. When you are addressing a number of the properties of a specific DataWindow object, this code is more efficient than long hand direct manipulation. Once critical thing to remember however is that you must explicitly destroy the DWObject variable. If it passes out of scope the object within it will become 'orphaned' and will remain in memory taking up space but serving no function.

10.7 DEALING WITH LARGE RESULT SETS

In client/server applications we strive to reduce the size of result sets that we request from the database. Large result sets tie up the server, the network and memory on our client. Reducing

10.7 Dealing with Large Result Sets   **337**

the size of the result set will improve the performance of the application and will improve the overall enterprise environment as less system resources are used. We have a number of different techniques that we use to either reduce the size of the result set, or try to deal with it in a more efficient way.

10.7.1 RETRIEVE AS NEEDED

Retrieve As Needed is a property of a DataWindow object that we can use to have the DataWindow only retrieve the result set in small blocks as the data is required by the user. When this property is set to true on the DataWindow and the Retrieve() function is called, a cursor is set up on the server and only enough rows to fill the available physical space (plus one) are fetched from the cursor. When the user cursors down or scrolls to the next page of data the next page is fetched and so on until the entire result set is retrieved.

This technique does not actually reduce the result set, but rather gives the user the perception that the performance of the application has increased because the first page of data appears very quickly. With a standard retrieval the first page of data will not appear until the entire result set is in memory. This option may reduce the result set retrieved because the user may only need to see a limited portion of data before finding what they require. At this point the retrieval can be canceled (the technique for doing so is described in section 10.7.6 —Canceling a Retrieval.

To activate this property you select from the menu in the DataWindow painter Rows → Retrieve → Rows As Needed. This can also be turned on in your script prior to issuing the Retrieve() function by coding:

```
dw_control.Object.DataWindow.Retrieve.AsNeeded = 'yes'
```

Developers Tip: Retrieve As Needed is automatically set to 'no' if you have any sorting or filtering of the result set on the client (does not apply to sorting or where clauses executed on the server) or if you are using any aggregate functions (such as sum, average or count). These conditions override the Retrieve As Needed property because by definition, PowerBuilder requires the entire result set in order to complete those conditions.

338   *Chapter 10: Advanced DataWindow Techniques*

Some of the functions that you use may be impacted by the Retrieve As Needed property. When used, the Retrieve() function will not return the total number of rows in the result set, but only the number of rows fetched in the first set (which is the number of rows it takes to fill the physical space allocated for the DataWindow control plus one). The RowCount() function will return to you the total number of rows that have been fetched into the client buffer so far. The only way to know how many rows are in the cursor on the server in total would be to perform a Count(*) embedded SQL statement prior to issuing the Retrieve() function (see section 10.7.3 for details on performing a Count(*) statement).

The events in the DataWindow are unaffected by this property. The RetrieveStart will be triggered at the beginning of the retrieval, the RetrieveRow will occur after each row is retrieved into the buffer and the RetrieveEnd will be triggered when the full result set is retrieved or the retrieval is canceled.

Developers Tip: When using Retrieve As Needed, you must be careful as opening and keeping open a cursor on the server may tie up system resources and stop other users from accessing the table that the current user is retrieving from. This lock will stay in place as long as the retrieval is incomplete. This is a bigger issue on databases that lock at the page level (like Sybase) than those that lock at the row level (like Oracle).

To help prevent users being locked out while the user holding the lock goes for lunch, you may want to code a script in the idle event which will check for incomplete retrievals and cancels them after a period of inactivity.

An approach that I recommend for providing the user with the perception of improved performance would be to begin your retrieval with the Retrieve As Needed property set to yes. After you have retrieved the first page of data, turn the property off with:

```
dw_control.Object.DataWindow.Retrieve.AsNeeded = 'no'
```

This will cause PowerBuilder to retrieve the rest of the result set in the background. The user perceives faster performance because the first page of data appears much faster than if they had to wait for a large result set to be retrieved (although the system will be a little sluggish until the entire result set is brought down) and the user can begin reading and looking at the data while the system continues to work.

10.7 Dealing with Large Result Sets **339**

If you code your retrieval in an event that has been posted to execute after the Open event (meaning that the window has been painted) then you can turn the Retrieve As Needed to no immediately after the Retrieve(). If you coded the retrieval in the Open event of the window you will not want to turn off the Retrieve as Needed property until the window has painted (meaning that you must post an event with the above code in it).

10.7.2 LIMITING THE USER'S QUERY

Limiting the user to using a more specific query is a generic concept that you can implement in many ways. The concept behind it is that users are often prone to ask for more data than they require, particularly if they are coming from the mainframe world where large result sets are common. You can require the user to be very specific in deciding what limiting criteria will be applied to reduce the result set to a smaller and more manageable size than they might otherwise select.

The advantages to this are obvious; improved performance, less network traffic and fewer system resources used. However there are tradeoffs as you are probably limiting the flexibility of the user by forcing them to take specific actions. Also, even with limiting criteria, this does not necessarily guarantee a smaller result set. To help alleviate this issue, this technique can be tied in with the Count(*) SQL calculation.

10.7.3 PERFORM A COUNT(*) CALCULATION

Executing an embedded SQL Count(*) calculation before trying to retrieve a result set will allow you to determine how many rows will be returned by the database. Then you have the option of deciding to cancel the retrieval and require the user to specify a more limited result set if the total number of rows to be retrieved exceeds some maximum threshold that you have established.

This type of a process can cost you in terms of server load as you are essentially having to execute the same SQL statement twice to get your result set. The first SQL call counts the number of rows and the second returns all the rows that were counted in the first call. This can effectively double the amount of server time necessary to complete the transaction.

340   *Chapter 10: Advanced DataWindow Techniques*

10.7.4 THE RETRIEVEROW EVENT

The RetrieveRow event is triggered after every single row that is retrieved from the database and placed into the DataWindow buffer. In this event you can keep count of all the rows that are coming back and stop the retrieval at any given point. You could also give the user the option of choosing to continue with the retrieval or stop with the data that they have so far.

This script will count the number of rows retrieved in the DataWindow and ask the user if they want to quit after every 250 rows (we are assuming the creation of an instance variable of type double called idb_rows).

RetrieveStart Event:

```
// Reset Row Counter
idb_rows = 0
```

RetrieveRow Event:

```
// Increment the row counter (which was set to zero in
// the RetrieveStart event)
idb_rows ++

IF ((idb_rows/250) - INT(idb_rows/250)) = 0 THEN

        // Exact multiple of 250 rows
        CHOOSE CASE MessageBox("Continue?","We have retrieved a total of "+&
string(idb_rows)+" rows. Do you want to continue?",& Question!, YesNo!,2)

                CASE 1 // Keep Retrieving
                     // Do Nothing
                CASE 2 // Cancel the retrieval
                     RETURN 1
        END CHOOSE
END IF
```

The biggest problem with the RetrieveRow event is that coding any script in this event (even a comment) will cause your retrieval to slow down noticeably because it is having to do work in between each row retrieved. I would not recommend this technique as a general practice, although it has its obvious uses in certain situations.

10.7.5 STORING DATA TO DISK

When you cannot avoid having to retrieve really large result sets you can avoid trying to store all that data in RAM by setting the StoreToDisk property. This will cause PowerBuilder to create a temporary file on your hard disk. This is a valid option that you can choose when you have no other option, but you have to remember that accessing data stored on disk is substantially slower than accessing data stored in memory.

You can turn this property of the DataWindow object on by selecting Rows → Retrieve → Rows To Disk from the menu in the DataWindow painter.

You can also toggle this property in your scripts with direct manipulation with:

```
dw_control.Object.DataWindow.Table.Data.Storage = 'memory' OR 'disk'
```

One final word about this option: it only works in 32 bit environments. If you are planning to roll out your application in a 16 bit environment, you can't use it.

10.7.6 PROVIDE A CANCEL RETRIEVAL OPTION

You can provide the user with a mechanism to cancel a retrieval in progress by using the function DBCancel() like this:

```
dw_control.DBCancel()
```

This function must be placed somewhere that a user can trigger it such as a command button. If you are using Retrieve As Needed, after each page of data is retrieved, the user can choose to go on as normal, or click on the 'Cancel Retrieval' command button with the DBCancel() function scripted in the clicked event. For regular retrievals, you must provide a way for the system to allow another action to be processed. This can be accomplished by placing a line of code in the RetrieveRow event (even a comment will do). This will force the DataWindow to yield to other processing messages as they come in.

342 *Chapter 10: Advanced DataWindow Techniques*

Developers Tip: Whenever you have a long running script and want to provide a way for other windows tasks to process simultaneously you can add a *Yield()* function to your code. This allows the system to check the message queue and execute them if they exist. This will function better in a 32 bit environment. In the 16 bit environment, Windows will try to 'timeslice' which can make your application jerk along in a rather unprofessional fashion.

You can also cancel a DataWindow retrieval by coding a

RETURN 1

in the RetrieveStart (to cancel before beginning a retrieve), SQLPreview or RetrieveRow events. This is the PowerBuilder 4.0 equivalent of a SetActionCode(1) function.

10.8 SHARING RESULT SETS

In PowerBuilder we have the ability to have multiple DataWindows share the same result set. This is extremely useful when you want to show two different views of the same data in different DataWindows.

An example of how this is often used in production enterprise applications is the list/detail paradigm. In this paradigm you have a window with two DataWindow controls on it. The first DataWindow control contains the entire result set, but only shows the necessary columns to differentiate one row from the next. The format of the first DataWindow is either tabular or grid. This DataWindow is called the list DataWindow.

The second DataWindow control is called the detail DataWindow. It displays all the information about the currently selected row in the list DataWindow, usually in a freeform format. Both DataWindows share the same result set, but display the information in different ways. This interface allows the user to move quickly through the data and perform updates on the rows that they want to change.

10.8 Sharing Result Sets

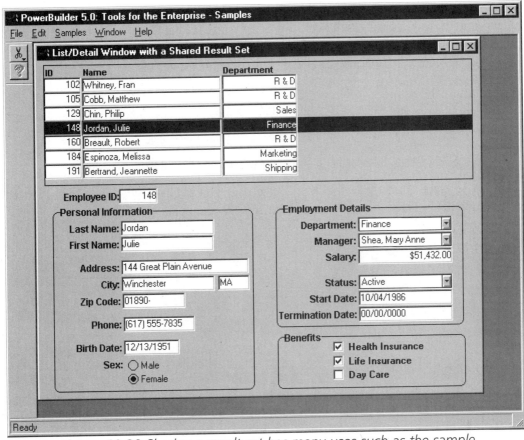

Figure 10.30 *Sharing a result set has many uses such as the sample List/Detail window on the companion CD.*

The sharing of result sets alleviates two problems with this type of retrieval. You only need to hit the database once to get all the information you need and you don't need to try and synchronize the data between the two windows. The two windows actually directly access the exact same set of buffers. When you make an update in one window, you are effectively updating them both. Sending a function call like Update() to a DataWindow control will cause the primary buffer to update regardless of which of the DataWindows you call the function on.

The result set actually belongs to one of the DataWindow controls. This control is called the Primary control. When you decide to link it to another DataWindow control, this control is the secondary control. You can share to as many secondary controls as you like.

Chapter 10: Advanced DataWindow Techniques

The critical factor when using ShareData() is that all DataWindows sharing the same buffers must have identical result sets. If you try to do a ShareData() function but no data shows up, check to ensure that the result sets are identical. The where clause and sort order statements in your SQL will not affect the share. For example, results sets from these SQL statements can all share data together:

1. SELECT emp_fname, emp_lname FROM employee
2. SELECT emp_fname, emp_lname FROM employee WHERE emp_id > 250
3. SELECT emp_fname, emp_lname FROM consultants ORDER BY consultant_id

Some developers like to use the query object as the data source when they know they will be sharing result sets to ensure that the result sets are identical.

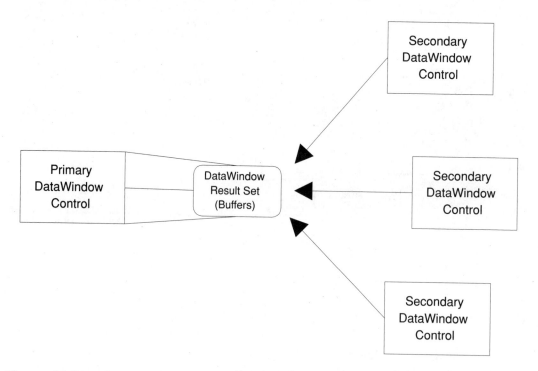

Figure 10.31 When sharing buffers between DataWindows, one DataWindow control is the primary control (it owns the buffers) all others are secondary controls.

The syntax for the ShareData() function is:

```
dw_primary.ShareData(dw_secondary)
```

where

dw_primary is the DataWindow control (with object) that will be the primary DataWindow. This is the DataWindow that has custody over the result set.

dw_secondary is the DataWindow control (with object) that will share the result set of the primary DataWindow.

To stop the link between a primary and secondary DataWindow you use the function:

```
dw_control.ShareDataOff()
```

where

dw_control is either the primary or secondary DataWindow control. If it is a secondary DataWindow control, then the link between those two DataWindows will be severed and the secondary control will appear blank. If it is a primary control then the links to all secondary DataWindows will be severed and they will all appear blank.

You can potentially gain performance improvements with ShareData by reducing the number of hits on the database server. Another common use is to have a single DataStore or DataWindow which contains the data for frequently used drop down DataWindows and to share the data with the drop down DataWindows whenever they are used. This technique is discussed in section 10.2.1.2.3 Buffering and Sharing Result Sets (for Child DataWindows) earlier in this chapter.

There is one thing to be aware of when using ShareData. Since the actual buffers are shared, if you filter one of the DataWindows involved, you are actually going to filter them all. This means that you cannot retrieve your entire code table into one DataStore and then simply filter it for each drop down DataWindow you have.

Developers Tip: You are not limited to sharing data only on the same DataWindow. You can, in fact, share data anywhere within an application. You can pass a DataWindow as a reference variable to another object and have the second object share data with the first. Of course, if the primary DataWindow is closed, the link to secondary DataWindows will be severed.

10.9 USING BITMAPS

Working in a GUI environment implies a strong use of visual cues and images. One way of adding to the visual side of your application is to take advantage of bitmap functionality in PowerBuilder. There are a number of different ways that you can use bitmaps in your applications. You can place them in picture controls, picture buttons, or in DataWindows as a visual enhancement, but you can also use them within the working area of a DataWindow to convey meaningful information.

10.9.1 DISPLAY AS PICTURE

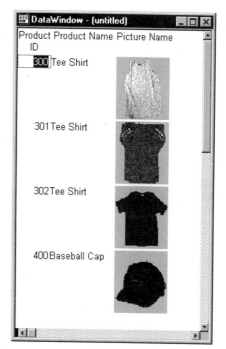

Figure 10.32 *Using Display As Picture to display a meaningful bitmap in a column in the detail band.*

Text columns in the database can be used to store the name of a bitmap file stored locally or on a network file server. To activate this option, you must turn on the Display As Picture property which is on the General tab of the properties page for the column that contains the bitmap name. When this property is set to true, the column will be a display only column.

10.9 Using Bitmaps 347

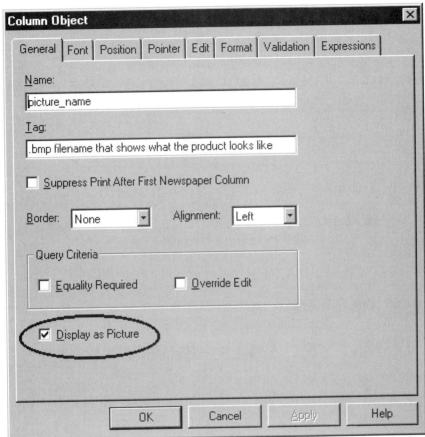

Figure 10.33 *The Display As Picture property will read a text column in the database and convert the text into a name for a bitmap file stored locally or on a networked server. The bitmap is displayed in the column space.*

10.9.2 PICTURES IN COMPUTED FIELDS

Display As Picture can also be used in combination with a computed field to relate information to your user. You can define an expression and then use the Bitmap() function to convert a string to a bitmap image. In the sample application on the Shared Result Set example, we examine the employees salary and if it is over $45,000 we put a happy face bitmap, if it is below that we put a blue sad face.

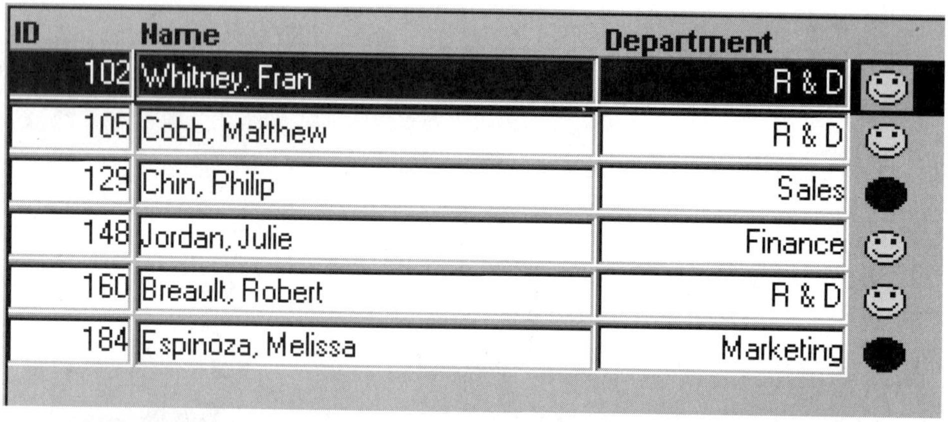

348 *Chapter 10: Advanced DataWindow Techniques*

ID	Name	Department	
102	Whitney, Fran	R & D	☺
105	Cobb, Matthew	R & D	☺
129	Chin, Philip	Sales	●
148	Jordan, Julie	Finance	☺
160	Breault, Robert	R & D	☺
184	Espinoza, Melissa	Marketing	●

Figure 10.34 *Computed fields can be used to display bitmaps based upon computed expressions.*

The syntax in the computed column is:

```
bitmap(if( salary >45000, 'happy.bmp', 'frown.bmp'))
```

10.10 USING THE SQLPREVIEW EVENT

The DataWindow has a special event called the SQLPreview event which fires immediately before the DataWindow sends a SQL statement to the database. In this event you can examine the SQL statement and decide to allow it to pass, stop it from going to the database, or replace it with a different SQL statement.

This event has a number of arguments that contain key information about the SQL statement that is being passed to the database:

request this argument will tell you which PowerScript function caused the current SQL statement to be generated. It will return an enumerated data type with one of the following values:

PreviewFunctionReselectRow!—SQL statement was initiated by the ReselectRow() function.

PreviewFunctionRetrieve!—SQL statement is from the Retrieve() function.

PreviewFunctionUpdate!—SQL statement is from the Update() function.

10.10 Using the SQLPreview Event   **349**

sqltype this argument will indicate what kind of SQL statement the current statement is. The value in this argument is an enumerated data type that equates to:

PreviewDelete!—SQL statement is a DELETE statement.

PreviewInsert!—SQL statement is an INSERT statement.

PreviewSelect!—SQL statement is a SELECT statement.

PreviewUpdate!—SQL statement is an UPDATE statement.

sqlsyntax this argument contains the complete SQL statement.

buffer this argument contains an enumerated data type that will tell you the identity of the DataWindow buffer that is either sending or receiving the data for this SQL statement. The possible values are:

Primary!

Filter!

Delete!

row this argument tells you the row number that is being updated, selected, inserted or deleted.

In your script for the SQLPreview event you can elect to continue, abort (if updating) or skip the current request and begin the next one (if one exists). This is accomplished through the return codes:

RETURN 0 - continue

RETURN 1 - Abort Update

RETURN 2 - Skip current request

You can also alter the current SQL statement by using the SetSQLPreview() function as follows:

dw_control.SetSQLPreview(new_sql_string)

All of the above concepts are demonstrated in the sample application. This example has been added to the User Events window. You will see a checkbox at the bottom of the window which says SQL Preview. When this is checked, the SQL Preview event will open the

SQL Preview response window (that is part of the sample application) where you can alter the SQL, Abort it, Skip it or Continue.

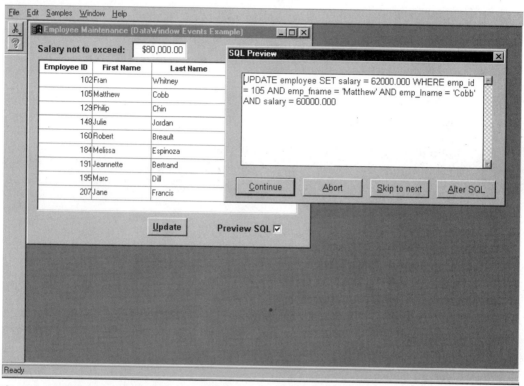

Figure 10.35 *The SQL Preview example in the companion CD application lets you preview and alter each SQL statement the DataWindow sends to the database.*

In the open event of the window we have set the DBParm attribute of SQLCA to

SQLCA.DBParm = "disablebind = 1"

to disable the use of bind variables. If we leave the bind variables enabled, our update previews would have all the values filled with question marks ('?'). Disabling the use of bind variables while previewing allows us to see the actual SQL statement.

10.10 Using the SQLPreview Event   351

The DataWindow control has the following script in the SQLPreview event:

```
s_sqlpreview lstr_sqlpreview

IF cbx_preview.checked THEN

        lstr_sqlpreview.s_sql = sqlsyntax
        IF sqltype = PreviewUpdate! THEN
                lstr_sqlpreview.b_update = TRUE
        ELSE
                lstr_sqlpreview.b_update = FALSE
        END IF

        OpenWithParm(w_sqlpreview,lstr_sqlpreview)

        lstr_sqlpreview = Message.PowerObjectParm

        CHOOSE CASE lstr_sqlpreview.i_return

                CASE 0  // Continue
                        RETURN 0
                CASE 1  // Abort the process
                        RETURN 1
                CASE 2  // Skip the current request, but continue with
                        // the next
                        RETURN 2
                CASE 3  // Alter the SQL then continue
                        THIS.SetSQLPreview(lstr_sqlpreview.s_sql)
                        RETURN 0
        END CHOOSE
END IF
```

The window w_sqlpreview has a multiline edit where the user can edit the SQL statement and the four buttons shown in Figure 10.35 above. Each one will specify a different return value. If the return value is 3, then we will use the SetSQLPreview() function as shown above to alter the SQL statement that the DataWindow is sending. Give it a try in the sample application.

352 *Chapter 10: Advanced DataWindow Techniques*

10.11 SUMMARY

Use the information in this chapter to take your DataWindows to the next level. With these techniques you can improve your user interface, speed up your application execution and manage your code more effectively.

There are still many more excellent DataWindow techniques that are in use, but this chapter has covered some of the most important. You should keep your eyes on the trade magazines where many new and emerging techniques are often featured.

CHAPTER 11

Advanced Reporting

*D*espite a wealth of third party tools for report generation on the market, most PowerBuilder projects choose to generate the bulk of their output directly from PowerBuilder. Why is this? Largely it is because of the flexibility and power of using the DataWindow to create reports. With the latest enhancements from PowerBuilder 4.0 and 5.0, almost any report that you can dream up can be constructed.

At this point, I am going to assume that you have already built standard reports with PowerBuilder. This implies that you are familiar with the DataWindow painter at a fundamental level and can perform all the basic operations. We will not be reviewing these here. Instead, we are going to focus on more advanced reporting techniques; nested reports, composite reports, graphs and crosstabs.

11.1 NESTED REPORTS

One of the tools that you have available to you for the building of sophisticated reports in PowerBuilder is the nested report. Nested reports are DataWindows that have other DataWindows embedded inside them. You can daisy chain as many of these DataWindows together as you desire and can effectively create a chain of DataWindows of different types and data sources within your parent DataWindow. Nested reports are sometimes referred to as 'Basic Plus' reports in PowerBuilder documentation.

Chapter 11: Advanced Reporting

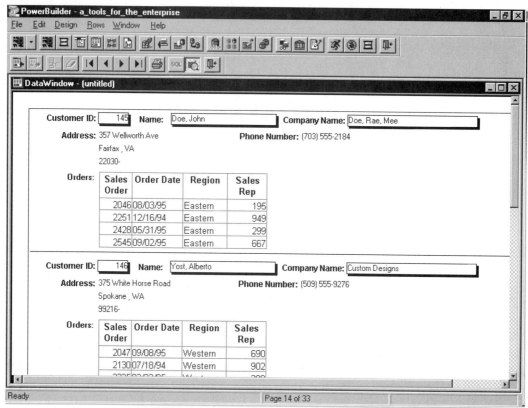

Figure 11.1 *A nested report is a DataWindow which has other DataWindows embedded within it.*

When you nest DataWindows, the object becomes exclusively a reporting object, you cannot use the data input and update DataWindow functionality in a nested report DataWindow object.

Your nested reports can be as many levels deep as you desire, or as your system resources can handle. You can accomplish this by building a nested report with an embedded DataWindow object, then you take that entire report and embed it into a new nested report, and so on. Each new report or DataWindow object can have its own presentation style and data source. You have the ability to link or daisy chain these reports through the definition of retrieval arguments that are linked to columns in the parent DataWindow. This will be demonstrated in section 11.1.1—Creating a Nested Report.

11.1 Nested Reports   **355**

Developers Tip: Nested reports can take a while to retrieve. Each level in the nesting can cause the retrieve time to increase almost exponentially. Try to keep the number of levels at a minimum, and for large reports, you will need to provide visual cues to the end user about what the system is doing.

If you have one nested report the DataWindow will first retrieve the master report. If this report brings back 100 rows then the DataWindow will need to execute 100 more retrieves (one for each instance of the nested DataWindow). This is a total of 101 retrieves. If the nested DataWindow itself contains a nested DataWindow, the retrieval effort could increase exponentially.

When you embed a DataWindow object into another (creating a nested report), you are adding an object to the parent DataWindow. This is accomplished by pressing the Nested Report icon in the DataWindow painter. The object that is created on the DataWindow cannot be treated exactly the same as other objects on the DataWindow such as columns, text fields and bitmaps. This is because within the embedded DataWindow there could be a number of rows of data, all containing multiple columns, and so on. This will restrict you from using the embedded DataWindow in a computed expression, filter, grouping, sorting or other activities which assume a much less complex object.

11.1.1 CREATING A NESTED REPORT

Nested reports are particularly useful for creating reports that rely upon a master/detail relationship in the data being reported on. Our example will use data from the PowerBuilder sample database that has just such a relationship.

We are going to build a report that will show all the sales orders for a particular customer, as illustrated in Figure 11.1. The database contains a table called Customer with the primary key cust_id. This links to the foreign key cust_id in the table Sales_Order. We will create a list of all the orders for a customer and embed that DataWindow into a freeform list of all the customers in the database.

Step 1   Create a DataWindow object to show all the orders for a specific customer. Open the DataWindow painter and select **New...** from the Select window. Then select SQL Select as the data source and Grid as the presentation style for your new DataWindow. Press **OK**.

356 Chapter 11: Advanced Reporting

Step 2   Build a SQL Select data source. Choose the sales_order table from the list. When the table appears, select the id, order_date, region and sales_rep columns.

Step 3   Define a retrieval argument. From the **Design** menu bar item, select **Retrieval Arguments...**. This will open the Specify Retrieval Arguments dialog window. Define a single numeric argument called ai_cust_id as in Figure 11.2. This will be used to link the embedded DataWindow to the parent DataWindow. When you are finished, press the **OK** button.

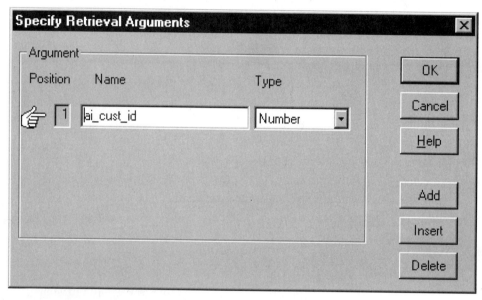

Figure 11.2 Define a numeric retrieval argument called ai_cust_id. This will be used to link the embedded DataWindow to the parent.

Step 4   Build the where clause. In the Where tab on the SQL Toolbox (at the bottom of your SQL Select painter) define a where clause to set the cust_id column equal to the argument defined in step 3. The result should appear as in Figure 11.3. Remember that all arguments are host variables and must be preceded by a colon (':').

11.1 Nested Reports

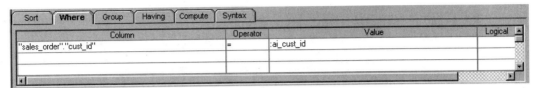

Figure 11.3 *Define a where clause in the SQL Toolbox where cust_id equals the argument defined in step 3.*

The complete SQL statement for this object is:

```
SELECT id,
    order_date,
    region,
    sales_rep
FROM    sales_order
WHERE cust_id = :ai_cust_id
```

Step 5 Go to the designer. Press the SQL icon in the painterbar to close the SQL Select painter and move to the DataWindow designer (sometimes referred to as the 'user interface painter').

Step 6 Customize to your specifications. Adjust the DataWindow object so that it conforms to your user interface specifications for reports. You can alter fonts, colors, column widths and other visual aspects. I have changed the edit style for region so that the drop down DataWindow arrow does not appear.

Chapter 11: Advanced Reporting

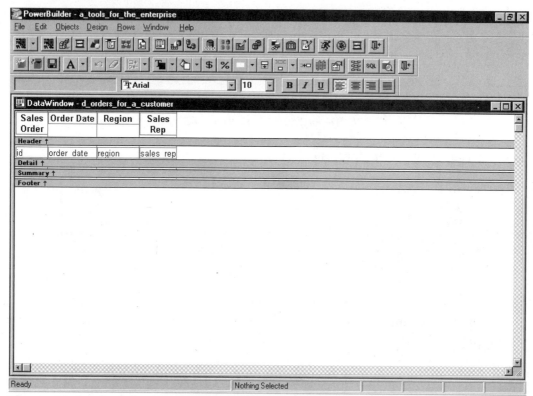

Figure 11.4 *Adjust the DataWindow object so that it conforms to your user interface specifications for reports.*

Step 7   Save the DataWindow. Save the DataWindow with the name d_orders_for_a_customer. You have now created the DataWindow object that we will embed into the parent DataWindow. Close the DataWindow painter.

Step 8   Create the DataWindow to show all the customers and their orders. Open the DataWindow painter. Select a new DataWindow and define it as having a SQL Select data source and a Freeform presentation style. Press **OK**.

Step 9   Define the SQL statement. Select the customer table from the Select Tables dialog window. When the table appears, select all the columns. The complete select statement for this table should be as follows:

11.1 Nested Reports 359

```
SELECT id,
    fname,
    lname,
    address,
    city,
    state,
    zip,
    phone,
    company_name
FROM customer
```

Step 10 Go to the designer. Press the SQL icon in the painterbar to close the SQL Select painter and move to the DataWindow designer.

Step 11 Customize the interface. Customize the interface to make room for the embedded DataWindow. You can alter the column layouts and design as I have in Figure 11.5.

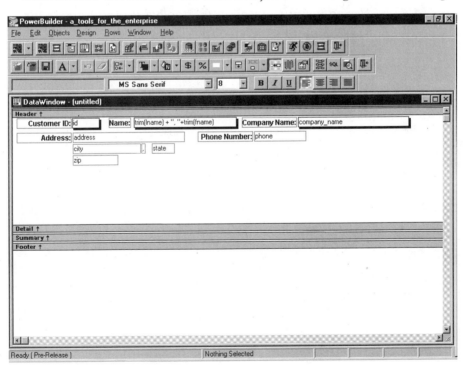

Figure 11.5 *Customize the interface allowing room for the embedded DataWindow and changing the fields to meet the report definition and standards.*

Chapter 11: Advanced Reporting

We have removed the first and last name columns and replaced them with a computed field called full_name. The computed field contains:

trim(lname) + ","+trim(fname)

We have also added a text field between the city and state fields which contains a single comma. Both this text field and the state field have been set to slide left and eliminate the gaps between city and state.

Step 12 Add the nested report. To embed the nested DataWindow in this one, we first select the Nested Reports icon from the objects drop down toolbar. The icon is pictured in Figure 11.6

Figure 11.6 *The Nested Reports button in the toolbar is used to place a nested DataWindow on the current DataWindow.*

Next you will select where in the current DataWindow you wish to nest another DataWindow. When you do this, a small box will appear and the Report Object dialog window will open as shown in figure 11.7.

The Report Object dialog window allows you to access and modify all the properties of the report object which you are nesting in the current DataWindow. The tab that comes up selected is the Select Reports. You will choose which DataWindow object you want to embed as a report in the current DataWindow. Select d_orders_for_a_customer from the list.

11.1 Nested Reports

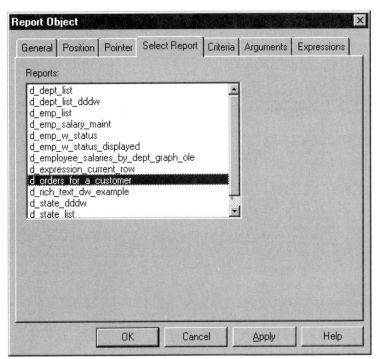

Figure 11.7 *The Report Object dialog allows you to access and modify all the properties of the report object which you are nesting in the current DataWindow.*

When you have done this, press the **OK** command button. Your designer should now show an object that has been resized to the width necessary to contain the report. The height of this object will be automatically adjusted at runtime to a height suitable to contain the number of rows being retrieved. Unfortunately, you don't see the DataWindow object that is nested inside the report object, although this isn't necessary for the object to function correctly.

362 Chapter 11: Advanced Reporting

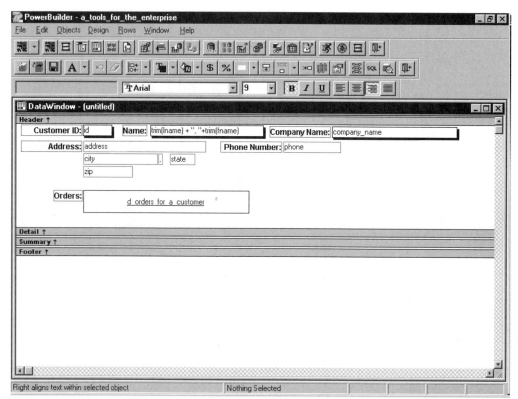

Figure 11.8 *The designer will show a report object on the current DataWindow that is wide enough to contain the nested DataWindow within.*

Add a text field with the label 'Orders:' as a header for the report object.

Step 13 Link the embedded DataWindow to the current DataWindow. We must provide a mechanism to relate the embedded DataWindow to the current row of the current DataWindow. This will allow us to only show the orders for a specific customer as their details are displayed in the report. We do this by linking the retrieval arguments on the report object to something inside the current DataWindow. In our case we will link ai_cust_id, the retrieval argument in the nested DataWindow, to the id column in the detail band.

Click on the report object with the right mouse button. A popup menu will appear containing options such as Modify Report, Cut, Copy and so on. Select the **Properties...** option. This will reopen the Properties page for the report dialog.

From here, select the **Arguments** tab as shown in Figure 11.9.

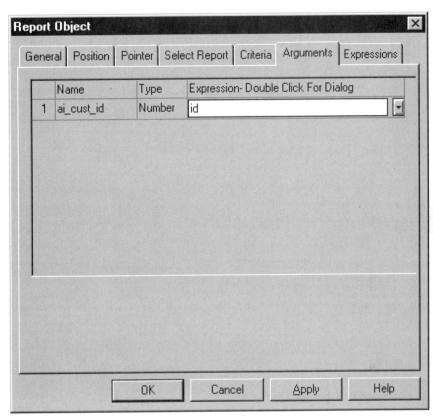

Figure 11.9 *The Arguments tab on the report object Properties page allows you to link the retrieval arguments of the nested DataWindow to an object or expression on the current DataWindow.*

This tab displays all the retrieval arguments defined for the nested DataWindow. You can link each retrieval argument to any referenceable object or valid expression on the current DataWindow. We are going to keep it simple and link the nested DataWindow retrieval argument ai_cust_id to the current value of the id column. Click on the drop down arrow and select id from the drop down list. For a more complex expression, double clicking in the entry field would open up the expression dialog window.

364   *Chapter 11: Advanced Reporting*

When you are finished, press the **OK** command button.

Step 14 Save the DataWindow. Save the current DataWindow object as d_customers_orders_report. You can now preview the report by selecting the Preview icon in the painterbar. Your DataWindow should appear similar to the one shown in Figure 11.1 at the beginning of this unit. Watch the row count at the bottom of the screen and you can understand why it takes longer to retrieve the data set for a nested DataWindow object.

11.1.2 USING THE REPORT OBJECTS PROPERTIES PAGE

All the properties of a report object are conveniently located on the Report Objects Properties page which you can open by clicking on the report object in the designer with the right mouse button and selecting **Properties...** off the popup menu. Alternatively, you could open the dialog window by selecting the report object and clicking on the Properties icon in the painterbar.

There are seven tabs in the tab control inside the properties page. They cover general, position, and pointer properties as well as allow you to select the DataWindow object associated with this report object, set retrieval criteria, set values and expressions for the DataWindow arguments and to define expressions to dynamically change the overall attributes for the report object.

11.1.2.1 General Properties

The General tab on the properties page allows you to access the general attributes that affect the overall embedded object.

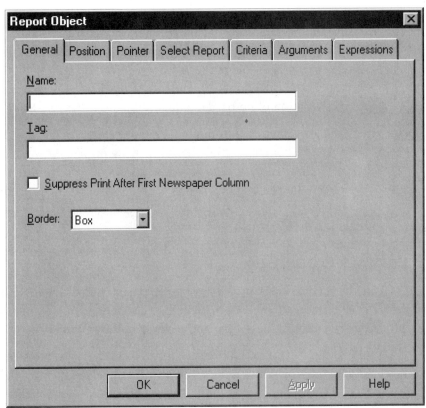

Figure 11.10 *The General tab on the properties dialog allows you to change the name, tag and border of the embedded report object. You can also enable the Suppress After First Newspaper Column attribute, which will stop this object from printing multiple times if the DataWindow is set to display in multiple columns.*

These properties are:

Name defines the name by which the embedded DataWindow will be referenced from within the parent DataWindow.

Tag defines the tag value for the embedded DataWindow object. This is a string value which can be accessed at runtime. By default, it will not cause or affect any specific functionality. It can contain any information you would like it to such as a text string for Microhelp. Some third party class libraries access this field to determine how to set protection, colors or other properties at runtime.

366   *Chapter 11: Advanced Reporting*

Border   defines what type of border will appear around the entire embedded
                           DataWindow. In addition to the standard borders of 3D Raised, 3D
                           Lowered, Shadow Box and Box, you can also use an Underline border
                           or a Resize border (the border does not provide resizing functionality,
                           but only the visual double line around the object). Of course, you still
                           have the option of no border at all.

Suppress Print After First Newspaper Column can be set to either TRUE or FALSE
                           (checked or not checked). When displaying or printing your
                           DataWindow using newspaper column formats, you can stop this
                           object from repeating in columns subsequent to the first by checking
                           this property. This is usually used in objects contained in bands other
                           than the detail band.

11.1.2.2 Position Properties

The Position tab on the report object properties page contains properties that control the
physical position of the embedded object in the parent DataWindow. Also contained on this
page are the properties that control the sliding and resizing of this object.

In most applications, the Y position and the height of this object are not significant, as
the object is repeated with multiple Y positions when it is instantiated, and the height is usually automatically sized at runtime based upon how much data is contained within the
embedded DataWindow. The X coordinate and the width are more significant, as they will
affect the physical position and size of the object. These attributes are not usually set on the
tab, but rather are set in the parent DataWindow designer, where you can use drag and drop
to position and resize the object.

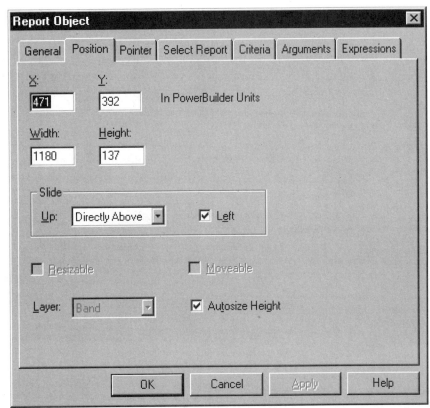

Figure 11.11 *The Position tab allows you to review and alter the physical position properties as well as the sliding and autosizing properties of the embedded DataWindow object.*

The Position tab properties are:

X   defines the distance of the embedded DataWindow from the left edge of the parent DataWindow in whatever units the parent DataWindow is defined in (by default this is PowerBuilder units).

Y   defines the distance of the first instance of the embedded DataWindow from the top edge of the parent DataWindow in whatever units the parent DataWindow is defined in. This attribute will dynamically change with each instance of the embedded DataWindow (assuming the embedded DataWindow is contained in the detail band) object, but

368   *Chapter 11: Advanced Reporting*

will automatically maintain is position relative to the other objects that are also repeated with each instance of the detail band.

Width   defines the width of the embedded DataWindow object in whatever units the parent DataWindow is defined in. The default width that will be assigned is the width of the embedded DataWindow object plus a small amount of space as a border (whether the border is visible or not).

Height   defines the height of the embedded DataWindow object in whatever units the parent DataWindow is defined in. By default, the height will be set to automatically change based upon how much data is retrieved in each instance of the embedded DataWindow (see the Autosize Height property below).

Slide Up   defines the upward slide properties of the embedded DataWindow object. The slide properties are similar to the slide properties for a column as discussed in *Chapter 10—Advanced DataWindow Concepts*. You can cause the embedded report to slide upwards, if there is empty space above it, or slide left if there is empty space to the left (see the Slide Left property below). The choices that you have for sliding up are:

None—the object will not slide up, even if empty space exists above it

Directly Above—the object will slide up if there is empty space directly above the space which it occupies.

All Above—the object will slide up only if the space above the embedded report is empty for the entire width of the parent DataWindow.

Slide Left	sets the DataWindow object to slide to the left if empty space or null fields exist to its left. It will slide until it finds an object that is not null. By default, this attribute is set to checked (TRUE). Setting it to unchecked (FALSE) will stop any left sliding from occurring. Slide up and slide left operate independent of one another.
Resizeable	this property is disabled for the embedded report as they cannot be resized by the user at runtime. You may notice the checkbox will become checked if you set the border to be Resize in the General tab, however, your embedded report will still not exhibit this functionality.
Moveable	this property is also disabled for the embedded report. The user cannot move the embedded report at run time.
Layer	this property is also disabled for the embedded report as all embedded reports must appear in the band layer.
Autosize Height	this property is by default set to TRUE. This will cause each instance of the embedded DataWindow to automatically adjust its height at run-time based upon the quantity of data which is contains. This will usually be left in its default state. If you uncheck this attribute (setting it to FALSE) each instance of the embedded report will be the fixed height defined in the height attribute, regardless of how much or how little data they have to show.

11.1.2.3 Pointer Properties

The Pointer tab for the embedded DataWindow object allows you to alter the pointer characteristics when the pointer is positioned above the embedded object.

Chapter 11: Advanced Reporting

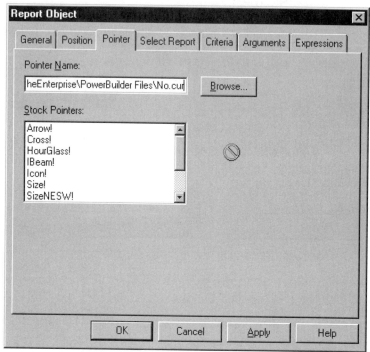

Figure 11.12 *The Pointer tab allows you control which pointer you want to appear when the mouse is positioned over the embedded object.*

The single Pointer tab property is:

Pointer Name   contains the name of the file which is a valid cursor file (.CUR) that you want to use for the pointer when the mouse is positioned above this object. The Browse button will allow you to search through your directories to find the cursor file, or you can use the Stock Pointers list box to select from the built in set of pointers. The standard windows pointers are built into the stock pointer set (i.e. Arrow, HourGlass, Ibeam). If no pointer is defined, the object will use whatever pointer is defined for the parent DataWindow.

11.1.2.4 Select Report Properties

The Select Report tab we have already seen during the creation of our nested report in Step 12 of the above example. This tab contains the Report property (which is the DataObject attribute when accessing this in your scripts). You select the currently associated report from the list of available DataWindows in all the libraries in the application object library search path.

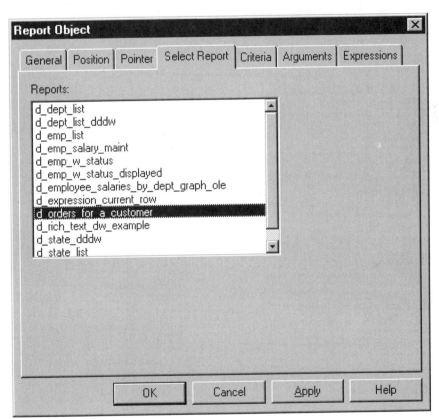

Figure 11.13 *The Select Report tab allows you to select or change which DataWindow will be contained within this embedded object.*

11.1.2.5 Criteria Properties

The Criteria tab allows you to define limiting criteria for the retrieval of data into this embedded DataWindow object. The method for doing so is very similar to the criteria window of a QuickSelect DataWindow.

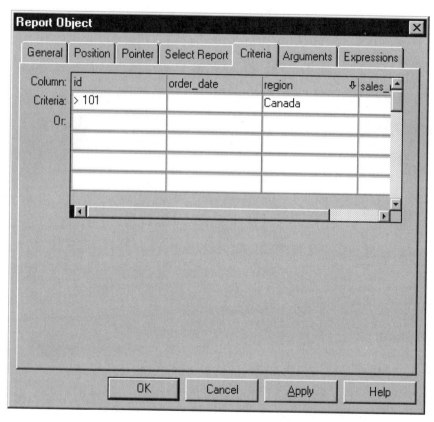

Figure 11.14 *The Criteria tab contains a table where you can enter limiting criteria for the retrieval of data into the embedded DataWindow object.*

Criteria entered across a physical line will be linked together using a logical AND, whereas, criteria placed on two different physical lines will be linked together with a logical OR. The example in Figure 11.13 would result in the query being limited by a where clause of:

```
id > 101 AND region = 'Canada'
```

11.1 Nested Reports 373

The actual where clause would contain the region code. The table automatically takes advantage of the predefined edit style to make our data entry easier. As you can see in Figure 11.14, the edit style defined for region allows us to pick the region from a Drop Down DataWindow.

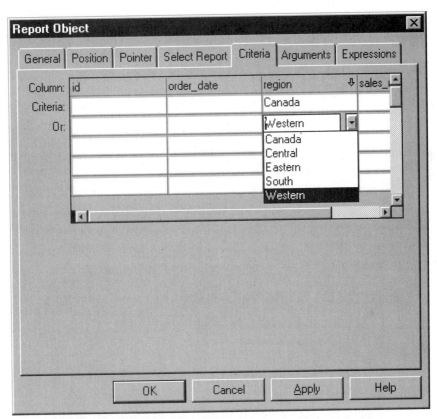

Figure 11.15 *Predefined edit styles are available to help you to enter criteria, like the Drop Down Listbox.*

In Figure 11.15, we see an example of a where clause that would be equal to:

region = 'Canada' OR region = 'Western'

Developers Tip: Criteria placed on the same physical line can be ORed together simply by typing 'OR' in front of the value. The same technique can be used to AND together criteria placed on two different physical lines.

11.1.2.6 Arguments Properties

The Arguments tab has been demonstrated in Step 13 of the example above. It is used to link any retrieval arguments defined for the embedded DataWindow object to columns and referenceable objects in the parent DataWindow. You can create any valid expression to pass information into the retrieval arguments for the embedded DataWindow. See Step 13 in section 11.1.1 Creating a Nested Report for more details.

11.1.2.7 Expressions Properties

The Expressions tab allows you to enter static and dynamic expressions for some of the general properties for the embedded DataWindow object. Although static expressions could be used, this tab is most often used to create dynamic expressions that are evaluated at runtime. An example might be to set the visible attribute to be

IF (state = 'CA',1,0)

This would have the effect of making the embedded DataWindow visible only if the customer was from California.

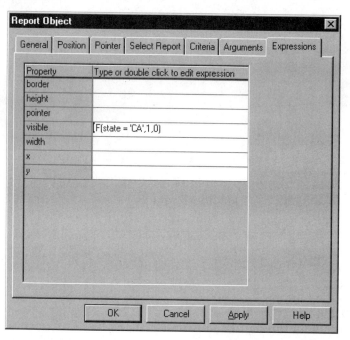

Figure 11.16 *The Expressions tab is used to enter dynamic (or static) expressions that will change the properties of the embedded object dynamically at runtime.*

> **PowerBuilder 4.0 to 5.0: This same functionality was available in PowerBuilder 4.0 through the popup menu that appeared when you clicked the right mouse button on a nested report.**

11.1.3 REFERENCING A NESTED REPORT IN YOUR SCRIPT

From the applications that I have been involved with, the need to access a nested report from your script arises very seldom. This is largely because nested reports are read only and don't allow any database updates. However, should you need access to a nested report the technique is very similar to accessing a DataWindow object inside of a Drop Down DataWindow with one notable exception; you can read the properties of a nested report, but you can only change a few of them such as the border or the list of arguments. The nested DataWindows are also child DataWindows, however, you cannot use the GetChild() function to get the handle of the nested report.

If you are unsure if the parent DataWindow actually possesses any nested reports, you can check the nested property. This is done through direct referencing as follows:

```
ls_nested = dw_control.Object.DataWindow.nested
```

This syntax allows you to determine the nested attribute the DataWindow object associated with the DataWindow control you name. The variable, ls_nested, will contain either 'yes' or 'no' after this line of code is executed.

> **PowerBuilder 4.0 to 5.0: Determining if the DataWindow associated with a specific DataWindow control contained a nested report was accomplished with the Describe() function in PowerBuilder 4.0. This syntax will still function in PowerBuilder 5.0. The PowerBuilder 4.0 equivalent expression would be:**
>
> ```
> ls_nested = dw_control.Describe("DataWindow.Nested")
> ```

Remember that we cannot alter a property within the nested DataWindow object. Trying to code

```
dw_nested.Object.order_list.Object.DataWindow.color = 255
```

376   *Chapter 11: Advanced Reporting*

will pass the compiler, but will cause your application to terminate. You could read the color value and store it in a variable like:

```
li_color = dw_nested.Object.order_list.Object.DataWindow.color
```

As a reminder: refer to the dwSyntax program to see what attributes of the nested report you can dynamically modify and the correct syntax for doing so.

11.2 COMPOSITE REPORTS

The primary purpose of the Composite presentation style is to allow you to create a DataWindow shell to act as a container for multiple DataWindow objects that you want to group together as a single report. The DataWindows that are included can be data independent. That means that they do not have to have expressions that provide a link between them, and could have completely unrelated data inside. This presentation style and the nested report functionality overcome what was a major liability of PowerBuilder prior to version 4.0; the inability to print more than one DataWindow on a page.

Since the composite DataWindow is only a shell, it has no SQL statement of it's own, and you will not be able to select a data source option. All the DataWindow objects that you embed into the composite DataWindow will have their own data sources. You can however define as many retrieval arguments as you like and those arguments can be linked to the individual retrieval arguments in the embedded objects. The technique to do this is the same as the attribute linking technique described in section 11.1.1 Creating a Nested Report, Step 13.

You can also add other objects to a composite DataWindow including static text, bitmaps, drawing objects and computed fields. The computed fields can incorporate values passed as retrieval arguments. This allows you to do things like customize report titles based upon parameters passed at runtime.

Each of the embedded reports in a composite DataWindow are child DataWindows. You can use the GetChild() function to get a handle for the embedded report. Once you have this you can manipulate the child from your scripts.

11.2.1 CREATING A COMPOSITE DATAWINDOW

We will walk through the steps of creating the composite DataWindow that is included in the sample application on the companion CD.

11.2 Composite Reports   **377**

Step 1   Create all the DataWindows which will be embedded within the composite DataWindow. We will be including a list of employees, a list of products and a graph summarizing employee sales by product.

If you are feeling adventurous, create the following three objects:

Employee List—A SQL Select / Tabular DataWindow showing the employee last and first name (concatenated, separated by a comma and space) and phone number.

Product List—A SQL Select / Grid DataWindow showing a list of product names and unit prices.

Graph of Product Sales by Employee—A SQL Select / Graph DataWindow showing a for each employee, the total sales for each product type in a bar graph.

If you prefer to focus on only the composite DataWindow at this time, these three objects can be obtained from the sample .PBL on the companion CD. The object names are d_emp_list_comp1, d_product_list_comp2 and d_emp_sales_by_prod_comp3.

Step 2   Create a new composite DataWindow. Open the DataWindow painter and choose to create a New DataWindow. Choose the Composite presentation style. The data source and **Options...** button will become disabled once you select the composite presentation style. Press the OK button.

Step 3   Select DataWindows to include. A list of all the DataWindow objects in the current library search path will appear. You should select the objects that you want to include in your composite report. These will be the objects you created in step one, or the objects provided on the companion CD.

Chapter 11: Advanced Reporting

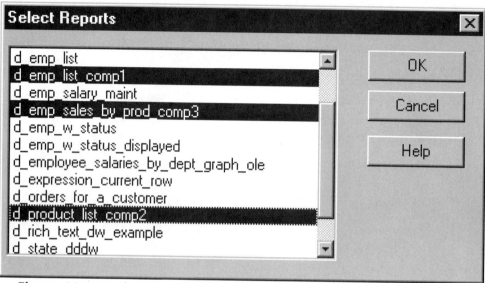

Figure 11.17 *In the Select Reports dialog window, you will choose all the DataWindow objects that you want to embed in the composite DataWindow.*

Step 4 Rearrange objects and alter the report. Press **OK**. Pressing the **OK** command button will take you to the designer. PowerBuilder will layout the selected objects in a default format. You will want to rearrange this in the fashion that you envisioned the report.

We want to move the objects to present their information in a more clear fashion. Let's place the graph at the top and resize it so that it takes up the width of the composite DataWindow. Place the employee list and the product list below it as in Figure 11.18

11.2 Composite Reports   379

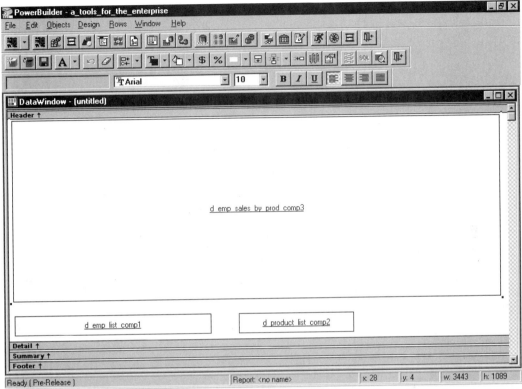

Figure 11.18 *We will rearrange the objects from their default positions to present our report in a more clear way.*

Step 5   Add headers and labels. Now let's add a header to the report which shows the date the report was run and who ran it (which we will pass as a retrieval argument). While we are at it, let's add static text labels for the list of employees and products.

To add the retrieval arguments, click with the right mouse button on an empty area of the DataWindow object. Select the **Properties...** menu option. This will open up a properties page for the DataWindow object. Select the Retrieval Arguments tab as shown in Figure 11.19. Define a retrieval argument called 'as_requested_by.'

Chapter 11: Advanced Reporting

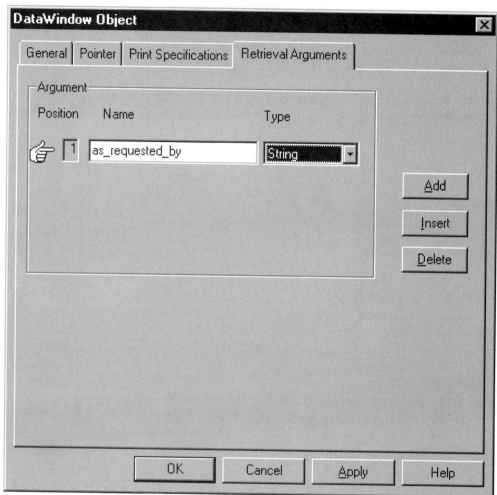

Figure 11.19 Retrieval Arguments are defined on the properties page for the DataWindow object.

Increase the size of the header band to allow room to insert a 'Printed Date' and 'Printed By' field. Adding the date field is quite easy. Select the Today's Date icon from the toolbar and place it in the header. Insert a static text field before it that contains the text "Printed Date:."

11.2 Composite Reports 381

Adding the Printed By field is a little trickier. You have to fool PowerBuilder. By default, the computed field icon is disabled, so you cannot place a regular computed field in your report. However, we can place another Today's Date field and then edit the expression to be whatever we want! Add a second Today's Date field now. Add a second static text field with the text "Printed By:"

Now click on the second computed field that you added with the right mouse button and open the properties page.

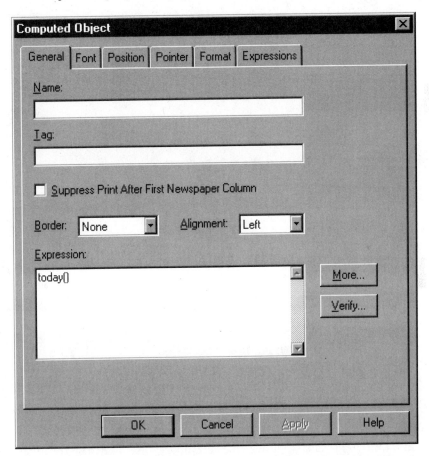

Figure 11.20 We can fool the composite DataWindow into allowing us to create computed fields by adding a predefined computed field and then modifying it to meet our needs.

Press the **More...** button to enter the expression editor dialog window. Clear the existing expression, Today(), and replace it with the retrieval argument listed in the columns box (you can do this in one step by highlighting the Today() expression and then clicking on the as_requested_by retrieval argument).

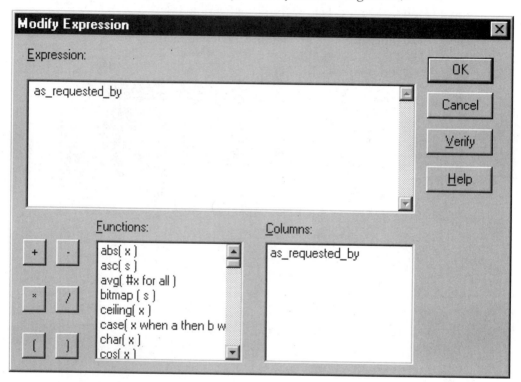

Figure 11.21 *Replace the Today() expression with the retrieval argument as_requested_by.*

Press the **OK** button on the Modify Expression dialog window to close it. Press **OK** on the Computed Object properties page to close it and apply the new expression to the computed field.

Add static text labels above the employee list and the product list. Your DataWindow should appear similar to the one in Figure 11.22.

11.2 Composite Reports

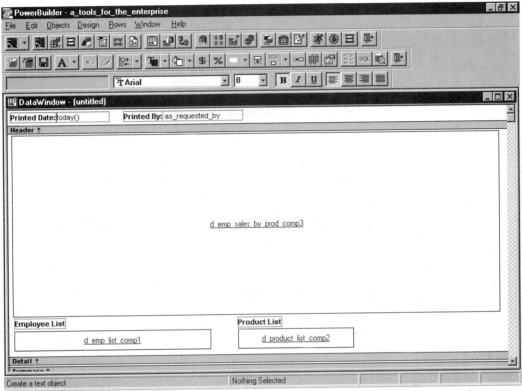

Figure 11.22 *We can add static text, computed fields, bitmaps and drawing objects to our composite DataWindows.*

Step 6   Preview the result. When you preview the DataWindow, it will ask you to fill in the retrieval argument. Enter your name. It will take a moment to retrieve all the data, remember, there are actually three DataWindows being retrieved. You should see a result something close to Figure 11.23.

Chapter 11: Advanced Reporting

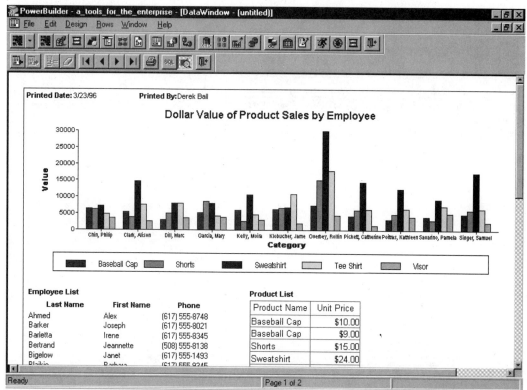

Figure 11.23 *Our finished composite DataWindow.*

11.2.2 PROPERTIES FOR COMPOSITE REPORTS

The properties for a composite report are very similar to those for a regular DataWindow. On the individual embedded reports, there are two new properties which you will find on the general properties tab. These properties are Start On New Page and Trail the Footer.

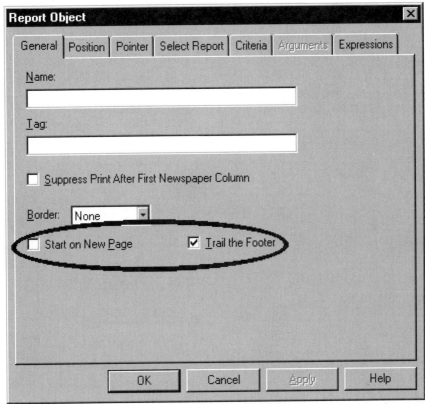

Figure 11.24 *The embedded reports on a composite DataWindow have two new attributes on the General tab, Start on New Page and Trail the Footer.*

The details of these new properties are:

Start On New Page When this option is checked (TRUE) each new instance of this embedded DataWindow object will print at the top of a new page. By default this is set to false.

Trail the Footer When this option is checked (TRUE) the footer for an embedded DataWindow will print immediately following the end of the embedded report. When this option is unchecked (FALSE) the footer will print at the bottom of each page of the report. You can see how this might cause problems if you had multiple embedded DataWindows each with their own footer! The default setting for this attribute is TRUE.

386 *Chapter 11: Advanced Reporting*

11.3 GRAPHS

Coming from an analytical and business background, I have long been an advocate of the power of graphs in application development. You have probably heard the axiom 'A picture is worth a thousand words'. That definitely applies to graphs which excel at conveying information in a quick, succinct an intuitive manner. From the picture it becomes easier to analyze data and determine trends and anomalies.

Everyone is familiar with the graph. We see them around us every day. From early childhood we understand how to read these information loaded pictures. Your users can glean information from a graph regardless of their level of technical expertise. These are major reasons for the tremendous amount of graphing in EIS (Executive Information Systems) and DSS (Decision Support Systems) applications.

In many EIS and DSS systems developed in PowerBuilder to date, graphs are tremendously under utilized. We expect our users to make their decisions based upon lists of data and summary values. This is truly a shame when you consider how easy the PowerBuilder graphing capabilities are to use. By simply specifying the data set that we wish to graph and what type of graph we wish to create, PowerBuilder will do the rest. It will extract the data from our relational database (the most common source) and present it to the user as a bar, line, column, pie or other type of graph.

PowerBuilder 5.0 continues the enhancement of the graphing capabilities of PowerBuilder first introduced in version 3.0. I am particularly pleased that the interface has been made more accessible by integrating a properties page that brings all the properties of the graph object together into one dialog window. The tab control is utilized to provide all this functionality in one window.

Developers Tip: The component gallery that comes with PowerBuilder 5.0 contains a graphing .OCX that will provide some advanced graphing functionality. This object can be used in an OLE DataWindow or an OLE 2.0 container on a window or DataWindow. At the time of printing, this object was not fully functional, so no examples are available.

11.3.1 How Do I Add a Graph to My Application?

Graphs can be added to your applications in one of three ways:

- In the window painter there is a graph control. The control can be placed on your window like any other window control. These controls are not specifically tied to a relational database, so you must pass the data to the control via a script. PowerBuilder has a long list of graph functions such as AddData(), AddSeries() and so on. This can become quite an arduous task unless your graph is quite simple. This is the least common use of PowerBuilder graphing capabilities because of this. This type of graph may be used to graph things such as system resources or other runtime information that is unrelated to the data being worked with.

- One of the DataWindow presentation styles is graph which allows you to make the entire DataWindow object a graph. Individual row details are not displayed to the end user.

- Graphs can be used to supplement and provide a pictorial summary view of data in a non-graph DataWindow. In this situation you can have both the low level detail information and the graph available to the user simultaneously. This type of graphing is quite flexible. It allows you to have the graph floating in the foreground layer of the DataWindow so that the user can move it around and keep it handy as they scroll through the data (of course, when it is in the foreground, then they can't print it). Alternatively, you could place in the background layer and you could have the graph display behind the printed detail rows. As another alternative, the graph could be placed right in the band layer and placed side by side with the detail rows.

11.3.2 Components of PowerBuilder Graphs

When you build graphs, there are a number of common elements. This is part of what makes a graph such a universally easy and effective tool to use. These elements have specific names in PowerBuilder:

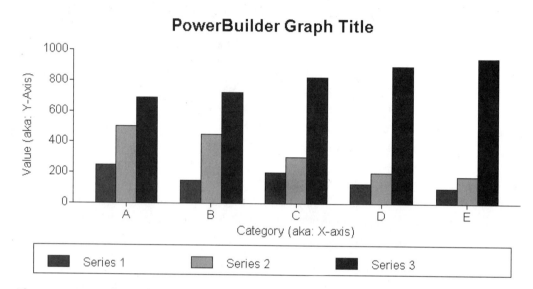

Figure 11.25 *All graphs have a number of common elements which help to make them such a universally effective tool.*

Category defines the major grouping of your data. This is also known as the X axis or the 'independent variable' in your graph. Our sample graph in Figure 11.24 shows a simple bar graph displaying employee salaries by department. Department is the category.

Value defines the dependent variable in your graph. This is also often referred to as the Y axis. In our sample graph this would be represented by the sum of the employee salaries for a given department.

Series adds a third axis (the Z axis) to provide an extra level of detail in your graph. The series is not a required element of your graph, you can graph by only the X and Y axis if you choose. Graphs with a series are sometimes referred to as 3D because they graph data using three dimensions. You must remember that this is different from a 3D presentation style which is strictly a visual change as opposed to a change in the data. In our example, we have added a series to break down salaries within a department by gender.

Titles and Legends Titles, labels and legends can be added to a graph as desired. They are useful for labeling the components of the graph. Legends are often only used if a series is included, or if you are using a pie graph.

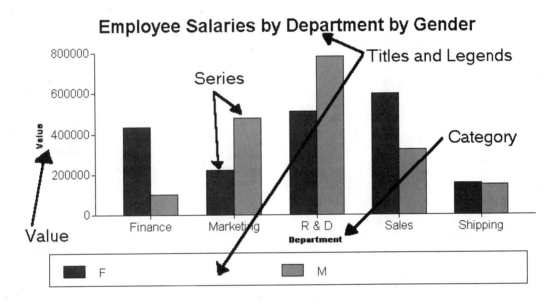

Figure 11.26 A sample graph showing total employee salaries within a department grouped by gender.

11.3.3 2 DIMENSIONS OR 3?

The expressions 2D and 3D get a little confused in the area of PowerBuilder graphs, because the same expressions are used to mean two different things. We can define both the number of data components or the graph type in terms of the number of dimensions.

In the case of the number of data components, a 2D graph will contain only a category (X-axis) and values (Y-axis). A graph showing the total employee salaries for each department (regardless of gender) would be a 2D graph. A 3D graph will contain a category, values and a series (Z-axis). The series further subdivides the information into smaller groupings such as our graph in figure 11.26, Employee Salaries by Department by Gender.

390 Chapter 11: Advanced Reporting

When referring to the graph type as being either 2D or 3D, this is purely a visual difference and has no functional or analytical implications. For most of the graphs types you can choose to show your graph rendered in a two dimensional or a three dimensional format as shown in Figure 11.27.

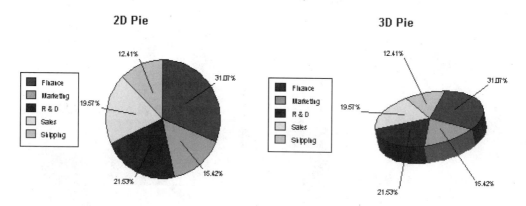

Figure 11.27 *Many of the available graph types can be visually rendered in two or three dimensions.*

> **Developers Tip:** Some 3D graphs can be difficult to read. For providing some of the slick visual effects of 3D without going overboard, try using the 'solid' graph types for bar and column graphs. These are discussed below.

11.3.4 GRAPH PROPERTIES

When you create a graph you will need to assign, at a minimum, values for its category and value properties. There are a vast array of properties that you can manipulate to customize the graph to your specific requirements. These properties are all located on the Graph Objects properties page. The page is divided into tab folders which group the properties into logical sets.

11.3.4.1 The Data Tab

The Data tab contains the most critical properties of any graph; the category, value and series. This tab does not exist on a window graph control as it is not linked to the database.

11.3 Graphs

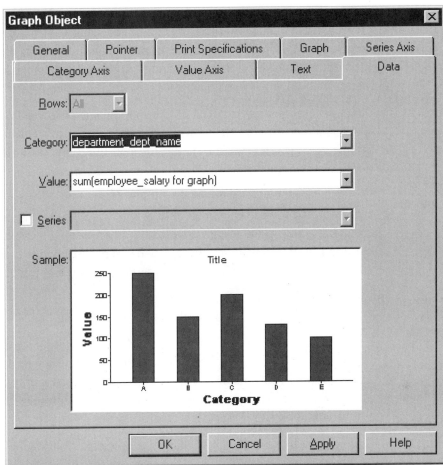

Figure 11.28 *The Graph Object properties page requires you to enter a category and value before you can modify any of the other graph properties.*

The properties contained on this tab are:

Category   defines what will appear on the major independent axis (as described in section 11.3.2). This field contains a drop down listbox. The list will contain all the possible categories that PowerBuilder thinks you may want to assign as the category. You can select from the list, or you can type in your own logical expression. Any valid expression will work. For example, you may decide to graph your accounts receivable into segments of 'Under 30 days', '30 to 60 days' and 'Over 60 days.'

392   *Chapter 11: Advanced Reporting*

Value   defines the expression used to evaluate the dependent, or Y axis, of the graph. Usually, some sort of mathematical or aggregate functions are involved. The drop down list box will provide you with a set of possible values that PowerBuilder thinks you may want to define as your value.

Series   defines the expression used to sub group the value property. For example, our graph showing the total salaries within a department is sub grouped into genders within the department. In order to be able to add a series expression (which by default is disabled), we must check (set to TRUE) the checkbox beside the series field.

Rows   defines which rows in the DataWindow will make up the data used in the graph. This option is only enabled if you are adding a graph to an existing DataWindow. If you are using the graph on a window control, or making the whole DataWindow a graph, it does not apply. The options in the listbox are:

> *All* —(Default) to include all the rows in the graph.

> *Page*—to have the graph display detail for the current page only. This means that the graph will have to dynamically change as you page through your data. If you decided to embed the graph in the footer of a report and only show the data for that current page, then this would be an option you would consider.

> *Group n*—to have the graph display the data from a specific grouping as defined by the group parameters of the DataWindow. Since a DataWindow could have multiple groups that you might choose to graph by, the n represents the group number.

The sample region at the bottom of the tab is use to remind the developer of the type of graph that is currently selected.

11.3.4.2 The Text Tab

The Text tab is used to control all the text fields that print on the screen. You have the ability to customize every label, font and color used in the text that appears. You can set a value for the graph title, category label and value label here, but you should usually change these three on the Graph, Category Axis and Value Axis tabs respectively. On these tabs you define the literal that will appear in the label, in the text tab, you can define a custom expression that includes the literal defined in the previous tabs.

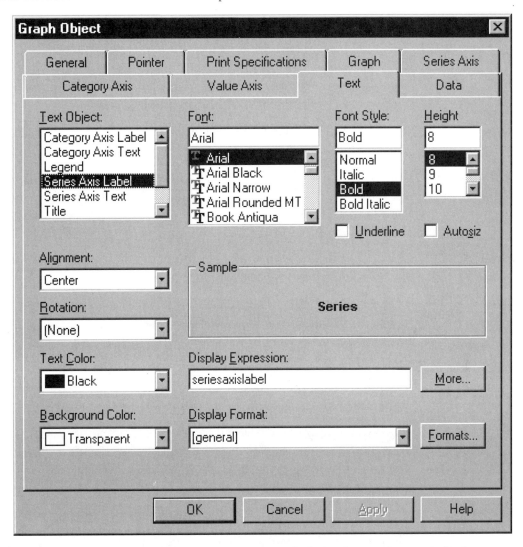

Figure 11.29 *The Text tab allows you to control all the formatting and display aspects for all text fields in the graph.*

394 *Chapter 11: Advanced Reporting*

The properties on this tab include:

Text Object   the currently select item in this list box is the text object from the graph that you are currently defining. All the other property fields on this page relate to the selected text object. The text objects that you can select are: Category Axis Label, Category Axis Text, Legend, Series Axis Label, Series Axis Text, Title, Value Axis Label and Value Axis Text.

Font   defines the currently selected font for the text object. All the available windows fonts will appear inside the drop down listbox.

Font Style   defines the style of the font for the current text object. You can make the font Bold, Italic, Bold Italic or Normal.

Font Height   defines the size of the font for the current text object. The standard sizes are listed in and can be selected from the drop down list box, but you can edit the size to be whatever size you prefer. This field is only enabled if Autosize is unchecked (FALSE)

Underline   when checked (TRUE) this will cause the currently selected text object to appear underlined, regardless of font style.

Autosize   when checked (TRUE) will automatically size the current text object font to the size that PowerBuilder deems to be most appropriate. When unchecked (FALSE) you must manually select the font size you desire from the font height field.

Alignment   allows you to left, center, or right justify the current text object. This option is not available for any of the axes text objects or for the legend.

Rotation   allows you to display the text of the current text object to some degree of rotation. The options available to you are: None, 45 Degrees Left, 90 Degrees Left, 45 Degrees Right, and 90 Degrees Right. This option is disabled for title and label text objects.

Text Color   allows you to select a color for the currently selected text object.

Background Color allows you to select a color for the background of the currently selected text object. The default color is *transparent*.

11.3 Graphs   **395**

Display Expression allows you to define a custom expression for what will display in the currently selected text object. This can be any logical expression. Pressing the **More...** command button will open up the Modify Expression dialog window and allow you to access all the DataWindow functions and fields that you can use in your expression. You can include any combination of the following fields (many of them are already defaults for specific text objects):

Title contains the string or expression defined in the Graph tab as the title for the graph.

SeriesAxisLabel contains the string or expression defined in the Series Axis tab as the label for the series.

CategoryAxisLabel contains the string or expression defined in the Category Axis tab as the label for the category.

ValueAxisLabel contains the string or expression defined in the Value Axis tab as the label for the value.

Category contains the actual category value for the current category. Only available in the Category Axis Text and Legend object.

Series contains the actual series value for the current series. Only available in the Series Axis Text and Legend object.

SumForGraph contains the numeric total of whatever is being evaluated as the dependent axis. For example, if the value axis is defined as 'sum(employee_salary for group)' then SumForGraph would be all the employee salaries added together.

SumForCategory contains the numeric total for the value axis for the current category. Only available in the Category Axis Text object.

SumForSeries contains the numeric total for the value axis for the current category. Only available in the Series Axis Text and Legend text objects.

SeriesCount contains the total number of series represented in the graph.

CategoryCount contains the total number of categories represented in the graph.

SeriesNumber contains the number of the current series. Only available in the Series Axis Text and Legend text objects.

CategoryNumber contains the number of the current category. Only available in the Category Axis Text object.

CategoryPercentForGraph contains a percentage of the value for the current category versus the total value for the graph (SumForCategory / SumForGraph). Only available in the Category Axis Text object.

SeriesPercentForGraph contains the percentage of the value for the current series versus the total value for the graph (SumForSeries / SumForGraph). Only available in the Series Axis Text and Legend text objects.

GraphType contains a number representing the type of graph that this is. This can be used in conditional expressions if you want the graph to display different expressions depending on the graph type. The number will match to a graph type as follows:

1	Area
2	Bar
3	Bar3D
4	Bar3DObj
5	BarStacked
6	BarStacked3DObj
7	Col
8	Col3D
9	Col3DObj
10	ColStacked
11	ColStacked3DObj

12	Line
13	Pie
14	Scatter
15	Area3D
16	Line3D
17	Pie3D

Some examples of expressions that you might use would include:

for title:	"Total Salaries Paid = " + String(SumForGraph)
for category:	category + String(CategoryPercentForGraph, "0.00%")

Display Format contains the formatting string for the value returned by the display expression. This defaults to [General] which will display the data exactly as it exists. If you are using a field that calculates a percentage, you could use a display format such as '0.00%' to format the percentage to two decimal places and add a percent sign at the end. Pressing the **Formats...** command button will open up a dialog window where you can select from existing display formats or create and test a new one.

11.3.4.3 The General Tab

The General tab contains properties that relate to the overall DataWindow object graph. These are high level properties and are essentially the same as other general DataWindow properties.

Chapter 11: Advanced Reporting

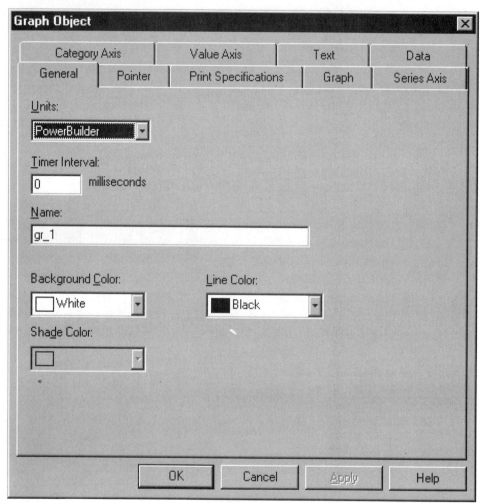

Figure 11.30 *The General tab contains properties that relate to the overall DataWindow graph object.*

The properties on the General tab are:

Units defines the type of units used to measure and layout objects on the DataWindow. The possible values are: 1/1000th of an inch, 1/1000th of a centimeter, pixels, or PowerBuilder units. PowerBuilder units (PBU) are the default and equate to 1/32nd of your system font size. PBUs exist to allow you to create applications that will look the same regardless of your terminal settings.

Timer Interval	defines the amount of time in milliseconds that you want to wait between timer events within the DataWindow object.
Name	the name for the DataWindow object (defaults to gr_1 for the graph object).
Background Color	background color for the graph (defaults to white).
Line Color	line color for the graph (defaults to black).
Shade Color	defines the color used for the 3D base in any 3D graph having a base (pie does not have a base, it floats). This option will be disabled unless you have defined the graph as 3D.

11.3.4.4 The Graph Tab

The Graph tab is where you will define the properties that affect the general type and appearance of your graph. You can choose your graph type, change its 3D properties (if applicable) and modify any other general appearance characteristics.

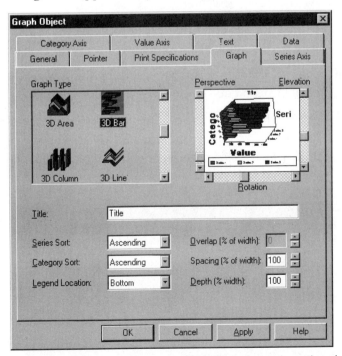

Figure 11.31 *The Graph tab is where you will define the properties that allow you to select the type of graph and how it will appear.*

400   *Chapter 11: Advanced Reporting*

The properties that you can work with on the Graph tab include:

Graph Type   defines the style of graph that you want to create. There are seventeen different types of graphs from line graphs to pie graphs. If you are unfamiliar with the different types of graphs that are available, they are all reviewed in section 11.3.5 Types of Graphs.

Perspective, Elevation, and Rotation all define the 3D characteristics of a 3D graph. These options are disabled if you are not using a 3D graph. You can use the slider bars to adjust these three attributes (relating to the roll, pitch and yaw) of the 3D object. The results can be viewed in the sample image.

Title   this is the title for the graph. Anything you enter in this field will appear in the title area of the graph, exactly as you type it. Expressions are entered in the text tab.

Series Sort   defines the sort order for the series axis. Valid choices are: Not Sorted, Ascending or Descending

Category Sort   defines the sort order for the category axis. Valid choices are: Not Sorted, Ascending or Descending

Legend Location   controls where in relation to the graph the legend will appear. Valid choices are: None, Top, Bottom, Left or Right.

Overlap   controls how much the different series overlap each other as a percentage of their width. For example, Figure 11.32 shows a bar graph with 35% overlap. This property is only valid for 2D bar and 2D column graphs.

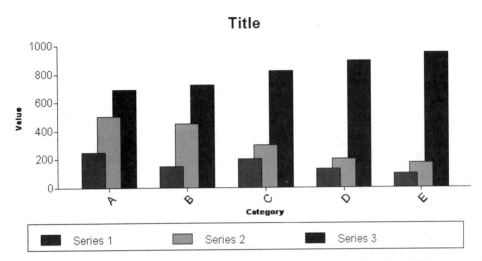

Figure 11.32 *This graph has an overlap property of 35% causing the different series to overlap each other by 35% of their width.*

Spacing controls how much space appears between the data markers for different categories. It is measured as a percentage of width of one data marker. For example, a bar graph with a spacing value of 150 would have a space equal to one and a half times the width of a bar between the categories. This property is not applicable to two dimensional scatter, pie, line or area graphs.

Depth controls how deep a 3D graph is in relation to its width. By default the graph will be equally deep as it is wide (depth = 100%).

11.3.4.5 The Category Axis Tab

Most of the attributes on the Category Axis tab will be disabled for most graph types. Only the scatter graph has any substantial degree of access to the properties contained on this tab due to its unstructured nature.

402 Chapter 11: Advanced Reporting

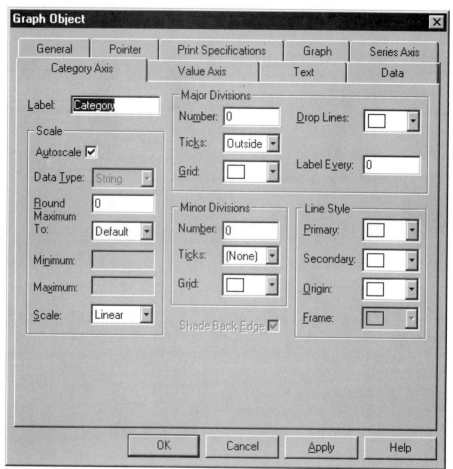

Figure 11.33 *The Category Axis tab properties are largely not accessible for most graph types.*

The properties on the Category Axis tab are:

Label This property is accessible for most graph types, with the exception of pie. It is the text label that you want to appear on the category axis. Like the Title property on the Graph tab, this is only a character string and will not evaluate expressions. If you want to use an expression for the category axis, you must define it on the Text tab.

11.3 Graphs **403**

Scale.Autoscale When checked (TRUE), PowerBuilder will automatically determine the appropriate scale for the graph. For most graph types, this is always set to true and is inaccessible.

Scale.DataType This property is only applicable for non-database graphs, such as those placed directly onto a window. Otherwise, the data type is determined by the expression that is used to define the category.

Scale.RoundTo specifies what value you want to round the category axis values to (i.e. 10).

Scale.RoundUnits specifies the units that the axis will be rounded in. The default is called 'units' which essentially means undefined. You can only define specific units if you are dealing with some measure of dates or times. There are seven possible unit types you can select when dealing with data of this type: Years (a value of 1), Months (2), Days (3), Hours (4), Minutes (5), Seconds(6) and Microseconds (7).

Scale.Minimum the minimum value for the category axis.

Scale.Maximum the maximum value for the category axis.

Scale.Scale specifies the type of scale used for the category axis. The possible options are: Linear (a value of 1), Log 10 (a value of 2) or Log e (a value of 3).

MajorDivisions.Number specifies the number of major divisions on the axis.

MajorDivisions.Ticks specifies the type of major tick mark. There are four possible values: None (a value of 1), Inside (2), Outside (3), Straddle (4).

MajorDivisions.Grid specifies the type of line used to draw the grid for the major tick marks within the graph. These lines are intended to make it easier to determine where data plots on your graph appear. This setting only affects the grid line for this axis (thus only vertical lines would appear). To have a true grid appear, you would need to define a value for this property and for the equivalent property in the value axis. The valid options all represent different variations of dots and dashes: None (0), Solid (1) , Dash (2), Dot (3), DashDot (4) and DashDotDot (5).

404   *Chapter 11: Advanced Reporting*

MajorDivisions.DropLines specified the type of line that will be used to draw the intersection point of a data point on the graph. Like the grid property, this line will only be drawn for the current axis. If you want to show intersection lines for both axis on the graph, you would need to define the same property for the value axis also. The acceptable values are the same as for the grid property.

MajorDivisions.LabelEvery specifies how often you want PowerBuilder to draw labels on the tick marks. The default (0) or a value of 1 will tell PowerBuilder to add a label to every tick mark. A value higher than 1 would cause PowerBuilder to only add labels to specific tick marks. A value of 2 would draw a label on every second tick mark, a value of 3 on every third, and so on.

MinorDivisions.Number specifies the number of minor divisions you want to appear on the axis. The default is none (0).

MinorDivisions.Ticks specifies the type of tick mark you would like to use for minor divisions. The options are the same as the are for major division tick marks.

MinorDivisions.Grid specifies the type of line that you want to use to draw grid lines for the minor tick marks. This property behaves exactly the same as the major divisions grid property, but for the minor divisions.

LineStyle.Primary specifies what style of line you want to draw for the axis itself. You can choose from the same styles that are available for drop and grid lines. If you specify None (which is equivalent to transparent) no lines will appear for the axis.

LineStyle.Secondary specifies the style of line you want to draw for lines other than the primary axis, that run parallel to the primary axis. The value options are the same as for all the other lines styles.

LineStyle.Origin specifies the style of line that you want to draw for the origin line. The origin line is the one that represents zero for this axis (if applicable). The value options are the same as for all the other lines styles.

LineStyle.Frame specifies the style of line that will be drawn for the frame of this axis of your graph, if your graph has a frame. The value options are the same as for all the other lines styles.

ShadeBackEdge allows you to choose whether you want to shade the back edge of your 3D graph or not. This property is either checked (TRUE) or unchecked (FALSE)

11.3.4.6 The Value Axis Tab

The properties on the Value Axis tab are identical to those properties that are on the Category Axis tab. Which properties are enabled and which are disabled will depend upon which graph type you have selected. Please refer to the property definitions in 11.3.4.5 The Category Axis Tab for the specifics of the value axis tab properties.

11.3.4.7 The Series Axis Tab

The properties for the Series Axis tab are also identical to the properties of the Value and Category Axis tabs. However, these properties will only be enabled if you have defined your graph as having a series in the Data tab. As the definitions for the properties are the same as in the previous two tabs, please refer to section 11.3.4.5 The Category Axis Tab for property definitions.

11.3.4.8 The Print Specifications Tab

The Print Specifications tab is only available if you have created a graph presentation style DataWindow. It does not apply to graphs created on a window or to graphs added to an existing DataWindow.

Chapter 11: Advanced Reporting

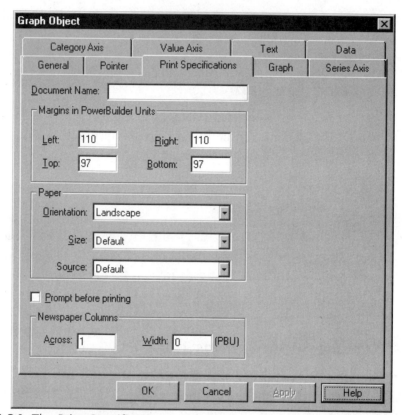

Figure 11.34 *The Print Specifications tab allows you to set the properties that define how the graph will print at runtime.*

On this tab you can specify all the details that relate to how the graph will print at runtime. The properties that you can control include:

Document Name specifies the name that you want to provide for the document to the print server. This name does not appear anywhere else and has no other useful function. If you leave this blank, the default will be no name at all.

Margins specifies the margins for the **Left**, **Right**, **Top** and **Bottom** of the page. These are specified in the same units as the DataWindow is set to use. By default this is set to PowerBuilder Units (PBUs), but remember that you can set the DataWindow to work in 1/1000th of an inch or of a centimeter if that is more convenient for you. The margins will default to 1 inch on each side regardless of the units you have selected. If you have left the DataWindow with all of its default settings, you will notice that 1 inch in PBUs is different for width than it is for height. This is because PBUs are based upon the system font size, which is taller than it is wide.

Paper.Orientation allows you to override the default orientation of the printer and print this graph in a specific way. Your options here are default (whatever the printer is set for normally), landscape (horizontal) or portrait (vertical).

Paper. Size allows you to specify the size of paper that the graph will be printed on. By default, it will use the standard settings of the printer. You can alter this to any of the built in paper sizes like letter, legal, executive, A4, envelopes, etc.

Paper.Source allows you to specify where the paper that the graph will be printed on will come from. By default, it will use the printers default paper source, but you can specify whatever valid sources are available for your printer.

Prompt Before Printing allows you to present the user with a popup print dialog box as shown in Figure 11.35. This dialog allows the user to select print options such as which printer to use, number of copies and print range. It also allows the user to cancel the printing of the current graph if they choose.

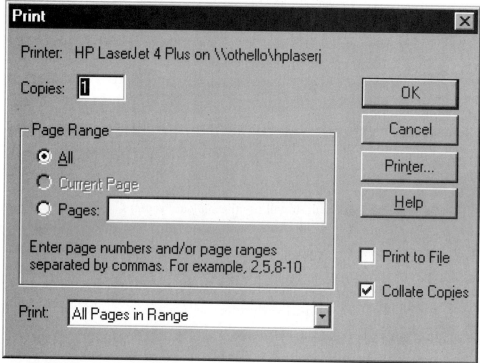

Figure 11.35 *The Prompt Before Printing property allows you to display a dialog window to the user to allow them to select print options or to cancel before printing.*

Newspaper Columns are intended to allow you to print your data in multiple columns. This does not really apply to graph DataWindows and should be disabled (it may be in the production version, but is currently enabled in mine).

11.3.4.9 The Pointer Tab

The Pointer tab works like any other pointer selection option in PowerBuilder. When the mouse passes over the graph, you can have the pointer change to a different icon. You can select from one of the standard stock icons, or you can select any valid cursor file (cursor files are those with .CUR extensions—these can be created using the Watcom Image Editor that comes with PowerBuilder).

11.3.4.10 The Expressions Tab

The Expressions tab is only available to graph objects that are embedded into an existing DataWindow. It allows you to dynamically modify some of the attributes of the graph object at runtime.

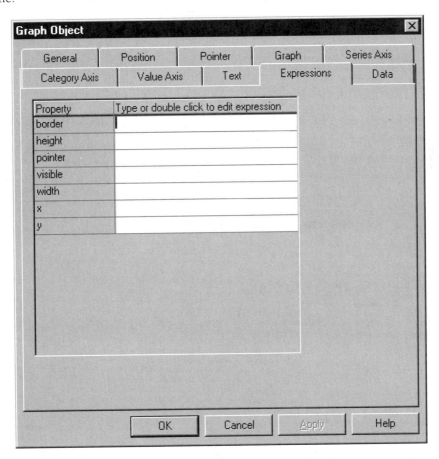

Figure 11.36 *The Expressions tab allows you to dynamically modify the attributes of a graph object that is embedded into an existing DataWindow object.*

The behavior of this expression dialog is identical to those that we examined in the last chapter. You can enter an expression that will be evaluated at runtime for each of the listed attributes. If you want to use the expression dialog window, you can double-click in the field that you want to create an expression for.

410 *Chapter 11: Advanced Reporting*

11.3.4.11 The Drag and Drop Tab

The Drag and Drop tab is only available to graph objects that are placed directly on a window, as opposed to those that are created as a DataWindow or embedded into a DataWindow. This tab is used to define the two drag and drop attributes of all dragable windows controls: DragAuto and DragIcon. For a full description of how to use drag and drop, refer to section 8.4—Implementing Drag and Drop.

The DragAuto attribute is checked (TRUE) if you want the graph to automatically enter drag mode when the user clicks on it with the mouse. If this attribute is set to false, you must manually initiate drag mode using the Drag() function if you want to drag and drop the graph.

The DragIcon attribute sets the icon that will appear in place of the cursor to indicate that the object is in drag mode. If you leave this undefined, the default icon is an outline of the current object (not particularly user friendly when dragging a large graph). You can assign one of the stock icons, or you can use any valid icon (.ICO) file.

An example of implementing drag and drop with a window graph would be to allow the user to drag a graph onto a bitmap of a printer to initiate printing.

11.3.5 TYPES OF GRAPHS

PowerBuilder has an ample supply of useful graph types. Most major graph types that you will need in a business environment are supported. In the event that you need some graph functions that are not supported in PowerBuilder, there are a number of third party vendors that make OLE 2.0 compatible graphing applications that you can integrate into your PowerBuilder application.

11.3.5.1 Column

When you first create any graph object, the default graph type will always be column. A column graph allows you to show your data as a range covered by the column on your graph area. Column graphs show increasing values on the value axis by increasing the height of the column.

11.3 Graphs

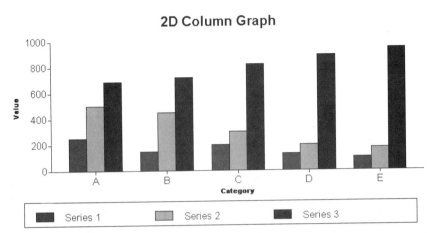

Figure 11.37 *The column graph is the default graph type for any new graph object. It will show data as a range covered by the column on your graph area.*

Column graphs can be either two dimensional or three dimensional.

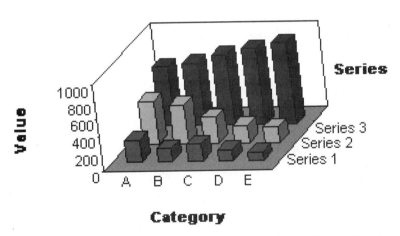

Figure 11.38 *Column graphs also come in a three dimensional variety.*

If you find three dimensional a little too 3D, then there is a graph type called 'solid' (available for both column and bar graphs) which takes the 2D graph types and gives their columns some depth. Only the columns themselves are 3D, the rest of the graph is drawn exactly the same.

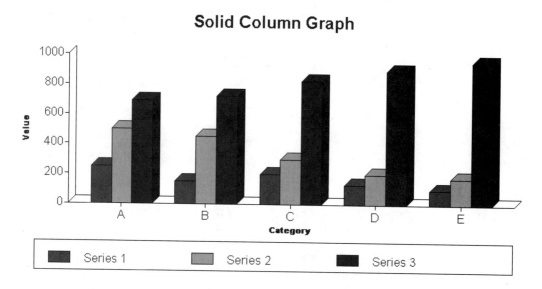

Figure 11.39 *A graph type of Solid Column gives the columns depth but the rest of the graph is drawn the same. This results in a partial 3D graph.*

For business graphing purposes, the 2D or the Solid Column graphs will provide the clearest message. 3D graphs tend to be more difficult to read, although they may look slick in your annual report!

11.3.5.2 Bar

Bar graphs are identical to Column graphs, but the value and category axes are swapped. The category is on the left (vertical) axis which the values are stretched across the bottom.

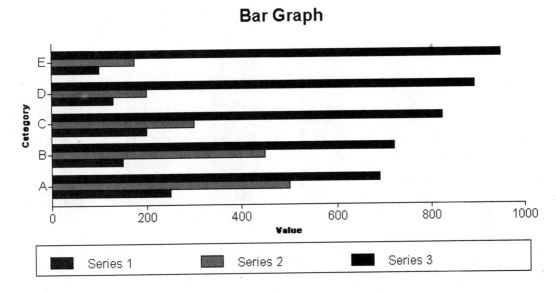

Figure 11.40 *The Bar graph is identical to the column graph however the category axis is the vertical axis and the value is the horizontal. This will make your bars (columns) stretch from left to right on your graph.*

Bar graphs are excellent for communicating information where there is a large range of values, but only a limited number of categories. The Bar graph comes in all the same flavors as the Column graph; 2D, 3D or Solid Bar.

11.3.5.3 Stacked Graphs

When you add a series to a graph, normally this implies adding new bars or columns extending from the appropriate axis, but grouped into a specific category. However, data from a series could also be stacked on top of data from other series within the same category. This allows you to build a cumulative total for all the series within the category.

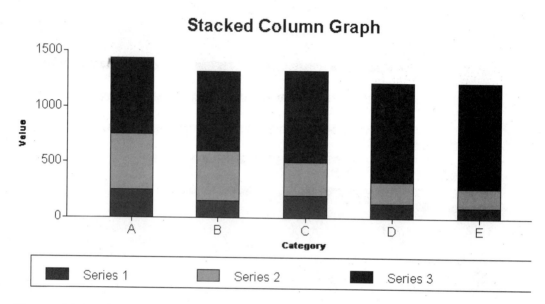

Figure 11.41 *The Stacked Column graph allows you to stack series on top of each other within a category building up a cumulative total.*

The stacked variety of graph is available for column and bar graphs only. You can select between 2D or 3D variations.

11.3.5.4 Line

Line graphs have discrete data points that are graphed against two axes, the value and the category. The related data points are connected together by a continuous line. If you add a series to a line graph, a separate line will be created for all the data points within that series. Each data point will be given a symbol that will match the symbol for the series as shown in the legend.

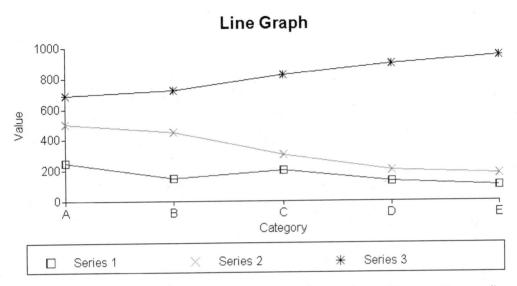

Figure 11.42 *The Line graph connects discrete data points with a continuous line. Multiple series are shown as separate lines.*

The line graph is most commonly used to show trend analysis. The category axis is often related to time or changes in time. A typical example of a line graph might be total sales of different products over 12 months. Each series would represent a different product.

11.3.5.5 Area

Area graphs are very similar to line graphs. They graph discrete points on two axes (category and value) and draw a line between the points. The difference between the two is that the area graph fills in the area under the line with a solid color.

An example of the use of this type of graph in a business application would be in the financial industry. Area graphs are often used to indicate financial performance or market share as the filled in area is easy to equate with a cumulative or increasing amount. Adding a series to an area graph would result in multiple lines, similar to the example in Figure 11.43.

Chapter 11: Advanced Reporting

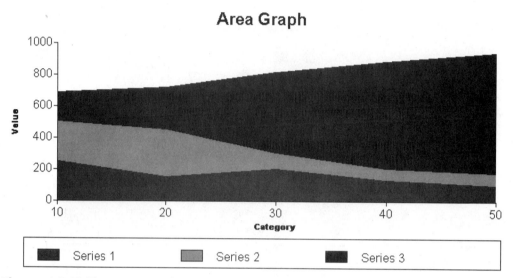

Figure 11.43 *The area graph is similar to a line graph except that the area under the line is filled in with a solid color.*

The area graph has both two dimensional and three dimensional variations. The two dimensional version is shown in Figure 11.43 and the three dimensional in Figure 11.44.

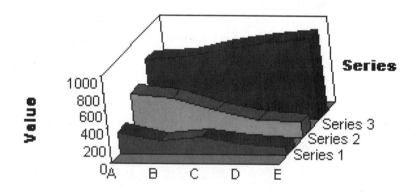

Figure 11.44 *The area graph can be created in both 2D and 3D formats.*

11.3.5.6 Pie

The Pie graph is a favorite of many business analysts. It is frequently used in decision support, executive information and market analysis systems. The data in a Pie graph is contained within a category. Each category shows up as a distinct piece of the pie. The size of the piece of pie represents the value for that category in relation to the cumulative total for all the categories (the entire pie).

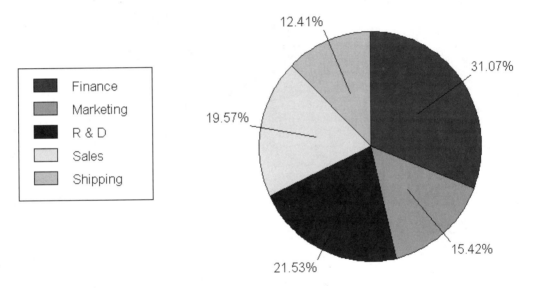

Figure 11.45 *The Pie graph displays the data within a category as a single slice of a pie (which represents the cumulative total of all the data in the graph)*

The Pie graph is also one of my personal favorites because of its flexibility. It comes in 2D and 3D varieties and you have the ability to add a series if you choose.

418 *Chapter 11: Advanced Reporting*

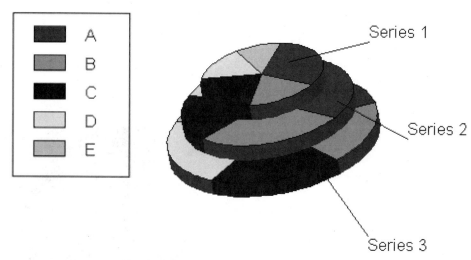

Figure 11.46 *The pie graph comes in 2D and 3D varieties and you can stack the pies up by adding a series.*

11.3.5.7 Scatter

The Scatter graph allows you to map out discrete points of data against two axes. This type of graph is most often used to provide a mechanism for visually ranking data.

11.3 Graphs 419

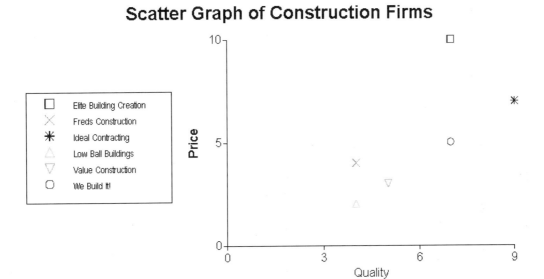

Figure 11.47 *The Scatter graph allows you to map out discrete points of data against two axes.*

Let's consider an example. We need to select a construction company to build our new office building. There are six construction companies in town and we have them in our database. Each construction firm is ranked for price and quality of work. We want to show a graph of this. The graph in Figure 11.47 allows us to examine which construction firm will give us the most value for our dollar.

Scatter graphs are also often used in research and testing environments where multiple test results from various test runs need to be referenced on the same graph.

11.3.6 BUILDING A GRAPH PRESENTATION STYLE DATAWINDOW

The techniques for building a graph are very similar regardless of whether you are adding a graph to an existing DataWindow, or creating a new graph presentation style DataWindow. We will base our example upon the latter, to keep things simple.

420   *Chapter 11: Advanced Reporting*

Step 1   Open the DataWindow painter. Open the DataWindow painter and select SQL Select as the data source and Graph as the presentation style. Press the **OK** button.

Step 2   Define your data source. In the SQL Select painter we must define the data set that will make up our graph. We will use two tables; department and employee. From the department table we will select the dept_name column. From the employee table we will select the emp_id, status, and salary columns. Press the SQL icon button on the painter bar (remember it appears as a push on/push off button)to close the SQL Select painter and move to the DataWindow designer.

Step 3   Define the category and value. The Graph Object properties page will appear. It contains a number of tabs with all the modifiable properties of the graph object. The Data tab is preselected for you and you are required to define a category and value before trying to select any of the other tabs.

For the category, we will be using the department_dept_name column. When you are dealing with multiple tables, PowerBuilder prefixes the name of the column with the name of the table and an underscore.

You can easily select the column from the list of recommended categories by clicking on the drop down listbox arrow in the category field. The list will contain all the items that PowerBuilder thinks you may want to use as a category, but you can enter any valid expression you desire (refer to section 11.3.4 above for a complete walk through of all the properties page tabs)

For the value, select sum(employee_salary for graph) from the drop down listbox. We will not be using a series at this point.

Step 4   Change the text labels. We could use the Text tab to change the labels for our graph. On this tab here we can change all the text on our graph including changing the font, color and expression. This tab is also addressed in detail in section 11.3.4 above.

Alternatively, the title could be changed on the Graph tab, the category label on the Category Axis tab and the value label on the Value Axis tab.

Change the title to "Employee Salaries by Department". Change the category label to "Department" and change the value label to "Amount."

Press the **OK** button.

Step 5 Preview the graph. Your graph should appear similar to the one in Figure 11.48.

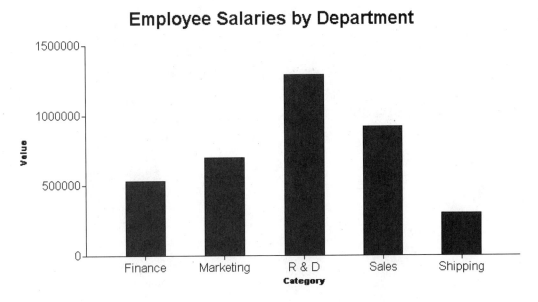

Figure 11.48 Your graph should look similar to this.

When you have finished, return to the designer.

Step 6 (Optional)—Change the formatting of the value column to provide currency formats to labels. Open the Properties page by clicking with the right mouse button and selecting **Properties...** from the popup menu.

Select the Text tab and change the display format to an appropriate currency setting as shown in Figure 11.49.

Chapter 11: Advanced Reporting

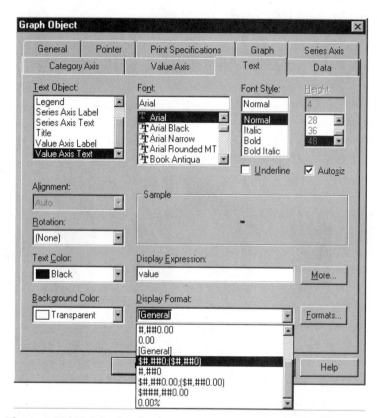

Figure 11.49 *Display format can be changed in the Text tab.*

Press the **OK** command button to apply the changes. Preview the results to see the new format.

Step 7 (Optional)—Change the title expression. Alter the title expression to include a dynamic evaluation of the total amount of all salaries paid in the company. Open the properties page and select the Text tab. Select the Title text object and change the expression to be:

title + " - Total Payroll: "+ String(sumforgraph ,'$0,000')

If you had used this field to change the graph title earlier instead of the Graph tab, then your expression will look like:

"Employee Salaries by Department" + " - Total Payroll: "+ String(sumforgraph ,'$0,000')

Apply the changes by pressing the **OK** command button. Preview your graph. It should appear similar to the graph in Figure 11.50.

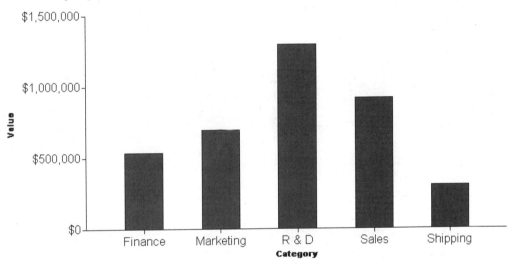

Figure 11.50 *After completing steps 6 and 7, your graph should appear similar to this.*

Step 8 (Optional)—Change the graph type. Open the Properties page and select the Graph tab. Select the 3D Pie graph option. Apply the changes and preview the graph. You should now see a 3D pie with all the same properties as you defined in the column graph.

11.3.7 USING OVERLAYS

It is possible in PowerBuilder to overlay a second graph over top of your first graph. The two graphs must be related. This allows you to identify trends or provide supporting information for the graph. You define an overlay in the Graph tab of the Properties page. This is demon-

424   Chapter 11: Advanced Reporting

strated below. The new data will appear as a line graph and will be added to the legend like a new series.

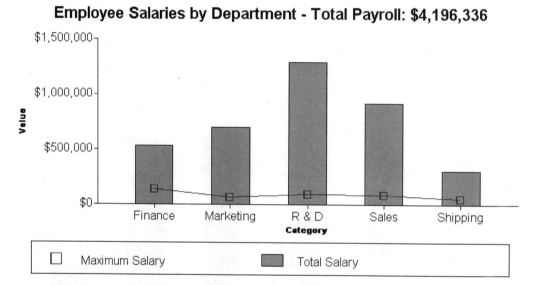

Figure 11.51 *Overlays allow us to show supporting information on top of an existing graph object. This is the result of the example steps in section 11.3.7.*

The example below uses the graph you built in section 11.3.6 as the primary graph. We will overlay the maximum salary in each department on our salary graph.

Step 1   Define the value axis for the overlay. We only define the value axis for our overlay and not the category as the overlay must use the same category in order for the data to make any sense. Open the Properties page and select the Data tab. In the value list box we are going to append the new expression for our overlay. We separate the two expressions with a comma. The complete new expression will be:

sum(employee_salary for graph),max(employee_salary for graph)

The first expression is our existing graph, the total employee salaries for a department. The second component will show the highest salary within a department.

Step 2 Define the series for the overlay. In order to make the overlay work, we must have a series defined. This is because PowerBuilder treats the overlay like a new series. The expression that we will use in our series is:

"Total Salary" , "@overlay~tMaximum Salary"

The first component gives a static label that will appear in the legend to show that our columns represent the total salary within a department. The second component instructs PowerBuilder to generate an overlay based upon the second component of the value axis and label it as 'Maximum Salary' in the legend.

Step 3 Preview your graph. Your graph should appear similar to the one in Figure 11.51.

11.3.8 RUNTIME GRAPH MANIPULATION WITH POWERSCRIPT FUNCTIONS

After you have created a graph object, you can manipulate and alter it at runtime through the use of various PowerScript functions. All aspects of the graph object can be altered. The full set of functions that can be used are listed in the PowerBuilder Function Reference manual that is part of your PowerBuilder documentation or in the online help.

11.3.8.1 Changing A Series Color

One function that I want to mention is the SetSeriesStyle function. I am often asked by students in PowerBuilder training how they can change the color for a graph. The default color for a single series graph is red, and some people don't want to have the bars showing up in red because of the negative financial connotations attached to red.

We can't change this color when we are painting the graph, but it can be altered at runtime through the use of the SetSereiesStyle() function. This function allows us to alter any of the style attributes for a particular series. The color attribute that we want to alter is referenced using an enumerated data type called ForeGround!

The syntax to change the color is:

control.SetSeriesStyle ({graph_control,} seriesname, colortype, color)

426   *Chapter 11: Advanced Reporting*

where:

control	is the name of the object that contains the graph control. This could be a graph control on a window, a graph type DataWindow or another DataWindow that has a graph object embedded in it.
graph control	is the name of the graph control within the object that you want to alter stored in a string. This is only applicable to DataWindow objects as with graph controls in a window the graph control name is the same as the control name.
seriesname	is the name of the series stored in a string for which you want to set the color.
colortype	is an enumerated data type containing which color attribute you wish to modify. The valid attributes are: ForeGround!, BackGround!, LineColor! or Shade! (applicable to 3D or Solid graphs only).
color	is a long containing the color that you wish to change the color type to. Remember that you can use the RGB() function to help you get the right color.

If we wanted to change the salary series of a graph to green instead of red, we would write a script such as:

```
dw_salarygraph.SetSeriesStyle("gr_1","salary", ForeGround!, RGB(0,255,0))
```

11.3.9 CREATING A DRILL DOWN GRAPH WITH POWERSCRIPT

Another series of functions that I find useful when working with graphs are those that allow me to turn the graph into a useful tool in the user interface. For example, the user can click on a section of a pie graph to get the detail of the data that is within that pie.

To accomplish this kind of functionality, we need to write a script for the clicked event on our DataWindow control. In this event, we need to find out which part of the graph the user clicked on. To do this we use the function ObjectAtPointer() which will return to us the object type that was clicked on and, through reference variables, will also provide us with the series number and data point that were clicked on.

11.3 Graphs   **427**

The syntax for ObjectAtPointer() is:

control.ObjectAtPointer({ graphcontrol, } seriesnumber, datapoint)

where:

control is the name of the object that contains the graph control. This could be a graph control on a window, a graph type DataWindow or another DataWindow that has a graph object embedded in it.

graphcontrol is the name of the graph control within the object that you want to alter stored in a string. This is only applicable to DataWindow objects as with graph controls in a window the graph control name is the same as the control name.

seriesnumber is an integer reference variable which, when the function completes, will contain the number of the series that the user clicked on.

datapoint is an integer reference variable which, when the function completes, will contain the number of the data point that the user clicked on.

The return value for this function is an enumerated data type called grObjectType (for 'graph object type') and has the possible values of:

TypeCategory! the user clicked on a label for a category.

TypeCategoryAxis! the user clicked on the category axis or in between the category labels.

TypeCategoryLabel! the user clicked on the label of the category axis.

TypeData! the user clicked on an individual data point or other data marker such as a bar.

TypeGraph! this is the catch all that is returned when the user clicked anywhere in the graph that is not represented by one of the other values for grObjectType.

TypeLegend! the user clicked inside the legend box, but not on a series label.

TypeSeries! the user clicked on the line that connects the data points of a series in a line graph, or the user clicked on the series label in the legend.

TypeSeriesAxis! the user clicked on the series axis (only applied to 3D graphs).

TypeSeriesLabel! the user clicked on the label of the series axis (also only applies to 3D graphs).

TypeTitle! the user clicked on the graph title.

TypeValueAxis! the user clicked on the value axis or the value labels.

TypeValueLabel! the user clicked on the label for the value axis itself.

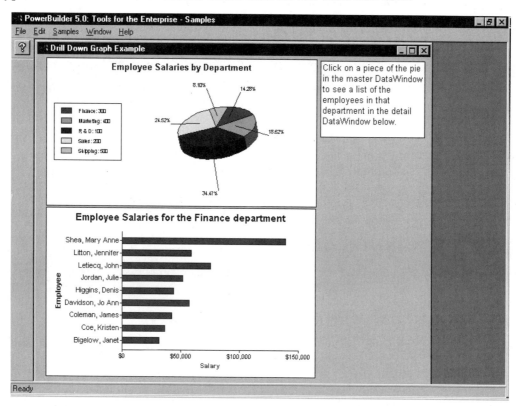

Figure 11.52 The sample application on the companion CD contains an example of a drill down graph.

You can examine the functionality of the ObjectAtPointer() function by looking at the drill down example on the companion CD. In this example, we have created two graph objects. The master object is a pie graph that shows all the departments and the total salaries

11.3 Graphs **429**

paid in the departments. The detail object shows all the employees and their salaries within a specific department as a bar graph. The example I deliberately kept as simple as possible so that you can see the functionality of the ObjectAtPointer() function. The only scripts on the window are in the open event and the clicked event on dw_master.

The open event sets up the transaction objects and retrieves the master:

```
dw_master.SetTransObject(SQLCA)
dw_master.Retrieve()
dw_detail.SetTransObject(SQLCA)
```

The clicked event calls the ObjectAtPointer() function and checks to see if the user clicked in either a data area (pie slice) or category (legend). If they did, then it gets the category name. It retrieves the detail DataWindow based upon the department id component of the category name and it changes the title of the detail DataWindow based upon the department name component of the category name.

```
// Declare local variables

grObjectType len_object
integer li_series, li_datapoint, li_dept_id
string ls_catname

// Where did the user click?

len_object = dw_master.ObjectAtPointer("gr_1", li_series, li_datapoint)

// Did the user click on a datapoint or category?
IF len_object = TypeData! or len_object = TypeCategory! THEN

        // User clicked in valid area
        // Get the Category name
        ls_catname = this.CategoryName("gr_1",li_datapoint)

        // Strip the department id from the category name
        li_dept_id = Integer(Mid(ls_catname, Len(ls_catname) - 3))

        // Retrieve the detail DataWindow
        dw_detail.Retrieve(li_dept_id)
```

430 *Chapter 11: Advanced Reporting*

```
            // Modify the title of the detail DataWindow to include
            // the department name
            dw_detail.Modify("gr_1.title= 'Employee Salaries for the "+&
                  Mid(ls_catname,1,Len(ls_catname) - 5)+" department'")
    END IF
```

11.4 CROSSTABS

Crosstabs are very useful tools when you need to perform analysis of your data. They allow you to scan through a large quantity of information and present a two dimensional summary of the results. The columns across the top of the cross tab represent the first dimension and the rows down the side of the crosstab represent the second. The intersection point in the grid between any individual row and column will contain the summary information about the data for that row/column combination. For example, in the crosstab in Figure 11.53, the first dimension is the product, the second dimension is the customer. At the intersection point between any row and column we see the total value of purchases made by that customer of that product.

Customer Purchases	Product					
Customer Name	**Baseball Cap**	**Shorts**	**Sweatshirt**	**Tee Shirt**	**Visor**	Grand Total
Agliori, Michael	$2,052.00	$1,080.00	$2,304.00	$108.00	$1,176.00	**$6,720.00**
Colburn, Kelly	$1,140.00	$1,620.00	$1,728.00	$1,668.00	$588.00	**$6,744.00**
Devlin, Michaels	$684.00	$360.00	$2,016.00	$1,992.00	$756.00	**$5,808.00**
Gagliardo, Jessie	$240.00	$900.00	$2,880.00	$1,332.00	$420.00	**$5,772.00**
Goforth, Matthew	$804.00	$180.00		$1,284.00	$252.00	**$2,520.00**
Mason, Meghan	$324.00	$1,080.00	$2,304.00	$2,220.00	$756.00	**$6,684.00**
McCarthy, Laura			$1,728.00	$984.00	$504.00	**$3,216.00**
Niedringhaus, Erin	$564.00	$180.00		$2,724.00	$504.00	**$3,972.00**
Phillips, Paul	$912.00	$180.00		$504.00		**$1,596.00**
Reiser, Beth	$780.00	$540.00	$576.00	$1,392.00	$336.00	**$3,624.00**
Ricci, Dylan	$1,356.00	$540.00		$276.00	$924.00	**$3,096.00**
Grand Total	**$8,856.00**	**$6,660.00**	**$13,536.00**	**$14,484.00**	**$6,216.00**	**$49,752.00**

Figure 11.53 *Crosstabs allow you to present the results of scanning through a large amount of information and summarizing it by two primary categories. The example above summarizes the total amount spent on each product type by each customer.*

Crosstabs have the look and feel of a spreadsheet. They use the basic grid format for displaying their information which means that the user has the ability to dynamically rearrange and resize columns at runtime. If you have a particularly large crosstab, you can enable split scrolling too.

Crosstabs can be found in many types of systems, particularly in decision support and analytical systems.

A system that I was involved with for a large university used crosstabs to analyze the number of applicants to each faculty within the university and break them down by their status: within state, out of state and foreign. This was important as they were required to report the ratios of in-state, out-of-state and foreign students who were attending to the government board that providing their funding.

11.4.1 CREATING A CROSSTAB

Let's walk through the steps of creating a crosstab DataWindow. We are going to create two crosstabs, the first one is a fairly simple crosstab, the second becomes a bit more complex. The first crosstab we will build will be the one shown in Figure 11.53.

11.4.1.1 Sample One—A Simple Crosstab

Step 1   Build the SQL statement. Open the DataWindow painter and select SQL Select/Crosstab. Select the Customer, Sales Order, Sales Order Items and Product tables. Remember to double check the table joins to be sure that they are correct! From these tables select the customer.fname, customer.lname, sales_order_items.quantity, product.name and product.unit_price columns. Close the SQL painter and move to the designer.

Step 2   Define the crosstab. Closing the SQL painter will cause the Crosstab Definition dialog window to open as in Figure 11.54. In this window you will define what data will represent the columns, rows and the intersection point between the rows and columns in the crosstab. Multiple data fields can be included in the definition and we will examine this in the second example. This example will use only one data field in each dimension.

Chapter 11: Advanced Reporting

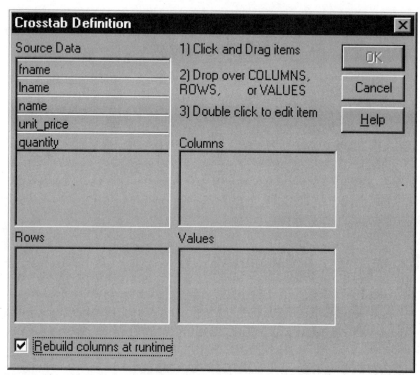

Figure 11.54 *The Crosstab Definition dialog window is where you define what data will represent the columns, rows and intersections in the crosstab.*

We want to use the product name as our first dimension (our columns). Drag the 'name' field from the Source Data listbox into the Columns listbox.

For the second dimension, the rows, we want to use the combination of first and last name. This will be a custom defined expression. To provide for this, we will drag the 'lname' field from the 'Source Data' listbox and drop it in the 'Rows' listbox. Now we must double click on the field with the left mouse button to open the Modify Expression dialog window.

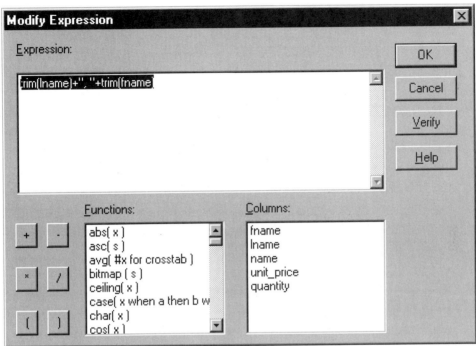

Figure 11.55 *We will double-click on the field to open the Modify Expression dialog window and change the field to a custom expression.*

Change the expression to combine the first and last name like:

trim(lname) +","+ trim(fname)

Now we have to define our intersection point. This is represented by the data displayed in the 'Values' listbox. Drag the 'unit_price' field from the 'Source Data' to the 'Values' listbox. PowerBuilder will take a guess at building an expression that you might want to use. In this case it will produce:

sum(unit_price for crosstab)

which is not really what we are after. What we really want to show is the sum of the (unit_price X quantity) for all the items that match the current product and customer. We need to double-click on the field and modify the expression to be:

sum((unit_price * quantity) for crosstab)

434   *Chapter 11: Advanced Reporting*

Now we have fully defined our crosstab. At any time in the designer, if you click with the right mouse button in an empty area of the DataWindow, you will see a popup menu with an option that says **Crossstab...** which will bring you back to the Crosstab Definition dialog. Press the **OK** command button to close the dialog.

Step 3   Modify the crosstab. Now you will see a DataWindow in the designer that appears very much like a grid DataWindow. In fact, it behaves very much like a grid. You cannot add overall titles, but you can add a title in the upper left cell of the grid. You can change the field types, alignments, colors and so on just like you would in a grid DataWindow.

You should change the column label to 'Products,' the row label to 'Customer Name' and the crosstab label to 'Customer/Products.' Apply a currency format to the intersection cell so that the amounts are formatted as currencies.

Step 4   Modify computed fields. By default, PowerBuilder will have created a grand total column for you that runs in both dimensions. In the summary band, you can create any computed field you desire. If you would rather show an average, you can use the AVG (#x for all) function. All the standard aggregate functions apply.

Where things become a bit different are when you want to add computed fields for the summary of a row. Notice the computed field in the detail band contains the CrosstabSum() function. This function will provide you with the sum of all the fields in the row that are part of the crosstab. The complete set of crosstab specific functions that you can use in computed fields on a row are:

CrosstabSum() sums all the fields in the row that are part of the crosstab.

CrosstabAvg() averages all the fields in the row that are part of the crosstab.

CrosstabCount() counts the number of values returned by the expression for rows included in the crosstab.

CrosstabMax() returns the maximum value for the fields in the row that are part of the crosstab.

CrosstabMin() returns the minimum value for the fields in the row that are part of the crosstab.

All of these functions have a simple and a complex syntax. In the simple syntax, they have a single parameter which is an integer. This integer indicates which expression that the function must act upon. Since our simple example has only one expression, this value will always be 1. Figure 11.55 demonstrates the use of the CrosstabSum() function in our example.

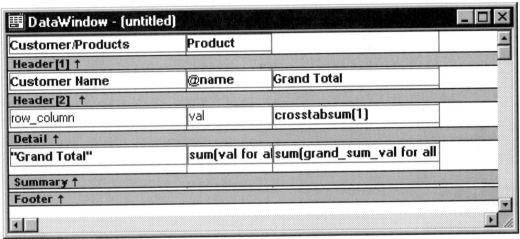

Figure 11.56 *The CrosstabSum() function is used in a computed field within the detail band in our example. This field is automatically generated by PowerBuilder for us.*

Step 5   Preview your data. Your finished crosstab should appear similar to the one in Figure 11.57.

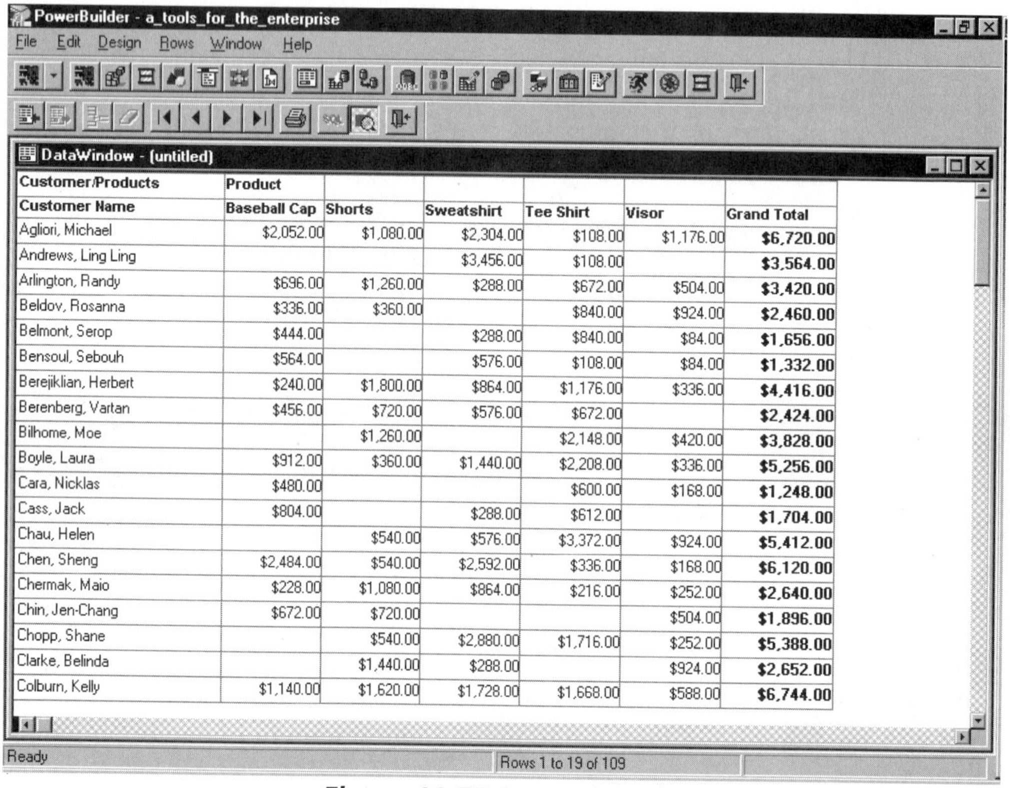

436 *Chapter 11: Advanced Reporting*

Figure 11.57 Our end result.

11.4.1.2 Sample Two—Crosstab With Complex Dimensions and Grouping

Now we are going to push our crosstab a little bit further by building one which has complex dimensions with multiple data elements. In our example we will build a crosstab that is going to tell us the purchases that each customer made for each product broken down by year and quarter (whew!). The result is shown in Figure 11.58. The whole crosstab didn't fit, so when you build yours, you can scroll back and forth, or you can see the result in the sample application on the companion CD.

11.4 Crosstabs **437**

Customer Purchases		1994		1994 Total	1995				1995 Total
Customer Name	Product	Q3	Q4		Q1	Q2	Q3	Q4	
Agliori, Michael	Baseball Cap	$1,020.00		$1,020.00		$108.00	$240.00	$684.00	$1,032.00
	Shorts	$180.00		$180.00	$360.00		$540.00		$900.00
	Sweatshirt			$0.00		$2,304.00			$2,304.00
	Tee Shirt			$0.00	$108.00				$108.00
	Visor		$924.00	$924.00				$252.00	$252.00
Agliori, Michael Total		**$1,200.00**	**$924.00**	**$2,124.00**	**$468.00**	**$2,412.00**	**$780.00**	**$936.00**	**$4,596.00**
Andrews, Ling Ling	Sweatshirt		$1,152.00	$1,152.00			$576.00	$288.00	$864.00
	Tee Shirt			$0.00		$108.00			$108.00
Andrews, Ling Ling Total		**$0.00**	**$1,152.00**	**$1,152.00**	**$0.00**	**$108.00**	**$576.00**	**$288.00**	**$972.00** $
Arlington, Randy	Baseball Cap		$360.00	$360.00	$228.00		$108.00		$336.00
	Shorts			$0.00		$720.00	$540.00		$1,260.00
	Sweatshirt		$288.00	$288.00					$0.00
	Tee Shirt			$0.00				$672.00	$672.00
	Visor	$336.00	$168.00	$504.00					$0.00
Arlington, Randy Total		**$336.00**	**$816.00**	**$1,152.00**	**$228.00**	**$720.00**	**$648.00**	**$672.00**	**$2,268.00**
Beldov, Rosanna	Baseball Cap	$216.00	$120.00	$336.00					$0.00
	Shorts		$360.00	$360.00					$0.00
	Tee Shirt	$336.00	$168.00	$504.00		$168.00		$168.00	$336.00

Figure 11.58 *Sample two builds a crosstab that will show us the total purchases that each customer made for each product broken down by year and quarter.*

Step 1 Build the SQL statement. Open the DataWindow painter and select SQL Select/Crosstab. Open the Customer, Products, Sales Order and Sales Order Items tables. Check the joins to ensure they are correct. There will probably be an incorrect join between the products and customers table. Delete this join.

Select the customer.fname, customer.lname, product.name, product.unit_price, sales_order_items.quantity, and sales_order.order_date columns. Your complete SQL statement should appear as follows:

```
SELECT "customer"."fname",
    "customer"."lname",
    "product"."name",
    "product"."unit_price",
    "sales_order_items"."quantity",
    "sales_order"."order_date"
FROM "customer",
    "product",
```

438   *Chapter 11: Advanced Reporting*

```
"sales_order",
"sales_order_items"
WHERE ("sales_order"."cust_id" = "customer"."id") and
  ("sales_order_items"."id" = "sales_order"."id") and
  ("sales_order_items"."prod_id" = "product"."id")
```

Close the SQL Select painter and move to the designer.

Step 2   Define the crosstab. The Crosstab Definition dialog window will open as you move from the SQL painter to the designer. We need to define the dimensions (rows and columns) and intersection (values) for this crosstab.

Drag the 'lname' field into the 'Rows' listbox. Double-click on it to open the Modify Expression dialog. Change the expression to:

```
trim(lname) + "," + trim(fname)
```

Close the Modify Expression dialog window. Drag the 'name' field into the 'Rows' listbox. Make sure that you drop it below the customer name field that we defined as we want the product name to be subordinate to the customer name. If we dropped the product name field above the customer name, then product name would become the primary group. We don't need to modify product name, we will use the field as it is.

Now drag the 'order_date' field to the 'Columns' listbox. Modify the expression so that we only use the year component of the date. To do this we use the Year() function in the expression as follows:

```
year(order_date)
```

Close the window. Now drag the 'order_date' field to the 'Columns' listbox a second time. Drop it after the year field. Modify the expression to provide us with the quarter that the order was placed in. We can do this by using the new PowerBuilder 5.0 case expression function as follows:

```
case(month(order_date)
when 1 to 3 then 'Q1'
when 4 to 6 then 'Q2'
when 7 to 9 then 'Q3'
when 10 to 12 then 'Q4'
else '??')
```

Now that we have both our dimensions defined, we have to define our intersection. Drag the 'quantity' field to the 'Values' listbox. Modify the expression to give us the unit price multiplied by the quantity for each cell in the crosstab. The expression will be like this:

sum((quantity * unit_price) for crosstab)

The expression is quite simple. PowerBuilder takes care of the more difficult grouping and interpretation of the expression.

Press the **OK** command button to close the Crosstab Definition dialog.

Step 3 Modify columns and text fields. PowerBuilder automatically generates all the necessary groups and fields for you (hurray!). All that you have to do is tweak them until you get the formatting that you desire.

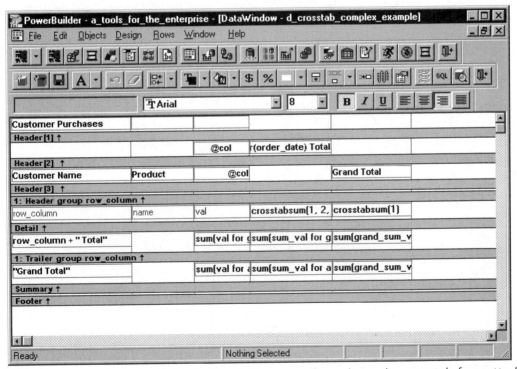

Figure 11.59 *Tweak the fields in the designer until you have the crosstab formatted as you desire.*

440 *Chapter 11: Advanced Reporting*

You can change the text field at the top of the crosstab to 'Customer Purchases' and remove the other fields from the header [1] area.

In the header [2] area, you should select the third column with the '@col' value and change its alignment to centered. This is the column that will display the year, and it looks better if the year is centered over the four quarters.

In the header [3] area, you should change the label above the customer name column to read 'Customer Name' and the label above the product column to read 'Product'.

In complex crosstabs, the volume of information can make it them difficult to read. Here is an excellent application for the use of color in your user interface. In the detail band, I have changed the customer name and product columns to have dark green text. You can't see it in the black and white picture above, but you can in the sample application. I also have changed the fourth column, the year subtotal, to a dark blue text.

In the group 1 trailer band, I changed all the text to a dark blue except the last column ('Grand Total') which I left black. The summary band I left unchanged.

You should alter the column widths to more appropriate settings, otherwise some of your columns will be difficult to read.

Step 4 Modify general settings. Clicking with the right mouse button in the unused area of the DataWindow will open up a popup menu. Select the **Properties...** option. This will open the Properties page for the DataWindow. On the General tab you will see a set of options that will allow you to change the grid settings.

11.4 Crosstabs

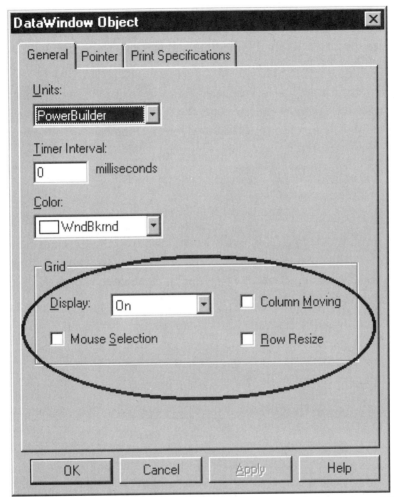

Figure 11.60 *On the Properties page you can change the grid settings for the crosstab.*

The Display drop down list box allows you to toggle the displaying of the grid lines for the cross tab. You can have them on, off, display only (not visible when printing), or print only (not visible when displayed on the screen. You can also enable or disable the end users ability to rearrange columns, select columns and resize rows at runtime.

442   *Chapter 11: Advanced Reporting*

Step 5   Preview your crosstab. Your end result should be similar to the original picture in Figure 11.58 previously shown. If you run the version in the companion CD, you can see the crosstab functioning in an application. Notice the built in functionality for horizontal split scrolling.

This example is a more sophisticated crosstab, but they can get even trickier. Notice in the above example, our subtotal columns use a more complex variation of the CrosstabSum() function. All the crosstab functions have an alternate syntax which is:

crosstabsum(value_exp, column_exp, groupvalue)

where:

value_exp   is the expression in the Values listbox of the Crosstab Definition window that you want to perform the function upon. In our example, this value is 1. This must always be a numeric value.

column_exp   is the expression in the Columns listbox of the Crosstab Definition window that you want to perform the calculation upon. In our example, we want the sum for each of our product lines, so our value is 2 (product is the second expression in our Columns listbox). This also must always be an integer.

groupvalue   is a string which is used to control the grouping for the calculation. Group value is usually a value from another column in the crosstab. In our example, we are wanting to group by the year. To define this, we would build a string for groupvalue that begins with the '@' symbol (which is a required element) and then add the name of the column (defined in our crosstab as 'year(order_date)'). The resulting groupvalue string is '@year(order_date)')

11.4.2 DYNAMIC VS. STATIC CROSSTABS

There is an attribute of crosstabs which is often overlooked by most developers. Consider this problem which I encountered at one client I was working with. They had to track ships that were coming and going from their dock. They wanted to build a crosstab that would show how many ships were scheduled on Monday through to Sunday broken down by the company that the ships belonged to. The crosstab would appear something like:

11.4 Crosstabs

Ship Schedule

	Monday	Tuesday	Wednesday	Thursday	Friday	Saturday	Sunday
Company A	0	2	5	1	0	3	2
Company B	1	0	3	1	0	2	1
Company C	3	1	2	1	0	1	0

They wanted to produce this schedule every week with all seven days listed. The only problem is that on days like the Friday shown above, the column would not appear at all. This is because by default crosstabs are dynamically rebuilt with every result set retrieved. If there is no data for Friday, the Friday column would be removed.

You can override the dynamic setting and build static crosstabs that will always come out the exact same way every time they are run. This is accomplished by deselecting the **Rebuild Columns at Runtime** checkbox in the Crosstab Definition dialog window as shown in Figure 11.61.

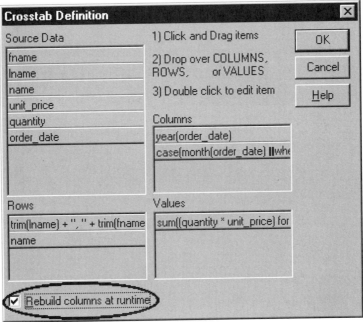

Figure 11.61 *Static crosstabs can be generated by deselecting the Rebuild Columns at Runtime checkbox in the Crosstab Definition dialog window.*

Chapter 11: Advanced Reporting

Now when you press the **OK** command button to close the Crosstab Definition window, PowerBuilder will retrieve the data from the database and will set up a series of static columns that will be the same for every retrieval of this crosstab. In order to ensure that all the columns that you want included will exist, there must be data in the database for each column (in our example, we must have at least one ship arriving each day). This is only necessary at the time that you create the crosstab. At runtime, it won't matter if there are no ships coming in on Friday, the Friday column will show up anyhow. You may need to create some fake data to meet your short term crosstab creation needs.

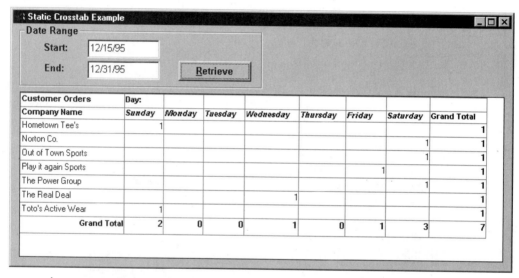

Figure 11.62 *Our Static Crosstab demonstration window on the companion CD allows you to pick a range of dates and then see which days orders were placed for each company.*

11.5 SUMMARY

Good quality reporting is an essential element of any successful business system. The ability to provide feedback to the users of the system is a key factor in why PowerBuilder has been so successful in the client/server business application development arena.

There are many advanced features in PowerBuilder that you can use to provide reports and feedback for your user. We have examined nested reports, composite reports, crosstabs and graphs. Rich Text DataWindows are also very useful advanced reporting feature of PowerBuilder 5.0. These are discussed in detail in Chapter 7, section 7.5.1.2—Rich Text DataWindow.

Take full advantage of these features to improve the quality of reporting that you integrate into your system. The features that are discussed in this chapter are some of the most powerful that PowerBuilder has to offer, yet they make up probably less than 10% of the reports currently in use in production systems.

CHAPTER 12

User Objects

A critical requirement to develop object-oriented applications within any environment is the ability to define and reuse your own object classes. In PowerBuilder, one of the vehicles for providing this functionality is the user object.

Although you are not required to utilize user objects when creating applications in PowerBuilder, they are essential if you want to build applications that are distributed, tiered and/or low maintenance. When you take advantage of user objects your development teams will be able to avoid repetitive coding, improve the maintainability of your application(s), standardize the interface and processing, and more!

User objects and be broken down into two general types: visual and class (non-visual).

12.1 VISUAL USER OBJECTS

Visual objects are objects that the user can see and will interact with in your application. In general, these objects are intended to be used as controls on window objects. You can use the visual user object to customize the appearance and behavior of standard PowerBuilder visual controls or you can integrate controls written in other languages like C, Delphi or Visual Basic into your PowerBuilder applications.

448   Chapter 12: User Objects

In PowerBuilder we have four different types of visual user objects; custom, external, standard and VBX.

12.1.1 VISUAL: STANDARD

Standard visual user objects allow you to customize the standard PowerBuilder visual objects such as command buttons, DataWindow controls, radio buttons and so on. These are particularly useful if you want to reuse this new object in multiple places. Consider the standard close command button. This button is used in many different windows throughout multiple applications. You could create a standard visual user object of this button encapsulating the button label and clicked method.

Let's walk through the process of creating the standard visual object cb_close.

Step 1   Open the User Object painter. Select the user object icon. The standard selection dialog window will open. Notice that it looks very much like the Window painter selection window. You can create a new user object or you can inherit from an existing user object. This allows you to inherit from and extend your own class definitions. Select the **New...** command button. This will open the New User Object window in Figure 12.1.

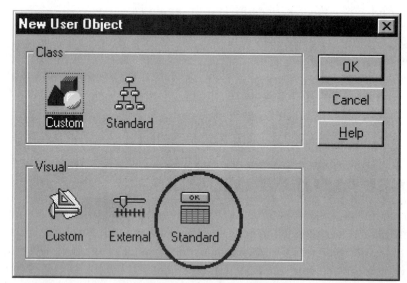

Figure 12.1 *The New User Object dialog window allows you to select the kind of user object you want to create.*

Select the standard visual user object and press the **OK** command button.

Step 2 Choose object type. The Select Standard Visual Type window will open. This window contains a list box with all the standard PowerBuilder visual objects that you can inherit from. Select the *commandbutton* from the list and press the **OK** command button.

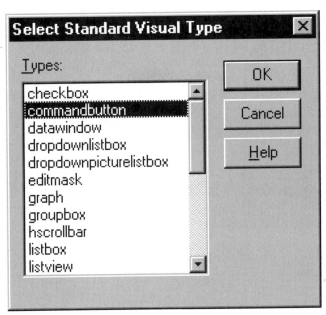

Figure 12.2 *The Select Standard Visual Type dialog window allows you to select the type of standard object that you are going to create from a list of all the standard PowerBuilder types.*

Step 3 Modify object. In the user object painter you will see a standard command button that has been created. You can now modify this object by altering its properties and adding methods and instance variables (which become new properties for this object when it is instantiated).

450 Chapter 12: User Objects

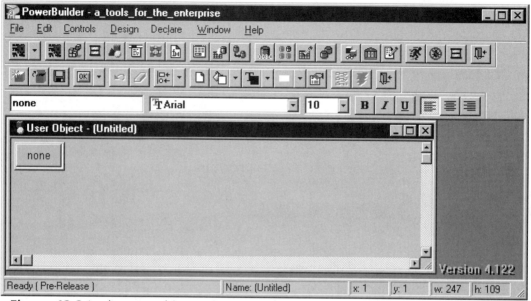

Figure 12.3 *In the user object painter you can alter the properties of the command button and add methods and instance variables.*

In the style bar, change the text on the button to '&Close' and make it bold (using the bold toolbar icon). Now resize the button to the size that you want it to be by default.

Next we want to add a method to the clicked event of this object. Click on the command button with the right mouse button and launch the script painter from the popup menu. By default, you will enter the clicked event. Like in any other instance of the script painter, you can move between events using the drop down list box at the top of the painter.

We want the clicked event to close the window that this object has been placed on. We want to code this script to be generic so it can be used on any Window. We will use the PARENT pronoun to accomplish this.

    Close(PARENT)

Save the object and give it the name u_std_cb_close.

12.1 Visual User Objects 451

Step 4 Create a new window. Open the window painter and create a new window (or use an existing window that has a Close button). To place the object on the window, select the user object control from the control palette. This will cause the Select User Object dialog window to open.

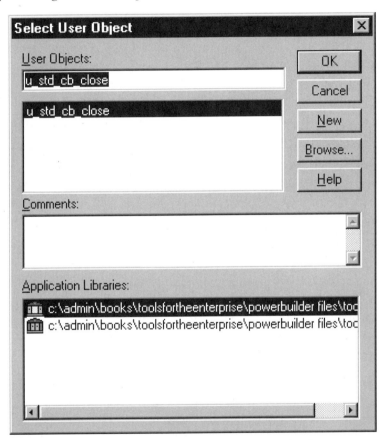

Figure 12.4 *When placing a standard user object on a window you will be presented with the Select User Object dialog window from which you will choose the object you want to work with.*

Choose your u_std_cb_close object. Place this object on your window. Give the object a meaningful name like cb_close. Save your window.

452   *Chapter 12: User Objects*

Step 5   Run your window. Run your window and observe the behavior of the user object that you placed. When clicked, it will close the window it is sitting on.

This user object could be used on any window in any application and it would function exactly the same. In order to use the user object we simply had to place it on the window and its encapsulated functionality did the rest.

This was a simple example, but you can think of many different uses, particularly for objects like the DataWindow control. If you are building a 'fat' two tiered application, you could build a DataWindow object that has all the logic for row selection, error handling, searching, sorting and so on built right in. Then all the DataWindows in your application could take advantage of all this functionality that you only had to build once!

If you are building a 'thin' three tiered or n-tiered application, or if you are taking advantage of a service based architecture, you could build your own standard visual DataWindow control that has built in links to all the required service objects and business objects.

12.1.2 VISUAL: CUSTOM

The custom visual user object can be though of as a way of grouping other objects together into one common container. This container is a fully encapsulated and reusable object. These objects are usually relatively generic in orientation. One project that I was involved with used a group of commandbuttons with the same functions as a custom popup toolbar throughout all their applications. When you clicked with the right mouse button, this user object was dynamically created (see section 12.3 Creating User Objects).

A common type of custom user object is a DataWindow VCR Controller. This type of a control combines a number of standard buttons that are combined into a custom visual object. This object can be used in conjunction with any DataWindow control as a user interface device for moving through the Data.

12.1 Visual User Objects

Figure 12.5 *A DataWindow toolbar, or DataWindow VCR Controller allows you to use everyday controls to navigate through the data in a DataWindow.*

We will walk though the construction of this custom visual user object.

Step 1 Open the User Object painter. As you did in the previous section, open the user object painter, and create a new user object. This time select the Custom Visual User Object Icon. This will open the user object painter window.

Step 2 Create the custom object. The workspace in the user object painter when creating a custom user object is very much like working in the window painter. You have the palette of standard PowerBuilder controls that you can build into your custom object. You can even embed other user objects into this custom user object.

Place four picture button controls in your workspace. Double-click on each picture button and change its properties as follows (set Original Size to true for all):

1. name: pb_first enabled picture: BFIRST.BMP (or you can use FIRST.BMP from your PowerBuilder directory)

2. name: pb_prev enabled picture: BPREV.BMP (or PREV.BMP from the PB directory)

3. name: pb_next enabled picture: BNEXT.BMP (or NEXT.BMP)

4. name: pb_last enabled picture: BLAST.BMP (or LAST.BMP)

Arrange these buttons in the top left corner of the workspace in the format of the toolbar pictured in Figure 12.5.

Step 3 Define an instance variable. We need to create a reference variable of type DataWindow that we can use at runtime to reference the DataWindow control that we want these buttons to work with. To do this we define an instance variable for the user object. This is done in the same fashion as in the window painter.

Define the variable as protected so that it cannot be accessed from outside this control. This keeps our object properly encapsulated.

Chapter 12: User Objects

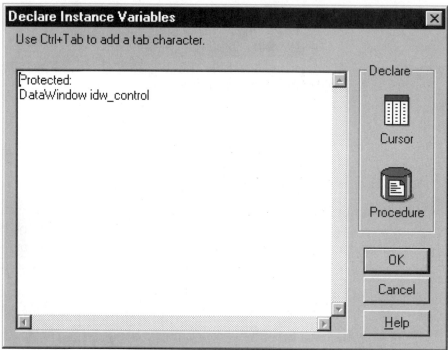

Figure 12.6 *Define a protected instance variable that will contain the runtime reference to the DataWindow control we want to tie this toolbar to.*

Step 4   Define a public function to set the runtime instance variable. We defined the instance variable as protected to encapsulate our user object. We need to provide a runtime interface to allow the parent object to interact with our toolbar. We will define an object level function called SetDW() which will accept a single argument of type DataWindow. This argument will be passed by reference and inserted into our protected instance variable. This will provide our methods in the picture buttons with a handle of a DataWindow control that they can work with.

The function declaration is shown in Figure 12.7. The script for this function is:

    idw_control= adw_dw

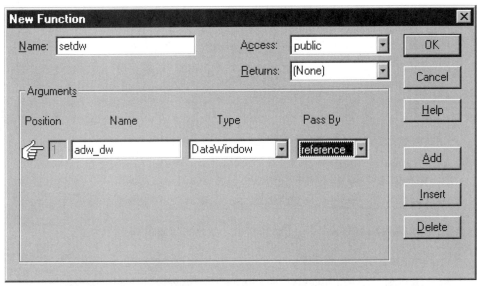

Figure 12.7 *Function declaration for the SetDW() method.*

Step 5   Add scripts to the buttons. We need to add a script to each button in the toolbar. The scripts will be as follows:

cb_first—will scroll to the first row in the DataWindow control. The script is:

idw_control.ScrollToRow(1)

cb_prev—will scroll one row up in the DataWindow control. The script is:

idw_control.ScrollPriorRow()

cb_next—will scroll to the next row in the DataWindow control. The script is:

idw_control.ScrollNextRow()

cb_last—will scroll to the last row in the DataWindow control. The script is:

idw_control.ScrollToRow(idw_control.RowCount())

456 *Chapter 12: User Objects*

Step 6 Fine tune the control. Change the background color of the control to a gray. Make sure that the border property is set to None. Resize the edge of the control so that it wraps neatly around the picture buttons.

Step 7 Save the control. Save the user object with the name u_cst_dw_toolbar.

Step 8 Place the control on a window. Select a window that has a DataWindow control on it. From the sample application you could select the w_emp_maint_dw_events window. Open the window and place the control on the window.

Step 9 Link the DataWindow control to the toolbar. We can link the DataWindow control to the toolbar by calling the SetDW() function that we defined in the user object. In the constructor event for our user object control enter the following script:

THIS.SetDW(dw_employees) // Use the name of the DW control on this
// window.

Step 10 Run the window and observe. Now that the object is created, it can be used on any window, anywhere with only one line of code to link it to the appropriate DataWindow control.

12.1.3 VISUAL: EXTERNAL

The external visual user object is used to bring objects and controls created in languages outside of PowerBuilder into a PowerBuilder application. The most common of these are probably controls written in C, C++ or Delphi, but you could encounter controls from any number of languages. Almost any language that builds a true windows .DLL (Dynamic Link Library) can be tied into PowerBuilder.

In order to use an external .DLL it is critical to have the appropriate documentation from the producer of the .DLL so you know the correct class name and style settings.

To define an external visual user object you select that option from the New User Object window. PowerBuilder will ask you to identify the .DLL file that will be the source for this object. Select it and press the **Open** command button.

This will open the External User Object Style dialog window pictured in Figure 12.8. The .DLL name will be filled in. This .DLL must be available at runtime which means it must be distributed along with your .EXE and other files to your end user. The Class Name comes from the documentation of the vendor. A single .DLL could contain multiple classes that you could use. The other critical property that you must set is the Style value. This value will control the attributes of the class. These values will also be specified in the documentation. If everything is set up correctly, when you press the **OK** command button, you should be able to see the control in the user object workspace. You will need to define custom user events that are linked to the appropriate windows messages (refer to Chapter 8, section 8.1—Setting Up Object Events) as specified in the vendor documentation.

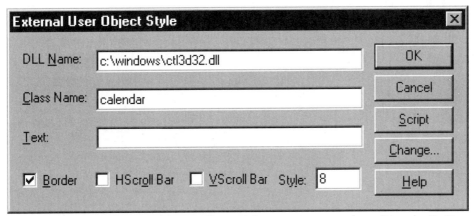

Figure 12.8 *External user objects allow to integrate controls written in C, C++ or another language into your PowerBuilder application.*

12.1.4 VISUAL: VBX

The VBX user object is only available if you are using the 16 bit version of PowerBuilder. These have generally been replaced by the 32 bit OCX controls. Chances are you won't be working with them, but here is how they work in a nutshell.

VBX controls are those written in Visual Basic. There are many third party VBX controls on the market for using in your applications. These objects work very similar to external user objects in PowerBuilder, except that they are a little easier to set up. You merely specify the VBX file to use, select from the list of control in that VBX file and that is all. You will automatically have a set of VBX events defined. You can continue to extend these methods as you see fit.

458 *Chapter 12: User Objects*

12.2 CLASS (NON-VISUAL) USER OBJECTS

Class, or non-visual objects are encapsulated containers for attributes and methods that the application will use but are never created visually or seen by the user. These objects are essential for distributed PowerBuilder, integrating OLE automation and the use of business objects and service based architectures.

12.2.1 CLASS: STANDARD

The standard class user object are objects that allow you to extend the properties and methods of standard PowerBuilder non-visual classes. The classes that you can build on are:

• Connection	• DataStore	• Dynamic Description Area (SQLDA)
• Dynamic Staging Area (SQLSA)	• Error	• MailSession
• Message	• OLEObject	• OLEStorage
• OLEStream	• Pipeline	• Transaction

The objects that you create from these ancestors can have expanded functionality that the ancestors don't have. For example, we could define our own transaction object that has all its methods encapsulated inside it. We could add a method that will automatically read in the property settings from an .INI file, another that will manage the connection process and so on (the current transaction object is very poorly encapsulated requiring you to do a great deal of work outside of the object).

Let's create our own transaction object as an example of how we create a standard class user object.

Step 1 Open User Object Painter. Open the user object painter and choose a new object. Select the Standard Class object from the Class group box. PowerBuilder will open up the Select Standard Class Type dialog window and let you select what kind of class to use as the ancestor for your object.

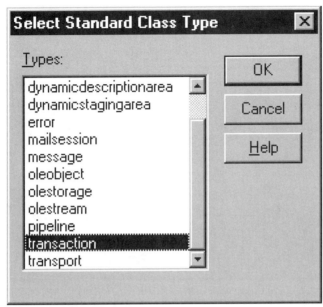

Figure 12.9 *Select the object to use as the ancestor for your standard class user object from the Select Standard Class Type dialog window.*

Step 2 Define any custom attributes and methods. The painter will open up with what looks like a window workspace, but you can't place any controls on it because it is non-visual! You can, however, define new attributes for the class (as instance variables) and new methods (as object functions).

We will define a custom method called GetINIParms() which will load the database parameters for the transaction object from an INI file. Select the **Declare → User Object Functions...** option from the menu. This will open the Select Function Window. Press the **New...** command button to create a new function.

In the function declaration window, declare your function as in Figure 12.10.

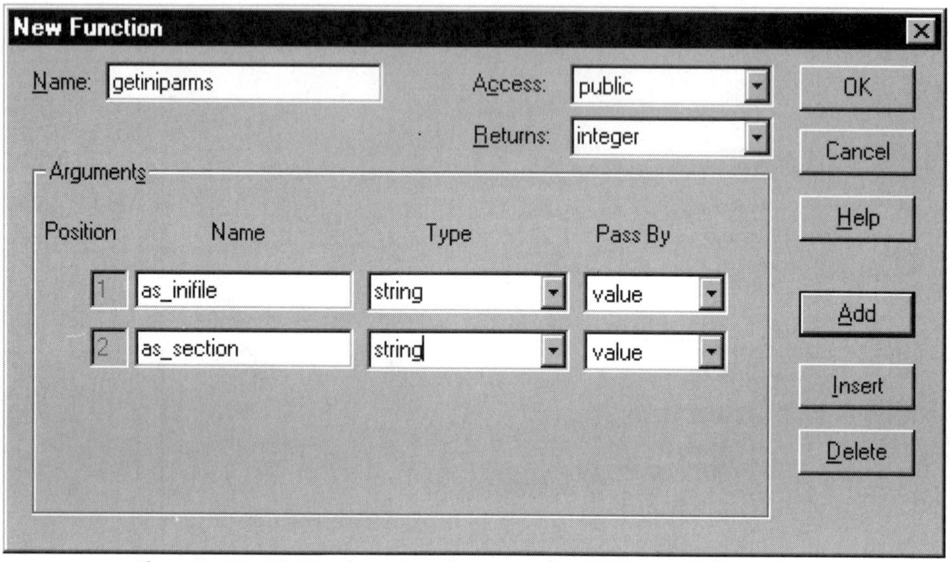

460 *Chapter 12: User Objects*

Figure 12.10 *Declaration for the GetINIParms() function.*

Define two string arguments, one to contain the path and name of the .INI file and the second to store the name of the section in the .INI file where the database profile can be found. The script for the function should be something like:

```
IF FileExists(as_inifile) THEN
        // Retrieve Parameters
        THIS.DBMS = ProfileString(as_inifile,as_section,'dbms','')
        THIS.Database = ProfileString(as_inifile,as_section,'database','')
        THIS.ServerName = &
                ProfileString(as_inifile,as_section,'servername','')
        THIS.Logid = ProfileString(as_inifile,as_section,'logid','')
        THIS.Logpass = ProfileString(as_inifile,as_section,'logpass','')
        THIS.Userid = ProfileString(as_inifile,as_section,'userid','')
        THIS.DBPass = ProfileString(as_inifile,as_section,'dbpass','')
        THIS.DBParm = ProfileString(as_inifile,as_section,'dbparm','')
        RETURN 1
ELSE
        // File Not Found
        MessageBox("Connection Error","Unable to read connection information."+&
                ".INI file '"+as_inifile+"' not found.",StopSign!)
        RETURN - 1
END IF
```

12.2 Class (Non-Visual) User Objects   **461**

This example reads even the user id and password from the .INI file. Most likely these would come from other places.

If you were to substitute this transaction object for the standard SQLCA transaction object (the technique for doing this is discussed in section 12.3 below) you would get SQLCA to populate itself from your .INI file simply by calling the following function:

SQLCA.GetINIParms("myapp.ini","[database]")

I am sure you can think of many other methods that it would be useful to have inside your standard transaction object such as a Connect() function that connects and checks for errors.

Step 5   Save the new object. Save the object as u_nvo_transaction.

12.2.2 CLASS: CUSTOM

The custom class user object is a place where you can build any kind of non-visual object you desire. This is the place where you will build your service objects, or your distributed objects for PowerBuilder.

When you first open a new custom class user object, it will have only one predefined property called *proxyname* that is used for distributed computing (as discussed in Chapter 7, section 7.2—Distributed PowerBuilder). The only functions it supports are ClassName(), GetParent(), PostEvent(), TriggerEvent() and TypeOf().

It is up to you to create the properties and methods that are necessary for what you intend this object to do. This is done in the same was as we have accomplished this in previous units, through instance variables and object functions.

Let's create a non-visual service object for handling errors.

Step 1   Open the user object painter. Open the painter and select Custom Class as the type of object that you want to create. This will open up the user object painter with a workspace that looks the same as it did in step one for the Standard Class object. Like that object, there is no visual component here, so you will not be able to place controls in the workspace.

462 Chapter 12: User Objects

Step 2 Define any custom attributes and methods. This is the meat of creating a non-visual user object as it serves no purpose without the specific attributes and methods that you define. For our example, we are going to define a two standard methods; one for checking for errors after embedded SQL calls, and a second for generic database error handling.

The generic error handling method will be created as HandleError(). The function definition for this is shown in Figure 12.11.

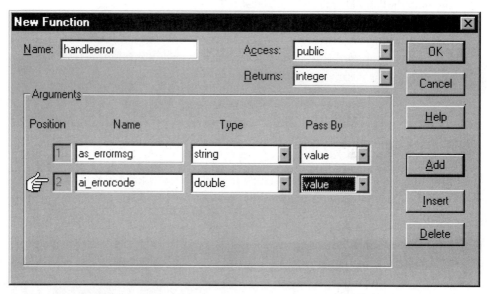

Figure 12.11 Function declaration for the HandleError() method.

The processing in this function could get quite complex. You could put in custom handling based upon error code and even use different non-visuals for different databases to allow for easier DBMS independent development. For our example, we will simply display the error message:

```
// Custom error handling based upon error code
// could be inserted here. Different non-visuals
// could be implemented for different databases
// simplifying database independent development.

RETURN MessageBox("Database Error","Error:"+as_errormsg + &
    "~n~rError Code:"+String(ai_errorcode), StopSign!)
```

12.2 Class (Non-Visual) User Objects 463

The second method that we will add is the CheckSQLError() method. This method could also be incorporated into the transaction object in the previous section, but for the purposes of demonstration it is included here. The function definition for CheckSQLError() is shown in Figure 12.12.

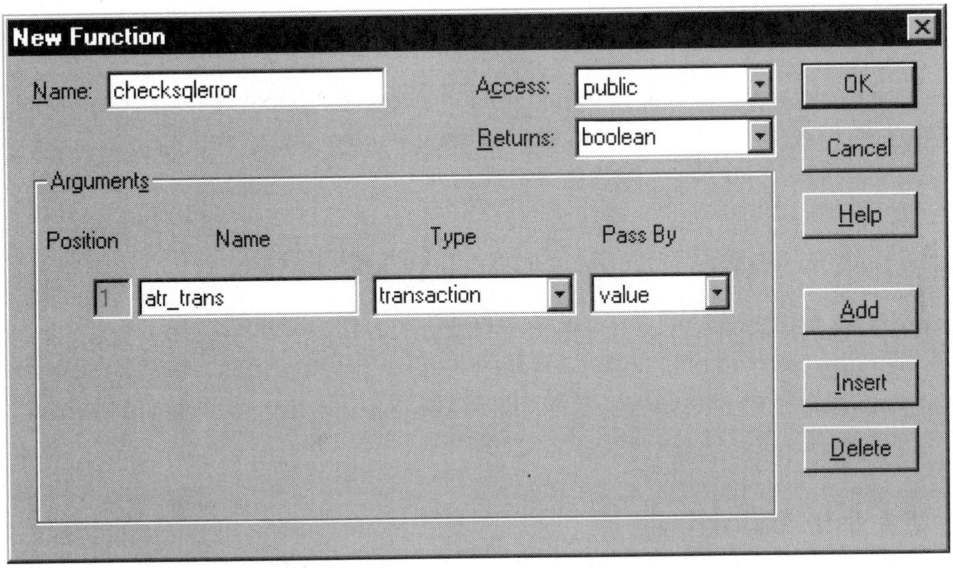

Figure 12.12 *Function declaration for CheckSQLError() method.*

This script will check the transaction object that was passed to determine if the SQL executed correctly. If not it will immediately rollback the transaction and call the error handling function (that is conveniently located within itself). The script for this is as follows:

```
IF atr_trans.SQLCode <> 0 THEN
        // Rollback immediately so that other users aren't
        // locked out of the table.
        ROLLBACK using atr_trans;

        // Call the Handle Error event to process error
        THIS.HandleError(atr_trans.SQLErrText,atr_trans.SQLDBCode)
        RETURN TRUE
ELSE
        RETURN FALSE
END IF
```

464   *Chapter 12: User Objects*

Step 3   Save the object. Save this object as u_nvo_errorhandler.

The next step to using this object is to create it in the location where it is required. Refer to the following section for details on how to do this.

12.3 CREATING USER OBJECTS

Creating user objects is only half of the skill that is necessary to realize their benefits. The second step is to integrate them into your application. The techniques for doing so are very different for visual and non-visual user objects.

12.3.1 INSTANTIATING A VISUAL USER OBJECT

Visual user objects play a critical role in interfacing with the user. You can think of them like a custom control that you place on a window. There are two methods for instantiating a visual user object; you can do it directly in the window painter, or you can write a script to dynamically create them as required at runtime.

12.3.1.1 In a Painter

To add a user object to your window in the window painter, you simply select the user object icon from the window painterbar (Be careful not to select the icon from the PowerBar as this would launch the User Object painter. Note that the icons are the same.). When you do so, you will be asked to select the object that you wish to paint on the window from the Select User Object dialog window.

> **Developers Note: Although non-visual user objects will appear in the list when you choose your user object to place on a window, attempting to place one will result in a warning message that you cannot place non-visual class objects on the window.**

Once you have chosen the user object that you want to place, you simply click on the window where you want it to appear. From that point it behaves exactly like any other windows control.

12.3.1.2 In a Script

If you are already familiar with instantiating non-visual objects, you will be familiar with the reserved word CREATE. This is the same reserved word we use to define our own transaction objects, which at this point I will assume that you are already familiar with. We could use the CREATE syntax to instantiate a visual class of object like this:

```
u_std_cb_close cb_close
cb_close = CREATE cb_close
```

This script would indeed create an instance of the class in memory. We could assign values to its attributes and so on. There is one critical reason why we don't do this; the object never appears on the window. Using the create statement on a visual class will not cause it to appear within the visible interface. To do this we need to use a special function called OpenUserObject().

The OpenUserObject() is specifically designed to allow us to instantiate and visually provide the user with a user object at runtime. The syntax for this function is:

```
window.OpenUserObject(user_object {, x , y })
```

where

window	is the window that you want the user object to be instantiated within
user_object	is the user object that you want to instantiate
x	is the x coordinate of where in the window you want the user object to open (the default if you don't specify is 0)
y	is the y coordinate of where in the window you want the user object to open (the default if you don't specify this is also 0)

This function will return a 1 if the open succeeds, a -1 if it fails.

Developers Note: When you open a user object dynamically at runtime, the object will NOT be placed into the window control array. Keep this in mind when you are cycling through the control array and performing an operation against all the objects in a window.

---

466 *Chapter 12: User Objects*

Developers Tip: If you issue an OpenUserObject() function for the same user object, PowerBuilder will open the object the first time, but only activate it the second time (not create a second instance). This behavior is the same as when you open a window. If you want to multiply instantiate a user object, use the same technique you would with a window. Declare a reference variable instead of opening up the object itself.

The OpenUserObjectWithParm() function works exactly the same way, but you are able to pass a parameter to the user object through the message object, just like you would with OpenSheetWithParm() or OpenWithParm().

If you want to close a user object that you have dynamically opened, you can do so with the CloseUserObject() function. The syntax for this function is:

```
window.CloseUserObject(user_object)
```

where

window   is the window that contains the user object

user_object   is the user object that you wish to close

This function also returns a 1 if successful and a -1 if not successful. When called, the object is removed from the window and removed from memory. You do not need to script a DESTROY statement in order to release the resources back to the system.

12.3.2 INSTANTIATING A NON-VISUAL USER OBJECT

When you want to instantiate a non-visual user object you must declare the object in your scripts so that the object manager will create the object in the appropriate memory pool. Some non-visuals are already declared for you. These are the system non-visual objects such as the error, message and SQLCA transaction object.

12.3.2.1 Default System Non-Visual Objects

You can change the standard system objects that PowerBuilder defines for SQLCA (communications area—transaction object), SQLDA (dynamic description area), SQLSA (staging area), the message object and the error object. If you would rather have SQLCA be created from the transaction object that we described above in section 12.2.1 we can switch it in the Application painter.

12.3 Creating User Objects   467

The definitions for these standard system objects is established in the application object. If you open the properties page for the application object you will see a tab marked Variable Types as shown in Figure 12.13.

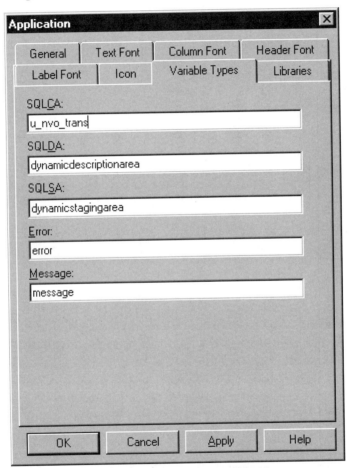

Figure 12.13 *You can substitute your enhanced standard non-visual user objects for the standard system objects that PowerBuilder creates in the application object.*

To use your object instead of the standard transaction object, simply replace the name of the object in the SQLCA field to your non-visual object name, u_nvo_trans.

468 *Chapter 12: User Objects*

12.3.2.2 In Script Creation

Most non-visual objects will be instantiated as required in your scripts. The usual process is to declare a reference variable that contains the handle for the object. This handle is how you will reference the object in your scripts.

The syntax for instantiating a non-visual object is:

```
u_nvo_errorhandler luo_errorhandler
luo_errorhandler = CREATE u_nvo_errorhandler
```

If you wanted to call a function in the error handler you would do so by using the reference variable like this:

```
luo_errorhandler.HandleError(dw_1.DBErrorMessage(), dw_1.DBErrorCode())
```

The scope of the reference variable that you declare will determine where you can reference this object. The error handler object example could be declared locally if you only needed the error handled within that object, or you could go to the other extreme and declare it globally so that the error handle could be used by any object in the application at any time.

Developers Tip: PowerBuilder 5.0 has a new variation on the CREATE syntax that allows us to be extremely generic when writing our scripts. We can now call CREATE and append the keyword 'using' to dynamically specify an object that we want to create.

For example, let's say that we have two ways of searching through a set of data on library books, by Author Name or by Title. We could have two specific search non-visual objects each inherited from the generic search non-visual object. We could dynamically determine which object we needed and instantiate only the appropriate object like this:

```
luo_nvo_search u_nvo_generic_search
string ls_specific_search
IF rb_searchbyname.checked THEN
    // Search by name
    ls_specific_search = "u_nvo_name_search"
ELSE
```

```
    // Search by title
    ls_specific_search = "u_nvo_title_search"
END IF

luo_nvo_search = CREATE USING ls_specify_search
```

Now calling the methods on the non-visual object luo_nvo_search will cause the appropriate Name or Title specific method to be implemented automatcally.

When you CREATE an object, you must remember to DESTROY the object when you are finished with it and before the reference variable passes out of scope. If you fail to destroy the object and the handle passes out of scope, then you have no way of removing this object from the memory pool. The object has now been 'orphaned.' It is occupying memory, but there is not way to reference it to use it or remove it. When your application exhibits this kind of behavior, we say that it has a 'memory leak.' The longer you run the application, the more orphaned objects are created and the fewer and fewer resources are available to the application.

The syntax to destroy our error handler object is:

```
DESTROY luo_errorhandler
```

Developers Note: If you issue multiple CREATE statements for the same object such as:

```
u_nvo_errorhandler luo_errorhandler
luo_errorhandler = CREATE u_nvo_errorhandler
luo_errorhandler = CREATE u_nvo_errorhandler
```

This will result in the creation of two instances of this object. The first one would be orphaned because the reference variable will point to the last object that was created. Be careful that you don't create any orphaned objects.

470 *Chapter 12: User Objects*

12.3.2.3 Without Reference Variables

It is possible to instantiate a non-visual user object (it must be a user object, non a system class) without explicitly declaring a reference variable first. PowerBuilder will automatically declare a global reference variable with the same name as the object class. For example:

u_nvo_errorhandler = CREATE u_nvo_errorhandler

would create an instance of u_nvo_errorhandler and provide us with a global reference variable of the same name to reference the object.

12.3.2.4 Autoinstantiate

In PowerBuilder 5.0, we have a new feature that is available for custom class user objects. The *autoinstantiate* property, when set to true, will cause PowerBuilder to automatically create an instance of the object in the appropriate memory pool when you declare a reference variable for it in your script. This eliminates the need for a CREATE statement.

This property can only be set in the user object painter. You access the property from the popup menu that appears when you right mouse click on the custom class object as shown in Figure 12.14.

12.3 Creating User Objects   471

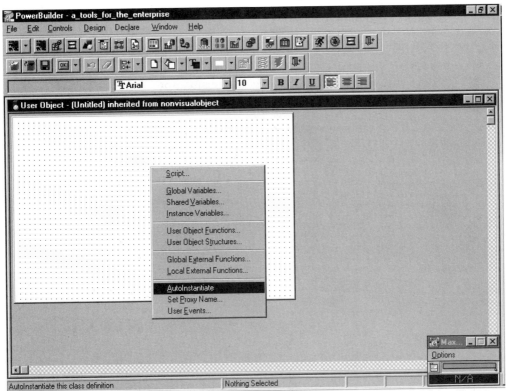

Figure 12.14 *The autoinstantiate option in a custom class user object will cause PowerBuilder to automatically instantiate the object in memory when you declare a reference variable of that object type.*

There is one behavior that you need to be aware of when using the autoinstantiate property. Usually if you set one reference variable to be equal to a second, the first reference variable merely picks up the pointer of the second object. When autoinstantiate is on, the entire object is copied and a new instance created when one reference variable is set to be equal to the second.

```
luo_errorhandler1 = luo_errorhandler2
```

would result in two separate instances of luo_errorhandler2. Note that if you already had an instance of your non-visual error handler in luo_errorhandler1 it would now be 'orphaned' and unreachable by you. This orphan will continue to consume system resources and can degrade the performance of your system.

472   *Chapter 12: User Objects*

12.4 SUMMARY

In any quality enterprise application built with PowerBuilder, user objects will play a critical role. They help with standardization, encapsulation, reduced maintenance and increased developer productivity. When used correctly, they can improve the performance of your application also.

Take a close look at the PowerBuilder Foundation Class library (PFC) that comes with PowerBuilder enterprise to see an example of extensive use of user objects.

Index

SYMBOLS

\# (pound sign), representing numeric characters, 304
% (percent) operator, 159
& (ampersand), for accelerator key, 321
: (colon), denoting host variable, 138, 356
:: (double colon), for global variable access, 172
? (question mark) value, 350
@ (at sign), representing any character, 304
[] (braces), denoting RTF fields, 139
\ (backslash), separating subkey from parent, 175
~t (embedded tab character), 336
Numerics
2D graphs, 389–390, 411, 413, 414, 416, 417–418
3 States property, 323
3D graphs, 389–390, 411, 413, 414, 416, 417–418
3D Look property, 320, 323
4GL tools, 95
16-bit environment, 97, 202, 231, 234, 342
32-bit environment, 97, 165, 231, 234
32-bit objects, 202
32-bit OCX controls, 457

A

abbreviations, storing in drop down list box, 324
abstract classes, 76
    See also inheritance
accelerator key, for display value, 321
Accelerator property, 314, 317, 325
ACE (Accelerated Client/server Enterprise) methodology, 10
    See also flattened spiral methodology
ad-hoc query storage, 331
Advanced PowerBuilder Utilities (APU), 306
ALIAS FOR keyword, 232
Alignment Drop Down Toolbar, 148
Alignment property, 394
Allow Edit property, 325
Allow Updates checkbox, 262
ALT key, with letter for accelerator key, 321
Always Show Arrow property, 325
Always Show List property, 325
ampersand (&), for accelerator key, 321
ancestor classes
    instantiating in memory, 77
    overriding methods in, 75
AND criteria property, 373
animation, with bitmaps, 203

474   *Index*

API (Application Program Interface)
  interprogram communications method, 103
  linking objects, 111
Application Functions... option, 225
Application painter
  creating object level functions, 225
  creating SQLCA transaction objects, 466–467
  described, 192
application server, 99–102
Application Service, 43
ApplicationName(string) property, 103, 106
applications
  See also architectures; user interface
  code modularity, 78
  compiling in machine code, 95, 96–97
  components in, 45, 111–113
  defining multiple docking toolbars, 192
  design decisions, 47
  with external functions, 227
  incorporating undefined system events,
      211–213
  libraries, 86–87
  non-enterprise, 46
  performance issues, 39–40
  productivity gains with object-oriented
      technology, 67–68
  robustness, 28
  RTF DataWindow objects in, 143
  security, 62–63
  tab folder implementations, 53
  testing, 113, 119
  tracing options for debugging, 105
  window types, 54–60
architectures
  defined, 37
  selecting, 44
  three-tiered, 40–41
  two-tiered, 38–40
area graphs, 415–416
Args... button, 213, 216
arguments
  altering PowerBuilder's default behavior, 274
  for custom events, 215
  defining in Event Declaration window, 216
  for events, 199–200
  examples, 221–224
  for functions, 220
  read-only function, 173, 220

specifying multiple options for, 104–105
  for SQLPreview event, 348
  triggering system events, 207
Arguments tab, Properties dialog, 363, 374
attributes
  See properties
attributes dialog, 152
audible cues, 62
audio files
  See .WAV files
Auto Horiz(ontal) Scroll property, 314, 325
auto indent, 165, 168
Auto Selection property, 314
Auto Vert(ical) Scroll property, 315
autoincrement (identity) columns, 261, 270–271
autoinstantiate property, 470–471
automatic scrolling, DataWindow designer,
      151–152
Autosize Height icon, DataWindow designer, 149
Autosize Height property, 369
Autosize property, 394
AutoSkip property, 317
.AVI files, 126

B

background color, 169, 226, 272
Background Color Drop Down Toolbar, 148
Background Color property, 394, 399
backslash (\), separating subkey from parent, 175
balloon help, 60–61
Bar graphs, 412–413
Bar Index field, Toolbar tab, 192
Basic Plus reports
  See nested reports
beeps (audible cues), 62
BETWEEN comparison operator, 158, 159
bidirectional edit styles, 310
bind variables, 350
Bitmap() function, 347–348
bitmaps
  for animation, 203
  in composite DataWindows, 383
  default red X picture, 188
  Display as Picture property, 346–347
  in List View controls, 185
  pictures in computed fields, 347–348

Index **475**

in Tree View controls, 184
BLOB (Binary Large OBject) data type, 194
Booch, Grady, 66
Border Drop Down Toolbar, 148
Border property, 366
braces ([]), denoting RTF fields, 139
buffer argument, 349
buffering rows, in temporary files, 164–165
buffers
    setting a value in, 162
    sharing between DataWindows, 344
    updating, 343
BufSize option, 104, 107
business logic
    in business objects, 92
    implemented as custom class user objects,
        110–111
    in server-based architectures, 43
    in three-tiered architectures, 41
    in two-tiered architectures, 39
    in visual objects, 62
business objects, 92, 100–102
business systems analyst (BSA), 21
Busy (boolean), in ConnectionInfo structure, 108

C

C code
    conversion chart, C data types to PowerBuilder
        data types, 230
    for external functions, 226, 228
    passed to embedded Watcom compiler, 95
    for user objects, 447, 456
calendar, in Component Gallery, 202
CallCount (long), in ConnectionInfo structure,
    108
Case() function, 156
Case property, 314, 325
Category Axis tab, Graphic Objects properties
    page, 401–405
Category property, 388, 389, 391
Category Sort property, 400
CD-ROM, 4–6
check boxes, 322–324
CheckSQLError() function, 463
child DataWindows
    See also DataWindows

assigning transaction object to, 292–293
GetChild() function, 291–298
linked, 298–299
managed by parent, 293
populating, 293–298
result set
    buffering and sharing, 295–296
    creating, 296–298
    retrieving, 294–295
child window, 55–57
CHOOSE CASE flow of control statement, 253
CICS (Customer Information Control System), 41
Cinderella, Dave, 99
class hierarchy
    defined, 76
    function names and, 220
class libraries
    advantages, 93
    building, 88–89
    described, 85–86
    purchasing, 89–90
    security mechanism, 32
class objects
    See non-visual user object (NVO)
Class Service, 43
classes, 71–74
    See also instances; non-visual object (NVO);
        visual objects
ClassName() function, 253, 461
clicked event
    arguments, 207
    coding, 247, 248
    playing .WAV files, 233–234
    return values, 208
ClickedRow() function, 207
client component, two-tiered architectures, 38
ClientId (string), in ConnectionInfo structure, 108
client/server applications
    See also enterprise PowerBuilder
    architectures, 37–44
    compared to object orientation, 67
    reducing size of result sets, 336–337
    two-tiered, 39
clock, in Component Gallery, 202
close event, for server window, 118
Close() global PowerScript function, 217
CloseQuery event, 199
CloseUserObject() function, 466

476 *Index*

Code Generations Options group box, 98
code modularity, 78
Code Table property, 318
colon (:), denoting host variable, 138, 356
color
    column background, 154
    customizing, 169
    DataWindow row, 272
    graphs, 425–426
    picture mask, 188
    with PowerScript painter, 165
    providing visual cues, 61
    RGB() function, 156, 157–158
column graphs, 410–412
Column keyword, 329
Column menu item, Objects menu bar, 141
column number, 161
column types, DataWindow painter, 152
Columns Across property, 320
command button
    customizing, 448
    encapsulation example, 78
    functions, 452
    properties, 450
companion CD, 4–6
comparison operators, 158–159
compiler warnings, 168, 220
Component Gallery, 202, 386
component library, 202–203
composite reports
    See also crosstabs; graphs; nested reports
    creating, 376–384
    presentation style, 376
    properties, 384–385
Computed Field... option, 140
computed fields
    in composite DataWindows, 381, 383
    displaying bitmaps in, 347–348
conceptual data model
    See data model
concrete classes, 76
    See also inheritance
concurrency issues, 263
connection object, 114
ConnectionBegin event, 109, 118, 192
ConnectionEnd event, 109, 118, 192
ConnectionInfo structure, 108
ConnectObject, 102–106, 113–115

ConnectString(string) property, 103
ConnectTime (DateTime), in ConnectionInfo
    structure, 108
ConnectToNewObject() function, 122
ConnectToServer() function, 105, 115
Console tracing option, 105
CONSTANT keyword, 171
controls
    See also objects; properties
    described, 75
    for drag mode, 245
    for List View, 185–187
    for Rich Text Edit (RTE), 183
    for tabs, 180–183
    for Tree View, 183–185
    for user objects, 447, 456
conversion chart, C data types to PowerBuilder
    data types, 230
CORBA (Common Object Request Broker
    Architecture), 41
corporate class library, 86–87
    See also class libraries
Count(*) SQL calculation, 339
Create() function, 330
Create Proxy Object... option, 108
CREATE reserved word, 334, 458–469, 465
Criteria tab, Properties dialog, 372–373
Crosstab Definition dialog box, 443
crosstabs
    See also composite reports; graphs; nested
      reports
    analyzing data, 430–431
    creating, 431–442
    data in columns, 444
    functions, 434
    grid settings, 441
    overriding dynamic with static crosstabs,
      442–444
CTLIB packet, 104
.CUR files, 249, 370, 408
Currency Format icon, DataWindow designer,
    148, 307
currency formatting, 148, 303, 304–305
CurrentRow() function, 154, 155
custom class user object methods, 114, 115
custom colors, 165
custom events, 200, 213–215
custom user objects, 461–464

custom visual objects, 452–456
custom visual user object, 181
cyclical approach, systems development, 13

D

daisy-chained DataWindows
   See nested reports
dashes, for grid lines, 403
data
   analyzing with crosstabs, 430–444
   copying and moving, 240–241
   copying directly to user object, 260–261
   direct manipulation of, 161–162, 257
   processing, 242
   storing
      in buffers, 257–261
      in database, 302
      to disk, 341
   viewing hierarchical tree of, 183–185
data format, with regular Edit Mask, 316
data integrity, 263
data model
   See also flattened spiral methodology
   creating, 45–46
   prototyping and, 22
   spiral methodology, 18–19
   for updating multiple tables from DataWindow,
      276
data (reserved word), 161, 162, 207, 208
data server component, two-tiered architectures,
   38
data sharing, 109
Data tab, Graphic Objects properties page,
   390–392
data types
   conversion chart, 230
   of display format, 304
   DWObject, 336
   with spin control, 318
Data Value property, 315
data warehouse, 18
database
   error handling with global functions, 223
   PowerBuilder 5.0 enhancements, 200–201
   predefined formats, 307

   storing of gender in, 311
   warnings, 168
Database painter, 303, 305
database server, 100
DataSource() function, 183
DataStore, 121, 279–281, 295–296, 345
   See also DataWindows
DataStore object, 107, 280
DataValue.Off property, 323
DataValue.On property, 323
DataValue.Other property, 323
DataWindow designer, 145–152, 328, 362
DataWindow Extended Attribute Synchronizer
   utility, 306
DataWindow keyword, 329
DataWindow Object Drop Down Toolbar,
   146–147
DataWindow painter
   automatic scrolling, 151–152
   expression enhancements, 152–159
   new column types, 152
   new toolbars and icons, 144–150
   with presentation styles, 132–133, 136–137,
      419–423
   Properties page, 150–151
   SQL formatting, 151
DataWindows
   See also bitmaps; DataWindow painter; edit
      styles; nested reports; objects
   buffers ·
      manipulating data stored in, 257–261
      types of, 255–257
   canceling retrieval in progress, 341–342
   changing attributes, 335–336
   child, 291–299
   columns, 262–263, 307
   computed fields, 381, 383
   controls, 56, 75
   data manipulation, 161–162, 257
   defining user events, 163
   display formats, 302–310
   Display Only, 139
   dropdown, 283–291
   dwo reference argument, 200
   dynamic, 327–331
   embedded fields, 139, 358–359
   labels, 139, 140

478 *Index*

modifying dynamically, 331–336
presentation styles
  graph, 419–423
  OLE 2.0, 120, 125–135
  Rich Text Edit, 135–143
previewing, 143, 348–351
QueryMode functionality, 124
result sets, 336–339, 342–345
retrieve functions, 163
RetrieveRow event, 340
rows
  expressions applied to, 333
  flagging, 61
  manipulating, 257–261
  selecting, 42
scrolling from side to side, 57
sliding columns, 299–301
SQLPreview event, 348–351
storing data to disk, 341
syntax definition, 329–330
updating
  advanced features, 261–271
  status flags, 271–279
DB Server Connect command button, 5
DBCancel() function, 341–342
DBErrorCode() function, 223
DBErrorEvent script, 223, 224
DBErrorMessage() function, 223
.DBF (dBase) files, 298
DCE (Distributed Computing Environment), 41, 108
DDE (dynamic data exchange), 135–143
debugging
  function overloading support, 194–195
  tracing options for, 105
Declare Instance Variables window, 80
Declare option, 225
delete buffer, 257
Delete icon, DataWindow designer, 147
DELETE statement, 261, 263
Deleted buffer, 162
DeleteRow() function, 162, 242, 252, 257
Depth property, 401
descendent classes
  overriding properties, 73
  sharing object functions, 226
Describe() function, 161, 309, 331–333, 375

describeless retrieve
  See static binding
The Design of Everyday Things, 46
DESTROY reserved word, 334–335, 466, 469
detail DataWindow, 342
direct manipulation
  of data, 161–162, 257, 309, 341
  of object properties, 159–161
direct referencing, 333
DisconnectServer() function, 105
Display as Picture property, 346–347
Display Expression property, 395–397
Display Format Maintenance... option, 303
Display format property, 397, 422
display formats, 302–310
Display Only property, 315
Display Value property, 315
distributed computing
  building applications, 109–119
  implementing in PowerBuilder, 99–102
  non-PowerBuilder components in, 120
  objects, 102–108
  OLE Automation support, 120–123
  planning issues, 109
distributed PowerBuilder, 5–6, 44
.DLL (Dynamic Link Library) files
  accessed by external functions, 226–227
  and class definitions, 72
  for DataWindow objects used with DataStores, 280
  distributing at runtime, 97
  external, 456
  external functions and, 226–231
  machine code generation and, 97
  with multiple classes, 457
Doc-To-Help, 64
document generation, 135–143
Document Name property, 406
documentation, training, roll-out, flattened spiral methodology, 34–35
Documentation button, 197
dot notation, 160
dots, for grid lines, 403
double byte characters, 202
double colon (::), for global variable access, 172
drag and drop capabilities
  changing properties, 241–242

Index **479**

code, 249–253
copying and moving objects or data, 240–241
events, 243–245
processing data, 242
properties, 245
setting the drag icon, 249
Drag and Drop tab, Graphic Objects properties page, 410
Drag() function, 246, 247, 248
DragAuto property, 245, 246, 410
DragDrop event, 244
dragdrop predefined system event, 251
DragEnter event, 244
DraggedObject() function, 252
DragIcon property, 245, 246, 249, 410
DragLeave event, 244
DragWithin event, 244
drawing objects, 243, 383
Driver(string) property, 103, 106
drop down DataWindow (DDDW), 283–291, 326
drop down list boxes, 324–326
Drop Down Picture List Box (DDPLB), 187–189
DropDown Toolbar, Menu painter, 189–191
Dropdowns tab, Properties page, 170
dw_control (DataWindow control), 161, 345
dwItemStatus enumerated data type, 273
dwModify() function, 152
dwo reference argument, 200
DWObject data type, 336
dwSyntax program, 160, 329, 334, 376

E

EDI (Electronic Data Interchange), 42
Edit... command button, 304
Edit Mask edit style, 315–319
Edit Style Maintenance... menu option, 311
edit styles
check box, 322–324
compared to display formats, 302, 310–11
defining, 311–312
drop down DataWindow edit mask, 326
drop down list box, 324–326
Edit Mask, 315–319
properties, 312–315
Radio Button, 319–322
Edit tab, Properties page, 311

Elevation property, 400
e-mail service, with service-based architectures, 42
embedded characters, 139
embedded tab (~t) character, 336
Empty String is NULL property, 314
Empty String is Null property, 325
encapsulation
for custom business rules or services, 280
effect on object, 77–78, 226
insulating methods and properties, 79
in OLE Automation technology, 122
tab control, 181
Encina (Transarc Corporation), 41
enterprise PowerBuilder applications
client/server development
ACE methodology, 10
evolution of, 9–10
flattened spiral methodology, 17–36
iterative methodology, 15–17
spiral methodology, 13–15
waterfall, 9–10, 11–13
color enhancements, 61
considerations, 1–3
creating form letters, 135–143
documentation window, 197
encapsulated objects, 78
error handling with global functions, 223
object libraries, 86–87
objects, 472
on-line help, 64
purchasing third party class libraries, 90
security considerations, 62–63
sharing result sets, 342
enumerated data types
dwItemStatus, 273
ForeGround!, 425–426
grObjectType, 427
for refused connection, 119
representing row status, 271–272
for SQLPreview event request argument, 348
EQUAL comparison operator, 158
ErrCode(long) property, 103, 106
error codes
for global functions, 223–224
returned
by Connection object functions, 106
by Transport object functions, 107
error processing, 109, 223, 461–464

480 *Index*

error tracking, 98
ErrText(string) property, 104, 106
evaluate (reserved word), 333
evaluation techniques, 158
Event Declaration window, 216
event list, 212
event script, 71, 198–200
events
    arguments for, 199–200, 236
    calling from scripts, 234–238
    drag and drop, 243–244
    return values for, 199–200
    types of, 200
Excel (Microsoft Corporation), 50, 51
exception handler, 109
.EXE files
    for DataWindow objects used with DataStores,
        280
    distributed with .DLL files, 456–457
    generating in machine code, 97
expressions
    DataWindow painter enhancements, 152–159
    defining for DataWindow, 272–273, 333
    modifying, 395–397
Expressions tab
    Graphic Objects properties page, 409
    Properties dialog, 374–375
extended attributes, 305–306, 311
    See also properties
external functions
    declaring, 226–231
    machine code generation and, 97
    platform considerations, 234
    playing a Wave file, 231–234
external subroutine syntax, 230–231
External User Object Style dialog box, 456
external visual objects, 456–457

F

fat-client syndrome, 39–40
feedback
    See user feedback
filter buffer, 256
Filtered buffer, 162
filters, 296
first level objects
    See primary objects

Fixedsys font, 167
flags argument, 250
flashwindow function, 226
flattened spiral methodology
    build phase, 22–23, 27–28, 32–33
    design phase, 20–22, 26–27, 31–32
    documentation, 34–35
    features, 17–19
    planning and analysis phase, 19–20, 25–26,
        30–31
    post production support, 36
    roll-out, 35–36
    test phase, 23–24, 28–29, 33–34
    time frame
        first iteration, 19
        second iteration, 24
        third iteration, 29
    training, 35
Font Height property, 394
Font property, 394
Font Style property, 394
fonts
    changing, 166–167
    color, 169
    with PowerScript painter, 165
ForeGround! enumerated data type, 425
Foreground/Text Color Drop Down Toolbar, 148
form letters, 135–143
Format Legend dialog box, 134
Format property, 314
Format tab, Properties page, 306–307
foundation window, 54
frameworks, 85–86
    See also object libraries; objects
full unit tests, 28
function overloading, 82–83, 194–195, 198
function posting, 198–200
functions
    See also names of specific functions
    access levels, 79–81, 219–220, 228
    adding, 450
    calling from scripts, 234–238
    creating, 71
    declaration window, 79, 219, 225–226
    naming, 219
    painter icon, 218
    posting, 237–238
    PowerScript, 217–218

Index **481**

supported, 216
triggering, 238
fuzzy search capabilities, 158

G

gender, storing in a database, 311
General tab, Graphic Objects properties page,
    308–399
General tab, Properties dialog
    accessing properties, 364–366
    adjusting tab indentation, 167
GenerateGUID() function, 121
GenerateRegFile() function, 121
generating machine code executables, 97–98
GetChild() function, 291–292, 376
GetClickedRow() function, 200
GetFormat() function, 307–308
GetINIParms() function, 459
GetItem() function, 162
GetItemStatus() function, 273
GetParent() function, 174, 461
GetRow() function, 155, 199, 250
GetSelectedRow() function, 252
GetServerInfo() function, 105–106, 106
GIS (Geographic Information Systems), 127
Global External Functions... option, 227
global functions
    calling from scripts, 234
    in PowerBuilder, 71
    public, 79
    user defined, 218–224
global identifier, for GenerateGUID() function, 121
global PowerScript functions, 217
global variables
    See also instance variables
    accessing, 172
    encapsulated objects and, 77–78
GO PBFORUM (CompuServe), 6
GPF (Global Protection Fault), 65
Graph tab, Graphic Objects properties page,
    399–401, 423
Graph Type property, 400
graphs
    See also composite reports; crosstabs; nested
        reports

adding to applications, 387
area type, 415–416
bar types, 412–413
building, 419–423
column types, 410–412
components, 387–389
default type, 410
dimensions, 389–390
embedded in DataWindows, 409
enhancements in PowerBuilder 5.0, 386
line type, 414–415
with Microsoft Graph, 126–135
overlays, 423–425
pie type, 417–418
properties
    Category Axis tab, 401–405
    Data tab, 390–392
    Drag and Drop tab, 410
    Expressions tab, 409
    General tab, 397–399
    Graph tab, 399–401
    Pointer tab, 408
    Print Specifications tab, 405–408
    Series Axis tab, 405
    Text tab, 392–397
    Value Axis tab, 405
runtime manipulation, 425–430
scatter type, 418–419
stacked column type, 413–414
tools in Component Gallery, 202, 386
grid DataWindow, 342
grid presentation style, 329
grObjectType enumerated data type, 427
Group keyword, 329
GUI (graphical user interface)
    design considerations, 47, 50
    drag and drop capabilities
        changing properties, 241–242
        code, 249–253
        copying and moving objects or data,
            240–241
        described, 238–239
        events, 243–245
        implementing, 243
        processing data, 242
        properties, 245
        setting the drag icon, 249

482 *Index*

guidelines
  GUI, 47
  radio buttons, 321–322

H

handle
  for child DataWindows, 291
  for referencing objects in scripts, 468
  for reports, 376
HandleError() function, 462
Height property, 368
help desk (post production support), 36
helpful tips
  accessing the properties page, 166
  advanced graphics capabilities, 386
  application partitioning, 50
  autoincrement columns, 271
  avoiding global and shared variables, 98
  building dynamic DataWindows, 328
  capturing activation of child windows, 56
  compiling applications, 72
  conversion chart for C data types to
        PowerBuilder data types, 230
  CREATE syntax variation, 468–469
  creating
    3D graphs, 389–390
    icons and cursors, 249
    object level functions in Application painter,
        225
  criteria properties, 373
  defining
    classes of objects, 70
    PowerTips for Tabs, 61
  documenting server applications, 119
  drag and drop
    implementing, 246
    sophisticated events, 253
  DWSyntax program, 160
  External source DataWindow, 287
  function overloading, 82
  generating machine code executables, 96, 97,
        98
  instantiating ancestor classes in memory, 77
  invalid drop zones for drag icon, 249
  managing long running scripts, 342
  naming functions, 219

OpenUserObject() function, 466
purchasing third party class libraries, 90
Radio Button edit style, 321
registry functions, 175
remote object functions, 108
Retrieve As Needed property, 337
retrieving nested reports, 355
RGB() function quick reference chart, 157–158
service-based architectures, 43
sharing data, 345
tab folder based interfaces, 53
triggering system events, 207
using DataWindow objects with DataStore, 280
hierarchical dot notation, 160
HKEY_CLASSES_ROOT key, 174, 175
HKEY_CURRENT_USER key, 174
HKEY_LOCAL_MACHINE key, 174
HKEY_USERS key, 174
Horiz(ontal) Scroll Bar property, 315
host variable, 138

I

IBM Corporation, CICS (Customer Information
        Control System), 41
.ICO files, 249
icon animation, 252–253
icons
  new, 144–150
  selecting from DropDown Toolbar, 190–191
  Window painter, 178–179
ImportClipboard() function, 298
ImportFile() function, 256, 298
ImportString() function, 298
information hiding
  See encapsulation
information technology (IT), 1, 99
  See also distributed computing
inheritance, 72, 75–77
.INI files, 174, 459–461
Insert button, selecting tree view functions, 185
INSERT statement, 261, 263, 279
InsertItemFirst() function, 185
InsertItemLast() function, 185
InsertItemSort() function, 185
InsertRow() function, 256, 287, 293, 296–297
Instance Service, 43

Index **483**

instance variables
    access levels, 79–81
    adding, 450
    declaring in the custom class object, 260–261, 453
    protected, 454
instances, 74–75
    See also classes
Interface Definition Language (IDL), 108
internationalization, 202
Internet spreadsheet plug, 202
ItemChanged event, 207, 208–209, 299
Items tab, Properties page, 188
iterative methodology, 15–17

J

Jacobson, Ivor, 66
JAD (Joint Application Design), 20, 25, 30
Join icon, SQL Painter, 145

K

Key and Modified Columns option, 263, 268–270
Key and Updateable Columns option, 263, 264–268
Key Columns option, 263, 264–265
Key Modification groupbox, 263
keys, treed hierarchy in registry, 174
keywords
    :: (double colon), for global variable access, 172
    CONSTANT, 171
    PARENT, 174
    for presentation strings, 329

L

Label property, 402
language support, 202
Large Icon view, of List View control, 185
LastCallTime (DateTime), in ConnectionInfo structure, 108
Layer property, 369
Left property, 301
Left Text property, 320, 323
LeftButtonUp event, 247, 248

Legend Location property, 400
level setting, for tracing options, 105
library list, 122–123
LibraryCreate() function, 331
LibraryExport() function, 331
LibraryImport() function, 331
LIKE comparison operator, 158
Limit property, 314, 325
Line Color property, 399
line graphs, 414–415
LineStyle.Frame property, 404
LineStyle.Origin property, 404
LineStyle.Primary property, 404
LineStyle.Secondary property, 404
list DataWindow, 342
List view, of List View control, 186
List View controls, 185–187
ListDetail window, 343
Listen() function, 106, 107
Local driver, 103, 104
Local External Functions... option, 227, 228
Local protocol, 114
Location (string), in ConnectionInfo structure, 108
Location(string) property, 104, 106
Log tracing option, 105
long data type, returned by Connection object functions, 106
Lotus' VIM (Vendor Independent Messaging), 43
Lower() function, 159
lparam argument, for custom events, 215

M

machine code, generating executables, 95–98
mailing labels, 299
main window, 55
MajorDivisions.DropLines property, 404
MajorDivisions.Grid property, 403
MajorDivisions.LabelEvery property, 404
MajorDivisions.Number property, 403
MajorDivisions.Ticks property, 403
MAPI (Messaging Application Program Interface), 43
mapped events
    See predefined system events; undefined system events
Margins property, 406–407

484 *Index*

Mask property, 317
Masks property, 317
MaxRetry option, 104, 107
MaxServerConnections property, 107
MaxServerThreads property, 107
MDI (Multiple Document Interface) applications
  frames
    as foundation windows, 54
    toolbars allowed on, 192
  user interface, 50–53
Menu Functions... option, 225
Menu painter, DropDown Toolbar, 189–191
MenuCascade property, 190, 191
messages, obsolete, 168
messages queue, checking, 342
methods, 70–71
  See also properties
MicroHelp, 60
Microsoft Corporation
  Excel, 50, 51
  MAPI (Messaging Application Program
    Interface), 13
  Microsoft Graph, 126–135
  Microsoft Word, 51, 53
  OLE (Object Linking and Embedding), 120
MinorDivisions.Grid property, 404
MinorDivisions.Number property, 404
MinorDivisions.Ticks property, 404
misbehaved client, 109
mock ups, 20–21
Modify Expression dialog box, 153, 154, 395, 433
Modify() function
  altering column display format, 309
  modifying DataWindow attributes, 331, 333,
    334, 335, 336
  partially replacing, 159–161
  pointing DataWindow toward access table, 277
mouse operations
  accessing menu of Undo functions, 165
  accessing Modify Expression dialog box, 153
  accessing OLE popup menu, 133, 134
  accessing script painter, 166
  changing background color of row, 272
  viewing object components, 196
MouseMove event, 247, 248
Moveable property, 369
multiple docking toolbars, 192

N

Name property, 313, 365, 399
Named Pipes protocol, 114
NamedPipes driver, 103, 104
native driver support, 201
NDX (Network Directory Services), 203
nested reports
  See also composite reports; crosstabs; graphs
  button, 360
  creating, 355–364
  described, 353–355
  with embedded DataWindow objects, 354
  properties
    Arguments tab, 374
    Criteria tab, 372–373
    Expressions tab, 374–375
    General tab, 364–366
    Pointer tab, 369–371
    Position tab, 366–369
    Select Report tab, 371
    types of, 364
  referencing in scripts, 375–376
NetBufSize property, 107
New... command button, 225, 304
New icon
  DataWindow designer, 146
  SQL Painter, 144
New User Object dialog box, 448
Newspaper Columns icon, DataWindow designer,
  149
Newspaper Columns property, 408
NoDelay option, 104, 107
non-enterprise applications, 46
non-visual user object (NVO)
  building, 116
  copying data directly into, 260–261
  custom, 461–464
  DataStore object, 107
  Datastores, 279–280
  described, 93, 458
  inbound OLE Automation and, 120
  instantiating, 466–471
  new classes inherited from, 102
  opening dynamically at runtime, 465
  proxy object, 108
  remote objects, 107–108

standard, 458–461
Novell, Inc., 41, 203
Now() global PowerScript function, 217
n-tiered architectures
    business objects in, 92
    business processes, 62
    defined, 42
    in distributed PowerBuilder model, 101

O

Object Browser, 129, 196–197
object functions, 217–218, 224–226
    See also methods
object hierarchy, 73–74
object libraries, 86
    See also frameworks
object (reserved word), 161
ObjectAtPointer() function, 426–430
ObjectCalls tracing option, 105
ObjectLife tracing option, 105
object-oriented technology
    changing ancestor objects, 76
    compared to client/server applications, 67
    described, 66–67
    flexibility, 65
    function overloading, 82–83, 198
    object level functions, 224–226
    PowerBuilder 5.0 enhancements, 198–200
    predefined system events, 200, 205–209, 212
objects
    See also frameworks; properties; user objects
    in Component Gallery, 202–203, 386
    copying and moving, 240–241
    creating, 27–28
    described, 68–69
    in drag mode, 245–248
    dragging, 151–152, 243–253
    effects of encapsulation, 77–78
    function declaration window, 79, 219, 225–226
    function overloading, 83, 198
    modifying, 153, 358
    orphaned, 336
    printing, 81–82
    properties, 159–161, 179–180
    rearranging, 379
    removing, 334–335
    sliding, 299–301

sound enabling, 232
obsolete messages, 168
.OCX files, 135, 202, 386, 457
ODBC (Open Database Connectivity), 201
OLE 2.0 presentation style, 125–135, 386
OLE DataWindow, 202
OLE (Object Linking and Embedding)
    application development tools, 41
    automation example, 6
    Automation technology, 120–123
    customizing objects, 134
    graphics, 386
    objects, 123
    point and click SQL interface, 120
    popup menu, 133, 134
    server objects, 130–131, 133
OLE Registry, 120
One-Off applications, 39
on-line help, 64
OOA (Object-Oriented Analysis), 66
    See also object-oriented technology
OOD (Object-Oriented Design), 66
    See also object-oriented technology
Open Client/OpenServer protocol, 114
Open() global PowerScript function, 217
Open icon
    DataWindow designer, 146
    SQL Painter, 144
OpenClientServer driver, 103, 104
OpenSheetWithParm() function, 466
OpenUserObject() function, 465
OpenUserObjectWithParm() function, 466
OpenWithParm() function, 466
Options... command, 329
Options... menu item, 165
Options(string) property, 104, 106–107
OR criteria property, 373
Oracle versions, supported, 201
original buffer, 162, 257
orphaned objects, 336, 471
Overlap property, 400
overlays, 423–425

P

packet sending delay, overriding, 104
PacketSize option, 104, 107
PAGE DOWN key, 143

486 *Index*

PAGE UP key, 143
Paper.Orientation property, 407
Paper.Size property, 407
Paper.Source property, 407
PARENT keyword, 174
PARENT pronoun, 450
partitioning, 40, 50
Password property, 314
Password(strong) option, 105
PBConsol application, 5
.PBD (PowerBuilder Dynamic Library) files, 280
   and class definitions, 72
   machine code generation and, 97
.PBL (PowerBuilder Library) files
   proxy objects in, 108
   for runtime ad-hoc query storage, 331
"pbm" prefix, for undefined system events, 210
pbm_dwnlbuttonup system event, 250
.PBR (PowerBuilder Resource) files, 280
PBServer application, 5
PBToolkit, 166
PBTRACE switch, 98
pb_trash picture button, 251
p-code
   generating executables, 95
   for library list, 122–123
   for testing, 98
percent (%) operator, 159
Percent Format icon, DataWindow designer, 148, 307
permissions, 62–63
Perspective property, 400
PFC (PowerBuilder Foundation Class) library
   advantages, 123–124
   contents, 124–125
   examples of user objects, 472
   extension layers, 125
   security processes and objects, 63
   third party class libraries, 90
phone number, 316
phone numbers, 302, 304, 310
picture clip control, in Component Gallery, 203
Picture ListBox, 189
picture mask, 188
Pictures tab, Properties page, 188
pie graphs, 417–418
Pipeline painter, 194

placeholders
   See stubs
Pointer Name property, 370
Pointer tab, Graphic Objects properties page, 408
Pointer tab, Properties dialog, 369–371
PointerX() function, 199, 200, 207
PointerY() function, 199, 200, 207
polymorphism, 81–82, 198
popup window, 58–59
Position tab, Properties dialog, 366–369
Position tab, Properties page, 300
PostEvent() function, 213, 215, 234–235, 237, 461
PowerBuilder
   See also applications; distributed computing; user interface
   See also enterprise PowerBuilder
   conversion chart, C data types to PowerBuilder data types, 230
   documentation window, 197
   fat-client syndrome, 39–40
   multiple function MDI application, 51, 52
   native compiled code, 95–98, 163–164
   object hierarchy, 73–74
   object-oriented technology, 65, 67–68
   performance enhancements, 163–165
   properties, 69, 166
   resources, 6
   sample files, 4
   third-party products, 41
   visual cues, 60
   window types, 54–60
PowerBuilder Advisor, 7
PowerBuilder Demo DB V5, 5
PowerBuilder Developers Journal (PBDJ), 7
PowerScript
   code enhancements, 171–178
   functions, 217–218
   painter, 165–171
Powersoft PAD, 7
Powersoft/Sybase products, 6
PowerTips, 60–61
predefined computed field, 381
predefined edit styles, 373
predefined system events, 200, 205–209, 212
presentation styles
   graph, 429–423

OLE 2.0, 120, 125–128
Rich Text Edit, 135–143
Preview icon
DataWindow designer, 150
SQL Painter, 145
primary buffer, 162, 256
primary objects, 75
primary window
See foundation window
Print Specifications tab, Graphic Objects properties
page, 405–408
private access level, 79, 81, 226, 228
process objects, 62–63
progress meter, in Component Gallery, 202
Prompt Before Printing property, 407–408
properties
See also extended attributes; objects
changing, 179–180, 242–242, 335–336
for composite reports, 384–385
described, 69–70
drag, 245
for edit styles, 312–315
effects of encapsulation, 77–78
for graphs, 390–410
for nested reports, 364–375
overriding in descendent classes, 73
Properties icon, DataWindow designer, 149
Properties... option, 150–151, 364
Properties page, 166
property sheets, 179–180
protected access level, 79–80, 226, 228
prototypes, 22–23
proxy object, 108, 113–114
proxyname property, 461
pseudo SQL operators, 158–159
public access level, 79, 81, 228
public object level function, 78, 226
publicly defined interface, 79

Q

quality assurance process, 23–24
query capability, 339
Query object, 194
QueryMode functionality, 124
question mark (?) value, 350
quick reference chart, RTB() function, 157–158

Quick Select data source, 194
QuickSelect DataWindow, 372

R

Radio Button edit style, 319–322
RAM (Random Access Memory)
compiling machine code executables, 97
storing data in, 341
Ramirez, Oscar, 309
RawData option, 104, 107
Read Only property, 318
read-only function arguments, 173, 220
READONLY keyword, 80
real world metaphor, 239
Rebuild Columns at Runtime checkbox, 443
reference variable
automatically instantiating objects in memory, 471
containing handle for objects, 468
instantiating ancestor classes in memory, 77
.REG (registry) file, 121
Registry functions, 121, 174–178
RegistryDelete() function, 177–178
RegistryKeys() function, 177
RegistryValues() function, 175–177
remote objects, 107–108
remote servers, 41
RemoteStopConnection() function, 106
RemoteStopListening () function, 106
Report Object dialog, 361
Report view, of List View control, 186–187
reporting
See also crosstabs; graphs; nested reports
request argument, for SQLPreview event, 348
Required property, 314, 318, 325
ReselectRow() function, 261, 270
reserved keywords
See also keywords; names of specific reserved
keywords
reserved words, 161
ResetUpdate() function, 275
Resizeable property, 55, 369
response window, 59–60
result sets, 295–298, 336–339, 342–345
retrieval arguments
in child DataWindows, 293, 294

488 *Index*

for DataWindow objects, 380
in nested reports, 356
values passed as, 376
Retrieval Arguments... option, 137
Retrieve As Needed property, 337–339
Retrieve() function
activating Retrieve As Needed property,
337–339
generalized, 163
moving data into primary buffer, 256
public function of DataWindow control, 217,
226
received by parent window, 293, 294
static binding and, 164
RetrieveRow event, 340, 341
return values
for events, 199–200, 208
for GetFormat() function, 308
for global functions, 220
for ObjectAtPointer() function, 427
for SQL statements, 351
RGB() function, 156, 157–158
Rich Text Edit (RTE)
controls, 183
presentation style, 135–143
Rich Text Format
See RTF (Rich Text Format)
Rich Text Input Computed Column Object dialog
box, 141
right-to-left cursor movement support, 202
RoboHelp, 64
robustness, 28, 45
roll-out, flattened spiral methodology, 35–36
root keys, in registry, 174
Rotation property, 394, 400
row argument, 250, 349
Rows property, 392
RowsCopy() function, 256, 257, 259
RowsDiscard() function, 252, 257, 259
RowsMove() function, 256, 257–258
.RTF files, 197
RTF (Rich Text Format)
See also composite reports; crosstabs; graphs;
nested reports
DataWindow object, 136–143
Rumbaugh, James, 66
runtime ad-hoc query storage, 331
runtime .DLLs, 97

runtime instance variable, 454

S

Save icon
DataWindow designer, 146
SQL Painter, 144
scalability, in two-tiered architectures, 39
Scale Circles property, 320
Scale property, 323
Scale.Autoscale property, 403
Scale.DataType property, 403
Scale.Maximum property, 403
Scale.Minimum property, 403
Scale.RoundTo property, 403
Scale.RoundUnits property, 403
Scale.Scale property, 403
scatter graphs, 401, 418–419
screen mock ups, 21
script painter, 166, 170, 200
scripts
calling events and functions from, 234–238
changing
color in graphs, 426
status flags, 277–278
for command buttons, 455
coordinating multiple DataWindow updates,
273–276
copying data directly into user object, 260–261
creating
child result sets, 297
DataStores, 280
GUID and generating a registry files, 121
customizing, 166
for drag and drop events, 250–253
for error handling, 463
with external functions, 230–234
icon animation, 252–253
instantiating visual user objects, 465
in ItemChanged event of DataWindow control,
208–209
playing .WAV files, 233–234
referencing nested reports, 375–376
RetrieveRow event, 339
retrieving
.INI file information, 460–461
result set for child DataWindow, 294

for runtime instance variable, 454
sharing a result set, 296
in SQLPreview event, 351
scrolling child window, 57
SDI (Single Document Interface) applications, 50–53
Seat of the Pants methodology, 10, 81
secondary objects, 75
See also controls
security
application design considerations, 62–63
class libraries, 90
embedded in login window, 110
Select Column dialog box, 142
Select Report tab, Properties dialog, 371
Select Reports dialog box, 378
Select Standard Class Type dialog box, 458, 459
Select User Object dialog box, 451
Series Axis tab, Graphic Objects properties page, 405
Series property, 388, 389, 392
Series Sort property, 400
server application
access control, 119
connection protocols, 114–115
creating, 116–119
name, 103
password, 105
service objects, 93
service-based architectures, 42–43
Set Proxy Name... option, 113
SetActionCode() function, 199, 208
SetFormat() function, 307
SetItem() function, 162, 279, 297
SetItemStatus() function, 279
SetPointer(Hourglass!) function, 62
SetRow() function, 217
SetSeriesStyle() function, 425–426
SetSQLPreview() function, 351
SetTransObject() function, 287, 292–293
SETUP.EXE program, 4
Shade Color property, 399
ShadeBackEdge property, 405
shared data store, 295
ShareData() function, 183, 344, 345
sheets, within MDI frame, 55
Show Focus Rectangle property, 315, 317
Show Parents Parent command, 174

Slide Above Drop Down Toolbar, 149
Slide group box, 301
Slide Left icon, DataWindow designer, 149
Slide Left property, 369
Slide Up property, 368
sliding columns, 299–301
Small Icon view, of List View control, 185
sndPlaySoundA() function, 232
software development
with distributed computing, 99, 100–119
with object-oriented technology, 67
quality assurance process, 23–24
Solid Bar graphs, 413
Solid Column graphs, 412
sort criteria, 296
Sorted property, 325
sound files
See .WAV files
source object, 243
Spacing property, 401
Specify Update Properties dialog box, 261, 262, 271
spell checker, 202
spin control, for Edit Mask, 318–319
Spin Control property, 317
Spin Increment property, 318
Spin Range Max property, 319
Spin Range Min property, 319
spiral methodology, 13–15
spreadsheet type control, 202
SQL Anywhere database server, 4
SQL Painter
fields selected in, 138, 140
icons, 144
moving to Design window, 128
SQL Select icon
DataWindow designer, 149
with Pipeline painter, 194
SQL Painter, 145
SQL (Structured Query Language)
Count(*) calculation, 339
formatting in syntax mode, 151
generating statements, 261–263, 328
result sets from, 344
SQL Toolbox, 138, 357
SQLCA (SQL communications area) transaction object, 292, 350, 461, 466–467
SQLPreview event, 342, 348–351

490 *Index*

SQLSA (SQL staging area), 466
sqlsyntax argument, 349
sqltype argument, 349
stacked column graphs, 413–414
Standard Visual Type dialog box, 449
Start On New Page property, 384, 385
static binding, 164
static crosstabs, 443
STATIC keyword, 236
static text, in composite DataWindows, 379, 380, 383
status flags
    changing, 272–273
    coordinating multiple DataWindow updates, 273–276
    creating templates, 278–279
    row status, 271–272
    updating multiple tables from DataWindow, 276–278
StopListening() function, 107, 118
stored procedures
    for business logic, 39
    with Pipeline painter, 194
StoreToDisk property, 341
string argument, 137
string matches, 159
string tests, 28
string variable, 308
strings, 327, 328–329
structure objects, 102, 197
stubs, 206, 214
Style keyword, 329
Style property, 314
subclasses, 72
    See also classes
subkeys, 175
subroutines, 220, 230–231
superclasses, 72
    See also classes
Suppress Print After First Newspaper Column property, 366
Sybase SQL Anywhere Developers Guide, 6
syntax mode, SQL formatting, 151
SyntaxFromSQL() function, 329–330
system delays, 62
system documentation, 35
system logic, implemented as custom class user objects, 110–111

T

tab controls, 180–183, 336
tab folder based interfaces, 53
Tab Sequence icon, DataWindow designer, 149
Table painter, 193
Table to Update drop down listbox, 262
Tables icon, SQL Painter, 144
tabular DataWindow, 342
Tag property, 365
target object, 243
TCP/IP services file, 5
technical writers, 64
teenager window
    See popup window
templates, creating with status flags, 278–279
temporary files, buffering rows in, 164–165
Test... command button, 305
Test property, 317
Test Results Document, 33
Text Color property, 394
Text keyword, 329
Text Object property, 394
Text property, 323
Text tab, Graphic Objects properties page, 392–397, 422
TFTE directory, 4
third party class libraries, 89–90
Thomson's Web Extra site, 47
ThreadLife tracing option, 105
3 States property, 323
3D graphs, 389–390, 411, 413, 414, 416, 417–418
3D Look property, 320, 323
three-tiered architectures, 40–41, 92, 452
TimeOut property, 107
Timer Interval property, 399
timeslicing, 342
Title keyword, 329
Title property, 400
Titles and Legends property, 389
to_column value, 162
Today() function, 382
Today() global PowerScript function, 217
toolbars
    allowed on MDI frame, 192
    in DataWindow designer, 145, 146–150

Index **491**

in DataWindow Painter, 144–150
multiple docking, 192
Window painter, 178–179
Toolbox icon, SQL Painter, 145
TOOLS.PBL library, 4
to_row value, 161
Trace(string) option, 105, 106
Trail the Footer property, 384, 385
training, roll-out, flattened spiral methodology, 35
transaction objects, 292–293, 458–461
Transarc Corporation, 41
transparent color, 394
Transport object, 102, 106–108, 116–117
Tree View controls, 183–185
trend analysis graph, 415
TRIGGER keyword, 236
TriggerEvent() function, 213, 215, 234–235, 461
triggering system events, 207
Tuxedo (Novell), 41
2D graphs, 389–390, 411, 413, 414, 416, 417–418
two-tiered architectures, 38–40, 62, 452
Type Of() function, 461
Type property, 317
TypeOf() function, 252, 253

U

UDT (Uniform Data Transfer), 127
uf_Print() function, 81–82
undefined system events, 56, 200, 210–213
Underline property, 394
undirectional display formats, 302
Undo icon, DataWindow designer, 147
Undo levels, 165
Unique Key Column(s) listbox, 263
United Method object modeling, 66
Units property, 398
Up property, 301
Update() function
arguments, 274–275
deleting rows, 162, 257
described, 261
manually controlling flags, 275
updating primary buffer, 343
UPDATE statement, 261, 263

Updateable Columns listbox, 262
Use Code Table property, 315
user analysis matrix, 48–50
user centric design, 46–47
user documentation, 34
user events
See also custom events; predefined system events; undefined system events
creating, 215–216
naming, 212
purpose of, 214–215
user feedback
audible cues, 62
system delays, 62
visual cues, 60–61
user interface
design considerations, 46–47
distributed computing and, 99–102
GUI-oriented, 50
prototype design, 22–23
tab folder based, 53
warning, 50
User Object Functions... option, 225
User Object painter, 448, 450, 458
user objects
See non-visual objects; objects; visual objects
user queries, limiting, 339
user-defined events, 200
user-defined functions
global, 218–224
object level, 224–226
passing arguments to, 198, 218
user-defined properties, 79
See also instance variables
UserID (string), in ConnectionInfo structure, 108
Userid(string) option, 105

V

Validate Using Code Table property, 315
Value Axis tab, Graphic Objects properties page, 405
Value property, 388, 389, 392
variables
calling events and functions from scripts, 234–235

492   Index

declaring, 173
for external functions, 228–229
in identifier names, 168
for SQL statements, 328
for storing data, 161
VBX (Visual Basic) user objects, 457
Vert(ical) Scroll Bar property, 315
Vert(ical) Scroll bar property, 325
video files
    See .AVI files
VIM (Vendor Independent Messaging), 43
virtual memory, 97
visible attribute, 374
Visual Components, 135, 202
visual objects
    building business logic into, 62
    custom, 452–456
    described, 91–92, 447–448
    external, 456–457
    inbound OLE Automation and, 120
    instantiating, 464–466
    standard, 448–452
    VBX (Visual Basic), 457

W

warnings
    creating inheritance, 77
    improper use of object-oriented technology, 68
    overriding packet sending delay, 104
    placing non-visual user objects in class window, 464
    purchasing third party class libraries, 89–90
    shutting down debugger during execution, 195
    user interface design, 50
Watcom compiler, 95
Watcom Image Editor, 408
waterfall methodology, 9–13
.WAV files
    as audible cues, 62
    in OLE 2.0 presentation style, 126
    playing with external functions, 227, 230–234
WaveOutGetNumDevs() function, 232
Web Extra site, 47
WHERE clause, 263
Width property, 368

wildcard, for string matches, 159
Window Functions... option, 225
Window object, OLE container on, 120
Window painter
    instantiating visual user objects, 464
    new toolbars and icons, 178–179
windows control, placing, 182
WinSock driver, 103
Winsock protocol, 114
wizards, 59
wparam argument, for custom events, 215
w_sqlpreview window, 351

X

X axis, 388, 389
X coordinate property, 366, 367

Y

Y axis, 388, 389
Y position property, 366, 367
Yield() function, 342

Z

Z axis, 388, 389

Go for the end zone *with full-contact* PowerBuilder 5.0 training.

Interactive courses let you train right at your desktop!

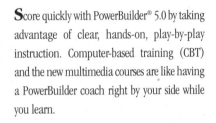

Score quickly with PowerBuilder® 5.0 by taking advantage of clear, hands-on, play-by-play instruction. Computer-based training (CBT) and the new multimedia courses are like having a PowerBuilder coach right by your side while you learn.

Each CBT lesson includes interactive, graphical exercises that walk you through the application development process. Multimedia courses combine sight and sound in "video" demos and instruction for a highly effective training program.

Best of all, you learn at your own pace — anytime, anywhere.

So before you tackle your next development project, order these self-paced training courses and take 15% off with this ad! See reverse for course topics and order form or call **800-395-3525** today.

Discount is valid only on purchases made through Powersoft from Jan. 1 - Dec. 31, 1996.

Save 15% on any PowerBuilder 5.0 self-paced training course.

Save 15% on PowerBuilder 5.0 Self-Paced Training (with this ad.)

Get up to speed quickly on the latest PowerBuilder® release with any of these highly effective, self-paced training courses. And be sure to check out the Powersoft® home page on the World Wide Web for full course descriptions, plus new video, multimedia, and CBT course offerings. Visit us at ***www.powersoft.com*** today.

Name
Title
Company
Address
City
State/Province
Phone
Zip/Postal Code
FAX

Qty	Course	Item #	Price Save 15%!	Total
	Making the Most of PowerBuilder 5.0 CBT	50300	~~$249~~ $212	
	Introduction to PowerBuilder CBT Series			
	• PowerBuilder: The Basics	50303	~~$249~~ $212	
	• DataWindow Concepts	50306	~~$249~~ $212	
	• Implementing a User Interface	50309	~~$249~~ $212	
	• Object Oriented Essentials In PowerBuilder	50312	~~$249~~ $212	
	• All four Introduction to PowerBuilder CBT modules	50320	~~$695~~ $591	
	Fast Track to PowerBuilder 5.0 Multimedia CD	50323	~~$649~~ $552	
	This series includes the following course topics:	*Available May, 1996*		
	• Preparing for Distributed Computing			
	• Developing PowerBuilder Applications in Windows 95™			
	• Extending PowerBuilder: Exploiting OLE and OCX			
	• Leveraging PowerBuilder 5.0 Object-Oriented Language Features			
	• Accelerating Development Using PowerBuilder Foundation Classes			

Note: All pricing is in U.S. dollars. To receive pricing and ordering information for countries within Europe, the Middle East, and Africa, please contact PW direct at tel: + 494 55 5599 or email: pwdsales@powersoft.com.
For all other countries, please contact your local Powersoft office or representative.

Subtotal
Applicable Sales Tax
Shipping ($8.50 per product)
TOTAL

ATR 40F6FU

Method of Payment:
Make checks payable in U.S. dollars to **Powersoft** and include payment with order. Please do not send cash.
❑ Check   ❑ Purchase Order   ❑ MasterCard   ❑ Visa   ❑ American Express

Credit Card number, Purchase Order number, or Check number   *Expiration date*

Name on Credit Card

Cardholder's Signature

THREE EASY WAYS TO ORDER!
#1 CALL Powersoft at **800-395-3525**.
#2 FAX this order form to **617-389-1080**.
#3 Or **MAIL** this order form along with payment to Powersoft, P.O. Box 9116, Everett, MA 02149.

Prices featured for each product include one personal-use license. Please allow 3-4 weeks for delivery. Discount is valid only on purchases made through Powersoft from January 1 – December 31, 1996. Copyright © 1996 Sybase, Inc. All trademarks and registered trademarks are property of their respective owners.